Acclaim for **Teresa N. Washington's**
Our Mothers, Our Powers, Our Texts

"Washington's book testifies to the author's impressive knowledge of Africana lore and literature, especially their feminine and feminist aspects, and is destined, deservedly, to become an authority for students of the Africana universe."
~ Oyekan Owomoyela, author of *Yoruba Proverbs*
University of Nebraska, Lincoln

"This important book will be welcomed into Black, women's, post colonial, and literary studies, but it deserves a still wider audience. Incorporating the work of earlier critics, yet reaching well beyond earlier findings, it delineates a system of traditional African cultural expression encrypted in contemporary literary forms and manifest to those with eyes to see it; but more importantly, it goes far toward re-empowering the Africana image of the female elder."
~ Menoukha Case, Empire State College

"Certainly readers will find new ideas here—surprising and illuminating readings that reveal the female protagonists' control of and by Àjẹ́. . . . Highly recommended."
~ C. A. Bily, Adrian College, *Choice*

"Blazes a new trail in Africana literary criticism by providing an insight into the soul and spirit of Africana womanhood."
~Anthonia Kalu, The Ohio State University,
author of *Women, Literature, and Development in Africa*

"Not only a brilliant study, but also a model to be emulated."
~ Ousseynou B. Traore, William Paterson University

"Patiently, Washington takes the reader through the complex cosmology and practices of Yoruba religion and philosophy. It is a much needed affirmation of feminine power and resource, and is essential reading for anyone attempting a greater understanding of the work of contemporary Africana writers."
~ Janie Franz, *Elevate Difference*

OUR MOTHERS, OUR POWERS, OUR TEXTS

OUR MOTHERS, OUR POWERS, OUR TEXTS

Manifestations of Àjẹ́ in Africana Literature

TERESA N. WASHINGTON

Revised & Expanded Edition

OYA'S TORNADO

Copyright © 2005, 2015, 2018
Teresa N. Washington
ALL RIGHTS RESERVED

This book is a publication of
ỌYA'S TORNADO
Books To Blow Your Mind
Orífín, Ilé Àjẹ́
oyastornado@yahoo.com

ỌYA'S TORNADO™, Books To Blow Your Mind™, and all associated tornado logos are trademarks of Ọya's Tornado.

ALL RIGHTS RESERVED

No part of this book may be reproduced, copied, or utilized in any form or by any means, electronic or mechanical, including photocopying, posting, and recording, or by any information storage and retrieval system, without permission in writing from the author and/or publisher.

Washington, Teresa N.,
Our mothers, our powers, our texts : manifestations of Àjẹ́ in Africana literature / Teresa N. Washington.

First Cloth Edition

p. cm.
Includes bibliographical references and index.

ISBN: 978-0-9964408-8-2 cloth; ISBN: 978-0-9910730-5-4 pbk

1. American fiction—African American authors—History and criticism. 2. Women and literature—United States—History—20th century. 3. American fiction—Women authors—History and criticism. 4. African fiction (English)—History and criticism. 5. African American women—Intellectual life. 6. American fiction—African influences. 7. African American women in literature. 8. Mothers and daughters in literature. 9. Yoruba (African people)—Religion. 10. Motherhood in literature. 11. Creation in literature. 12. Women in literature.

For Odùduwà…
*Every*thing for Odùduwà

I am the first and the last
I am the honored one and the scorned one
I am the whore and the holy one
I am the wife and the virgin
I am the barren one
And many are my daughters
I am the silence that you cannot understand
I am the utterance of my name

   —Julie Dash, *Daughters of the Dust*

CONTENTS

Preface / ix

Note on Orthography / xi

Introduction / 1

PART ONE / ÀJẸ́ IN AFRICANA ORATURE

1. Àjẹ́ in the Yoruba World   13

2. Àjẹ́ across the Continent and in the Ìtànkálẹ̀   56

PART TWO / ÀJẸ́ IN AFRICANA LITERATURE

3. Word Becoming Flesh and Text in Gloria Naylor's *Mama Day* and T. Obinkaram Echewa's *I Saw the Sky Catch Fire*   113

4. Initiations into the Self, the Conjured Space of Creation, and Prophetic Utterance in Ama Ata Aidoo's *Anowa* and Ntozake Shange's *Sassafrass, Cypress & Indigo*   141

5. Un/Complementary Complements: Gender, Power, and Àjẹ́ in Selected Works by C. L. Adeoye, Octavia E. Butler, Zora Neale Hurston, Wole Soyinka, and Amos Tutuola   165

6. The Relativity of Negativity: Àjẹ́ in Jean Pliya's "The Watch-Night," Zora Neale Hurston's *Jonah's Gourd Vine*, and Gloria Naylor's *Mama Day*   198

7. The Womb of Life Is a Wicked Bag: Cycles of Power, Passion, and Pain in the Mother-Daughter Àjẹ́ Relationship   217

8. Twinning across the Ocean: The Neo-Political Àjẹ́ of Ben Okri's Madame Koto and Mary Monroe's Mama Ruby   245

Coda-Continua   273

   Appendix / 280

   Glossary / 285

   Notes / 289

   Works Cited and Selected Bibliography / 321

   Index / 338

PREFACE

Our Mothers, Our Powers, Our Texts: Manifestations of Àjẹ́ in Africana Literature exists because of my desire to learn all I could about the lives and texts and powers of my progenitors.

When I was a young child I knew that my maternal mothers were extraordinary. These women could successfully split storm clouds, could see the wind, and could store food so it never spoiled. They were master meteorologists and renowned healers. My Great Grand Mother Donnie Harris was so skilled at curing thrush that community members of various ethnicities would line up before her great white oak tree (which I named The Wicked Tree as a child) to receive her guaranteed cure.

Everyone admired and respected my great-grandfather, Dock, Donnie's husband, but Donnie was the head. She was the Force. I would often gaze upon my mother with awe simply because she had been loved, hugged, educated, and cured *directly* by Donnie.

Because many parts of my family's history have been locked in a vault of secrecy and silence, a large portion of my life has been dedicated to discovering and restoring the presence and powers of Donnie and her mother Ann to our family's continuum. When my Motherdear (my mother's mother) told me that Momma Donnie made everyone drink Rabbit Tobacco, also known as Life Everlasting, tea every year to keep them from catching colds, I directed the restoration of two family rituals: 1) the annual search for and collection of Life Everlasting and 2) the mandatory imbibing of Life Everlasting tea. Motherdear always refused to drink her tea. When I reminded her that the herb's name signified that its drinkers would enjoy longevity, she declared she'd rather go on to glory than have to drink that tea again. We could feel Momma Donnie laughing with us.

The woman who was born into slavery but left her progeny 80 acres of land that she and her husband Dock secured despite America's unrelenting racist oppression captivated my consciousness. *My mothers are women who do the impossible with elegance*, I often mused. *I can too.*

One of Momma Donnie's most endearing legacies is that she never used violence to discipline her children. In an African American world in which extension cords, steel-toe boots, backhands, fists, shaving strops, staves—any handy objects—are readily used on children, Momma Donnie stands as a Paragon of Perfect Parenting. As a child, my summers were divided between staying with my paternal grandmother, a woman whose childrearing techniques came straight from the core of the cruelest enslaver and whose routine method of discipline included naked front-porch display beatings, and being shown immeasurable patience, guidance, wisdom, and reserve from two of Momma Donnie's daughters, Mother Dear and Sister B who, like my own mother, never hit me. The thought never entered their minds. Momma Donnie's message is clear: When it comes to family, violence need not be the *last* resort; it need not be considered at all.

My life-long love of literature and my need to better understand the characters who were like my mothers but who critics assigned to the realm of imaginary was fueled by Momma Donnie. When I read about the power of Àjẹ́, it was as if I were receiving wisdom from her own breasts. Every gift, power, curse, cure, testimony, tribulation, and revelation of my family found a complement or a twin in Àjẹ́: from growing hands to talking trees to the ability to curse up a storm to the power of Hoodoo—and more. Within Àjẹ́ and Àwọn Ìyá Wa are all of the skills, abilities, threats, and treasures in which I had been immersed throughout my life. And there was nothing magical but everything real about it.

Momma Donnie is the reason this book exists. She is the reason that I exist. She is the reason that my daughter exists. All praise to you, Ìyánlá Donnie! "You brought us to this place; it is Your influence we are using."

When I was younger, my oríkì was The Child of Many Mothers. I knew the importance of finding a Mother to love, guide and protect you wherever you are. I needed a Mother when I went to Nigeria to study Àjẹ́. Momma Donnie led me to Ìyá Oyeronke Igbinola Awo Oòduà Ìyálájẹ́ ti Ifẹ̀, who opened her truth and her soul unto me and allowed me to enter her àṣiri. The part of that àṣiri that I can share with you is the *Ìtàn-Oríkì Ìyàmi Òṣòròngà*. It is exclusive to this book and cannot be found in any other publication. Behold, with care, this rarest of gems from my Mothers.

One of my saddest and most helpless periods came when I learned my Ìyá had died. I lamented that she would never hold in her hands the book that she brought into being. However, the day before I received notification that this book, my book, *our* book would be liberated so that I could finally publish this long-awaited revised edition, my Ìyá came to me, sat across from me and, with shining eyes, said, "I didn't die. I have always been with you, and I will always be with you." She could not die because she is immortal: *àikú pariwà*. And she has always held and will always hold me and her book in her empowering hands.

Writing a book is a monumental undertaking, and because my motivations are deeply personal, spiritual, political, and lastly, academic, I approach the writing, publication, and revision of this book carefully. Because of the weight of the subject matter, an additional layer of care and caution envelops my work. My goal is to ensure that every page of this book, and of all my books, is loaded with truth, wisdom, power, triumph, and passion, just like all of the mothers who live in these pages.

I derive great pleasure from the fact that the wisdom-workers who I knew first and know best I refer to in this book alongside internationally known historians, writers, and scholars. It is imperative that we understand that our mothers' and fathers' truths are vital to our evolution —whether they are ever name-dropped or not.

The most rewarding aspect of this book, by far, is the fact that it is a testament to my daughter who informed me at two years of age that she is, in fact, Odùduwà. The knowledge she shares with me could only come from Ọmọ Ọrun. I am honored to be the recipient of her cosmic wisdom, her nebulaic hugs, and her Dark Star kisses! I now understand that she is the master architect of all my works. As I place in my daughter's hands the books whose writing she directed from the Cosmos, I know she will have all the tools she needs to repair the world she created.

This book's layers of significance are innumerable, but the paramount reason for this book's success is *You*. I will be ever grateful for your support, encouragement, and excitement regarding the first and only full length definitive studies devoted to Àjẹ́: *Our Mothers, Our Powers, Our Texts: Manifestations of Àjẹ́ in Africana Literature* and *The Architects of Existence: Àjẹ́ in Yoruba Cosmology, Ontology, and Orature*. I am overjoyed that so many people from diverse walks of life have found my research and analyses helpful, engaging, revelatory, and revolutionary.

I am honored to present to you, on the ten year anniversary of its publication, the revised and expanded edition of *Our Mothers, Our Powers, Our Texts*! I am confident that you will find this edition even more profound than its predecessor and also tighter and more forthright.

Thank you for inspiring me and challenging me, and thank you for joining me on an exploration of the simply extraordinary: *Our Mothers, Our Powers, Our Texts: Manifestations of Àjẹ́ in Africana Literature*.

NOTE ON THE ORTHOGRAPHY

The orthography used for Yoruba words in this book is that of modern Yoruba. Tone marks are consistent in each usage, with the exception of direct quotations. Proper Yoruba names and places are neither tone-marked nor italicized, with the exception of the Òrìṣà. All African words, with the exceptions of proper nouns and certain quoted passages, are italicized in the first usage only.

I am grateful to Oyin Ogunba and Adebayo Ogundijo for their generous assistance in helping me perfect the Yoruba orthography in this book. However, I take full responsibility for any and all errors in this text.

OUR MOTHERS, OUR POWERS, OUR TEXTS

> Neo-hoodoo is "your mama."
> —Larry Neal, quoted in *Conjure*

Introduction

Ishmael Reed anointed and appointed himself the high priest of Neo-Hoodoo during the height of the Civil Rights struggle and Black Power movement. Quincy Troupe, Ted Jones, Toni Cade Bambara, and a host of other Hosts joined Reed in the sacred circle and courageously continued the ancients' holistic spiritual work. Literary critics, moved by the arts, also found themselves "catching sense" and the spirit. Marjorie Pryse and Hortense Spillers were caught *Conjuring* in 1985 with a number of devotees. Joyce A. Joyce was found conspiring with *Warriors, Conjurers, and Priests* in 1993. And in 1991, Houston A. Baker was discovered working the Mother Spirit of theory:

> One might say . . . that a poetics of Afro-American women's writing is, in many ways, a phenomenology of conjure. In any case, the field most decisively analyzed by such a poetics is decidedly not one where pathological or aversive images dominate. Rather, what are revealed are felicitous images of the workings of a spirit.[1]

When I came of age, Neo-Hoodoo had *been* manifest, but having styled myself a radical-in-waiting and born "under the trickster's sign" to boot, I was not feeling it.

I remember reading Toni Morrison's *Song of Solomon* for the first time as an undergraduate student. Guitar and the Seven Days, as contemporary Nat Turners or initiates of an ancient African secret society, fascinated me to no end, but Milkman's soaring ascension left me dry. I did some research and read testimonies about the flying Africans and thought there might be a *bit* of truth therein. But I quickly placed flight into my subconscious—or dismembered it from my contemporary reality. What, I wondered, did marked children, shape-shifters, and two-headed folks have to do with literary arts, social evolution, and political revolution?

Black feminism, which had long been carving out its position in the critical and political world, spoke directly to me. The now classic Gloria T. Hull, Patricia Bell Scott, and Barbara Smith effort *All the Women Are White, All the Blacks Are Men, But Some of Us Are Brave* (1982), Claudia Tate's *Black Women Writers at Work* (1983), and the works of Barbara Christian, Barbara Smith, bell hooks, Gloria Hull, and Mary Helen Washington all seemed to be saying to me, "You're right on time, daughter! Come in!" I entered and reveled in the literary and theoretical quilts my mothers had knotted. My soul soared as I read their words, but I yearned for something deeper. Our timeless, torturous, and triumphant journey to our empowered selves deserved, in my opinion, something more authentic than the adjectival appendage offered by "Black feminism."

I turned to womanism, which was historically sound and personally, politically, and linguistically revolutionary. With Alice Walker's lyrical prelude to *In Search of Our Mothers' Gardens: Womanist Prose* (1983), Clenora Hudson-Weems's attempts at balance in *Africana Womanism: Reclaiming Ourselves* (1995), and Mary E. Modupe Kolawole's historically rich *Womanism and African Consciousness* (1993), I was well on my way to myself. However, there were many aspects of Africana literature that womanism did not fully elucidate. Always an inquisitive individual, now immersed in the study of African cultural and linguistic continuity in America, I wanted to know how these textual entities and realities came to be. If Womanism was, by degrees, the mother of feminism, who, I wondered, was womanism's Mother? From what queenly and all-encompassing womb did the purple of womanism spring?

What I sought was a definitive, holistic African-based model to elaborate the profusion of Africana cultural and spiritual properties in Africana texts: those elements that Western theoretical models ignored altogether, traced to the plantation, or described as "magical realism" (as if the Mothers had the time or inclination to pull rabbits from hats). Marjorie Pryse whispered, "The way back links Black women's biological heritage with their powers of naming each other as literary models."[2] But what was the origin of that "biological heritage"? I wondered. What was the source of the African American model of critical conjuration? Who was the Mother of the Text?

Gay Wilentz's *Binding Cultures: Black Women Writers in Africa and the Diaspora* (1996) shed light. Wilentz asserted that Africana women's literature is

> informed by a consciousness of what must be passed on to future generations; *the telling of the tale is paramount to the survival of the culture.* Like their African sister-storytellers, these writers create oraliterature in their written works. They (re)assemble the fragmented sounds of their foremothers' voices, rendering explicit the implicit memory of African orature.[3]

If I could handle the tools used to (re)assemble the fragments and hold the whole before it became fragmented, and more, witness the original source of the oraliterature that spoke through written works, I would have the critical model I desired, the model I thought Africana literature—at least that which sang to my soul—needed. The trickster had had me caught up in riddles, and, like Milkman, I had been seeking what was in me all along. After forays in Black feminism, deconstruction, womanism, and other theories, I was finally ready to enter at the beginning.

Spiritualist Luisah Teish gave me a reading and some soul food with *Jambalaya: The Natural Woman's Book of Personal Charms and Practical Rituals* (1985):

> We have learned the true definition of words, which have, in the past, been shrouded in fear and perverted by misinterpretation. Words such as witch have been re-defined in the light of their true origin and nature. Instead of the evil, dried-out, old prude of patriarchal lore, we know the witch to be a strong, proud woman, wise in the ways of natural medicine. We know her as a self-confident freedom fighter, defending her right to her own sexuality, and her right to govern her life and community according to the laws of nature. We know that she was slandered, oppressed and burned alive for her wisdom and her defiance of patriarchal rule.[4]

Such a definitive spiritual and political affirmation was what, in my mind, Black feminism and womanism lacked. For if we are ashamed of some of the herbs growing therein, how can we fully appreciate "'our mothers' gardens'? However, I doubted that "witch" was the word "we" Africana women had been seeking to claim. While the attempt of Caucasians to reappropriate the word "witch" by empowering its Old

English root word "wicca/wicce" is admirable, wiccan philosophy—with its distinct cultural differences—and wiccan adherents—with a typical tendency to misappropriate Africana concepts while exhibiting racism toward African people—were simply not worthy of my consideration.[5] Such constructs as "witch," "witchcraft," and "wicca" have nothing to do with my mothers, my powers, or my texts.

After reading to me from his Jesus/Èṣù poems, my mentor Charlie R. Braxton took me to the doorway of origins by telling me, "You gotta read Gates's *The Signifying Monkey.*" When I did, I met Èṣù and understood that home had defined itself millennia ago and merely awaited re-membering.

Ayodele Ogundipe's description of Èṣù as a defining definer was a revelation:

> Being result and issue, [Èṣù] inherits the nature of all ancestors, the Egun Irunmale, as well as those of the female Iyam-mi Aje. By compounding their morphologies, he partakes indifferently of either group and can circulate freely between all.[6]

Although Èṣù entered Western philosophical and analytical circles as a male, thanks to Caucasian gender bias, Ogundipe asserts that Èṣù "certainly is not restricted to human distinctions of gender or sex; he is at once both male and female. Although his masculinity is depicted as visually and graphically overwhelming, his equally expressive femininity renders his enormous sexuality ambiguous, contrary, and genderless."[7] One could find Èṣù, crafty "devil," sitting at the crossroads, awaiting sacrifice with eyes aglow, and holding either his breasts or the vagina that waits patiently under his erect penis. What, I wondered, was that vagina for? Does Èṣù get salty when one overlooks "his" vagina? Doesn't the pronoun "he" at least deserve an "s" with a punning slash, when it comes to Èṣù? And most important, I wondered, could that hidden vagina be a gateway to the Origins?

It was Èṣù's cosmic-physical relationship to the "female Iyam-mi Aje" that provided me with both an interpretive turning point and an analytical linchpin. Among the Yoruba of Southwest Nigeria, "ìyá mi" literally means "my mother"; with tonal changes, "ìyá mi" becomes Ìyàmi, My Mysterious Mother. Àjẹ́ is the furtive force the Great Mother used to create life and ensure evolution. She shared her force with Deities and select humans so that they might ensure that the world maintains its structure and balance. I began to study the Ifá spiritual system of the Yoruba, and the deeper I delved into this ancient Way of Knowing and Doing, the more Àjẹ́ impressed me with its centrality. Thanks to the efforts of numerous scholars, elders, and artists, there was abundant evidence of Àjẹ́'s ancient and contemporary influence on ritual drama, orature, music, visual arts, and literature. But it was Zora Neale Hurston's *Mules and Men*—a cosmological, auto/biographical, revolutionary treatise disguised as entertaining anthropology—that best illustrated how Àjẹ́'s covert and resilient properties connected ancient Africa and the fractured but shining African Americas.

Ever-ready Èṣù lent me a copy of *Mules and Men,* and the Trickster placed in my hands a plethora of signs and symbols when I could appreciate and interpret them. Here were forcibly dislocated African mothers and fathers—dismissed as mere fractions of pieces of property—signifying, naming, creating, making, Hoodooing, outwitting someone else's concepts of God and Devil, killing, and dying and living to tell it! Hurston's works became artistic and critical roots that moved stones of Western ideology out of my path. She also lent me her shoes with the sky-blue bottoms so I could fly to Nigeria and better understand the power inherent in Africana women that makes it a forgone conclusion that they will create and recreate and texture, color, and enliven nearly everything they touch no matter where they are.

Hurston didn't concern herself with the theoretical flavor or aesthetic edict of the month. She knew there was something deeper, larger—there was a Yewájọbí—a Mother of all Òrìṣà (Gods) and life forms.[8] Her name is disremembered, but Her visage is only a clear lake away. Overlooked and ignored, She is the ink of the text, and She is the framing reflective margin. She wears an Afro like Queen Tiye. She is as vain as Erzulie but as shy as Odù. Her arms are as long as Yeye Muwo, and She smells just like creation.[9] The Isley Brothers caught a glimpse of Her and asked, "Who's That Lady?" Robert Johnson rifled through Her nation sack only to emerge with a nickel and loneliness. She had shrines all over Europe until Constantine dismantled some and whitewashed others in 333c.e. Yet she survived subjugation, exile, slavery, colonialism, and imperialism. She is the red earth we till—that which soaks up the blood of lynching victims. It is in Her womb that the ancestors are reborn. And although She smiles when you do it, She begs you on her knees not to call Her out of Her name.

THE EURO-PHALLOGOCENTRIC CONSTRUCTION OF "AFRICAN WITCHCRAFT"

Despite the centrality of Àjẹ́ to the Yoruba ethos, most academic descriptions of the force and its bearers are steeped in negativity. In *Sixteen Great Poems of Ifá* (1975), Wande Abimbola argues, "The Àjẹ́ represent a negation of all that human beings cherish." He further declares, "Helping the Àjẹ́ or doing them a favour does not stop them from their path of eternal opposition to the òrìṣà and the human beings."[10] In *Yoruba Beliefs and Sacrificial Rites* (1980), J. Omosade Awolalu asserts, "Witches [meaning Àjẹ́] are seen as the personification of evil, as innately wicked people who work harm against others. They are capable of their nefarious deeds through their possession of mysterious powers unknown and unavailable to ordinary people."[11] I had finally found a force deep and wide enough to elucidate those intricate and encoded aspects of Africana art, but it was covered in academic and cultural offal, as the erroneous translation of "Àjẹ́" as "witch" and the upheaval caused by the European social, economic, and ideological colonization of Africa led to the social construction of "African witchcraft."

In order to solidify the mental slavery and social death of Africans and facilitate territorial expansion and economic control, European colonizers slated traditional African spiritual systems and their devotees for eradication. In Nigeria, the British targeted Àjẹ́ and Ifá spiritualists because their covert and indigenous revolutionary works threatened the colonial order:

> When the British colonized the Yoruba Nation, they made a deliberate effort to ridicule and abolish indigenous forms of religion. The effects of that campaign are still apparent in modern day Nigeria. Missionary groups provide much of the available education outside of the large cities. Indoctrination against Ifá is a part of the curriculum in many of the Christian schools.[12]

Many Traditionalists challenged political-religious domination outright or nestled resistance covertly,[13] but the destruction left incomplete by colonizers was taken over by African religious zealots. These Continental "witch hunters" focused largely, but not exclusively, on spiritual entities and objects of a particular gender:

> During the 1950's missionary groups from the Congo entered Nigeria and accused large numbers of traditional women of practicing "witchcraft." As a result of the accusations, many of the shrines used by female secret societies were burned and destroyed.[14]

Although Àjẹ́ is a biologically derived force that Africana men and women can inherit, in the grip of alien, patriarchal, imperialist indoctrination, it apparently became important to differentiate spiritually empowered females from their male counterparts. Consequently, a binary opposition of evil female "witches" and good male "wizards" was constructed. Such bifurcation is evident in Barry Hallen and J. Olubi Sodipo's insightful study, "A Comparison of the Western 'Witch' with the Yoruba 'Àjẹ́': Spiritual Powers or Personality Types?" (1986).

Dealing with the myths up front, Hallen and Sodipo state that the "popular stereotype of Àjẹ́ is that it is èníyàn burúkú—a malicious, extremely secretive person whose aim is to [harass] or to do serious injury to usually innocent victims."[15] However, their fieldwork disproves this assertion. *Oníṣègun* (doctors) and *babaláwo* (diviners) have indispensable functions in Yoruba society, and the oníṣègun and babaláwo they interviewed—all of whom were male—all necessarily possess and utilize Àjẹ́. In fact, the researchers found, "The reason a person is one of the most powerful and successful of the oníṣègun is because of his own special abilities, *and those abilities derive from the fact that he has the Àjẹ́.*"[16] Despite this, societal fear and hatred of Àjẹ́ are so strong that "no oníṣègun who has any reasonable concern for his own personal safety would admit in an explicit manner to having the power of Àjẹ́."

Describing their male informants as "distinguished and reasonable members of their community," Hallen and Sodipo argue that the scope of Àjẹ́ "must be broadened to take such people into account."[17] The researchers reveal Àjẹ́ to be a respectable and facilitating force in the hands of men, but no mention is made of the original owners of Àjẹ́ who endure the greatest persecution—women. With their reluctance or inability to analyze or address Àjẹ́ in relation to its female bearers, the researchers' findings appear to tacitly validate a male = good : female = evil dichotomy.

While some studies ignore women with Àjẹ́, others focus on the "witch's personality." In *Nupe Religion: Traditional Beliefs and the Influence of Islam in West African Chiefdom* (1954), Siegfried F. Nadel argues that "African witches" are commonly perceived to be "abnormal" "social deviants" who resent jokes, get "angry over trifles," and are "always morose and forbidding and never cheerful." A woman acting in such a manner is one who "belies the common precepts and ideals of conduct; she is ill conditioned, eccentric, 'atypical'" and must, then, be a witch.[18] Nadel also finds the "African witch" to constitute the "enemy of men and of male authority; she seeks to dominate men . . . and her evilness is often directed against a husband and his kin."[19] However, assertions about "evil" women reveal more about the aberrations of a patriarchal society than about a particular type of woman. Researchers Akin Omoyajowo, Geoffrey Parrinder, and Nadel agree that many accusations of witchcraft in Africa result from "deep-rooted sexual antagonism" harbored against women by men.[20] To put it succinctly, "In being made the witches of the society, the women are made to carry its fault or failure."[21]

With the phrase "in being made," Nadel alludes to the role patriarchy plays in the social construction of the "African witch." The pervasive myth of "African witchcraft," imported from Europe with all its attendant evil, patriarchal iconoclasm, and devilishness, finds constant validation in the African mass media, which feeds off of and into societal indoctrination.[22] Rarely do artists, researchers, or theorists make distinctions between the concept of "African witchcraft" and Yoruba Àjẹ́ or similar forces, and, until recently, discussions of "African witchcraft" supplanted attempts to objectively analyze Àjẹ́ and its African sister forces. Furthermore, as Hallen and Sodipo argue in their remarkable study, *Knowledge, Belief, and Witchcraft: Analytic Experiments in African Philosophy* (1986/1997), racial and ideological biases often taint Western discussions of African spiritual powers:

> The Western intellectual's attitude is more or less a "Thank goodness we don't believe in *that* anymore," and that a society that does is primitive, sick and inhuman. But, as we have indicated, this pejorative attitude depends upon an incomplete, misleading and thereafter erroneous translation and definition of a term like the Yoruba Àjẹ́.[23]

Many of the scholars whose invaluable findings I quote in this book use the terms "witch" and "Àjẹ́" as if they are synonymous. The erroneous translation of Àjẹ́ and the misguided assumption that complex African concepts can and must be defined by false European language equivalents has led to much confusion and impeded a true understanding of Àjẹ́ and similar powers.

Rather than continue to attempt to find definitive meaning in the terms and tongues of others, Àjẹ́ deserves to exercise its ability to define itself, speak its own piece. Furthering the arguments of Hallen and Sodipo, Diedre Badejo makes a significant step in the process of linguistic and conceptual reclamation in *Ọṣun Ṣẹ̀ẹ̀gẹ̀sí* (1996):

> Some writers have interpreted the *Àjẹ́* as witches, which connotes a negative use of power only. However, the *Àjẹ́*, as we find in the cosmology of *Ọ̀ṣun* and in the *Ifá* corpus, are given this power by *Olódùmarè* and it is used variously. My colleagues and informants made it clear that any person of ability, insight, leadership or other forms of observable power

can be considered Àjẹ́. Consequently, the translation, "witch", is singularly misleading and conceptually incorrect.[24]

Conceptualizations of Àjẹ́ are also complicated by the fact that it is not a one-dimensional concept or figure with a neat definition or concise exposition. Ubiquitous, ambiguous, and invisible, Àjẹ́ is everything; it is nothing. Its depth, breath, and shroud of taboo may be the reason *Our Mothers, Our Powers, Our Texts* is the first book-length exposition on Àjẹ́. However, this force of artistic, biological, spiritual, and ecological creation, maintenance, destruction, and re-creation is profoundly influential in contemporary Africana arts. And as an analytical tool, it can elucidate often overlooked but profoundly important aspects of Africana literatures.

ENTERING THE SPHERE OF THE MOTHERS

Our Mothers, Our Powers, Our Texts is a two-part study. Part I of this disquisition consists of a survey and analysis of the ancient and historical forms and figures of Àjẹ́ as revealed in Africana oral literature. The Yoruba conceptualization of Àjẹ́ constitutes the foundation of this study, and its elaboration in chapter 1 is segmented into two parts that correspond to Àjẹ́'s duality. The term Àjẹ́ denotes both a spiritual power and spiritually empowered humans: "The Powers of the Mothers" explicates the various forms and methodologies of the power; "The Mothers of Power" explores the attributes and signature activities of Òrìṣà and humans who have or are Àjẹ́. I follow the discussion of Àjẹ́ in its Yoruba place of origin with a survey of Àjẹ́ manifestations in Africana communities outside of Yorubaland. The cross-cultural comparative analysis of the orature of Àjẹ́ elucidates the force's proliferation and evolution and highlights significant aspects of cultural specificity. Most important, part I's analysis of Àjẹ́ in Africana orature establishes the critical and artistic foundation for part II's examination of Àjẹ́ in Africana literature.

Archetypal Àjẹ́ and their modern literary descendants provide wonderful examples of life and art reflecting, gleaning from, and growing with one another. To better reveal this continuity, I undertake thematic analyses of contemporary literature in part II, chapters 3 to 8. Chapter 3 focuses on the solidification of sacred space and the translocation of power of the word to power of the text and flesh in Gloria Naylor's *Mama Day* and T. Obinkaram Echewa's *I Saw the Sky Catch Fire*. In chapter 4, I examine the prophetic potential and power of Anowa and Indigo of Ama Ata Aidoo's *Anowa* and Ntozake Shange's

Sassafrass, Cypress & Indigo, respectively. Using the works of Amos Tutuola, C. L. Adeoye, Zora Neale Hurston, Octavia E. Butler, and Wole Soyinka, chapter 5 focuses on Àjẹ́'s struggle to institute gender balance and harmony. Focusing on Ayele of Jean Pliya's "The Watch-Night," Hattie of Zora Neale Hurston's *Jonah's Gourd Vine,* and Ruby of Naylor's *Mama Day,* chapter 6 mines the nuances of the most feared and reviled aspects of Àjẹ́. Using Audre Lorde's *Zami: A New Spelling of My Name* and Jamaica Kincaid's "My Mother" to frame an in-depth analysis of Toni Morrison's *Beloved,* chapter 7 explores the intricacies of the Àjẹ́ mother-daughter relationship. To better understand the methodology and application of neo-political Àjẹ́, chapter 8 turns to twin sisters separated by the sea: Mama Ruby of *The Upper Room* and Madame Koto of Ben Okri's *The Famished Road* and *Songs of Enchantment.* By analyzing manifestations of Àjẹ́ in literature of various genres by male and female Africana writers from the Continent, America, and the Caribbean, I hope to reveal this ancient power's vast contemporary influence. As a force that is central to Pan-African continuity and one that marries ancient orature and Òrìṣà to contemporary literature and literary characters, Àjẹ́ lies at the center of an unbroken circle of power that is ever-relevant and effortlessly signifies from blood to ink.

Part One

ÀJḖ IN AFRICANA ORATURE

Ọmọ mi, Tèrésà, ó fẹ́ẹ́ mọ̀ bí Àwọn Ìyá ṣe ń ṣiṣẹ́.
Ó fẹ́ẹ́ mọ̀ ìtàn àwọn Ìyàmi Àbẹ̀ní....
Bí wọ́ ṣe ń ní,
bẹ́ẹ̀ ni mo ṣe ń ní ìí
Kó o ṣàánú

(My child, Teresa, she wants to know how the Mothers operate.
She wants to know the story of My Mysterious Mother,
The One We Beg To Have....
Just as they say it,
so am I saying it now.
Please have mercy)

—Oyeronke Igbinola

Neo-hoodoo is a litany seeking its text.

—Ishmael Reed

> Ohùn èmi ná à kọ́.
> Ohùn ìyá mi ni...
>
> (This is not my voice.
> It is my mother's voice...)
> —Oríkì Àjẹ́[1]

1

Àjẹ́ in Yorubaland

THE POWERS OF THE MOTHERS

OVERVIEW

The Yoruba have many praisenames for the fertile, protective, and creative Mothers who people the earth, protect their children, and ensure evolution: Àwọn Ìyá Wa (Our Mothers); Àwọn Ìyàmi Òṣòròngà (The Great and Mysterious Mother); Yewájọbí (The Mother of All the Òrìṣà and All Living Things);[2] Àgbàláàgbà (Old and Wise One); and, succinctly, Ayé (the Earth). Whatever appellations they are given by their "children," these women are recognized as the spiritual and terrestrial "gods of society" and "the owner[s] of everything in the world."[3] The Mothers enjoy suzerainty because of a force called Àjẹ́.

Although Àjẹ́ resists English language definition, as do many African concepts, Diedre Badejo defines it as "an embodiment of power and an expression of the matrix of potentiality from which that power emanates."[4] Yoruba cultural analyst Ayo Opefeyitimi asserts that Àjẹ́ endows women with "celestial, terrestrial [sophistication] and unrivaled powers" that surpass "those of men."[5] Henry Drewal and Margaret Drewal define it as women's possession of "the secret of life itself."[6] An "always-already" force—that has always existed and is ever prepared for action—Àjẹ́ is depicted in Yoruba mythistories[7] and Odù Ifá (divination verses of the Ifá spiritual system—the Yoruba Way of Knowing) as a biological, physical, and spiritual force of creativity and social and political enforcement.

A vastly influential African power that is inclined toward paradox and multiplicity, Àjẹ́ is holistic and neutral and can be used in myriad ways depending upon the entity wielding the power and the circumstances and motivations dictating the actions. In addition to being a cosmic force that originates with Great Mother Deities, Àjẹ́ is a naturally-occurring property of select human beings. Àjẹ́ have many significant attributes and roles in society. They may be bestowed with spiritual vision, divine authority, power of the word, and *àṣẹ,* the power to bring desires and ideas into being. As "children" of Imọlẹ̀, the Mother of Earth, they control agricultural fertility and plant life. Holistic healing is an important aspect of Àjẹ́, and its wielders use their incomparable knowledge and ownership of flora and fauna to create nourishment, healing elixirs, and poisons. Àjẹ́ also enact spiritual communication through divination and *Ọ̀rọ̀,* power of the word. Most important, Àwọn Ìyá Wa are teachers whose gifts, lessons, trials, and punishments compel their communities to seek higher levels of spiritual evolution and redirect misguided destiny, direction, or power.

Part of their evolutionary educational and social work involves dispensation of justice. Àjẹ́ are feared for their astral "outings," which are undertaken largely to punish trespassers of cosmic and terrestrial laws. The following are possible retaliations for offenses committed against the Earth Deity:

> In addition to cases of inexplicable deaths, a female victim may have her menstrual blood stopped or trickling for years, her foetus may be spirited out of her and hung high over an iroko tree. . . . [A] man's penis may lose its erections or may be denuded of sperms or active spermatozoa, there may be eruptions of mysterious illnesses, etc.[8]

Spiritually and physically powerful women using their astral forms to slay offenders and deliberate on communal and political issues may sound harrowing. But it is important to note that Odùduwà, who is heralded as the progenitor of the Yoruba peoples,[9] is the embodiment of Àjẹ́, and Àjẹ́ is one of the essential components she used to create the earth.

Odùduwà's "daughters," Àwọn Ìyá Wa, act under her auspices, and they also use their power with discretion and in accordance with ordained rules of which no breech is allowed. In addition to rules involving group consensus for astral punishments, Àjẹ́ must adhere to simple but important terrestrial laws:

1. Do not dabble in herbalism (do not use herbs without thorough knowledge of their nature and use and divine authorization).
2. Do not display wealth.
3. Share everything.[10]

Yoruba spiritualist Samuel M. Opeola contends that "Àjẹ́ balance the social fabric" and are "against class systems" and "exploitation." He finds that Àjẹ́'s tolerance contributes to a healthy and expansive society.

The tolerance to which Opeola refers is an aspect of *iwà-pèlé,* superb composed character. In contrast to "witches," who are described as temperamental, vicious, and quick to take offense, Àwọn Ìyá Wa are typically cool, patient, composed, and disinclined to emotional outbursts.

> These elderly women and priestesses are considered neither antisocial nor the personification of evil. Rather, they form an important segment of the population in any town and tend to be shown much respect and affection. Because of their special power, they have greater access to the Yoruba Deities. They occupy a position subordinate to those of the supreme deity, Olodumare, and of Orunmila, god of the Ifa divination system, and equal or superior to that of the gods.[11]

The iwà-pèlé of Àwọn Ìyá Wa is directly related to their ability and authority to cool and heal or strike and destroy as necessary. True power needn't advertise itself, and even when abused, Àwọn Ìyá Wa retain their composure. The elders state that an offended Àjẹ́ will "just look at you and beg you. Then some time later another thing will happen."[12] Melding power of the word, paradox, and astral power, the kneeling position that an Àjẹ́ assumes to beg an offender is also the optimal pose from which to "curse or to invoke retributive justice on anyone who disrespects motherhood."[13]

As its praisenames indicate, Àjẹ́ is essential to biological creation. Many argue that the force is acquired in vitro and that male and female children can be born with Àjẹ́. It is also said that latent Àjẹ́ can also be developed and intensified in children through consistent training in symbols and rituals.[14] Evidence of Àjẹ́ in males gives rise to gender-neutral oríkì (praisenames) such as Elders of the Night, which refers to a collective that includes individuals of both genders. However, Àjẹ́ is decidedly woman-owned and woman-administered. Female ownership of Àjẹ́ can be attributed to the life-giving, highly spiritual, and sacred womb; indeed, Our Mothers' wombs are literal doorways to existence and the terrestrial origin-sites of Àjẹ́. Consequently, all Africana women, as the genetic progeny of Odù, inherently possess some degree of Àjẹ́. Because Yoruba women boast the closest genetic and phenotypic relationship with Odù, Yoruba women stand as paragons of Àjẹ́.

While Àjẹ́ knows no age restrictions, elderly Africana women, endowed with wisdom that is tempered by life's vicissitudes, are considered the most evolved, balanced, and powerful. Henry Drewal and Margaret Drewal find that "any elderly woman, her longevity implying secret knowledge and power, may be regarded as an aje, as are all who hold important titles in cults for the gods and ancestors. The feeling is that in order to fulfill her role properly she must possess such power."[15]

Àgbàláàgbà Obìrin, a Yoruba praisename and euphemism for Àjẹ́, denotes a stately and reserved, respected elder woman of control, composure, and reticence who is recognized as having reached a social, psychological, and spiritual pinnacle. Among the Yoruba, the postmenopausal era does not signify obsolescence; instead, when lifebearing ends, spiritual magnification begins. An elderly woman is heralded as "the one with the vagina that turns upside down without pouring blood."[16] With the acquisition of the beard of old age, an Àgbàláàgbà Obìrin acquires not masculine aspects but dual spiritual-material mobility. She is *abáàra méjì*, one with two bodies, and *olóju méjì*, one with two faces: Her spirit becomes a force equal to or greater than her physical being.

Perhaps as a result of their incalculable invisible power and the hidden potential of the life-giving or powerfully inverted womb, Àjẹ́ is considered by many to be a taboo word that is rarely uttered publicly[17] for fear the Mothers will hear the utterance and take offense. To praise the unmentionable, the Yoruba cloak the motherforce in euphemisms and stage the Gẹ̀lẹ̀dẹ́ festival to honor, placate, and praise the owners of the world. As a devotee explains,

> The gods of Gelede are so called "the great ancestral mothers.". . . The power of the Great Mother is manifold. . . . The Great Mother has power in many things. . . . [She] is the owner of everything in the world. She owns you. We must not say how the whole thing works.[18]

POWER OF THE WORD

Òrìṣà Odùduwà, or Odù, who is praised as Yewájọbí, The Mother of All the Òrìṣà and All Living Things,[19] is an important source of Àjẹ́'s far-reaching power. Modupe Oduyoye argues that Odùduwà's influence is historical, spiritual, material, individual, and communal and originates with the womb and power of the word:

> When . . . the Yoruba say that all Yoruba people are *omo Odùduwà*, "children" of *Odùduwà*, some interpret this politically to mean that *Odùduwà* was the first *Ọba* [King] of Ilé Ifẹ̀ . . . and that the other Yoruba *ọba* were his sons. But there is a cosmological interpretation which [describes] this "parent" of all Yoruba people as a goddess; and as all life springs ultimately from the earth, *Odùduwà* is said to be an earth goddess. Since a goddess cannot bear children without a god, she is partnered with *Ọbàtálá*! From the simile that the first *Ọòni* of Ifẹ̀ is politically ancestral as the earth is naturally ancestral, we [arrive at the belief] that the first *Ọòni* of Ifẹ̀ is an earth goddess. *Odùduwà*, as we have said, is *Odù-ó dá ùwà*, "Oracular utterance created existence."[20]

Odùduwà used her self, her "oracular utterance," to create existence; consequently, the Àjẹ́ of Odùduwà has, on some level, influenced and is a part of all living entities—human beings, flora, and fauna alike. Indeed, Ọ̀rọ̀ (power of the word), which manifests itself in many ways, including *ọfọ̀ àṣẹ* (the power to pray effectively), *àyàjo* (power of incantations), and *aásàn* (the power to curse and drive insane),[21] is inextricably linked to Àjẹ́.

In *Ìwà-Pẹ̀lẹ́: Ifá Quest*, Awo Fatunmbi elucidates the connection between Àjẹ́ and Ọ̀rọ̀, and he makes an important distinction between masculine and feminine acquisition of spiritual power, further validating my assertions about the phallogocentric construction of "African witchcraft":

> The power of the word itself comes from an elemental spirit known as *Àjẹ́*. Anthropologists usually translate *Àjẹ́* to mean "witch" and this inaccuracy has caused serious confusion regarding the theological foundation of *Ifá*. Both *Àjẹ́* and *Oro* are found at the *iroko* tree. *Oro* is the manifestation of the power of the word. *Àjẹ́* is the force that gives the power of the word the intensity needed to effect change. It is the polarity between *Àjẹ́* and *Oro* that makes effective prayer possible. The ability to pray effectively is called *ọfọ aṣẹ*. *Ifá* scripture suggests that women have *ọfọ aṣẹ* as a consequence of menstruation. Men receive *ọfọ aṣẹ* as a consequence of initiation. Because the power of the word is a natural birthright of women, this power has been

erroneously associated with "witchcraft" by those who have tried to give it a negative connotation.[22]

The power that Odù and Àjẹ́ wield is complex, elemental, and profound. What is more, it is not merely the biological act of giving birth but the entire concept of *creating,* and the mysteries surrounding how to sustain and develop creation, that signifies Àjẹ́ Odù and her ownership of Ọ̀rọ̀.

To ensure continuous human creation and evolution, Odù shared her powers with Òrìṣà (lit. Select Head, Deities) and Àwọn Ìyá Wa.[23] Using the oracular power of the Mothers, human beings create ritual dramas, proverbs, divination texts, healing rituals, and other forms of artistic and spiritual expression, including contemporary literature, music, and visual arts, that honor the Mother's original utterance and sustain, flavor, and structure society. Consequently, the orature and literature of Àjẹ́ elucidate its elusive being and constantly revise and codify its ever-shifting forms through culturally, artistically, and politically relevant art befitting Odùduwà.

THE TEXTS OF THE MOTHERS

Perhaps the best way to comprehend the magnitude of Àjẹ́ is through its literature, and in this section I use the orature of Àjẹ́ to elucidate the various properties and methodologies of this force. The text that forms the heart of this discussion is the *Ìtàn-Oríkì Ìyàmi Òṣòròngà*[24] (Historical Praisesong of the Deity of Àjẹ́). Recited by Oyeronke Igbinola[25] of Ife, Nigeria, who proudly heralds her Àjẹ́, the *Ìtàn-Oríkì Ìyàmi Òṣòròngà* (*Ìtàn-Oríkì*) is a profoundly important contemporary exposition of Àjẹ́ by an owner of the power. However, because the paradoxical nature of Àjẹ́ suffuses its literature, it is necessary to foreground the analysis of the orature of Àjẹ́ with a discussion of the type of *ìtàn* (texts) it produces.

In the article "In Praise of Metonymy: The Concepts of 'Tradition' and 'Creativity' in the Transmission of Yoruba Artistry over Time and Space," Olabiyi Babalola Yai elucidates the full meaning of *pa ìtàn,* which has been "inadequately" translated in English as "to tell a story" (*pa,* "to tell or speak," and *ìtàn,* "story"). As Yai explains, "*Pa ìtàn* is actually to 'de-riddle' history, to shed light on human existence through time and space." Yai describes three primary dimensions of incorporative totality at work in pa ìtàn: (1) the chronological dimension; (2) the geographic dimension, which includes sites of origin and natural migration and expansion; and (3) the "discursive and reflexive dimensions" of the ìtàn.[26] Yai's elucidation of the intricacies of

Yoruba orature is profoundly important. However, in the process of illuminating its figures and features, the ìtàn and oríkì of Àjẹ́ add more layers of complexity. Encompassing and transcending the constructs of time, space, and text around which human existence, pa ìtàn, and literary analysis revolve, the verses of Àjẹ́ are conceptual conundrums that pa ìtàn (de-riddle, decode) as they *pa àlọ́* (lit., "tell a riddle," or "encode").

ÀJẸ́ AND COSMIC CREATION

The tutelary Òrìṣà of Àjẹ́ are Odù and Ìyàmi Òṣòròngà. These Deities' names are synonymous with the concept of Àjẹ́, and both have individual and communal attributes: Terrestrial Àjẹ́ inherit Odù's power, and Ìyàmi Òṣòròngà heads the Ẹgbẹ́ Àjẹ́ (group of empowered women) called Àwọn Ìyàmi Òṣòròngà. Odù and Ìyàmi Òṣòròngà share so many attributes that they are not unlike twin sisters, Odù being the introvert, Ìyàmi Òṣòròngà the extrovert. At other times they are an amalgamated force. Many mythistories detail the origins of Àjẹ́. Depending on the origin text and the stage of creation, the Creator Mother may be Odù; the Womb of Origins, who is *the* Àjẹ́; or Ìyàmi Òṣòròngà, the Great and Mysterious Mother.

That Òrìṣà of Àjẹ́ are central to the formation of the earth and are credited with the creation of existence reveals the centrality of Àjẹ́ in Yoruba cosmology. The *Ìtàn-Oríkì* also reveals the esoteric and exoteric origins and function of this force. Lines four to thirteen reveal Àjẹ́ to be

> 4   One from Orífín, one from Odò Ọbà
> ....
> 6   They go on outings to bring sunrise and sunset.
>   Where do you meet her?
>   You meet her at the crossroads
>   You meet her at the crossroads of sixteen roads
> 10 Eight go to the ayé (the earth),
>   Eight go to ọ̀run (the cosmos).
>   What does she hold?
>   She holds sixteen long livers.

Àjẹ́ originates in what would seem contradictory places. Odò Ọbà (a river named after Òrìṣà Ọbà; see chapter 2) is a tributary of the Ọ̀ṣun River; its source is in the town of Igbon in Igbomina (North of Ibadan). In the Ijesa Yoruba dialect, Orífín means "the Heavens." That Àjẹ́ originates in an actual river and in the cosmos illustrates the force's paradoxical nature and ubiquity. Àjẹ́ is also elusive. Although Àwọn Ìyá

Wa have spiritual meeting places on the earth, such as the three-road junction and ìrókò and baobab trees, they are not relegated to specific places. To add complexity to paradox, one is not directed to go to Orífín or Odò Ọbà to meet Àjẹ́ but to "the crossroads sixteen of sixteen roads."

The sixteen crossroads and sixteen long livers are the most richly symbolic concepts in the foregoing passage. In the Ifá spiritual system, sixteen is a number associated with completion; it is a spiritual prime number.[27] Even with modern technology, sixteen crossroads is improbable outside of a spiritual context. Such a place can be found only where the physical and the spiritual worlds meet—at the boundary between heaven and earth or between the astral and material realms.

At the sixteen crossroads, the Mothers hold sixteen long livers, which represent the pinnacle of humanospiritual dominion. The liver is one of the primary organs Àjẹ́ attack, but in addition, the liver, the umbilical cord, the ọ̀ja (cloth for wrapping and carrying one's child on one's back), the ọ̀kẹ́ (amnion), and the gèlè (the cloth headtie) are all intimately and inextricably connected to their human owners, and they are controlled or "held" by Àwọn Ìyá Wa and cannot be untied or wrenched away by any force. Thus, the Mothers are physical women who boast cosmic control of existence through sacred objects that span the spiritual and material worlds. An ẹsẹ Ifá (divination poem) recorded by Osamaro Ibie describes the supremacy of Àwọn Ìyá Wa by referring to their majesty and their tying and binding totems:

> Who can claim to be bigger than the buffalo?
> Who can boast of being more influential than the king?
> No head-tie can be wider than those used by the elders of the night!
> No rope can be as long as the one used by the witches![28]

Administering life, death, destiny, and transcendence with sixteen sacred objects, Ìyàmi is One Who Knows When Man Would Cease to Exist.[29]

Àjẹ́ encompasses myriad forms, actions, and entities, and it is so multifaceted that even explication by a member is a supreme act of artistic encoding. The re-riddling of the Ìtàn-Oríkì is apparent in the seamless weaving of sacred and terrestrial times and places. Re-entangling through disentangling is also apparent in oríkì that span from seemingly aesthetic praise—"one with captivating eyes"—to gratitude for spiritual endowment—"It is Ìyàmi who gave me àṣẹ!" The oríkì move from awesome grotesque power—"One who eats bile from the belly"—to mystic abilities—"When they fly, they pay homage to Olọ́run"—to the ambiguous—"One who kills without motivation of inheritance." Ìyàmi Ọṣòrònga is the essence of riddling. She is the spiritual and biological Mother. She is also a supernatural and terrestrial taker or reclaimer of the lives she grants. She has full mobility in all realms, and she is also a collective, a "we."

Yai argues, "The essence of art is universal bifurcation. Yoruba verbal art, oríkì, abundantly display this bifurcation." However, the *Ìtàn-Oríkì Ìyàmi Òṣòròngà* riddles concepts of "orí (individuality) and ìyàtọ̀ (difference, originality)"[30] in intriguing linguistic and humanospiritual ways. The *Ìtàn-Oríkì* is an utterance riddled with deceptively simple pronoun shifts. In every "they" there is an implied "we"; in every "you" there is an implied "I," and these identifications are literal and cosmic and encompass various levels. Ìyàmi Òṣòròngà is a historical and spiritual entity, and she is also every terrestrial member and those who will come to be. Thus, Igbinola's recitation is at once cosmic biography of the M/Other and auto/biography of the Self. The melding occurs not only as a result of a She/I/We confluence but also because Àwọn Ìyá Wa are actually the forces they themselves praise. Àwọn Ìyá Wa are not vessels Ìyàmi possesses, nor are they priests or devotees of the Mother—they are the actual living embodiments of Ìyàmi; they are Àjẹ́. Furthermore, because of the forces of invocation and unification that suffuse the ritual utterance, the *Ìtàn-Oríkì* involves not only re-membering through oral literature but also a polyvocal grand verbalization in which the self is the literature and the literature is the self.

The complex union of individual, group, Deity, and text is evident in Igbinola's affirmation-supplication: "Just as they say it / so am I saying it now / Please have mercy" (lines 56 to 58). And although Igbinola was speaking to and for me, I was not the entity from whom she sought mercy!

The following passage also melds ritual praise of the M/Other with recognition of a vastly empowered communal Self with declarative spiritual ecstasy:

>   Ìyàmi, I give you respect
> 115 Ancestors, I give you respect
>   I give respect to sunrise and sunset
>   Àwọn Ìyàmi herself gives me àṣẹ!

Born with Àjẹ́ and endowed with àṣẹ, Igbinola has powers, sources, and obligations that are cosmic, ancestral, and literally and figuratively astronomical.

The fact that creation, compassion, killing, and composure are nurtured as a single kernel in the single palm of a conglomeration of women that is one is a recurring theme of the *Ìtàn-Oríkì*:

>   When they fly
>   They pay homage to Ọlọ́run
> 150 They say *alálàfunfun, alálàfunfun, alálàfunfun*
>   [immaculate white]
>   They are going out
>   May they go well
>   And come back well.
>   A composed collective, we appear with the day,
> 155 A composed collective, we appear with the moon [night],
>   A composed collective, they [or we] meet Ìyàmi.
>   Ambassadors of the sun;
>   Ambassadors of the afternoon; Ambassadors of the night;
> 160 A composed collective, they [we] meet Àwọn Ìyàmi.

As the ambassadors of the sun, afternoon, and night, the Mothers originate and boast control of terrestrial and spiritual realms and sacred and linear time. Àjẹ́'s control of time is also recounted in Yoruba orature.

In *Ifism*, Ibie describes Ọlọ́run (the God of the Sky) entrusting Ìyàmi Òṣòróngà with the administration of *ọ̀run* (the cosmos) while Ọlọ́run bathes. Not only is she the only entity permitted to see Ọlọ́run naked but she is also charged with informing the cock to crow when the bath is over, thereby initiating the day.[31] Thus, the work of Àjẹ́ on ayé begins in ọ̀run, and Ìyàmi Òṣòróngà's methodology encompasses and surpasses chronological time. Àwọn Ìyá Wa have adapted to modernity and keep their vigilance not only with the sun and moon but also by "one p.m. and one a.m." (line 60). These cosmic-terrestrial beings are by no means arrogant about their power but carry out their duties with dignity and aplomb, as a "composed collective."

In *Yurugu*, Marimba Ani explicates the phenomena at work in Àjẹ́'s melding of linear and sacred time:

> In the African conception, sacred, cyclical time gives meaning to ordinary, lineal time. The circle/sphere adds dimension to the line as it envelops it. The sphere is multidimensional, and it is curved. Sacred time is not "past" because it is not part of a lineal construct. The ancestors live in the present, and the future lives in us. Sacred time is eternal and therefore it has the ability to join past, present, and future in one space of supreme valuation.[32]

Àwọn Ìyàmi Òṣòròngà can be described as the spiritual-material owners of the "space of supreme valuation"; this is evident in such descriptive oríkì as "One who reigns in the night," "Ambassadors of the sun," and "She holds sixteen long livers." Àjẹ́ textures linear time and terrestrial space and their spiritual counterparts. Given the holistic linear and cyclical authority of Àjẹ́, one must be prepared to "move beyond ordinary time and space to a higher level on which events can become meaningful in terms of cosmic or universal causation"[33] in order to comprehend this force and its owners.

SPIRIT BIRDS OF THE MOTHERS

Àjẹ́ assume many astral and material forms to enact "cosmic . . . causation," but they are most commonly linked to birds, especially doves, vultures, pigeons, and owls. Indeed, Àjẹ́ are known as Ẹléyẹ, the Owners of Birds. While all Àjẹ́ embody birds, Odù is the paramount Ẹléyẹ, and she makes her entrance at the Gèlèdé festival as the phenomenal Ẹyẹ Òrò, the Spirit Bird with the bloody red beak:

> Spirit Bird is coming
> Spirit Bird is coming . . .
> The One who brings festival today
> Tomorrow is the day when devotees of the gods will worship
> You are the one who brought us to this place
> It is your influence we are using
> Ososobi o, Spirit Bird is coming.[34]

Honored as the source of creative expression, Ẹléyẹ rises with each sunset and sunrise to influence and bless her progeny whether or not there is a festival.

It is only fitting that the emissaries of Ẹléyẹ Odù are gifted with their own Spirit Birds. In another praisesong, Igbinola heralds her bird of power:

Ìyàmi Àbèní	My mysterious mother Àbèní
Mo léyẹ nílé	I have a bird in the house
Mo léyẹ níta . . .	I have a bird outside . . .
Mo rìnde òru	I walk in the night
Mo rìnde òsán	I walk in the afternoon
Ti mo bá lo sóde	When I go on outings
E fòwò mi wò mí o.	Give me my proper respect.[35]

From the ancient time of Odù to this day, an ẹyẹ (bird) enclosed in a calabash has symbolized Àjẹ́.³⁶ According to J. R. O. Ojo, women receive their Spirit Birds through the Ìyálóde (lit. "Mother of the Outside," a powerful station and title among the Yoruba). It is "to her [that] other women who want to become witches come with their calabashes in which they will keep the birds which the Iyalode will give to them."³⁷ Igbinola's praisesong of personal power reflects the authority invested in Àjẹ́ as a result of their cosmic affiliation with Odù. The song also implies that the Spirit Bird is resident inside the human body and has unlimited access to both the astral and physical worlds. The threatening plea of the last line, "Give me my proper respect," alerts the listener/reader to the potentially fatal power that is accorded Àjẹ́ through ẹyẹ.

Ẹyẹ Àjẹ́ are often described as the evil familiars of Àjẹ́, and the complicated social perceptions about and complex methodologies of Ẹyẹ Àjẹ́ are described in many divine texts. The first stanza of an oríkì recorded by Ayo Opefeyitimi describes Ẹyẹ Àjẹ́ as desired and ubiquitous:

> My passion the-flying-beings
> the mysterious bird (ẹyẹ funfun) to my right hand
> the mysterious bird (ẹyẹ funfun) to my left hand
> the mysterious wild bird (ẹyẹ mafunmafun) in the centre of the boundary between heaven and earth³⁸

Death and death imagery is juxtaposed with longevity and immortality in much of the orature about Àwọn Ìyá Wa. This is apparent in the second stanza of Opefeyitimi's verse which highlights Ẹyẹ Àjẹ́'s duality through praise analogies:

> They are the eaters of human liver without vomiting
> The hunter who dips the hand into the charm-purse to bring out poison
> Master medicine being who brings charms out of the pocket
> Snake who is not accompanied by its young ones on secret expeditions

The passion and power described in these lines are sufficient to prevent death or cause it. Not only does this stanza illustrate the magnitude and detail the prowess of Ẹyẹ Àjẹ́ but the grotesque images of death, rich with significant references to hunters (who are closely linked to Àjẹ́) and animals, go far in inducing fear and confusion into the mind unprepared for the multiplicity of Àjẹ́. When it seems the verse will spin into oblivion, the oríkì ends simply: "You are the beings in whose hands this life is placed." This open-ended conclusion bespeaks a confidence born of trepidation and admiration. Because the ritual words of praise detailing the awful and awesome methodology of the Mothers have been uttered, the speaker can be certain that the mysterious birds will not devour the life they hold but will use their stupendous hunting, healing, and harming abilities to protect, bless, and assist.

An ẹsẹ Ifá of *Ọ̀ṣẹ́-Méjì* recorded by William Bascom also illustrates the cosmic-terrestrial sanctuary that Ẹyẹ Àjẹ́ provide. The ẹsẹ Ifá reveals that at one time "evil spirits of the world" (*ibi gbogbo inu aiye*) wanted to kill Ọ̀rúnmìlà, the Òrìṣà of divination. Ọ̀rúnmìlà told the "evil spirits" that he "had a master as they did and that his master would deliver him."[39] Bascom states that Ọ̀rúnmìlà's master is his "ancestral guardian soul." His ancestral guardian must be on intimate terms with Àjẹ́, for Ẹyẹ Àjẹ́ deliver him from evil. Ọ̀rúnmìlà, consulted the same Ẹyẹ Àjẹ́ mentioned in Opefeyitimi's verse: "He went to the white birds ["eye fin-fin"] inside the termite hill, to the white-spotted birds ["eye ma-fin-ma-fin"] on the left side, and to the white birds who flew to earth from inside the termite hill."[40] Following this he sacrificed white kola, red kola, and alligator pepper to the three types of Ẹyẹ Àjẹ́. The birds used these items to make *egiri* ("not-see-death medicine") for Ọ̀rúnmìlà. It is significant that one of the diviners Ọ̀rúnmìlà consulted is "Akoda, the diviner of 'One who owns soil.'" "One Who Owns Soil" could easily be a praisename for either Ìyá-Àyé, the Mother of the Earth and principal Òrìṣà of Àjẹ́ (see discussion below), or Odù. With the Mother of the Earth furtively and Ẹyẹ Àjẹ́ actively overseeing his destiny, Ọ̀rúnmìlà gained immortality. Far from being the embodiment of evil (*ibi*), Ẹyẹ Àjẹ́ are instrumental to salvation.

THE COLOR OF POWER

In addition to rendering void assertions about the inherent maliciousness of Àjẹ́ and Ẹyẹ Àjẹ́, both of the foregoing ẹsẹ debunk a prevalent myth. In line with the Eurocentric racial hierarchy, there are three types of Àjẹ́ discussed in contemporary Yorubaland. *Àjẹ́ funfun* (white) are said to perform benevolent acts, such as imparting wealth, prosperity, good health, and protection. *Àjẹ́ dúdú* (black) are said to cause misfortune and bad luck and to induce people to commit criminal offenses and suicide. *Àjẹ́ pupa* (red) are said to specialize in bloodletting, car wrecks, cuts—any incident that will result in bloodflow.[41]

The ęsę Ifá refer to Àję́ as Elders of the Night, People of the World, Owners of the World, Bird Women, and Our Mothers; Àję́ are described as a collective working toward the same goal, as is evident in the orature describing various birds of Àję́. There is no hierarchical scaling of white, red, or black Àję́ in traditional orature, and Yoruba cultural historians Bade Ajuwon and Adebayo Faleti posit that the color-coding of Àję́ occurred during the eras of colonialism and neocolonialism.[42]

With the encroachment of an alien imperialistic Western worldview that designated African traditional beliefs as "pagan" and defined Africans as inferior because of melanin and in a misogynistic world that abhorred women's power when not used for the benefit of European patriarchal supremacy, it may have been expedient for Àję́ to camouflage its timeless force under the Western concept of "whiteness." Igbinola made it clear that her Àję́ is funfun, and she may not have felt secure discussing Àję́ without that qualification. Furthermore, lines 60 to 71 of the *Ìtàn-Oríkì* differentiate the work of Àję́ funfun from Àję́ pupa and Àję́ dúdú in terms of motivation and the times when each is active. In Igbinola's recitation, Àję́ pupa and dúdú come onto the astral scene two hours after Àję́ funfun have had their deliberations. While this may be the case, applying the Western white is "good," black is "evil" hierarchy to Àję́ is misleading and reductive, especially given the original and contemporary roles of Àję́ in ordering society; the perplexing and complex force and infinitude of Ìyàmi Òṣòròngà, who is the Mysterious Mother We Beg to Have and the mother from who mercy is pleaded; and the oríkì and the ęsę Ifá recorded by Opefeyitimi and Bascom, respectively.[43]

In contrast to a worldview centered on racist bifurcation, respect for multiplicity and diversity emerge as cornerstones of the traditional Yoruba ethos. A Yoruba proverb suggests we *"mọ ìwà fún oníwà"* (recognize existence in respect of the one existing); idiomatically, "concede to each person his or her own nature of existence."[44] The dominant genetic and phenotypic "nature of existence" is Blackness as imparted by melanin, and Àję́ is a melanin-related pigment-activated force.

Melanin and its genotypic and phenotypic properties are central to Yoruba philosophy and cosmology because the human being who boasts immaculate melanin is a direct reflection of Odù and her immaculately created cosmos. As I elucidate in *The Architects of Existence: Àję́ in Yoruba Cosmology, Ontology, and Orature*: Odù, which means Colossal Womb of Infinite Blackness and Creative Power, is *the* Àję́ and she is the cosmos.

Perfect and unadulterated pigmentation has historically been a source of great pride in Yoruba culture. In "The African World and the

Ethnocultural Debate," Nobel laureate Wole Soyinka discusses the cultural philosophy of the Yoruba in which Blackness is indicative of life, energy, vitality, and, most important, correctness.[45]

Soyinka's assertions are validated by many ancient sources, including an ẹsẹ Ifá that states that when Ọbàtálá made human beings, he created three vats of color. One vat was black (dúdú), another was red (pupa), a third was white (funfun). The Yoruba soul awaiting creation begged Ọbàtálá:

> Make me black,
> Do not make me red
> Make me black,
> Do not make me white
> Dye me with my ìwà first
> At the dawn of creation.[46]

More than a mere hue or ethnic marker, dúdú means profound depths. This infinitude originates in the Pot or Womb of Odùduwà, the immaculately Black daughter of Odù, who epitomizes the creative energy of dúdú (black). When the speaker of the ẹsẹ demands "Dye me with my ìwà first / At the dawn of creation," the request is in part for aesthetic beauty but it ultimately refers to the spiritual and cultural completion that cosmic, genetic, and phenotypic Blackness impart.

In Yoruba cosmology, the colors in question signify on even deeper levels and are cosmically connected. Odù's sibling aspects are Ìyàmi Òṣòròngà—who, like Ọbàtálá, is Òrìṣà funfun (a Deity symbolically represented by white)—and Ìyánlá, the Great Mother—who bears a white beard, which symbolizes wisdom and longevity.[47] Additionally, the Great Mother mask is wrapped in "a spotless white cloth called oloya or aṣo funfun [that] envelops her completely."[48] The white beard of Ìyánlá, the white hair of Ọbàtálá, and the immaculate white cloths of Ìyánlá and Ọbàtálá reflect *all* the characteristics, destinies, probabilities, powers, and methodologies that originate from the black depths of Mother's Womb of Life. Furthermore, the Great Mother's Ẹyẹ Ọ̀rọ̀ (Spirit Bird) is "immaculately white" but bears a blood-reddened beak that serves as a threatening promise to balance society by any means necessary. In lines 148 to 150, Igbinola describes Àwọn Ìyá Wa as paying homage to Ọlọ́run through one of the praisenames of Ọbàtálá, alálàfunfun (immaculate white), while on an outing. These lines confirm the inherent unity of Òrìṣà who have been recently disassociated from one another, and they indicate that the all-reflecting properties of white include the promise of blood retribution and blackness's creative-destructive-regenerative totality.

An oríkì of Àwọn Ìyá Wa is aláàwọ̀ méjì, one with two colors. These colors could be any combination of the dúdú of Odùduwà—the depth of knowledge and origins and the capacity to absorb, create, and recreate; the funfun of Ọbàtálá—the power to reflect, signify, and give individuality to every creation; and the pupa of Ẹyẹ Ọ̀rọ̀—the blood of life and death and all the àṣẹ in between.

Ọbàtálá is a perfect "reflector" for this discussion. Like Èṣù, Ọbàtálá partakes of both genders and has Àjẹ́ but has been subjected to patrification and Christianization. The Deity's white cloth has led to minimizing comparisons with the Christian God, and Ọbàtálá's Àjẹ́ and "equally expressive femininity," to borrow Ogundipe's phrase, is often overlooked. However, Ọbàtálá's multitudinousness makes a mockery of false equivalents.

In Pepe Carril's drama *Shango de Ima*, Ọbàtálá's self-description is faithful to spiritual reality and contains copious references to Àjẹ́:

> I was always sanctified and old. I was never able to be a child, to live the life of an ordinary woman. . . . But I have sixteen roads. I have humility. I am loving, vengeful, voluptuous, and simple. I am father, mother, king and queen. I am wise and serene. I am the mistress of destiny. And I am also nothing. . . . this white hair of mine reflects all mysteries. I have the power of all minds, and I bring retribution to those whose minds are evil.[49]

As lyrical and accurate as Carril's description is, an ancient oríkì of Ọbàtálá shared by C. L. Adeoye is more forthright and of even greater depth:

> Olufọ́n Adé, King fully adorned with white beads
> Those who label you Àjẹ́ are not liars
> It is the skull of another human being that you use to drink water
> For *osùn* (camwood) to rub your body, you use the blood of humans
> The water in the clay pot (*oru*) given to you
> Is placed on somebody else's head.[50]

This verse associates Ọbàtálá with the three colors of creation: The red blood of àṣẹ covers Ẹyẹ Ọ̀rọ̀'s beak and serves as Ọbàtálá's body lotion; Odù's earthen pot holds healing waters; and, symbolizing great wealth, Ọbàtálá is covered in her-his signature white beads. This verse also reveals the multifarious nature of Àjẹ́ in characteristically paradoxical form, as Adeoye explains, "In the old days, whenever [Ọbàtálá's] water pot was to be placed, a whole human being would have been buried there alive. The top of the head of the victim was where the big water pot was placed." An oríkì recorded by Yemi Eleburuibon reveals that Ọbàtálá's drum is made of "dwarf skin," and says that "The bone of the hunchback is the one we use to beat / Ogidan for the father [Ọbàtálá]."[51] While all this may sound terribly inhumane, what we are witnessing is the pinnacle of humanospiritual reciprocity.

A popular creation text describes how when molding human forms, Ọbàtálá got inebriated on palm-wine and molded misshapen figures. Rather than destroy these creations, Ọbàtálá asked Olódùmarè to endow them with life like all the others. The significance of Ọbàtálá's indiscretion and his-her rectification thereof is profound: Not only did the Creator stop drinking palmwine, but, as Rowland Abiodun reveals, "The hunchback, albino, and other deformed beings, all the hand-work of Ọbàtálá, received their 'license' or right to be respected and admired by virtue of their relationship with their creator, the cause of their existence."[52] It is said that when you see persons who have what Cee-Lo Green would call "perfect imperfections,"[53] you are actually seeing Ọbàtálá. Nikki Giovanni might say that Ọbàtálá is "so hip, even [her-his] errors are correct."[54] It is fitting that when Ọbàtálá's spiritual-physical charges die, their bodies are recycled for her-his worship.

Ọbàtálá both makes mandatory and epitomizes the Yoruba respect for a plethora of ìwà (character, characteristics, manners of existence), harmonization of forces, and appreciation of diversity. As the Òrìṣà of the white cloth, Ọbàtálá is a reflection of everything and reflects everything, including the rich profundity of Àjẹ́. Ọbàtálá functions like the prism, which bends, separates, and reveals the spectrum of possibilities lodged in the beam of "white" light. Transforming the linear prism into a circular rainbow, what comes from Ọbàtálá's creative Àjẹ́ and àṣẹ—all human forms—returns to Ọbàtálá in sacrificial and symbolic forms, only to be recreated again in cyclic infinitude. Ọbàtálá molds the heads of the yet-unborn and "will not allow his offspring to die." And just as it is in the hands of Àwọn Ìyá Wa that lives are confidently placed, Ọbàtálá, owner of all destinies, mysteries, and heads, who uses sacred water stationed on the head of a living human being to heal and protect, is fittingly beseeched, "Take care of my head for me."[55]

The color black represents perfection, vitality, and infinite depth. Red is often symbolic of blood, the fluid that holds and releases àṣẹ, the power to make things happen. The hue of spiritual transcendence is white. Òrìṣà of Àjẹ́ take on all the attributes and utilize all properties of these hues because these colors and their powers represent the totality of the cosmos. Recall that Ẹyẹ Àjẹ́ of two hues and three places of origin use a combination of white kola, red kola, and alligator pepper, which is black in color, to prepare the medicine of immortality for Ọrúnmìlà.[56]

The effectiveness of the medicine seems to depend on the melding of three elemental items that are connected to and integrated by three types of Àjẹ́. Similarly, Odù, Ọbàtálá, and Ìyàmi Òṣòròngà are three interconnected aspects of one force. From the Yoruba ontological perspective, manners of existence are infinite, and this plentitude is symbolized in the interrelated spiritual properties of the colors black, white, red; the various powers that result from combining elements with these hues; and the Òrìṣà and human beings who work with and through those colors and elements to ensure the sustenance of the world.

ÀJẸ́ AND THE ADMINISTRATION OF JUSTICE

The Ifá spiritual system of the Yoruba is holistic and comprehensive, encompassing cosmology, cosmogony, ontology, divination, ancestor reverence, science, and medicinal healing.[57] Àṣẹ and Àjẹ́ are central to this inclusive way of knowing and being. However, while Ifá and àṣẹ enjoy social appreciation and academic respect, Àjẹ́ remains swaddled in taboo and negativity. The societal perception of Àjẹ́ is directly related to its authority, invisible astral mobility, and social and political work. In discussing the administration of justice—the delicate and fear-inspiring duties of Àjẹ́—it is helpful to turn again to the *Ìtàn-Oríkì*:

> My Mysterious Mother, Whom We Beg to Have (Ìyaà-mi Àbẹ̀ní),
> The one with captivating eyes
> One who reigns in the night
> One from Orífín, one from Odò Ọbà
> 5   One who kills without motivation of inheritance

As is evident in line 1, the phrase Ìyá-mi (lit. "my mother") becomes transformed linguistically and connotatively under Àjẹ́. The mother becomes a Mysterious Mother whose presence is much desired and sought after, the proper name Àbẹ̀ní meaning One We Beg To Have. The mythistories make it clear that Ìyaàmi Àbẹ̀ní is analogous to Ẹdan, the Òrìṣà that the inhabitants of Ifẹ̀ Oòyè literally begged to come and cleanse the community when deceit and wickedness had caused upheaval.[58]

Ẹdan is "the Child of the Mother of the Earth," so she is a perfect mediator between human beings and the Earth Òrìṣà. Ancient sources reveal that when Ẹdan arrived on earth she prescribed ritual cleansing and sacrifice for everyone in addition to making everyone swear an oath of unity. In this way, Ẹdan initiated all inhabitants of Ifẹ̀ Oòyè into the

Mọlẹ̀, the Cult of the Earth, which is also known as Imọlẹ̀, Ògbóni Ibílẹ̀ and Ògbóni. C. L. Adeoye reveals important information about the origins and relationships of Ẹdan, Àjẹ́, and Ògbóni:

> When Ẹdan came to Ifẹ̀, she gave birth to Àjẹ́, and all the people who know the "mystery" of Ẹdan are elders called Ògbóni. Ẹdan is an Òrìṣà; Ògbóni is a cult or an association. The complete name for Ẹdan is Ẹdan Ògbóni. . . . There is an important association between Ẹdan, Ògbóni and Àjẹ́. It is because of this partnership that Àjẹ́ must not do anything that is harmful to Ògbóni. If Ògbóni offends Àjẹ́, Àjẹ́ is supposed to report them. Both Ògbóni and Àjẹ́ have to pay homage to Ìyá-Ayé, who is Ẹdan.[59]

Àjẹ́ and Ògbóni are not unlike fraternal twins of Ìyá-Ayé[60] who work together to enforce the laws that keep society on the path Ẹdan established millennia ago. Line 140 of the *Ìtàn-Oríkì* describes Àjẹ́ has "holding sixteen long Ẹdan," and with these profound emblems of power that unite the material and cosmic realms, Àjẹ́ direct, control, and hold the destiny of the Yoruba world.

Brass-cast male-female figurines joined at the head by a brass chain symbolize Ẹdan, the tutelary Deity of Ògbóni society. Ẹdan symbolizes the Yoruba expression "*Èta ni ti awo èjì ni ti ọgbẹ̀rì*" ("Threeness is to the initiate as twoness is to the uninitiated"). Babatunde Lawal contends that in addition to implying that members of sacred societies and those in possession of spiritual powers have deeper insight and knowledge than others, "this saying implies that the bond between two friends is not so strong as between two initiates sharing an oath of secrecy witnessed by a Deity, who is the invisible third party to all occult transactions and who will not spare a traitor."[61] Ẹdan contains the power of the ancestors, Mother Earth, and forces such as Àjẹ́ and àṣẹ—all figures, forms, and forces.

The comprehensiveness of Ẹdan facilitates dispensation of justice, as do the unique, politically structured eyes of Ẹdan and Àjẹ́. Ẹdan's eyes are described as large, yellowed, all-seeing, and ever open; Àjẹ́'s eyes are "mysterious" and "captivating." In contrast to the gouged-out or blindfolded eyes of Western justice, the eyes of Àjẹ́ witness *all* actions, particularly wicked ones, and ensnare offenders and traitors.

Àjẹ́ and Ògbóni are also the keepers of esoteric knowledge. Opeola expounds upon the centrality of Àjẹ́ and Ògbóni to Ifá specifically and to the Yoruba ethos in general:

In the past, nobody except he or she who belonged to the Cult of Incarnation could possess the true secret of Ifá or other similar systems of divination developed by the Yoruba, because the Ifá Arithmomancy (the literary corpus inclusive) was developed through the co-operation of the Ogboni cult and the Fraternity, to which most of the witches belonged. In the past, all people possessing secret knowledge of the universe, including Orunmila and his followers (the Babalawos), belonged to the Cult of Incarnation.[62]

Although Àjẹ́ are often shunned as mercurial destroyers, males with Àjẹ́, male members of Ògbóni, and Oṣó (a male force subordinate to Àjẹ́) are often lauded as noble. This dichotomy is the work of a power-hungry patriarchy. Kolawole Ositola echoes the findings of Opeola, asserting that Àjẹ́ and Ògbóni are "partners in progress, in status, in objective, in achievement." He goes on to say, "The foundation of Òṣugbó [another name for Ògbóni] is Àwọn Ìyá Mi Òṣòròngà."[63] Ògbóni or Òṣugbó society is constituted of males and females who have Àjẹ́. These "partners in progress" undertake holistic work that includes enforcing laws and developing society through application of spiritual knowledge. The foundation Ositola mentions is maternal, cosmic, and quite literal: A maxim of Ògbóni members (male and female) is "*Omú iya dùn ú mu*" ("Mother's breast milk is sweet"), which implies the unity of all members through both their biological mothers and the Great Mother of the Earth, who gave birth and sustenance to humanity.[64]

Oṣó is an intriguing group about which little has been written. Àjẹ́ and Oṣó have similar powers; they have also both been denigrated. The following group prayer/request is included in many Yoruba Christian services:

Ba wa ṣègún Àjẹ́	Help us destroy Àjẹ́
Ba wa ṣègún Oṣó	Help us destroy Oṣó
Ba wa ṣègún lóògùn	Help us destroy all herbalists and all their works [65]

Ironically, these three entities help ensure communal fertility, harmony, justice, and evolution.

Both Oṣó and Àjẹ́ (and babaláwo and oníṣẹ̀gun) were subjected to great oppression under Christianity and Islam; however, Oṣó was able to retain its respectability. Oyin Ogunba states that before Christianization, Oṣó did not connote negativity, and contemporary acceptability is evident in common Yoruba names that herald Oṣó such as Ṣoyínká (Oṣó yí mi ká; "I am surrounded by Oṣó"); Ṣodipọ̀ (Oṣó di púpọ̀; "Oṣó have become many"); Ṣotadé ("Oṣó to adé"; "Oṣó is as important as the king"); Ẹ̀ẹ̀rinoṣó ("I am well born; I thrive among Oṣó"); and Esuruṛoṣó ("a titled man of Oṣó wearing royal beads").[66] Oṣó's retention of its original meaning may be partially due to the fact that it is an exclusively, male power.

Oṣó operate a system akin to that of Àjẹ́: Their "secret guild" meetings at the base of the apa (African mahogany) tree correspond to Àjẹ́'s spiritual union with the ìrókò tree.[67] Additionally, Àjẹ́ and Oṣó are active in the astral realm and work closely together. Gẹ̀lẹ̀dẹ́ orature mentions the relationship between Àjẹ́ and Oṣó, saying, "Something secret was buried in the mother's house / A secret pact with a wizard."[68] With regard to this spiritual "pact," Yoruba elders say, "The mothers (aje) conceive a plan and their male counterparts (oso) carry it out."[69] However, for all their cooperative work, Oṣó are the subordinates of Àjẹ́. Unlike male Àjẹ́, Oṣó do not attend the deliberations of the Ẹgbẹ́ Àjẹ́; Oṣó are "knife-holders" who immolate those guilty of breaking cosmic laws.[70]

The apparent Àjẹ́-Oṣó hierarchy is subtly intimated in the Yoruba proverb "Oṣó l'oko Àjẹ́" ("Oṣó are the husbands of Àjẹ́"). In a patriarchal society, defining the male through the female indicates matriarchal authority rather than equality or intimacy. Apọkọdọ̀su, meaning The One Who Killed Her Husband in Order to Take the Òṣu Title of Òṣugbó,[71] also emphasizes Àjẹ́'s superiority to patriarchal entities. Furthermore, with this oríkì we can understand better why husbands in particular might fear their wives! The praisename also underscores the fact that spiritual relationships take precedence over terrestrial ones, as a husband provides a (requisite?) physical means to a spiritual end. Despite hierarchical distinctions, Àjẹ́ and Oṣó are above all "partners in progress" who work in conjunction with Ògbóni under the direction of Ẹdan, who is their tutelary Òrìṣà, to enforce the law of the Earth Mother, Ìyá Ayé.

The work of Oṣó, Àjẹ́, and Ògbóni, the enforcement of cosmic law, is exacting. At certain sacred trees, road junctions, or spaces in the astral realm, Àjẹ́ hold meetings to gauge the path of societal evolution and deliberate about offenders. According to Awolalu, "These meetings are held at different levels, local, divisional, regional, interregional, national and international. Communications are maintained between one level and the other."[72] The *Ìtàn-Oríkì* describes a meeting of the Ògbóni, Oṣó, and Àwọn Ìyá Wa collective:

> ... My Mothers,
> When they are going out
> When they wish to undertake their work

	They inform the owner of the house
40	That they are going
	When they come back
	They will proclaim they have arrived well
	They arrive safely
	They will say, "Ògbóni"
45	The response, "Ògborọ̀."

. . . .

91	[Call] "Ìyàmi, o! Ìyàmi, o! Ìyàmi, o!"
	[Affirmative response] "Hòóò! Hòóò! Hòóò!"
	How do they answer?
	Àjẹ́ respond three times.
95	Oṣó speak three times.
	Àwọn Ìyàmi respond three times.
	They will knock
	They will enter
	They will greet the owner of the house
100	When they want to eat intestines,
	When they want to eat liver,
	When they want to eat arms,
	When they want to eat legs,
	They knock three times
105	They enter to meet the victim
	They eat and eat
	Then they leave
	Afterward, they feel pity for the person and engage in lamentations:
	"O Ìyàmi o, please don't feed on me! Please Ìyàmi, don't feed on me!"

Àwọn iyá mi are astounding hunters. They can eat human bile and liver without flinching and devour arms and legs without vomiting. Their ability to undertake such acts is due to the fact that there is no physical extraction and ingestion of limbs and organs. After a successful "hunt," an offender's organs are astrally removed and retained by Ẹgbẹ́ Àjẹ́. From this time, the offender is granted a "grace period" of seventeen days to rectify his or her misdeed so the sentence can be repealed.[73] If the sentence stands, the "eating" of the organ(s) is *astral* but has definite physical consequences. The punishment is the equivalent of removing the soul, or àṣẹ, of a person. The excision of the offender's spirit will result in the physical decline of the body and death.

It is important to note that the *Ìtàn-Oríkì* depicts many figures and forces working for one goal under Àjẹ́. Lines 30 to 43 describe the Ẹgbẹ́

Àjẹ́ informing the owner of the house (*onílé*) of the astral mission they are about to undertake and bidding him or her farewell. However, lines 91 to 99 describe Àjẹ́, Oṣó, and Àwọn Ìyá Wa entering and greeting the owner of the house before they begin their work. Given the familiarity of address, the free movement to and from both astral and material domiciles, and the fact that the astral agents use the same ritual knocks and greetings upon departure and arrival, the homeowner who is bid farewell by the collective could easily be the homeowner the collective later visits and attacks. Because the inevitability of justice stands as a warning to all, the subject of an astral attack could easily be an Àjẹ́. For these reasons, the outings' participants "pity" their victims, engage in "lamentations," and encourage them to seek help.

The pleas of Àjẹ́ on behalf of their victims are not sarcastic or facetious. Àwọn Ìyá Wa assist in the exoneration of trespassers. As a Yoruba proverb makes wonderfully clear, "*Àjẹ́ òngbìjà ènìyàn ni ó di kòkó délé wí*" ("An Àjẹ́ attends the meeting and fights on your behalf, but when she sees you, she doesn't say a word"). The *Ìtàn-Oríkì Ìyàmi Òṣòròngà* also makes this point. Speaking of the enforcing Mother/Group/Self, lines 126 to 127 state, "You are the one who is devastating the affected / You are also the one who delivers the affected from devastation." Because they are "our Mothers" and because they could find easily themselves on the receiving end of Àjẹ́'s enforcement, they would rather teach lessons than slay. Indicative of their mobility in all realms and the power they consistently wield, Àwọn Ìyá Wa are called *abáàra méjì*, one with two bodies: one astral, one terrestrial. They know when to reprimand and when to destroy because, as their oríkì proclaims, *Arínú róde* ("They see the inside; they see the outside").

Àjẹ́ work under the auspices of Ìyá-Ayé, Ẹdan, and Imọlẹ̀, forces that cannot be tricked, bribed, or overruled. Contrary to popular belief, Àwọn Ìyá Wa cannot use their powers to maim or kill for fun or to satisfy a personal vendetta. While an Àjẹ́ may antagonize a person, that person cannot be astrally (and then physically) destroyed unless he or she has broken the spiritual and terrestrial laws governing the universe and his or her death has been approved collectively by the Ẹgbẹ́ Àjẹ́. As Ibie explains,

> Normally, the rule of the club is that no victim is punished without the benefit of a fair trial and conviction. In fact it is well known that no matter however much witches may hate a person, they do not strike until the person has been tried and found guilty. For as long as the person cannot be charged and convicted, they will not touch him.[74]

Àwọn Ìyá Wa are the "owners of society," but they are also representatives of the Earth Mother (Ìyá-Ayé), who is the ultimate judge: "God himself proclaimed that the ground (Oto or Ale) should be the only force that would destroy any witch or divinity who transgresses any of the natural laws."[75] Aware of the Mother's watchful eyes, Àjẹ́ pray for balance and overall correctness as they undertake the cosmic administration of justice:

> 85 We will not say what we are not supposed to say
> We will not make false steps upon the earth
> We will not make false steps during our outings
> We will not make false steps during our outings in the afternoon
> We will not make false steps during our outings in the midnight
> 90 We will not make false steps during our outings at night.

The system of checks and balances within Yoruba cosmology is logical and ordered. No matter the alleged color or the stereotyping moniker, Àjẹ́ is recognized as being "the most disciplined cult in the world."[76]

THE MOTHERS OF POWERS

One of the things that makes Àjẹ́ so overwhelming a concept is that it is not relegated to spiritually inclined humans. Many Òrìṣà have Àjẹ́ or were given Àjẹ́ to magnify and solidify their power. According to Opeola:

> Any Òrìṣà [involved] in creation, childbirth, or protection of a town . . . possesses the power of Àjẹ́. That is why Ọbàtálá is said to have Àjẹ́ because he created human beings; Ọbalúaiyé with prevention of disease is said to have Àjẹ́; war, defense, [and] everything associated with Ògún is also associated with Àjẹ́; [and] Odùduwà with growth, food supply—*everything*—giving birth and protection of children and crops. All [of these Òrìṣà and their attributes] are part of Odù and they share part of Àjẹ́.[77]

Àjẹ́ is an integral component of Ifá cosmology, and the following discussion will examine the Òrìṣà of Àjẹ́, or the Mothers of the Powers, and their influence on terrestrial life, ritual, and ritual literature.

ÌYÁNLÁ ODÙ—THE GREAT MOTHER

In the creation of earth, the genesis of the Yoruba people, and the origin of Ifá, Odù is the force of origins. She is the Great, Grand Mother of Àjẹ́, and she utilizes her force in many ways, including covenant-making, communication/signification, divination, and aesthetic, cosmic, terrestrial, and biological creativity. Fatunmbi calls Odù the "Womb of Creation."[78] She is also known as Ìyá Agbè (Mother of the Gourd or Mother of the Closed Calabash).[79]

In addition to representative praisenames, the profundity of the Ìyánlá (Great Mother) is apparent in the variations on her name that designate her various roles and attributes. She may be known as Odù, Oòdùa, Odùduwà, or Odúdùa.[80] Her vast power is evident in her oríkì:

> Great mother with whom we dare not cohabit
> Great mother whose body we dare not see
> Mother of secret beauties
> Mother who empties the cup
> Who speaks out with the voice of a man.
> Large, very large mother on the top of the iroko tree,
> Mother who climbs high and looks down on the earth
> Mother who kills her husband and yet pities him[81]

In a secondary tier of cosmic creativity, Odù is paired with the male aspect of Ọbàtálá. However, just as the oríkì above describes an ultra-fecund and life-giving Mother who is celibate and a Mother who takes on male attributes and eventually makes a male sacrifice, the Ìyánlá's relationship with Ọbàtálá is as complicated as the cosmic twinning of their black and white associative hues. John Mason describes the pair's complexity in *Orin Òrìṣà*:

> Odùa is reputed to have given birth to all the Ọbàtálás and is connected to the earth and the underworld of spirits. She is the mother creator of the human species and owner of all heads. Odùdúà and Odùa are called to cure the dying and help women have an easy birth. All of these attributes are also claimed by Ọbàtálá. Odùdúà, who is said to ride on the back of Ọbàtálá, is given, when preparing his medicine, only herbs that grow on top of another herb in a parasitic relationship. . . . Odùdúà is represented by two gourds that have been sealed and painted white. The medicine that is contained inside is said to blind you if the gourd is ever opened.[82]

As the flora that symbolizes them suggests, Ọbàtálá and Odùduwà are often depicted as adversarial complements.[83] However, creation outweighs conflict. J. Olumide Lucas reveals that the Òrìṣà consecrate their union in the cosmos and are depicted as being "locked in inseparable embrace symbolizing the union between earth and sky."[84]

While the Mother is often paired with Ọbàtálá in more recent ìtàn and origin texts, Odù is the Cosmos and the Womb of *All* Existence, and she needs no assistance. As Lucas reveals in *The Religion of the Yorubas*: "In the earlier myths Oduduwa is credited with priority of existence as compared with Obatala. She is regarded as having independent existence, and as co-eval with Olorun, the Supreme Deity with whom she is associated in the work of creation." Even more telling, Lucas's transliteration of Odùduwà is "Odu ti o da wa," the "self-existent personage."[85]

That John Mason attributes to Odù the creation of all humanity, including "all the Ọbàtálás," emphasizes the centrality and supremacy of Àjẹ́. Opeola emphasizes this point:

> Odù was given power over all men. Olódùmarè gave all the power of the word to Ọbàtálá in the form of àṣẹ. But he gave Odù power over everything done by men. . . . If Odù has power over everything done by men and Ọbàtálá is a man, Odù has power over àṣẹ. . . . Odù is Àjẹ́.
> . . . She is the Great Mother. Nobody can do anything on the earth without consulting her.[83]

One of Odù's most significant origin texts (one she shares with other Òrìṣà of Àjẹ́[86]) recounts her role in the creation of the earth. The elders reveal that Odù was the only woman among the sixteen Òrìṣà that Olódùmarè, the Great Creator, commissioned to make the earth habitable and secure for humanity. Rather than work as a unit, the fifteen males decided to disregard the female principle, Àjẹ́ Odù.[87] With this act, the males rendered themselves biologically and creatively impotent. After integrating Odù into the creative process, the collective instituted life, humanity, and social structure on earth.[88] In addition to Àjẹ́ being a force essential to creation, the Àjẹ́ of Odù is independent of and complementary to masculine forces. Most significant, although her power surpasses that of the fifteen male Deities, Odù used her power with discretion and deliberation. As the descendants of Odù, Àwọn Ìyá Wa inherit the Mother's attributes and continue her struggle against sexual oppression and for holistic harmonization.[89]

Odù has been described as vindictive and reclusive, but she is also generous; she provided humanity with the means to communicate with her and gain esoteric knowledge. One of her gifts constitutes the "keys of life" of the Yoruba. An ẹsẹ Ifá reveals that after instituting life, spiritual force, and social harmony on earth, Odù prepared to return to the cosmos. Before she departed, she instructed three of the primary Òrìṣà to prepare sacred calabashes. Ọbàtálá brought a calabash of ẹfun, white chalk, symbolizing spiritual transcendence. Ògún contributed a calabash of èédú, or charcoal, symbolizing the carbon of existence and technology. Ọbalúaiyé placed osùn, or camwood (red in color), indicative of vitality, in his calabash. Odù's own contribution was a calabash of ẹrẹ̀, mud or earth, representing agriculture, abundance, and the ancestors. Odù placed the four sacred calabashes, which notably include the three hues of Àjẹ́ and the earth of origins, into a cylinder that serves as her cosmic seat and the means by which communication with her is achieved.[90]

The powers of signification and communication are also manifest in an important but often-overlooked gift of Yewájọbí to humanity, the Odù Ifá. In addition to her other roles, Odù was the wife of Ọ̀rúnmìlà, and she loved and respected him so much she "revealed to him the knowledge of divination so that man could communicate with the spirit realm."[91] Odù also bore sixteen children with Ọ̀rúnmìlà. These children became the sixteen Olódù (human embodiments of the primary divination verses) of Odù Ifá, in a remarkable example of word becoming flesh and flesh becoming word and word becoming *text*.[92]

Odùduwà has been translated as Oracular Utterance Created Existence, and as is revealed in the *Oríkì Ilẹ̀* (below), her gifts of Ọ̀rọ̀ are infinite and eternal. She endows her daughters, Àwọn Ìyá Wa, with Ọ̀rọ̀ and Àjẹ́, and she literally shared the sons she bore with Ọ̀rúnmìlà with the world so that all human beings could attain their destiny. Accordingly, her divine gifts bear her name, Odù Ifá.

ÌYÁ-AYÉ—THE MOTHER OF THE EARTH

The Earth Òrìṣà is known by many names: Ilẹ̀, Onílẹ̀, Àpẹ̀pẹ̀-Alẹ̀, and Ìyá-Ayé. She is heralded as the "brave and courageous . . . representative of Olódùmarè," and she is obviously central to existence. Yoruba orature reveals that in order to create the world, Olódùmarè told Àpẹ̀pẹ̀-Alẹ̀ to place some earth (her element), a chicken, four pigeons, and one chameleon in a basket and follow Ọ̀rúnmìlà to the small portion of earth upon which he was residing. After Àpẹ̀pẹ̀-Alẹ̀ poured the earth of self to create the firmament, Olódùmarè told her to dispatch the fowls to scatter the earth about and to allow the chameleon to walk on the earth to ensure its stability. By fulfilling her duties, Àpẹ̀pẹ̀-Alẹ̀ magnified herself and ensured humanity its home.[93] Furthermore, her use of a container and pigeons provides yet another powerful image of Àjẹ́'s Womb of Life and Spirit Bird solidifying creation.

With her essential role in creating the earth and existence through Àjẹ́, Ìyá-Ayé is the terrestrial twin of Odù. She ensures sustenance, fertility, and holistic development. As the origin, final resting place, and source of regeneration of life, Ìyá-Ayé is the reservoir of all forces: spiritual, ancestral, terrestrial, and cosmic. The following diagram[94] depicts the interconnectedness of Odù and Ìyá-Ayé and Àwọn Ìyá Wa.

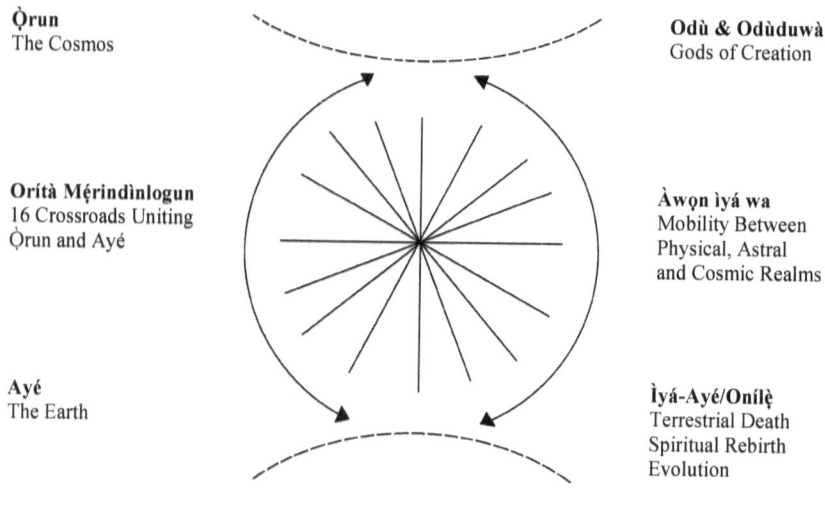

Interrelated Domains and Dominion of Àjẹ́

Odù, a decidedly spiritual entity with worldly dominion, is stationed at the top of this diagram. As the embodiment of the earth, Ìyá-Ayé is logically positioned at the diagram's foundation. The earth (ayé) and the cosmos (ọ̀run) are represented by broken lines to signify their porosity, the free access that Àjẹ́ have to these realms, and the fact that Àwọn Ìyá Wa are intermediaries who share aspects of both Ìyá-Ayé and Odù. The crossroads of sixteen roads, a perfect symbol for Àjẹ́, stationed at the center of the diagram, reflects Àwọn Ìyá Wa's full spiritual-physical, terrestrial-astral mobility and authority. Each of the sixteen roads is opened and overseen by Odù and Ìyá-Ayé, and as Àwọn Ìyá Wa administer Odù's covenant with humanity, they use their Àjẹ́ to send offenders to the tombs of Ìyá-Ayé, the only entity to whom Àjẹ́ are accountable.[95]

As discussed earlier in this chapter, the Mother of the Earth plays an important role in the enforcement of justice. Ìyá-Ayé is the Mother of

Ẹdan, who is also known as Imọlẹ̀ (Child of the Mother of the Earth).[96] Mọlẹ̀ was the original name of the Ògbóni society of elders who use the cosmic Àjẹ́ of Odù and Ìyá-Ayé to enforce social order. Members of Ògbóni refer to themselves as Omo Ìyá, children of the same mother,[97] and that Mother is Ẹdan or Imọlẹ̀. *Oríkì Ilẹ̀* (Praisesong of Mother Earth) reveals the esoteric compositions and judicial functions of Ìyá-Ayé and Ẹdan-Imọlẹ̀ and their connection to Àjẹ́ and Ògbóni society.

Oríkì Ilẹ̀

   Mother Earth, The Slippery One (Ilẹ̀ Ogẹ́rẹ́),
   One who uses the hoe to style her hair (Afọkóyẹrí)
   The owner of wicked bags (Alápò-Ìkà)
   One who has a stomach to swallow people
5 One whose curse has immediate effect (Àkété perí)
   One who eats Ọ̀ràngún without vomiting
   Òdù [huge pot] rolls and rolls without breaking
   He is the father of Lánní Pòrúkú poóyè
10 He is the father of Àbẹ̀ní
   Olódù Ifẹ̀ is the father of Àjẹ́
   All of them are children of Àpẹ̀pẹ̀-Alẹ̀
   Lánní is Ẹdan
   He never goes blind in Ilédì
15 He stares at you, stares at you
   Focuses his gaze on you
   Àbẹ̀ní is Àdè
   Who opens his mouth to swallow deceitful people
   Who arranges the skulls of the dubious for conference
20 Who hastens to pass judgment on people
   Who uses honesty
   To scatter the possessions of the wicked
   Àbẹ̀ní, the child of Oótùye Ifẹ̀
   Slippery One is the Mother of Ajíbọ́lá, whose name is Ẹdan
25 Don't let us step on you wrongly
   Let us walk on you for long
   For long the feet are destined to walk the earth
   Don't let us step on you Ilẹ̀
   Where it will cause you injury.[98]

Before analyzing this oríkì, it is necessary to address the gender incongruities in this text. It appears that the elders who rendered this oríkì attempted what I like to call a patriarchal shift in referring to Ẹdan,

Àbèní, Odù, and Ilè as fathers and endowing them with masculine gender. However, in the cosmology, the standard oríkì of the first seven lines, and Adeoye's discussions, it is clear that these entities are female. The close relationship between Àjé and Ìyá-Ayé is illustrated in lines 1 to 5 of the oríkì.[99] Both share the praisename Ilè Ògèrè, Mother Earth, the Slippery One. This oríkì is a reminder that *anyone* can "slip" on the earth and break a taboo or law, and anyone who does so, rank, title, and spiritual or physical power notwithstanding, will be punished. Afòkóyerí, One Who Uses the Hoe to Style Her Hair, refers to the enormity of the Mother and the fact that what provides humanity with sustenance beautifies her. Both Àjé and Ìyá-Ayé are Alápò Ìkà, the Owners of Wicked Bags mentioned in line 3. These bags contain healing salves, poisons and, most important, tombs.[100] The bags are "wicked" because one never knows which of their many skills—curing, cursing, or devouring—the Mothers will employ. Line 7 affirms that Òdù is, in fact, the Earth, itself. Her unending revolutions in the cosmos cyclically replenish and extinguish life eternally. Àjé Òdù is the source of all earthly existence.

In addition to detailing enigmatic attributes and stupendous deeds, the oríkì reveals lineage connections of Òrìsà of Àjé. Olódù (lit. "the Owner of Odù") is clearly recognized as the progenitor of Àjé. But the work of Àjé has many tiers. Line 23 states that Àbèní is the child of Oótùye Ifè, the reputed place of origin of the Yoruba peoples. This line refers to Àbèní and Èdan's action of arriving at and cleansing Oótùye Ifè of all rogues, thieves, liars, and double-dealers. Èdan is described in lines 13 and 24 as the child of the "Slippery" Earth, who, with "captivating" eyes, "focuses his gaze on you" and "never goes blind in Ilédì [the Ògbóni meeting house]." After witnessing infractions, Àbèní "uses honesty / To scatter the possessions of the wicked," passes judgment quickly, and devours traitors in her ever-ready earthen tombs. In Yoruba cosmology, justice is as sure as existence.

The first oríkì of Ìyá-Ayé constitutes a warning that is acknowledged in the praisesong's prayerful conclusion (lines 25 to 29) and in the *Ìtàn-Oríkì Ìyàmi Òsòròngà* (lines 85 to 90). Terra firma is filled with cosmic pitfalls, landslides, pots of riches, and regenerative tombs. Because everything is contained in the earth on which we live and walk, it is necessary to pray for correctness at all times and in all actions. Reminiscent of Àjé Òdù and her primal pot of creativity, which is the mother of all àpo ìkà, a praisesong of Ìyá-Ayé reveals, "Elephant died in the farm and the pot ate it up / Buffalo died in the farm and the pot ate it up."[101] No matter how large, small, overlooked, or powerful, the womb of Òdù and the tombs of Ìyá-Ayé give life, take it away, and dispose of the corpses completely, but they also reincarnate life through the comprehensive and cyclic power of Àjẹ́.

ÒṢÙMÀRÈ—THE RAINBOW SERPENT

Òṣùmàrè is the "Rainbow Serpent" or "Serpent in the Sky,"[102] and this important God literally elucidates the Àjẹ́ of Olódùmarè, or Odù, for humanity. In *Orunmila Magazine,* Solabade S. Popoola interprets the word "Olódùmarè" as "Olodu-Ikoko-ti-enikan-ko-le-re—The owner of the giant pot that nobody can surpass." Olódùmarè has also been translated as "Olodu-Ikoko-to-ntan-Osumare—meaning, the owner of the giant pot where Rainbow emerges."[103] Cosmically and etymologically, Olódùmarè, the architect of existence, is Odù the Womb of Creation and is revivified through Òṣùmàrè's light. Indeed, Fatunmbi interprets the word Olódùmarè as "The light of the Rainbow comes from the Primal Womb."[104]

In addition to their connections to Olódùmarè, Odù and Òṣùmàrè share important symbolic and terrestrial attributes. Both simultaneously provide and are symbolized by unending cycles of creation, destruction, and re-creation. Odù is the pot of life and the wicked bag of death; Òṣùmàrè is symbolized by the brilliant but intangible rainbow and a serpent that devours its own tail. Discussing the ravage-renewal motif of Òṣùmàrè, which is also manifest in Àjẹ́, Yai asserts, "Perhaps we must discern in this poetics a permanent will to conjure death, to prolong life ad infinitum, by the simultaneous interaction of the voice and the body periodically fitted into a plurality which is reassuring because it promises immortality."[105] Fatunmbi's translation of Òṣùmàrè as "the deity to whom I shall return"[106] supports Yai's assertion. Òṣùmàrè represents the brilliant light of the rainbow and its spectrum of possibility and enlightenment. Among the Yoruba, enlightenment is both conceptual and tangible: Òṣùmàrè's terrestrial form, the Rainbow Python, is said to deliver the "covenant between Olódùmarè and the people of Earth." The python also represents the ability of human beings to "become transformed and experience rebirth" or attain immortality.[107]

While the appearance of the rainbow and visitation of the serpent are sufficient reminders of eternal life, the Rainbow Python is physically equipped with the tangible light of transformation. It is said to hold in its mouth a mystic stone. When the python goes blind with old age, it discharges this stone which it uses as radar. Much sought after by spiritualists, the serpent's stone is said to be able to illuminate the darkest surroundings and endow its owners with wealth and good fortune.[108] Just as Àwọn Ìyá Wa utilize Odù's Àjẹ́ and assist her in the administration of law, so too does Òṣùmàrè have daughters who share the physical light of transformation and immortality with humanity, and their exploits are detailed in ẹsẹ Ifá.[109]

A sixteen cowry divination verse describes the marriage of Ọṣẹrẹgbo (Ọbàtálá), who owned "power of vision," and a woman named "Erè," which means python. Erè gave birth to three children, Elerin and Elegunrin, and, notably, Olódù. However, Erè and Ọṣẹrẹgbo's union dissolved when she swallowed his "power of vision." When Ọṣẹrẹgbo saw it glowing inside of Erè, he cursed her, causing her limbs to disappear and forcing her to walk on her chest. In this way, Erè became Òṣùmàrè, the Rainbow Python, the owner of the mystic stone and guardian of the cosmic covenant symbolized by the rainbow. The conclusion of the divination verse—"'Olodu, child of Python.' / They called him Olódùmarè"[110]—confirms etymological interpretations that Olódùmarè is the result and issue of Òṣùmàrè and Odù. Not only do Odù and Òṣùmàrè naturally have Àjẹ́ and acquire the àṣẹ of the "power of vision" but their merger creates Olódù, the cosmic knowledge that is the Odù Ifá, and it solidifies the promise of immortality manifest in Olódùmarè.

YEMỌJA—MAJESTIC MOTHER OF MANY GODS

> We are three whom the mother has born and placed into the world:
> The first one inherited the cloth (Egungun)
> The second one inherited the bloody buba (Aje)
> The third one looks in the house, and looks on the road, but finds nothing to inherit;
> That is why he [possibly she] has inherited the voice and the dance (Gelede).[111]

It has been previously stated that Odù is Yewájọbí, The Mother of Us All. This title is also used in reference to Yemọja, whose name is literally translated as "the Mother of Fishes." The Mother of Fishes and Mother of Us All is also the Mother of Many Òrìṣà. Yemọja gave birth to Ṣàngó (Òrìṣà of Thunder), Dàda, Ṣònpònná (Òrìṣà of Smallpox), Ògún, Ọya, Olókun (Òrìṣà of the Ocean), Ọṣun, Ọbà, Òrìṣà Oko (Òrìṣà of the Farm), Òṣùpa (The Moon), Ọ̀ṣóòsì (The Tracker), and Ajé Sàlúgà (Òrìṣà of Wealth).

Ìyá Yemọja's Àjẹ́ is as diverse as her "roads," or manifestations, are many. Yemọja Mayé'lé'wo is a healer "known for her knowledge of medicine and her close relationship with Òsanyìn [Lord of the Leaves],

Ògún, Òṣun Ikòlè and the Àjẹ́."[112] Yemọja is also a master diviner, an Iyaláwo (literally "Mother of Mysteries"). Yemọja Àsàbà (Yemọja, the One Chosen for Homage) was married to Òrúnmìlà, the father of divination, and under his tutelage she mastered different methods of casting Ifá. Àsàbà "was hailed, by the people, for being well versed in divination and medicine. Her predictions always come true and her medicines are always effective."[113]

As the "vaginal fluid of the earth,"[114] Yemọja is the water of life who makes the body of Ìyá-Ayé fertile. Her two most revered roads are Yemọja Òkuntè (Yemọja Who Laid Down the Ocean) and Yemọja Ògùntè (Yemọja Who Laid Down the Ògùn River).

> She is always found in the virgin forest and desolate places that hunters frequent. . . . Ògùntè has a violent and exacting nature and can be challenging and offensive. When she fights she carries the knife and other tools of Ògún on a chain around her waist. She also has a great knowledge of herbs and medicines and is expert in the preparation of Àfòṣe (charms for causing harm). Ògùntè is a fearless and tireless worker who dances with a snake wrapped around her arms.[115]

The fierce dancing of Yemọja, a woman of much style and many heads, became the signature of her Àjẹ́.

The mythistories reveal that when Yemọja came to earth, she became Ṣàngó's third wife and that she made a sacrifice so she could reach her destiny. Ṣàngó also consulted Ifá about his destiny, and he was directed to sacrifice a parrot's feather to ensure his success. He had the feather but refused to sacrifice it. On the day of a grand festival, Ṣàngó left his compound and was dancing and spinning "like a top throughout the town."[116] When Òṣun, Yemojí, and Yemọja tired of waiting for their husband to return, they commenced their festival, and Yemọja began to dance.

> Everyone in the neighbourhood gathered at Yemọja's home compound. After hearing an uproar from Yemọja's compound, the two elder wives decided to go and see what the matter was. The wives saw Yemọja dancing in a unique fashion . . . and . . . when everyone saw the parrot's feather on Yemọja's head they were astonished, and they said she was Ṣàngó's favourite wife.[117]

From spiritual, symbolic, and anthropological standpoints, Yemọja's dance, crowned by the parrot's tail feather, is the dance of Àjẹ́.

Raymond Prince finds that "the red tail-feather of the parrot is used as a sign of witchcraft power, and may be placed in a calabash or in the tree containing the witchcraft power."[118] Ṣàngó had the force of Àjẹ́, but by refusing to sacrifice—and magnify—it, he made a path for his wife's ascension.

Ṣàngó's gyrations through town are mundane in comparison to the spiritual, kinetic, creative force generated by Yemọja's Àjẹ́-crowned dance. In fact, her dance galvanized so much spiritual energy it stopped being creative and wrought destruction. Feeling slighted and dishonored, Ọṣun and Yemojí ran out of the compound with water pitchers, stumbled, fell, and became rivers. When Yemọja realized that her force had shattered her home, she fled with water, fell, and became the Ògún River. However, Àjẹ́, like matter, cannot be created or destroyed. Yemọja actually solidified her destiny through seeming destruction. "Water takes a crown," an oríkì of Yemọja, is literally manifest in her adornment with the parrot's feather and her becoming Ògùntè. But Yemọja's reign did not end with the river. She resurfaced, married Oluweri, and continued dancing.

As an Òrìṣà, Yemọja was the mother of many wonderfully endowed children, but as a woman, she had no issue for Oluweri. To have children, Ifá asked Yemọja to make one of the signature sacrifices of Àjẹ́, "plenty of mashed corn (ègbo) and clay dishes (awo) and . . . dance about with wooden images on her head and metal anklets on her feet."[119] Yemọja bore two children; the male she nicknamed Èfè because of his proclivity for joking. The female child was called Gèlèdé "because she was very fat and was an excellent dancer like her mother."[120] Yemọja founded the Gèlèdé festival held in honor of Àjẹ́ with her sacrifice and dance and through her progeny Gèlèdé and Èfè, who is the principal masker of the Gèlèdé festival. Mason describes Yemọja "as the ultimate manifestation of female power [and] the patron of the Gèlèdé society, who honor 'Our Mothers' so that they will lend their tremendous power to the uplifting . . . of society."[121] Entire communities stage Gèlèdé festivals, the epitome of pragmatic art, because Yewájọbí and Àjẹ́ "love the performing arts" and "favor all those who honor them with music and dance."[122]

There is also a cosmological bond connecting Gèlèdé, its implements, Yemọja, and spirit children. Community women who are infertile or are having difficulty conceiving attend Gèlèdé to ask the Mothers for children. The children given these women may be ẹlẹ́gbẹ́, children who belong to a spiritual group of Àjẹ́, and they can even be àbíkú children, who are literally "born to die." Honoring commitments they make in the spiritual realm, àbíkú children die quickly after they are born if they are not persuaded to remain on earth. Parents adorn àbíkú children with metal anklets because the rhythmic clinking they produce is thought to frighten the child's ever-present and alluring spiritual companions. Àbíkú are the charges of Yemọja Akúààrà (Yemọja Whose Abode the Dead Frequent), who "is said to tie up the àbíkú and keep them with their mothers in the world of the living."[123] Yemọja Akúààrà may give spirit children to women who are having difficulty conceiving,[124] and the irony of Àjẹ́ giving women children who are "born to die" and who may quickly return to the Mothers is obvious.

Àbíkú and ẹlẹ́gbẹ́ children symbolize Àjẹ́'s ravage of impending death and the promise of renewed life in various ways. Indeed, once they are born, these children are called *elére,* "children of the wooden image," for they are considered to be the living embodiments of the wooden dolls infertile women carry at the Gẹ̀lẹ̀dẹ́ festival.[125] Additionally, adult Gẹ̀lẹ̀dẹ́ dancers wear the iron anklets of àbíkú, which suggests a dual cosmic-birth tie to Àjẹ́ and Yemọja Akúààrà, just as children born with cauls over their faces, twins, and surviving àbíkú and ẹlẹ́gbẹ́ children have unique ties to Gẹ̀lẹ̀dẹ́ festival and the males may become maskers.[126] In a compelling blend of power dialectics, Yemọja's original maternity-inducing acts of supplication, ritual praise, and dance result in an amalgamated festival centered on the mothers' ability to give and take life.

ỌṢUN—ÒRÌṢÀ OF FERTILITY, ABUNDANCE, AND POLITICAL POWER

Òrìṣà Ọ̀ṣun is the spiritual and aquatic daughter of Yemọja; her name means "spring" or "source." Ọ̀ṣun is the inspiration for existence, and she is the force that motivates or soothes sentiment, longing, pride, pleasure, and pain. Like many Àjẹ́, Ọ̀ṣun has marine and winged aspects. She is a true Ẹlẹ́yẹ; the vulture, quail, and peacock are her winged messengers. Through the vulture, Ọ̀ṣun carries prayers directly to Ọlọ́run, and she is the only Òrìṣà with the authority to arrange a meeting with the Sky God.[127] She is also Ọ̀ṣun Ìkólé (The Stream That Builds the House). Her waters represent fertility, abundance, and development, so it is fitting that she is the owner of the Ọ̀ṣun River and that her town, Òṣogbo, is built on its banks. Ọ̀ṣun is also an expert pharmacist, and her medicines are given their potency through ọfọ̀ àṣẹ. Commanding powers of Ifá, ọfọ̀ àṣẹ, Ọ̀rọ̀, and Àjẹ́, Ọ̀ṣun boasts guardianship of spiritual, biological, material, and social spheres of life.

As is her mother Yemọja, Ọ̀ṣun "is the champion of women and the protectress of mothers" and Our Mothers, for "the Àjẹ́ are her associates."[128]

> As a woman who knows the agony of birthing humanity, she bonds with other women who share this painful responsibility to maintain the world. . . . *As a female deity, she possesses the power to withhold the life-force which activates humanity through the male principle. That singular power emphasizes that without the female principle, the male principle is rendered impotent.*[129]

Given her influence in spiritual and social realms and her importance to Àjẹ́, it is logical that Ọ̀ṣun can be a fierce warrior when necessary. Like Yemọja and Onílẹ̀, she has a close relationship with Ògún and wields his implements of war. Ọ̀ṣun Ibú Àparò is described as "tall, very neat, extravagant, antagonistic, and pugilistic."[130] However, Ọ̀ṣun's preferred weapons are grace, cunning, and dignity. An ẹsẹ Ifá recounts a time when, with only a drum and a song

> Sewele sewele,
> Oshun is coming to play;
> Oshun does not know how to fight
> Sewele sewele[131]

Ọ̀ṣun was able to do what Ṣàngó, Ọbalúaiyé, Egúngún, Ògún, and Ọya all failed to do—establish social and spiritual harmony and balance.

Another ẹsẹ Ifá describes how Ọ̀ṣun reintegrated segregated genders with a Gẹ̀lẹ̀dẹ́-like dance. At one time, "Four Hundred and One Deities . . . were making war on the Town of Women," and it was "an unsuccessful war that they could not win."[132] Several Òrìṣà stormed in and were promptly defeated by the Àjẹ́. Ọ̀ṣun was the only Òrìṣà with the presence of mind to consult Ifá and make the sacrifice of cowries, a pigeon, a cock, a calabash, and a skein of thread. The thread symbolizes umbilical cords, headties, and long livers, all of which are owned by Àjẹ́ and connect them to human beings. Ọ̀ṣun used this thread to bind the Àwọn Ìyá Wa to their community. Melding the masculine power of the cock with the female force of the pigeon, she captivated and captured the warring women. Beating Odù's calabash and pulling Àjẹ́'s rope, which spans from heaven to earth, Ọ̀ṣun announced the return of the Mothers with a dance and song: "I have brought them; / Long, long rope, / I have brought them, long."[133]

Confounding the division of myth and history, the ẹsẹ Ifá concludes:

> This is how they took power
> And gave it to women until today;
> And that women became the husbands,

And have more power than men in the presence of the king.
Since a woman won the war for him
They are
The ones who live with him.[134]

Her oríkì queries rhetorically, "Who does not know that it is the Òṣun Òṣogbo, who helps the Ọba manage/rule Òṣogbo?"[135]

Òṣun is the essence of political Àjẹ́ and represents "females in power, controlling not only law and economies but the ability to market their own natural resources."[136] She is the "consummate woman," who founded and defended towns, whose name may have become a title for lineage queens,[137] and who continues to liberally distribute Àjẹ́ to her progeny. Her devotees honor her force and their inheritance with an oríkì riddled by a deceptively simple simile:

> My Ọ̀ṣun of healing waters, one who is as effective as salt.
> When we are as effective as salt in using the healing waters,
> When I am Àjẹ́, I am as effective as salt,
> I proudly grow long arms and hands for dancing.[138]

ỌYA—THE GOD OF TRANSFORMATION

Òrìṣà Ọya is one of the most undervalued but significant Òrìṣà of Àjẹ́. Her influence spans from the unborn to the ancestors to the domestic realm, and her totems and symbols are essential to many rituals in the itànkálẹ̀ (lands to which Africans were forcibly exiled). Enslaved Africans relied heavily on the transformation and transcendence Ọya's Àjẹ́ promised.

A self-directed example of Ọya's transformational force is recorded in the divination verse Òdí Òbàrà and concerns the battle that ensued when she left Ògún, her first husband, for Ṣàngó. Ògún, the master ironsmith, developed countless implements of war, including a staff that would reduce a man to seven pieces or a woman to nine pieces with one blow. Fascinated by the tool, and thinking ahead, Ọya asked Ògún to make her an identical staff, and she took the weapon with her when she left him for Ṣàngó. When Ògún hunted the lovers, he took his staff of disintegration. When Ṣàngó saw Ògún approach, he fled, but Ọya battled her ex-husband. When the two simultaneously struck each other, "Ògún immediately disintegrated into seven parts. Ọya broke into nine parts. That is the source of the saying: Ògún meje, Ọya mesan-an" (Ògún seven, Ọya nine).[139] Eventually Ògún and Ọya were resurrected, but in their battle there was no winner or loser, only transformation and symbolic solidification: Ògún's number is seven, which relates to his seven roads of worship, and Oya's number relates to her nine roads of worship.

Oya also used her transformative power usher Sàngó to his ultimate destiny as Divinity. Oya ruled the Oyo Empire alongside Sàngó, who grew bored in his peaceful and prosperous kingdom. To amuse himself, he ordered his two brothers (or favorite generals, depending on the origin text) to fight. When one was killed, Sàngó was so remorseful that he hanged himself from an ìrókò tree. Oya discovered his body and proclaimed, "*Oba kò so*" ("the king did not hang," or "the king is not dead"). Fatunmbi explicates the enigmatic pronouncement: "Oya has passed judgment on her husband's state of enlightenment. She is saying that he has learned the lesson of not abusing power and that he has taken the wisdom of the experience with him into the next life."[140] Seeing her husband's lifeless body entwined with the ìrókò tree, Oya spoke the Òrò that unleashed the winds of change and propelled Sàngó to immediate ancestral transmigration and Òrìsà status; hence, the importance of offerings to the Spirit of Òrò made at the ìrókò tree. Fatunmbi's assertion that Òrò "is the manifestation of the power of the word" and that "Àjé is the force that gives the power of the word the intensity needed to effect change" is magnificently manifest in Oya.

Whether wielding Power of the Word or a man-disintegrating staff, Òrìsà Oya is the embodiment of purposeful transmogrification and this is apparent in her dress, style, bearing, and childbearing. An ese Ifá informs us that "a cloth of many colors is the cloth of [Àjé]."[141] A cloth of many colors is also the cloth of Oya.

> There was a time when all the children of Oya were still-born or born premature. She went to Ifá and was told to make a sacrifice with $18.00, cloth of many colors (aso wínni-wínni), and a ewe (abo àgùtàn). She completed the sacrifice and ate the medicine made from the meat of the ewe. This medicine allowed Oya to give birth to nine children, the youngest being Egúngún (many colored cloths). From then on she was known as Ìyasan (Mother of Nine).[142]

Oya is called "Olomo [Owner of Children], who bore small children in a caul" and Ìyánsàn.[143] The circumstances surrounding the birth of her children are also spiritually significant. Gèlèdé leaders, speaking about the import of children born in the amnion (òké) say, "The sack tied by the gods cannot be untied by anyone."[144] The "sack tied by the gods" refers to Àjé's connection with spiritual children, and this connection manifests itself in the òja, or child-wrapping cloth; the èdò gbórogbóro, long livers; the Ẹdan gbórogbóro, long Ẹdan; the umbilical cord; the gèlè, or headtie; and the ọ̀kẹ́, the caul tied by Ọya.

Ọya's connection to the unborn and newborns is closely tied to her relationship to death and the ancestors. Egúngún is the spiritual society of the ancestors, and Ọya literally gave birth to the society through her child Egúngún and through her personal ascension. As is apparent in her relationship with Ṣàngó, from the moment of death, Ọya is present. Her purpose at funeral ceremonies is to "invoke Iku [Death Òrìṣà], who initiates the transformation that occurs at death. Ọya also opens the gates to the realm of the ancestors."[145] She stands at the center of humanity's two most profound transformations, life and death.

In addition to having Pan-African import, Egúngún rituals are important to the Pan-Yoruba nation, because "everybody has at least one ancestor to call upon."[146] Fittingly, Ọya's terrestrial daughters assist human beings in their quest to appease and honor their ancestors. In *Egungun among the Oyo Yoruba,* S. O. Babayemi reveals that "Iyámode and Yèyésòrun are the most senior women titles in the [Egúngún] cult. In Egbado, the female title-holders in the cult are the Iya Agan, Otun Iya Agan and Iyameko."[147] The title Ìyá Agan refers to Ọya's praisename, Áàjálayé, the Winds of the World, and her face, which "is so terrible that none dare to behold it; likewise, her wrath so devastating that it must be absolutely avoided."[148] The cloaked visage and the wrath of whirling wind are manifest in both the actual whirlwind and the spiritually intense Agan:

> You must not see my face
> No one can ever see Orombo
> Whenever the Agan comes out at noon
> (A gale will rage) toppling trees upon trees
> And palms falling upon palms
> Dense forests are set ablaze
> And savanna fields are burnt down completely
> This Ifa divination is cast for Mafojukanmi
> Don't see my face—Who is called Agan.[149]

Agan could be defined as a pure force of Àjẹ́ and àṣẹ. Ọya's Àjẹ́-rich Agan is the force of the Egúngún that "rids the society of all forces of instability."[150] At the calm center of the ancestor's gale of justice is yet another woman of Àjẹ́.

PROFILES IN POWER

Elucidation of the Òrìṣà of Àjẹ́ is important to this discussion. These figures and their forces recur in Africana literature, and their contributions to the Yoruba ethos and worldview are profound. It is important to emphasize the fact that the Òrìṣà have both mythical and historical aspects, as is evident in the ìtàn and oríkì. The comprehensive power of Àjẹ́ permeates all aspects of existence, and its proclivity for balance may well have contributed to African social organization. In *The Cultural Unity of Black Africa,* Cheikh Anta Diop argues that historically the vast majority of African societies were matriarchal. To avoid false Western comparisons, Diop precisely defines African matriarchy:

> Matriarchy is not an absolute and cynical triumph of woman over man; *it is a harmonious dualism, an association accepted by both sexes,* the better to build a sedentary society where each and [every one] could fully develop by following the activity best suited to his [or her] physiological nature. A matriarchal régime, far from being imposed on man by circumstances independent of his will, is accepted and defended by him.[151]

Harmonious gender dualism in Yorubaland resulted in empires founded and ruled by women. Pupupu is the acknowledged founder of Ondo;[152] Adetirin, a daughter of Odùduwà, is the founder of Igbomina;[153] Òṣun is the founder of Òṣogbo; and Ile-Ife was founded by Odùduwà. There is also evidence that several women ruled Ife after Odùduwà, including Moropo, Oluwo, Bebooye, and Omogbogbo.[154]

With the influx of Indo-European settlers, traders, and enslavers and the spread of Islam and Christianity, a patriarchal shift occurred in Africa. In Yorubaland, the shift occurred between the 1600s and the 1900s. Whether the society remained matrifocal or not, "Northern crescent," Indo-European, or Western beliefs that women are at best inferior to men and at worst base, lowly harbingers of evil, infected the African male psyche. The patriarchal shift, along with the adoption of a Eurocentric psychosexual ideology, contributed significantly to the male: good, female: evil dichotomy and promoted the social and political devaluation of women.

In the attempt to realign history with patriarchy, recent male rulers have tried to obliterate women rulers from Yoruba history,[155] and debate about the gender and import of many spiritual and historical female figures in Yorubaland continues to this day. And although a reduced female political presence saw a corresponding rise in female ritual activity,[156] as the pronouns of the *Oríkì Ilẹ̀* and other texts reveal, women's roles as originators and key players in important societies such as Orò, Ògbóni, and Egúngún have been minimized or inverted.[157] However, Àjẹ́ cannot be destroyed, and countless women used their timeless and resilient inheritance to fight the patriarchal shift and colonialism and attempt to restructure their communities. Three of the most notable Yoruba warriors are Tinubu, Efunsetan Aniwura, and Olufunmilayo Ransome-Kuti.

The title Ìyálóde (Mother of the Outside) garners much respect in Yorubaland. It is a social-political-spiritual title, and its bearers are all Àjẹ́. Madame Tinubu was the Ìyálóde of Abeokuta in the middle 1800s. She initially rose to prominence in Lagos and Abeokuta because of her wealth and status. But her vast dealings in "slaves, arms, ammunition, palm oil, salt, and tobacco"[158] firmly cemented her social and political power and gave her leverage as a key player in matters of state.

Tinubu refused to honor the decrees of the British government. She was so strong an adversary of the British that they expelled her from Lagos in 1856.[159] Because Àjẹ́ is subject to the laws of the earth and not the interests of the British, Madame Tinubu was able to refortify her finances and assist in the Abeokuta-Dahomey war of 1864 by providing soldiers with necessary artillery. Tinubu also served as the head of a peace party that demanded the termination of the Ijaye war in Abeokuta and the resumption of trade in goods. Ìyálóde Tinubu is heralded as "the first woman to play a part in resistance to British rule."[160]

The Ìyálóde of Ibadan, Efunsetan, followed the dynamic Tinubu. "One of the biggest wholesale traders in Ibadan," Efunsetan used her financial gains to solidify her political station. She was so wealthy that she was able to provide warriors to assist Chief Latosa in his campaign in the Ado War of 1872. However, when she gathered with a group of chiefs to withdraw support from Latosa, her political, spiritual, and social influence was so formidable that Latosa had to have her deposed from the position of Ìyálóde in order to regain political control.

> Efunsetan was especially significant not because of her wealth or power as iyalode, but because she was one of the few women in southern Nigeria before 1900 to have engaged in open political opposition to the indigenous government. *Efunsetan was not acting as the representative of the women but as the representative of a political group consisting of male chiefs.*[161]

Nina Mba's finding is significant, as many discussions of women's roles in Yoruba and other African societies often describe women in positions of "female" (as opposed to comprehensive sociopolitical) power. If it were the case that the ìyálóde was an office constructed to placate women, there would have been a decided lack of political power attached to it. But with the acumen of Ọ̀ṣun and the military might of the Àjẹ́ of the "Town of Women," Efunsetan and Tinubu wielded comprehensive political power and exerted unquestionable social force. However, the power of the ìyálóde is not restricted to holders of the title.

Legendary musician Fela Anikulapo-Kuti proudly heralded his mother Olufunmilayo Ransome-Kuti as an Àjẹ́ and "the only mother of Nigeria." Because of her educational and financial status, her charismatic nature, and the fact that she was oblivious to class divisions, Ransome-Kuti was a vastly influential activist. In 1944, she founded the Abeokuta Ladies Club (which later became the AWU, Abeokuta Women's Union), which consisted of a spectrum of women gathered to fight for many humanitarian concerns, especially "raising the standard of womanhood in Abeokuta . . . [and] encouraging learning among the adults and thereby [wiping] out illiteracy."[162] Most significant, Ransome-Kuti fought against the colonial disenfranchisement of African women. Contrary to the political power wielded by women during the era of "harmonious dualism,"

> [Ransome-Kuti] argued that under the colonial system Nigerian women had lost their traditional economic and political power, and that they were oppressed by the colonial system and its agencies. . . . Not only were they denied suffrage . . . but in Abeokuta they were forced to pay [taxes] which they could not afford and were not given basic amenities. . . . The only way to stop women from being exploited was to organize them to gain political power and demand suffrage, participation in government and, if necessary, changes in the system.[163]

Fighting colonialism's patriarchal shift through nonviolent agitation, Ransome-Kuti and the AWU staged effective campaigns against discriminatory and excessive tax hikes and forced the end of rice control and seizure by government officials in Abeokuta in 1945. In 1946, the AWU worked to unseat Ademola II, ruler of the Egba Council of Native Administration.

The AWU's primary weapons against Ademola were songs of Àjẹ́ that asserted women's traditional sociopolitical authority:

> This *oro* festival has no regard for men;
> This *oro* could carry men away even from their rooms;
> There is no regard for men;
> We are celebrating

It is significant that in order to threaten colonial agents, Ransome-Kuti reclaimed and invoked the original Òrò, a spirit-woman who killed her husband on the day of their marriage and whose marital assault resulted in Yoruba men literally hiding from their new brides rather than meeting them at home.[164] By invoking the highly secretive Òrò masquerade, which is said to fight Àjẹ́, Ransome-Kuti reminded her listeners of Òrò's female origin and debunked the myth that women are excluded from and terrified and terrorized by Òrò.

The spiritually laden political songs of Ransome-Kuti's Ẹgbẹ́ grew more specific and damning as the women reached deep into Odù's pot for the Ọ̀rọ̀ to destabilize Ademola and his colonizing minion:

> O you men, vagina's head will seek vengeance;
> You men, vagina's head shall seek vengeance
> Even if it is one penny, If is only a penny
> Ademola, we are not paying tax in Egbaland
> If even it is one penny.[165]

Even if Ademola and his administrators hide in their rooms, as Yoruba men hide from their brides, the council cannot escape the vengeance of "vagina's head."

In another song, Ransome-Kuti used her own name to threaten the ruler and his multicultural council:

> Anyone who does not know Kuti will get into trouble:
> White man, you will not get to your country safely
> You and Alake will not die an honourable death.[166]

Without weapons or an honorific title, Ransome-Kuti cowed British colonizers and their African administrators. But she was not exceptional: She was one of many historical Àjẹ́ with a deep spiritual ancestry.

Entwining myth and history, the relationships of the Òrìṣà of Àjẹ́ reveal the depth of Yoruba cosmology, which seamlessly integrates the cosmic, ancient, genealogical, and historical for holistic personal and communal development. The Deities of Àjẹ́ provided perfect role models for historical women, and their deeds continue to inspire sociopolitical movements. However, the power of Àjẹ́ is not exclusive to the Yoruba. Àjẹ́ sister-systems exist throughout Africa, and together these powers have contributed to the social, political, and spiritual evolution of Africans on the Continent and throughout the world.

> The Yoruba have always conceived
> of their history as diaspora.
>
> —Olabiyi Babalola Yai

2

Àjẹ́ across the Continent and in the Ìtànkálẹ̀

CONTINENTAL CONNECTIONS

In this chapter's epigraph, Yai highlights the importance of physical migration and cross-cultural exchange to the Yoruba. These concepts are also important to Yoruba Deities, for Ẹdan's praisename is She Is Well Placed Around the Earth.[1] One might say that during her travels to protect her Mother's dominion and spread the force of cosmic justice, Ẹdan exchanged knowledge with the peoples of many lands, especially her divine siblings on the African continent. Perhaps human beings followed the lead of the Deities or took them along on their travels, because the sociocultural, spiritual, and linguistic similarities among West African ethnic groups are obvious. I use Àjẹ́ as a Pan-African paradigmatic descriptor because the Yoruba exposition of this force is, at present, the most detailed and elaborate. However, there are similarities among Àjẹ́ sister-systems throughout the African continent that are important to the overall conceptualization of Àjẹ́ and to understanding this force's impact in contemporary Africana literature.

What appear to be linguistic cognates of Àjẹ́ and Oṣó abound in West African languages, and this is especially true of Nigerian ethnic groups. The Igbos use the term Amusu to describe Àjẹ́, and the term Ajalagba signifies Oṣó. Ajalagba, which kills by falling on and smothering its victims,[2] could be a linguistic cognate of Àgbàláàgbà, a Yoruba praisename of Àjẹ́, which means "wise and strong elder." In Hausa language, male Àjẹ́ are called Maye; the term for females is

Mayya; and the plural form is Mayyu. Among the Bini, whose home land is to the East of Yorubaland, Àjẹ́ is called Azẹn. The Nupe peoples call Àjẹ́ Ega; a woman with the power is called Gaci; male holders of the force are called Eshe. As do Àjẹ́ and Oṣó, Gaci and Eshe have political and judicial duties. Òrìṣà Oya comes from Nupeland, which is to the north of Yorubaland, and it is interesting to note that the material magnifier of Ega, called *cigbe,* uses Oya's totem, the buffalo.[3]

Many ethnic groups associated with countries other than the nation known as Nigeria state that their place of origin is Ile-Ife.[4] Spiritual and linguistic ties to the Yoruba are evident in many of these groups, and this is also true of terms related to Àjẹ́. The Ewe people, largely of Togo, Benin, and Ghana, refer to Àjẹ́ as Dije. Among the Akan largely of Ghana, Ayen is a term reserved for violent Àjẹ́, while Nzima Baye, signifying an ethnic group and a locality, indicates benevolent force. Ayen and Nzima Baye both state that they come from "the cosmos,"[5] the equivalent of Àjẹ́'s Orífín.

While linguistically distinct, Central African Àjẹ́ forms are similar to those in West Africa. Simon Bockie defines *Kindoki* in terms similar to Àjẹ́:

> Kindoki signifies power or force. The usual meaning denotes this power as evil. But it is susceptible to being exercised in any sense, in a good sense as well as evil. It is a question of an ambivalent, ambiguous power, which arouses fear; or a dangerous and good power, capable of harming but also protecting.[6]

The BaKongo recognize two types of Kindoki: *Kindoki Kia Lunda* ("protecting kindoki") and *Kindoki Kia Dia* ("eating kindoki"). Similar, but not identical to Àjẹ́, Kindoki Kia Dia are usually elders who regulate society by punishing trespassers.[7] Although there are distinctions between "protecting," or "day," Kindoki (which is apparent to and can be admired by all) and "eating," or "night," Kindoki (which is secret, mysterious, and "half-hidden") Bockie finds that "[s]ometimes the 'day' and 'night' leaders in a family end up being the same person."[8]

Kindoki and its owners, *Ndoki,* do not conform to Western dichotomy; they can only be properly understood from the holistic African worldview. As Bockie reveals:

> An evildoer is ndoki, a benefactor is ndoki as well. They are both ndoki in their undertakings and approach to the community. They are ndoki for what they do; that is, their particular specialty cannot be handled by any other member of the society.

They are ndoki both by their acts and by their uniqueness, which can only be explained by their having unusual powers.⁹

Bockie's description of Kindoki is similar to those of Àjẹ́. Furthermore, like the Yoruba, BaKongo diviners, healers, ancestors, and Gods are all thought to be Ndoki and to use some aspect of Kindoki.¹⁰

In chapter 1, I discuss how Tinubu, Efunsetan, and Ransome-Kuti used their unique manifestations of Àjẹ́ to exert profound influence in Nigerian politics. Such spiritual-political dynamism was not restricted to the Yoruba world. In Ghana, Yaa Asantewaa was the warrior-mother who battled the British, and Queen Nzingha of Angola struggled against the Portuguese. Sarraounia, whose praisename is Sarraounia Aben Soro, Queen Who Terrifies Her Adversaries, rallied the Hausa of Niger against the French using militaristic and spiritual Mayya/Àjẹ́.¹¹ In Uganda, Muhumusa was a staunch adversary against the British colonials,¹² and Nyabinghi, whose name has become a praisename and a call to order for Rastafarians, fought oppression with astral Àjẹ́. These historical Great Mothers and others, such as Queens Bakwa, Amina, and Zaria of Zaria (Northern Nigeria) and Madam Yoko, who expanded the Mende kingdom of modern-day Sierra Leone,¹³ rose to prominence despite slavery, colonialism, and attempts of patriarchs to usurp their power because they sprang from a fertile spiritual-political foundation that had been long steeped in what Diop calls "harmonious dualism."

GREAT MOTHERS OF THE WIDELY DISPERSED EARTH

It is not surprising that peoples who neighbor the Yoruba have similar spiritual philosophies, Gods, political structures, and linguistic systems. However, there are intriguing connections between Yorubaland and Kemet (Ancient Egypt).¹⁴ The Kemetic Deity Ast (Greek translation, Isis) is identical in form, phenotype, and function to Odù, and through Ast the depth, breadth, and timelessness of Àjẹ́ become more clear.

Scriptures of *The Book of Coming Forth by Day* (antithetically termed *The Book of the Dead*) describe Ast in terms similar to Àjẹ́: "In the beginning there was [Ast], Oldest of the Old. She was the Goddess from whom all becoming arose."¹⁵ Credited with all "becoming," Ast bears cosmological resemblance to Odùduwà, the "self-existent personage" who is also Yewájọbí, The Mother of All Òrìṣà and All Living Things. Like Ẹlẹ́yẹ with the bloody red beak, Ast is heralded as "Mistress of the gods, thou bearer of wings, thou lady of the red apparel." Entwining the dual origins of Àjẹ́, the oracular utterance of

Odù, and the supremacy of the "owners of everything in the world," Ast is "queen of the crowns of the South and North, [the] only One . . . superior to whom the gods cannot be, thou mighty one of enchantments."[16] The parallelisms continue as Ast's oríkì grow more specific:

> Thou who art pre-eminent, mistress and lady of the tomb, Mother in the horizon of heaven. . . . Praise be to thee, O Lady, who art mightier than the gods, words of adoration rise unto thee from the Eight Gods of Hermopolis. The living souls who are in their hidden places praise the mystery of thee, O thou who art their mother, thou source from which they sprang, who makest for them a place in the hidden Underworld, who makest sound their bones and preservest them from terror, who makest them strong in the abode of everlastingness.[17]

As "lady of the tomb" who is mightier than all other Netcherw (Gods) and the source of their existence, death, and regeneration, Ast's attributes are identical to those of Odù and Ìyàmi Òṣòròngà.

Just as many Òrìṣà have politically and socially significant historical realities, Ast is said to have "invented agriculture" with the cultivation of corn and wheat.[18] Most important, Ast's monogamous marriage with Ausar (Osiris) and their co-rulership of Kemet seems to place harmonious matriarchal dualism squarely within the world's first civilization.[19]

Àjẹ́'s use of astral trials and violent retribution to order and cleanse society is also evident in Ast's sister Nebhet (Nephths, or Nephthys). As a unified force, Ast and Nebhet are the original "creating-and-destroying" Mothers. In the following praisesong, it seems that Nebhet-Ast's wings are lifted by the winds of Ọ̀rọ̀ (power of the word). With all the multiplicity of Ìyàmi Òṣòròngà, Ast is "the Goddess from whom all becoming arose" and she is

> Terrible one, lady of the rain-storm, destroyer of the souls of men, devourer of the bodies of men, orderer, producer, and maker of slaughter. . . . Hewer-in-pieces in blood, Ahibit, lady of hair . . . pure one, lover of slaughterings, cutter off of heads, devoted one, lady of the Great House. . . . Her name is Clother, hider of creations, conqueror of hearts, swallower of them. . . . Knife which cutteth when its name is uttered, slayer of those who approach thy flame.[20]

Ọya and Agan, her transforming whirlwind, swirl in the storm of Nebhet-Ast. "Knife which cutteth when its name is uttered," conjures Nana Bùrúkù, who cuts life without a knife. Ast's praisename "Clother, hider of creations" recalls the symbols and masks of Ẹdan, Odù, and the Ìyánlá, all of which are clothed in white, hidden from view, and lodged in the innermost recesses of shrines. Ìyá-Ayé, who interrogates the skulls of traitors and swallows wicked people, is also a sister of Nebhet-Ast, who loves to slaughter and decapitate. Interspersed throughout the oríkì are such appellations as "pure one," "lady of the Great House," and "devoted one," making Nebhet-Ast just as paradoxical and perplexing as Ìyàmi Òṣòròngà and Ìyàmi Àbẹ̀ní.

Àjẹ́'s proclivity for social harmonization also surfaces in Kemetic philosophy. Òrìṣà Odù received knowledge to organize the world and tempered that knowledge with "Mercy, Justice and Compassion."[21] In Kemet, such works are the domain of Maat, the winged woman who oversees the seven cardinal virtues (antithetically revised as "seven deadly sins")—truth, justice, propriety, harmony, balance, reciprocity, and order—that are the "keys to human perfectibility."[22] The forty-two *Admonitions of Maat* are "the guidelines of correct behavior and the standard against which the soul of the deceased would be judged."[23] Maat's keys of civilization and perfectibility act as an ontological bridge balancing the nurturing and slaughtering of Ast and Nebhet. Furthermore, in her gender, winged form, and political directives, Maat bears a striking similarity to the Spirit Bird of Àjẹ́, Ẹdan, and Ògbóni society.

Representations of the Spirit Bird of Àjẹ́ can be found on the staves of Òsanyìn, the shoulder of Egúngún, and royal scepters because "the bird, the woman, was the one who had been granted the precedence of vision—before all else. She was therefore the first one to see and know before all else; even before Obarisa [Ọbàtálá], the grand patriarch."[24] Employing the same "precedence of vision," Maat weighs the hearts of the dead against a feather to determine earthly correctness and ancestral destiny. The significance of Spirit Birds is also evident in Ba. Depicted, like Maat, as an entity with the body and wings of a hawk and a human head, Ba is the "world-soul" that represents humanity's oneness with the universe. Ba also symbolizes astral mobility, or "the soul's ability to move between heaven and Earth. It is the life-giving power of the Netcherw."[25] Ba's twin force is Ka. An "activator of cosmic forces," Ka contains "all of the powers of creation," such as àṣẹ, Òrò, and Àjẹ́, and Ka determines character and destiny. Similar to Odù and Òṣùmàrè's covenant with humanity, "the soul becomes enlightened when it is liberated by both the Ba and the Ka."[26]

Just as there is spiritual knowledge-sharing among West African peoples, so too did the people of Kemet use the wings of Àjẹ́ and astral-terrestrial Spirit Birds to share their wisdom. Greek historian Herodotus described the founding of the legendary oracles of Dodona in Greece and Ammon in Libya by Kemetic Ẹyẹ Ọ̀rọ̀:

> Two black doves flew away from Egyptian Thebes, and while one directed its flight to Libya, the other came to [Dodona]. She alighted on an oak and sitting there, began to speak with a human voice, and told them that on the spot where she was, there should thenceforth be an oracle of Jove [or Ammon].[27]

Ẹyẹ Ọ̀rọ̀, the Spirit Bird, is the supreme manifestation of Ìyánlá and the spiritual-terrestrial familiar of Àwọn Ìyá Wa. That black doves from Thebes alight on an oak, a twin of Àjẹ́'s ìrókò tree, and speak words of Ọ̀rọ̀ with a human voice could be a cosmic coincidence, but it is more likely evidence of Àjẹ́'s Pan-African scope and continuity.

The similarities between Yoruba Àjẹ́ and Ast, Nebhet, and Maat are such that had they been in Yorubaland, the Kemetic Netcherw would have been heralded with all the praisenames of Àjẹ́. Additionally, the cosmological structure and philosophical tenets of Kemet and Yorubaland resonate in many African societies. Most traditional African cosmologies honor a Mother Creator, a melded Mother-Father Creator, or male and female Deities who work cooperatively. Just as Ast is paired with Ausar and Odùduwà with Ọbàtálá, Asase Yaa is the Akan Earth Mother who is partnered with Sky God Onyame. As Peter Sarpong elucidates, Asase Yaa is not a one-dimensional token God but a source of vast and nearly unfathomable power similar to Ìyá-Ayé:

> She is not simply the symbol of fecundity but she is the fertile woman *par excellence;* she is impersonal, but alive. . . . Incalculable like all mystical agencies, the cause of prosperity, fertility and health as well as of drastic retribution for sin or sacrilege, witting or unwitting, she is regarded with great awe. She usually has no priests.[28]

With spiritual pragmatism, the Akan say, "Earth, whether I am dead or alive, I depend on you." Respect for Asase Yaa's vengeance is evident in the praisenames "Every-Ready Shooter" and "Killer Mother." Also, the Ga people of Ghana "look upon God as both masculine and feminine—*Atta Naa Nyomo*[.] meaning Grand Father–Grand Mother God."[29]

Images of life-giving, justice-granting Great Mothers who work without Great Fathers also abound in Africa. The Ijọ of the Nigerian Delta honor Tamara as "Mother, the one who moulded us all."[30] The Herrero of Southwest Africa cloak the Mother in riddles: "God has no father and is not a man."[31] The Igbo of southeast Nigeria have a Yewájọbí in Idemilli, who gave life to more than ten Deities. Ani, the Igbo Earth Mother, is often depicted as an ever-ready Àjẹ́, "carrying a child in one hand and holding a knife in the other."[32] Reminiscent of tributes to Yoruba Àjẹ́, the Igbo say of Ani, "Earth Mother owns men / The Earth owns everybody."[33]

Although Àjẹ́ is resident in the womb and great emphasis is placed upon the gift of life, childbearing is not a prerequisite for attaining a supreme manifestation of Àjẹ́. While "mothers" have been the subject of discussion up to this point, there are significant Òrìṣà of Àjẹ́ who bore no children. For these entities, infertility is not the stereotypical African curse; the decision to bear no children or the inability to do so seems to magnify their resident Àjẹ́. Yéwà, Ọbà, and Nana Burúkú are "old and powerful 'eternal aunts' who promote and protect society yet are as respected and feared as 'Àjẹ́—Our Mothers.' Though they have no children, the Yorùbá see them as 'Mother-Ideals.' Mother-attitude does not depend on how many children one has given birth to."[34] It is interesting that each of these three "eternal aunts" is of Yoruba origin but has larger significance to communities outside of Yorubaland.

Yéwà is both the "daughter" of Odùduwà and the wife of Ọbàtálá. She is known as Yèyé Ìwara, The Mother of Marvelous Character, and not only does she fully embody the stately grace (iwà-pẹ̀lẹ́) of Àwọn Ìyá Wa but she enters only the heads of upstanding individuals. Only dignified community elders who are no longer engaging in sexual activity and "are of impeccable character" can be one with/in the Mother of Marvelous Character. The majority of Yéwà's devotees are elder women who are virgins or infertile—women who give the spiritual precedence over the physical. Although her name and attributes seem to indicate gentleness and compassion, to her and her children's enemies, Yéwà is lethal: "The Lùcùmí call her AFÍRÌMÁÀKỌ̀—The greatest, strongest elder who if touched kills (the sacrilegious one) by magic."[35] However, like Ọ̀ṣun, Yéwà prefers to conquer through wisdom and understanding, and she is a bastion of applied knowledge and grace for her children. Her oríkì proclaims, "Wisdom is the understanding of correctness / It is correctness [exemplary character] that sustains the children of / the mother with character."[36]

Ọbà, whose river is a source of Àjẹ́, is the "first and legitimate wife of Ṣàngó," and she is described as "a superb warrior who is said to have taught Ṣàngó the use of the long sword and Ọya the use of the cutlass."[37]

However, when both were married to Ṣàngó, Oya deceived Ọbà. She persuaded Ọbà to cut off her ears and feed them to their husband in a stew seasoned with her blood. Rather than tying Ṣàngó to her heart, Ọbà's actions and meal repulsed her husband, who banished her from the kingdom. She became a recluse who wore a mask to hide her deformity, shame, and anger. However, she did not become a vindictive destroyer; she used her force to buoy her children. Ọbà is the embodiment of strength born of suffering; one of her praisesongs asks, "Whose head is blunted? Whose head is broken? / The one we take refuge with is whose head is broken."[38] With her physical deformity and her warped and twisted destiny, it is not surprising that Ọbà has special significance for tragically dislocated Africans of the ìtànkálẹ̀. Her displaced devotees sing, "To cure you use gloomy misery to teach the habit of the mystery." Her home was wrenched away from her and her kindness used to destroy her, but Ọbà utilized her Àjẹ́ in the same progressive manner as her forebears to keep the circle of evolution unbroken.

Transgeographic Nana Bùrúkù may well be the most influential Àjẹ́ in West Africa. She is known in Yorubaland as Earth Mother Nàná Búkúù; in Igboland, she is called Olisabuluwa, who literally supports the world.[39] In the lands of the Akan, Fon, and Ewe and in the ìtànkálẹ̀, she is Nana Bùrúkù or Nana Buluku, The Mother of All Deities. The exact meaning and origin of Nana Bùrúkù is difficult to ascertain: "Nana" is an Akan title of authority; "Bùrúkù" means wicked in Yoruba language. However, her power is phenomenal. An ẹsẹ Ifá recalls her arrival in Yorubaland:

> Ọ̀yẹ̀kú swings here
> Ọ̀yẹ̀kú swings there
> Divined for Nàná Búkúù
> On the day when from the cosmos
> She was coming to earth
> As a stranger to earth
> Nàná Búkúù is not a stranger to earth.
> She is a true child [of the earth]
> She made heavy thunder
> She set up commotion in the streets
> They were shouting her name on the right
> They were shouting her name on the left
> In the centre of the earth
> There Nàná Búkúù was fighting[40]

When Nana Bùrúkù, Child of the Earth, came to earth, all entities stopped to witness the spontaneous generation of this Àjẹ́. This is the "wickedness" of Nana Bùrúkù—not evil, but sublime, self-generated strength; personal and communal protection; and supreme military acumen.

Mason finds that Nana Bùrúkù is part of another spiritual trinity that includes Òkè Ìlú and Orélú. As "the sacred three," they represent "our aged mothers, who oversee the administration of the community, the assurance of full [bellies], and the responsible use of the earth."[41] Represented by a human figure cast in brass, Nàná is "an earth force that must be placated in order to assure continued health and productivity."[42] Fulfilling her role as the grantor of bounty, Nàná Bùrúkù shared significant gifts with humans and Òrìsà.

Just as Odù organized Ògún, Ọbalúaiyé, and Ọbàtálá to give humanity the keys of life, Nana gave Ọbàtálá, Ọ̀ṣun, Ọbalúaiyé, and Ògún cosmically relevant gifts of protection, which became their signature totems. Yoruba origin texts reveal that Nàná gave Ọbàtálá a large amount of òjé (metal similar to lead) to use against his enemies, and she gave Ọ̀ṣun ide wewe (copper bangles): "Nàná Búkúù told her that once she beats any of her enemies with these copper bangles, they would suffer from bloated arms, legs and stomachs."[43] Nàná Bùkúù gave iron to Ògún, the Òrìsà of iron and technology. She told him to use it to "free himself from the machinations of his enemies." Nàná Búkúù asked Olódùmarè for and was given the materials to inflict and cure smallpox, and this knowledge is what she shared with Ọbalúaiyé for use against his enemies.[44]

The Ketu Yoruba honor Nana Bùrúkù through the *ileeshin* staff, which consists of raffia, palm fronds, cowries, leather, camwood, and blue dye. The ileeshin staff is apparently pure Àjẹ́ and cannot be held by a man. When a woman holds the staff, she must take care not to "speak any evil of any animal or man," for it makes her Òrò magnificently lethal. It is said that if a man is hit with the ileeshin staff, he will immediately swell and die.[45] Truly, Nana is "wicked"; she kills and cuts without use of a knife. As one of the paramount Earth Mothers, the enslavement of her children is a direct crime against the earth and her; consequently, Nana Bùrúkù's Àjẹ́ was an essential element of African survival in the ìtànkálẹ̀ as much as in Africa. Yet, like Ọbà and Yéwà, Nana is a quiet educator of gentle character who eradicates evil and mends the spirits of her children.

The Fon people of Benin Republic consider Nana Buluku to be the "grand ancestress of all the Yoruba-derived (Anagonu) deities of the pantheon of Fon." As the creator of all must be all-encompassing, Nana Buluku is "one God who is at the same time both male and female" who created the world.⁴⁶ After creating the earth, Nana Bùrúkù created a holistic Deity, MawuLisa, to further order her efforts:

> Mawu is one person but has two faces. The first is that of a woman, and the eyes of that part which belongs to the woman is the Moon. That face takes the name of Mawu. The other side is the side of a man. That face has for its eyes the Sun, and it takes the name of Lisa. The part called Mawu directs the night. Where the Sun is, Lisa directs the day.⁴⁷

Mawu is the cosmic daughter of Nana Bùrúkù, and she is the Mother who houses the Father, Lisa. Together, as MawuLisa they create life and oversee earthly rotations and evolution from the cosmos.

The power and ecstasy of Mawu and Lisa's union are readily observable: "When there is an eclipse of the moon . . . the celestial couple [is] engaged in love-making; when there is an eclipse of the sun, Mawu is believed to be having intercourse with Lisa."⁴⁸ Such sensual-spiritual unification recurs in African cosmology in the "conception of Ọbàtálá and Odùduwà as being locked in inseparable embrace symbolizing the union between earth and sky,"⁴⁹ and in the Central African supreme Deity, Mani. Synthesizing the qualities of Òṣùmàrè and the union of Ọbàtálá and Odùduwà, Mani consists of two interconnected bundles: "The light-coloured bundle on top is the male god Yende, the dark bundle underneath is the goddess Ndasu."⁵⁰ As the "double snake" *kelema*, Yende and Ndasu can be seen "lying with one another in the sky." It is said that when the couple is not visible, they have continued consecrating their union in the waters.⁵¹ From Mani to Mawu, sensual Deities astronomically renew their vows and recharge the world with their power.

After using her Dije (Àjẹ́) to create the world, Nana Bùrúkù instructed Mawu to organize the sphere. Mawu delegated to serpent Loa (Deity) Aido Hwedo important duties that unite Aido Hwedo with Yorubaland's Òṣùmàrè and Igboland's Olisabuluwa and elucidate the central role of serpents in African cosmology. After Mawu created the world, she rode in the mouth of Aido Hwedo to shape her dominion: "Wherever the Creator went, Aido-Hwedo went with her. That is why the earth is as we find it. It curves, it winds, it has high places, and low places. That is the movement of the serpent Aido-Hwedo."⁵² In an inversion of Loa riding humans, Creator Mawu rides Aido Hwedo, and with their combined Dije they infuse the world with all of its danger, beauty, and form.

Following the beautification of the world, Mawu worried that her creations were too heavy and could destroy themselves and the earth.

She summoned Aido Hwedo again and told her, "Crawl beneath the earth. Curl yourself up as round as a reed mat and like a platter that holds the food . . . hold up the weight of the earth so that it shall never fall. . . . The earth is heavy with my creation and you must hold it up."[53] Aido Hwedo used her Dije in connection with Nana Bùrúkù and Mawu to prepare the world for habitation. In this respect, Aido Hwedo mirrors Dan, the Fon Rainbow Serpent of the Sky, and the Igbo Olisabuluwa, who is "spread out everywhere and carrying the world."[54]

In addition to creation and structure, Mawu brought the world wisdom, knowledge, and understanding. Like the Odù Ifá for the Yoruba, Mawu or Fa represents the way of knowing and doing for the Fon. Just as Odù Ifá is named after Odù, the Fa divination system of the Fon is called Mawu, and the "[Fon] take Mawu, or Fa, as the author of man and his destiny. . . . Fa is Mawu and Mawu is Fa."[55] Furthermore, "The prophets said that Fa is the writing with which Mawu creates each person." Mawu is Mother, Creator, Initiator, Master of Oral and Written Texts, Three in One. Legba (Yorubaland's Èṣù Ẹlẹ́gbára), the privileged seventh child of Mawu and "linguist-messenger" of the Fon, administers the divine writing, reading, and critiquing to humanity.[56] Legba is a composite of MawuLisa: an entity with two heads of power, one male and one female, comprising all spiritual forces, including Àjẹ́/Dije. The unified nature of Èṣù/Legba is essential, for the link between the male-female, spiritual-earthly, and oral-written must be unlimited. Notably, Legba has a linguist-trickster sister in Afrekete, who is also the seventh-born, youngest, most intelligent child of MawuLisa. Although she was born through spiritually empowered human parents, Afrekete knows all the secrets of her terrestrial parents, Agbe and Naete, and those of MawuLisa.[57] Like Legba, Afrekete is a messenger and link between the material and spiritual worlds; but her medium is the sea.[58] Afrekete is a "daughter" of Yemọja, or more, Mami Wota, the Pan-African Oceanic Mother, and she exerts great influence as a contemporary spiritual medium and divine linguist.

TWO GRAND MOTHERS

West African Nana Bùrúkù, her Fon daughter Mawu, and Mawu's daughter Aido Hwedo constitute a triumvirate of Dije, and their social influence is profound, as is evident in Christian Gaba's *Scriptures of an African People: Ritual Utterances of the Anlo*. In scripture LXXIII, Mawu and her Anlo Ewe priest rid 10-year-old community member Naki of illness and tribulation:

> Naki, as I dip your hands into this water today,
> All the misfortunes that have been after you,
> They all have departed whence they came.
> Today your tongue is cleansed,
> It is only Mawu, the Great determiner of destiny,
> the Ground of all being,
> That can cleanse you completely.
> Stretch out your tongue and receive the white clay.
> Look!
> Mawu, the Great Determiner of destiny,
> the Ground of all being himself now cleanses you.
> Therefore all the misfortunes that have been after you
> All have departed whence they came.[59]

The phrase "Mawu, the Great Determiner of destiny" is a direct reference to the Book of Fa and Mawu's role in protecting and avenging her progeny; the phrase is also Gaba's translation for Mawu Segbo Lisa, the owner of all souls. The Ground of All Being is a powerful oríkì that recalls Ìyá-Ayé, the magnified power of all life forms sprung from the earth and all powerfully transmigrated ancestors resting within the earth. Consequently, all that is necessary to cleanse Naki is sacred water, the white clay of Mawu, and words of power uttered by a Dije. It is interesting that the white clay of The Ground of all Being, which "cleanses completely," is called *pemba* by the BaKongo and signifies "the mountain of the dead"; in Igboland, white clay is *azu igwe,* the first food and spiritual food of humanity.[60] In Yorubaland white clay is *efun,* and it and sacred water symbolize Ọbàtálá. In this scripture, Pan-African symbols meld with Dije to cleanse and renew communal members.

Powerfully transmigrated ancestors are of supreme importance in the African worldview. They are as accessible as Òrìṣà and are thought to be profoundly influential. Far from a contrived phrase signifying nonsense, "*mumbo jumbo*" is a corruption of the phrase "Mama Dyumbo," which means "protective spirit of the Khassonkee tribe." This protective spirit is recognized as being a "Grandmother."[61] In Scripture XLIX, Grandmother surfaces as perhaps the most significant ancestral Deity of the Anlo, and her influence is directly related to her Dije.

> O my spouse, Grandmother,
> The Red Substance which is always present in a woman's bathroom.
> Breaker of spears and forge-hammers,
> Mighty rivers that cannot be artificially blockaded,
> Red-hot drink that cannot be served to children,

> A Deity who smiles and also frowns,
> The sea-water which is not drinkable,
> Lover of peace,
> You who demand both money and human beings from an offender,
> Destroyer of whole households,
> O, my spouse, I invoke your presence
> . . . .
> Here is the water, please
> Put out all the fires of misfortune
> And may peace abound forever.[62]

Grandmother is a study of profundity and paradox. She is the water of life that cannot quench thirst. She is both a "destroyer of whole households" and a "lover of peace." Her countenance is inscrutable, but she is the "spouse" of the community. As "a single firewood that cooks a meal for thousands,"[63] Grandmother is at once fundamental and phenomenal. While she nourishes her nation, like justice-imparting Àjẹ́, Grandmother demands human sacrifice to balance monumental imbalances.

Ìyàmi Òṣòròngà is a God of multitudinous manifestations, and Grandmother exhibits the same multiplicity of form. Ìyàmi Òṣòròngà is a God, is the collective Àwọn Ìyá Wa, and is the controller of the blood of existence. Grandmother is also a God, and she is every menstruating woman, and she is the potent menses. Gaba states that the praisename "Red Substance which is always present in a woman's bathroom . . . is intended to symbolize the ever-abiding presence of the Deity with her worshippers."[64] Combining the àṣẹ and Àjẹ́ of menstrual fluid with the amalgamated power of the post-menopausal womb, Grandmother embodies the curvilinear covenant of spiritual, biological, destructive, and creative Dije (Àjẹ́), and she extends that covenant to all the women of her community.

As in Yorubaland, Àjẹ́ sister-systems across Africa are both feared and revered and are lavished with praise. The respect these Mothers receive is not born of terror. As with praise of Ìyàmi Òṣòròngà, Grandmother is beseeched with the pride and confidence that comes from knowing that praise of the Mother facilitates actualization of the Self. Such cyclic praise and spiritual confidence are apparent in the Ịjọ oral epic *The Ozidi Saga*. Ozidi is a spiritually inclined male born to avenge the murder of his father. However, without Ọrẹamẹ, Ozidi's Grand Mother, there would be neither Ozidi nor saga.

In Ịjọ language, Ọrẹamẹ is called Krọ or Bengbai ("Sorceress") or Oloko ("Oracle Woman"); the Yoruba would say Àjẹ́. Ọrẹamẹ is a shapeshifter like Ọya, she has extensive herbal knowledge, and her cooking pot is the origin of powerful cures and fatal poisons. Of herself, she says, "I am Ọrẹamẹ[;] what I cannot endure does not exist in this world"; "I am she that surpasses a city"; "I am queen of the earth."[65] Ọrẹamẹ's power is most evident in her fan, which is used in an Àjẹ́-like manner to soothe, cool, and placate or stir the winds of destruction with debilitating medicines.[66] Ọrẹamẹ's fan, in addition to being a weapon of war, propels her flight. Ojobolo, the saga's griot, recalls the family's trip to their homeland: "Immediately they tied one cloth to the other and [Ọrẹamẹ] lashed out with her magic fan, striking them both . . . yes all of them, she flew off with all in full tow, wings beating the wind. They flew for a long time, straight to the city of Ozidi."[67]

The epic reflects societal realities. The Ijọ of Central Nigeria adhere to a matrilineal family structure in which "a man's *fatu* or 'final womb' is his mother's ancestral home."[68] Matrilineal alignment is not merely filial; it extends to Deities. The suffix "Ziba," when applied to the founder of a clan, "more often than not connotes a mother-goddess of the clan."[69] Extending the suffix to the Great Creating Mother, Zibaru is an appellation for Tamara, "the mother from whom all knowledge flows." Like Ìyá-Ayé, Tamara is the final judge of humanity, and "there is no appeal against her judgment."[70] Extending creative Mother-force to human women, Oyin is another name for Creator Tamara, and *yin* is the word for mother in Ijọ language. Both the mythical Ọrẹamẹ and all mothers are invested with Tamara's force on linguistic and spiritual levels, and Ọrẹamẹ also has human counterparts.

Revered as "one of the greatest, if not the foremost, prophetesses Kumbo-Ziba has ever produced," Afaro was the oracle of the fertility Deity Oziara. She cured children, divined by touching wombs, and, reminiscent of Ọ̀ṣun's relationship with the buzzard, Afaro "had the power to receive messages from her deity and other divinities through the agency of sacred birds."[71] Afaro was one of many humanospiritual emissaries of Oziara. Oziara's prophets are characterized by their "immaculately white" dress and are called *oyinara*, "our mother." As the "'mother' of the clan and daughter of Oziara," these priestesses engage in no manual labor. The community provides them with material sustenance in symbiotic return for spiritual sustenance. Egbe Ifie concludes that the prophet of Oziara "is sacred and has around her so great an aura of reverence from her 'children' that one would often feel that she was the goddess herself."[72] Like her divine predecessors and successors, Afaro lived in the shrine with the Deity during her life. With Tamara, Ọrẹamẹ, and Afaro, the lines that bifurcate Deity/human being, myth/reality, and folklore/history collapse under the unifying forces of African holism and Àjẹ́.

It is important to discuss the similarities and aspects of cultural specificity in Àjẹ́ forms across the African Continent because the Africans who were forced through the Middle Passage came from almost every region of Africa, including Madagascar. While some displaced groups' linguistic and ritual gifts bear clear stamps of particular Continental ethnic groups, it is often the case that African rituals and beliefs were so deftly blended and revised that they can be considered neo-African. However, at the center of ìtànkálẹ̀an rituals, liberation strategies, and divine utterances is Àjẹ́, ever urging proliferation and evolution in remarkably alien and oppressive lands.

ÀJẸ́ IN LATIN AMERICA AND THE CARIBBEAN ISLANDS

Africa's most blighted era occurred from 1442 to the middle 1800s, as tens of millions of Africans were stolen, enslaved, and exiled. The spiritual, psychological, social, and physical destruction remains beyond measure. For example, with all their similarities, the Fon and the Oyo empires, with all of their spiritual, cultural, and linguistic similarities turned upon one another in a series of wars that created thousands upon thousands of war captives who were sold as slaves. So successful were European divide-and-conquer strategies that regions of modern-day Nigeria, Togo, and Benin were designated the "Slave Coast."

While enslavers did not discriminate, according to Ogunsola Igue, "The elites, the poets, and those who patronised art were captured by raiders and sold off as slaves along the Benin coast."[73] Given the pragmatic nature of African art, it is unlikely that Igue refers to bourgeois elite; the "elite" were most likely activist-artists. The healers, artists of speech, and owners of Àjẹ́ and àṣẹ, who stood against the dominating order would have been quickly sold and forced into exile and slavery.[74] Once the warriors, activists, and artists were banished, the African social structure eroded: "The intensity of the slave trade not only caused the downfall of the cities but also led to cultural trauma among those who had escaped capture."[75]

All Africans, those on the Continent and those forced from their land of origin, suffered psychological, spiritual, cultural, and social trauma. Africans destined to live in alien lands had to withstand the physical dislocation, unimaginable sexual and physical brutality, and attempts at cultural genocide—including efforts to obliterate African familial, linguistic, and community bonds—that were the cornerstones of Caucasian racism and oppression. In order to survive, African spiritual organizations, Deities, and devotees had to either go underground or they had to undergo cosmetic conversion.

Possibly as a result of the influence of the Vatican, which sanctioned the exile and enslavement of Africans in 1442, 1444, and 1452, Catholicism was the mandated religion for most of the Caribbean Islands and Latin Americas. However, the religion readily lent itself to merger with African spiritual systems. Catholicism had a pantheon of saints whose figures, exploits, iconography, and authority could easily be associated with those of African Òrìṣà and Loa. The saints also provided an effective shield for Òrìṣà worship. By customizing a religious mandate to fit their spiritual realities, Africans also gave Àjẹ́ room to blossom and thrive. Between 1720 and 1785, Chico Rei, a self-liberated African, financed and organized the building of a Catholic church in Ouro Preto, Brazil.

In "Cultural Tourism to Slave Sites," Sandra Richards describes the iconography of Egreja da Santa Efigênia:

> In addition to the profusion of images, of angels, Jesus, and the Virgin Mary . . . the Egreja da Santa Efigênia also contains iconography that suggests a relationship to the Yoruba *orisa*. . . . Carved into some of the side altars are sixteen cowrie shells, a fan (associated with the riverine goddess Osún), and water (symbolic of the mother of all gods, Yemọja). Also visible on another side altar is the statue of a pregnant saint, demonstrating . . . the importance of fertility to Africans.[76]

Many of the symbols and entities carved into the sanctuary are representative of Àjẹ́. The sixteen cowries on the altar represent Yoruba women's preferred method of divination: Indeed, Oyeronke Igbinola is Awo Oòduà, a diviner of sixteen cowries. As described in Thompson's *Flash of the Spirit* and Bekederemo's *The Ozidi Saga* and as is evident on the ceilings and the walls of Ewe praisehouses in Kissehman, Ghana,[77] fans are a powerful assuaging/inflaming tool of Àjẹ́. The covenant established between Yemọja (The Mother of Waters) and her human progeny took on heightened significance as a result of the Middle Passage, and the church's water symbols signify both the exile of enslaved Africans and Yemọja's promise of protection and evolution. In the light of the praisenames Àwọn Ìyá Wa, Ìyàmi, Yewájọbí, Ìyánsàn (Mother of Nine), and Òrìṣà Ọlọ́mọwẹ́wẹ́ (God of Small Children), the pregnant woman is the clearest representation of Àjẹ́. The pregnant saint, not unlike a stationary Gèlèdé masker, is the ultimate promise, shrine, and sign of survival and evolution against all odds. Through an artistic text of spiritual permanence, the constructors and worshippers of the Egreja da Santa Efigênia were not serving two Gods; they were praising the power of many, especially the Àjẹ́ extant without and resident within.

In discussing the ìtànkálẹ̀, it will become clear that although spirituality and higher powers remained at the heart of the dislocated African's existence, the power within—to liberate, signify, outwit, and overcome—takes precedence; this is logical because self-actualization is a cornerstone of Àjẹ́.

When Africans were confronted with Christian religious mandates, they responded with proclamations from the divinely empowered and fully actualized self. The Vatican demanded that enslaved Africans show respect for the Christian God, whether they were adherents of the religion or not. However, because they were born with the means to exert their spiritual authority, enslaved Africans showed their oppressors that respect must be earned. Africans enslaved in Mexico engaged in the spiritual-linguistic strategy of signifying on the church's mandate and its deity at a most significant time—while they were being beaten. The violated Africans would declare, "'Mal grado aya Dios' ('May it spite God'), 'Pese a Dios' ('May God regret'), 'Reniego a Dios' ('I renounce God'), 'Descreo de Dios' ('I disbelieve in God')." With these utterances, Africans spit in the faces of the church and its god. What the Catholic church defined as "blasphemy" was logical to the Africans because any "God who failed to offer 'protection' or to work 'a miracle' when the situation demanded it was not playing the role ascribed to him and so could be renounced."[78]

Leonor de Isla was a free African of Mexico whose oracular utterances, self-actualization, and Àjẹ́ were exemplary. De Isla acted as seer, prophet, and healer for her community. In addition to assisting community members with conjure, she could conjure community members. She spoke with the spirits regularly and could make them appear. De Isla worshipped Yemọja, Olókun, Mami Wota, and Afrekete outright through "the spirits that live in the sea" and under the guise of St. Martha.[79] De Isla also worshipped Èṣù so fervently that she was accused of being a "devil worshipper." The charge against de Isla is that she would "go to the intersection of a certain street at midnight and there 'she would *go* around in circles . . . and call and invoke the devil.'"[80] The intersection is the home of Èṣù, guardian of the crossroads, and spinning around counterclockwise three times is the way Èṣù is saluted.

De Isla's authentic and unapologetic worship of African Gods left Christian religious officials mystified and terrified. De Isla was accused of "witchcraft" and went on trial before the Holy Office of Inquisition in 1622. As part of her testimony, she recited two personal prayers. In the following excerpt, de Isla uses the linguistic mastery of Odù to invoke

African Òrìṣà to protect and empower her while she prays to Catholic saints:

> Our Lord, Jesus Christ, by the holy cross on which you were hanged and crucified on Mount Calvary, and you who fixed your eyes on the thief at your right hand, you who may subject all men and women to do my will and make them walk where I desire and aid me, and in my heart, men as well as women, let them see me and praise me as much as I may desire or command, so that whatever I choose to do they may come to my aid and defense against my enemies. May Our Heavenly Father and the Holy Spirit and the Virgin Mary and the court of angels and patrons and dominions and all the court of Heaven be with me. Saint Raphael be with me Saint Paul and all the saints and heavenly court, and the priests who say Mass in vestments, and all the saints and ministers who commune with the Holy spirit and the Virgin Mary. May they wish to aid me wherever I may go, in the name of the Father and God, the Son and the Holy Spirit. May they never love God more [than] your servant Leonor [and] may they approve all that I may desire to order in the name of God and the Holy Spirit. Amen.[81]

Maneuvering between religious mandate and spiritual reality, de Isla's prayer is rich with syncretism and linguistic dissembling. Not only does de Isla dissemble as she conceals Ifá in Christianity, but she is also *disassembling* the construct of a Christian prayer as she assembles a linguistic shrine to the Òrìṣà, herself, and her Àjẹ́.

Africana linguistic skills are diverse and multitudinous, and they traversed the Middle Passage. In addition to outright signifying, enslaved Africans would encode their words and infuse two or more meanings in one statement. They would also engage in specifying, which is to expound upon either an encoded or a signified concept or utterance. De Isla was a master of signifying, encoding, and specifying. While on trial, de Isla offers a renunciation of the Christian God that she shields by addressing African Deities with Catholic names and offering them effusive praise. Furthermore, she crafts a prayer that follows the religious decrees of the Holy Office of Inquisition by mimicking the selfish prayers Africans regularly associated with Caucasians.[82]

Weaving the mandate of the Holy Office of Inquisition, the hypocrisy of an enslaving religion, and her spiritual needs into a unified whole, de Isla begins her prayer with the classic *ijúbà,* the introductory ritual homage that opens the doors of the spirit world. To have started asking "Our Lord" for favors without ritual recognition and homage would have been a severe breech of form that would have either rendered her prayer fruitless or yielded the opposite result. However, de Isla deftly melds praise to Jesus with the galvanization of her personal spiritual power. While de Isla often mentions Jesus, literally and figuratively concealed in the word "Jesus" is the ubiquitous Èṣù, the divine linguist, trickster, and mediator between humans, Deities, and ancestors. Èṣù, who has àṣẹ and Àjẹ́ and is invoked first and foremost lest she-he twist one's words and confound destiny, performs the same path-opening duties for de Isla as she-he does for devotees in Yorubaland. It is not the placid lamb but the ever-ready seventh son who can subject persons to de Isla's will, make them walk where and how she commands, and defend her against enemies.

Alternating between mandatory place markers and powerful signifying forces, de Isla massages her Àjẹ́ while invoking a pantheon of "sainted" Òrìṣà. It is said that no Òrìṣà is senior to Àjẹ́; fittingly, de Isla's ultimate desires are that human beings "never love God more [than] your servant Leonor [and] may they approve all that I may desire to order in the name of God and the Holy Spirit." What is most significant about her Ọ̀rọ̀ Àjẹ́ is that de Isla recited her layered prayer when she needed her force most catalyzed—while on trial.

It is important to note that while de Isla conceals many Òrìṣà behind Catholic saints, Àjẹ́ stands forth without cloaking. There is no need to conceal Ìyàmi Òṣòròngà in a saintly figurine because she exists in and as de Isla, and this makes de Isla's references to personal power and her requests for obedience from members of the community even more profound. It is also telling that de Isla does not ask for destruction of oppressors or evolution of the community. She asks no favors on behalf of a client. She seeks only the physical and spiritual amplification of her Àjẹ́ so that she can *continue* doing all of these things herself.

The spirit that kept Àjẹ́ alive and that ordered existence in Latin America struck with fury in the Caribbean as Akan, Igbo, Yoruba, Wolof, BaKongo, and other African forces of retribution united for revolution. Haiti was filled with freedom fighters who used veiled and unconcealed African rituals and Àjẹ́ for revolutionary purposes. Prior to her truncation as the Virgin Mary,[83] Ast was heralded as "pre-eminent, mistress and lady of the tomb, Mother in the horizon of heaven" and "orderer, producer, and maker of slaughter. . . . Hewer in pieces of blood." Riviere of Haiti, known as the "godchild of the Virgin Mary," channeled Ast's power. Riviere "used to say mass, torture the whites, and maintain all he did was in accordance with the orders of the Virgin."[84] Although colonized by Catholicism, diluted by religious mandate, and debased to precipitate oppression of Africans, Ast apparently remained devoted to her progeny and accepted enslavers' blood as libation.

Freedom fighters Hyacinthe and Halaou used the highly developed art of bullet deflection along with other African powers to ensure that their battles against enslavers were victorious.[85] And power brokers such as Court of Antigua and Boukman of Haiti initiated members of impending insurrections with Ayen-rich rituals.[86] In 1791, Boukman and his followers held an Akanian group initiation. Following this, with a prognosticating storm cloud overhead—possibly the watchful form of Oya—an elderly woman, indubitably of Àjẹ́, danced while brandishing a cutlass, perhaps invoking Ògún to bless their revolutionary undertaking. After the invocative juba, a black hog was sacrificed and its blood was shared for group solidification.[87] Six days later, Boukman and "the slaves of the Turpin plantation, near Cap Francais, indiscriminately massacred every white man, woman, and child upon whom they could lay their hands."[88]

In Jamaica, an Àjẹ́ led hundreds in an armed struggle for freedom. Queen Nanny, the leader of the Eastern Jamaican Maroons, appears to be a direct spiritual descendant of Odù and Ìyàmi. In 1739, guided by Oya's Áàjálayé (Winds of the World), Nanny led 500 Windward Islands Maroons into successful battles against 5,000 British soldiers: "Queen Nanny did indeed kill many British soldiers, and . . . had many put to death."[89] The most important tools in her arsenal, like those of Nana Bùrúkù, Nyabinghi, and Sarraounia, were military acumen and Àjẹ́.

Known as a "powerful obeah woman" (obeah is the Jamaican equivalent of Àjẹ́) and a "ritual specialist," Nanny borrowed a page from Odù's text and erected a massive spiritual pot that, without fire, produced boiling water that mesmerized and swallowed British soldiers.[90] Like Hyacinthe and Halaou, Nanny was a bullet catcher. Said to have boarded a slave vessel on the Gold Coast of her own volition to arrive in Jamaica and fight for her people's freedom, Queen Nanny is praised as the "Messiah" of the Maroons.[91] The pride and power of African Caribbeans facilitated their freedom from oppression and provided a fertile foundation for the culturally specific evolution of traditional African spiritual systems, as is evident in Voodoo, Santería, and Lùcùmí.

ÀJẸ́ IN AFRICAN AMERICA: UNITED STATES OF SALVATION

In contrast to the Caribbean and Latin America, it is widely held that Africans in the United States, other than those of the Sea Islands and New Orleans, generally adopted Christianity and the ways of their oppressors. Due to the violently oppressive tactics American enslavers employed, such assumptions seem valid. However, while there was little opportunity for widespread overt retention of Òrìṣà among Africans enslaved in America, covert revival was ongoing. George P. Rawick found that given the absence of a serious attempt to Christianize Africans during the first 100 years of slavery, "there was sufficient time and opportunity for the establishment in North America of generalized West African religious forms."[92] He also found that "[s]ome slaves never became Christian in any sense." Despite the fervor of the Great Awakenings, some oppressors refused to allow Africans to practice Christianity; this, coupled with the comprehensive force of African spiritual systems, facilitated the development of a holistic self-affirming faith known as the African Cult.

THE AFRICAN CULT AND THE POT RESISTANCE

Melding the rituals, tenets, and practices of many spiritual systems into one, the African Cult was the spiritual gumbo of America. Cult members were characterized by their ability to "catch sense," a phrase that signifies one's having added spiritual sense to common sense or worldly knowledge. Practitioners, although often empty-handed, were said to "carry power." In other words, as had their Yoruba predecessors, they toted wicked bags of medicinal, killing, or protective power on or within their person.

Worship in the African Cult took various personal and communal forms, depending upon the prevailing ethnic groups of an area. Although visual evidence of the Cult can still be found in southern rituals and protective art,[93] Africans were unable to reproduce and worship at overt shrines to Òrìṣà. However, always-already Àjẹ́, which has no specific shrine elements or locales except for the evolved Self, was inherently prepared to heal, curse, unify, and politically restructure on behalf of the African Cult. In "Singing Swords: The Literary Legacy of Slavery," Melvin Dixon explicates the psychological and social import of the African Cult and Àjẹ́ in the enslaved African community:

> Knowing the deep need for community and the deprived sense of belonging for slaves isolated in bondage, and knowing the utter contempt with which whites regarded black spiritual welfare (despite a very false "Christian" religious education), it is obvious that through the religious organization in the slave quarters, the slaves were not converting themselves to God, but *were converting themselves to each other. As a result, slaves*

> *converted God to their identity and community in the New World and made God active in their struggle for freedom. . . . Both God and man experienced conversion.*[94]

As did de Isla, enslaved Africans of the United States summoned the Òrìṣà and Àjẹ́ within and became their own saviors. This was necessary because, in comparison to Ifá or Vodun and the revolutionary Deity therein,[95] Christianity had few readily accessible paths to liberation. Furthermore, as Minnie Fulkes and countless others recalled, Africans were often denied any form of worship:

> Dey would come in and start whippin' an' beatin' the slaves unmerciful. All dis wuz done to keep yo' from servin' God an' do you know some of dem devils wuz mean an' sinful 'nough to say, 'Ef I ketch you here agin servin' God, I'll beat you. *You haven't time to serve God. We bought you to serve us.*' Un um.[96]

Attempts to excise the African spirit actually strengthened the soul. And soul-power is the breeding ground of Àjẹ́. African Cult rituals began with the bare essentials of the plantation: a pot, water, and the word:

> They would get a big ole wash kettle and put it right outside the door, and turn it bottom upwards to get the sound, then they would go in the house and sing and pray, and the kettle would ketch the sound. I s'pose they would kinda have it propped up so the sound would get under it.[97]

William Bascom finds that among the Yoruba, "There is a special kind of pot for each of the hundreds of Deities," and among the Fon, ancestors are remembered and honored with individual pots "into which a young chick is placed as a sacrifice."[98] Recalling the pot of Odù, the Womb of All Existence from whence the covenants of Òṣùmarè and Olódùmarè come, enslaved Africans adroitly compounded the use and meaning of the pot. The holistic nature of the African worldview, which includes the inherent unity of sacred and secular realms, was fully manifest in the iron and clay pots, which were used for the practical tasks of washing and cooking during the day. However, the domesticity of the pot was upended with the evening, when it became a pragmatic spiritual vehicle.

Many elders asserted that the upended pots were "catching" the sounds of worship, which is shrewd and practical. I also agree with Rawick that the ancestors employed the African practice of using pots to direct and facilitate prayers and ensure, in the greatest of ironies, the transcendent destiny of those deemed utterly destitute.[99]

In some cases, rather than being upended, the pot would be filled with water. As depicted in the iconography of Egreja da Santa Efigênia, water is a staple of African spiritual systems: It is essential to life, fertility, and abundance, and it is the original liquid of libation. Additionally, the enslaved African knew—all too well—that water is a means of travel.

The water and the pot, then, were not only tools of sympathetic conjure used to keep the word contained among the supplicants and away from the oppressor's ear, but they were also used to hasten the speed with which requests reached to the Òrìṣà and the spiritual realm. The pot also gave adherents physical and psychological protection from being beaten. What better place to pray than in a sacred grove where the Òrìṣà descend, and what better vehicle to use than the fluid of Yemọja, the Mother of Waters, who transported the traumatized Africans and ensured their survival despite everything? What tool could be more effective for those forbidden to pray than the innocuous cooking pot converted into and consecrated as Odù's Pot of Origins?

The empowerment granted by prayers and pots at night inspired acts of resistance in the day. Similar to Africans in Mexico who would renounce the Christian God while they were beaten, African Americans would condemn the oppressors who styled themselves God's emissaries. One enslaved African simply informed the plantation mistress, "You no holy. We be holy. You in no state of salvation."[100] In addition to dispatching "all bad slaveholders" to hell, demystifying racist sermons with simple truths and declaring, "No white people went to Heaven,"[101] Africans celebrated their oppressors' deaths with laughter and final pronouncements: "Old God damn son-of-a-bitch, she gone down to hell."[102]

The pot's dual utilitarian-spiritual role was also expanded into a tool of retribution, as Amy Chapman reveals in her discussion of a woman's retaliation for a merciless beating:

> She got so mad at him [the plantation owner] dat she tuk his baby chile what was playin' roun' de yard and grab him up an' th'owed it in a pot of lye dat she was usin' to wash wid. His wife come a'hollin' an run her arms down in de boilin' lye to git de chile out, an' she near bout burnt her arms off, but it didn't do no good 'cause when she jerked de chile out he was daid.[103]

African American women contributed in so many ways to the upbringing of Euro-American children. They were forced to breast-feed the offspring of their oppressors while giving their own children "sugar tits" or a little bit of nothing.[104] To add insult to injury, these children, nourished on African breast milk, would likely grow to become oppressors, as Boukman and Nat Turner hypothesized. The woman discussed by Chapman is cognizant of slavery's ensnaring web. Therefore, the entity she was helping to create, who would have continued her oppression, she destroys. In the words of oríkì Onílẹ̀, "[A child] died on the farm and the pot ate it up." With an impromptu sacrifice to Odù's ever ready "wicked bag," this woman exerted her authority and facilitated the reshaping of her destiny.

Academic discussions of abolition usually feature Caucasian Americans and their literature; however, abolition was an inextricable component of Africana existence, and it permeated *every* aspect of existence at all times. Furthermore, just as Ọṣun and Ast's holistic Àjẹ́ has been minimized and trivialized, so too has the contribution of African American women in fomenting insurrection and precipitating their own freedom and that of their communities been marginalized. Discussions of Africana women abolitionists are usually limited to Harriet Tubman and Sojourner Truth, but these women are part of a continuum of Pan-African abolitionist Àjẹ́ who, by galvanizing the divinity within and without, fanned individual and communal flames of freedom on plantations.

One of the most common forms of resistance involved the destruction of the African-built facilities that maintained slavery. Nana Bùrúkù and her fire were staunch allies of enslaved Africans, as an Afri-Cuban praisesong to the God reveals:

> Wicked Mother, mother kills life and she does not use a knife
> . . . .
> You cut the world you did not use a knife
> Gently cut this evil you who do not use a knife
> . . . .
> Mother uses fire to trap you, wicked mother
> . . . .
> Fire unloosed severely on the plantation
> Mother uses fire to trap you[105]

In "Reflections on the Black Woman's Role in the Community of Slaves," Angela Y. Davis reveals that Nana Bùrúkù's daughters lit revolutionary flames and cut lives without knives from Louisiana to New York. In Charleston, South Carolina, in 1740, an African American woman set her plantation ablaze. In Maryland in 1776, as Euro-America was celebrating its independence from Britain, "A slave woman was executed . . . for having destroyed by fire her master's house, his outhouses, and tobacco house."[106] In York, Pennsylvania, in 1803, "Margaret Bradley was convicted of attempting to poison two white people." She was already reputed to have eliminated several "respectable white men" via poison. Upon Bradley's conviction, "the black inhabitants of the area revolted en masse"; they held siege to the city for three weeks and burned eleven buildings defending their Ìyá.[107]

Given their close proximity to their oppressors and the fact that they were entrusted with the preparation of foodstuffs, it was only logical for Africans, such as Bradley, who were domestic workers to use Àjẹ́ to poison the food of their oppressors. Alice Green revealed, "Old folks used to conjure folks when dey got mad at 'em. . . . Dey went in de woods and got certain kinds of roots and biled 'em wid spider webs, and give 'em de tea to drink."[108] If a person did not know which herbs would kill, Àjẹ́ would systematically season food with finely ground glass.

Even saliva was used to political advantage by those who in Yorubaland would be called The Elders of the Night. In Africa, spittle can be used to curse, cure, or bless,[109] and the power resident in the mouths of the elders, whether utterance or spittle, survived the Middle Passage. George Leonard declared, "An old person could punish anybody by taking a piece of chip and spitting on it and den dey would throw it on 'em. Dey said dat in two weeks time maggots would be in 'em."[110] Africans used saliva for healing and to locate lost objects. Amanda Styles described how Africans also used saliva to "fix" plantation masters.[111] Once a whipping time and date was set, the intended victim would spit as far as he or she could. When the master approached the spittle, he would forget his mission.[112] Africans' repertoire of skills—from saliva to herbs, from the pot to the word—reflects Àjẹ́'s ownership of everything in the world and the ability of human Àjẹ́ to compound and catalyze the spiritual properties of their possessions.

WORKING THE SPIRITS: FROM HOODOO TO WHODO(?)

African American rituals and conjure cannot be discussed without elaboration on the contemporary evolution of the African Cult, Hoodoo, which is the African American spiritual system that includes cosmology, divination, rootwork, conjuring, power of prayer, the ability to heal, and the power to curse. Hoodoo is a melding of numerous African spiritual systems, including Yoruba Ifá, Ewe Afa, Igbo Afa, Fon Vodun, Haitian Voodoo,[113] and BaKongo and Akan spiritual systems. The word Hoodoo is derived from Voodoo, which comes from Vodun; these terms all mean

Spirit. Far from a conglomeration of superstitions or magic tricks, Hoodoo simply involves working the Spirit. The boundless and comprehensive nature of Àjẹ́ is manifest in Hoodoo, which, like Voodoo, has two aspects. The *Rada* (benevolent) aspect of Hoodoo is used to tie lovers together, assist in healings, aid initiations, and make desires reality. The *Petro* (retributive) aspect of Hoodoo is used to drive insane and kill.

Hoodoo provided tragically dislocated Africans with the means to even odds. Given the frequent usage of the term "fixed" in relation to works of Hoodoo, one could define Hoodoo as "that which fixes." The "fixers" of Hoodoo are known by many names. The Yoruba have oníṣẹ̀gun: African America has root doctors or root workers. The sibling of the babaláwo is none other than the conjure man or woman. If the discussion turns to Àjẹ́ or Oṣó, the ancestors used the terms haints, spirits, hags, witches, or witchmen as a result of linguistic imposition and depending upon the context. But for the all-around specialist in spiritual work, the term two-headed doctor is used. Reflecting the oríkì of Àjẹ́, the term describes a person who has the knowledge of two heads in one or owns a spiritual in addition to the physical head. In Central Africa, the two-headed doctor's equivalent is the *nganga*. Simon Bockie described the nganga's vast power and multidimensionality:

> Nganga is neither a magician, witch, faker, nor sorcerer; yet he is all of these and much more. As used by BaManianga, the term nganga denotes a physician or medical man. Pharmacist, prophet seer, visionary, fortune-teller, priest *and ndoki*. . . . [W]orking closely with an ancestral spirit, *he sits above any imaginable kind of human power.* He becomes a factotum and guardian of the community secrets. . . . He is humanospiritual; he is possessed by a spirit without being a spirit himself. Remaining constantly in touch with the spirit, he connects the two communities.[114]

We can compare Bockie's description to that of W. E. B. DuBois, who wrote that the two-headed doctor

> early appeared on the plantation and found his function as the healer of the sick, the interpreter of the Unknown, the comforter of the sorrowing, the supernatural avenger of the wrong, and the one who rudely but picturesquely expressed the longing, disappointment, and resentment of a stolen and oppressed people.[115]

In comparing the words of Bockie and DuBois, we arrive at a clearer understanding of the inviolable but malleable composition of African spiritual powers and power-wielders.

While two-headed doctors and nganga held "power unequal to man," every African had some degree of personal access to Continental ways of knowing and doing. Personal power extended from basic knowledge of herbal preparations and interpretation of signs to the power to create and destroy. A worldview centered on communal knowledge-sharing made it even easier for one to be one's own babaláwo and oníṣègun.

Justice is a cornerstone of Àjẹ́ and is a right of existence in traditional African societies. However, Africans found themselves enslaved in a republic where a Caucasian man could chop an elder's head open with an axe and then pour cold water into the bashed cranium while the elder moaned herself to death.[116] Africans survived in a society where a Caucasian woman would sit down with a pipe and leisurely whip an African for an hour or more: It is important to note that women (and children) were as cruel, often more so, as men.[117] Enslaved women had to submit to rape or "get a killing."[118] And after freedom was decreed in the "land of the free," Confederate soldiers "shot niggers and chopped their heads off, and [stuck] their heads on poles" and stood "slaves backwards to the river and [shot] them off in the river."[119] In order to survive these and countless other terrors, those who had Àjẹ́ used it; those who did not sought the help of those who did.

A man went to see a two-headed doctor because he had been severely beaten and wanted retribution. The conjurer employed Àjẹ́. The next morning the master was chipper; however, "[a]s soon as de sun was down, he down too, he down yet. De witch don dat."[120] Another victim had his retribution established *before* his beating: "Wen' to a witch-man. When his master 'mence to whip him, eve'y cut he give de man, his [master's] wife way off at home feel de cut. Sen' wor' please stop cut lick de man. When [the master] got home, his wife was wash down wid blood."[121] In *Mules and Men,* Zora Neale Hurston describes how Old Dave brought African justice to his family. When a racist planter killed Old Dave's daughter by bashing in her temple with a rib roast, two-headed Dave, using the blood of his dead daughter as a catalyst, Hoodooed the planter's wife and two children and drove them insane, one by one. Their minds deranged, they would try devotedly but unsuccessfully to kill their patriarch, who spent the rest of his life experiencing the justice of Àjẹ́.[122] We can compare Old Dave to Old Julie, who was responsible for so much "maiming" and "death" that the master put her on a steamboat headed for the Deep South. That night, Julie used her Àjẹ́ to make the ship sail backward. In the morning, she was at the point of departure, ready to return to her home.[123] And indicating the scope of insurrectionist Àjẹ́, in 1816 George Boxley, a Caucasian storekeeper, began planning an insurrection because "a little white bird had brought him a holy message to deliver the slaves from bondage."[124] It seems that the Mysterious Mothers and their ubiquitous Spirit Birds could move anyone.

Because Àjẹ́ is not locked in rigid rituals, it expanded and proliferated freely. The song "Hoo-dooism" highlights Àjẹ́'s ability to adapt to any environment as it instructs dislocated Africans to use the objects and forces at hand to re/determine their destinies.

Hoo-dooism

A snake head an' er lizard tail, Hoo-doo;
Not close den a mile o' jail, Hoo-doo;
De snake mus' be er rattlin' one,
Mus' be killed at set uv sun,
But never while he's on de run, Hoo-doo.

Before you get de lizard cot, Hoo-doo;
You mus' kill it on de spot, Hoo-doo;
Take de tail an' hang it up,
Ketch de blood in a copper cup,
An' be sure it's uv a pup, Hoo-doo.

Wait until sum stormy weather, Hoo-doo;
Put de head and feet together, Hoo-doo;
In a dry ol' terrapin shell,
Let 'em stay fer a good long spell,
But don't you ever try to sell, Hoo-doo.

De rattlers mus' be jus' seben, Hoo-doo;
But mus' not be over leben, Hoo-doo;
He mus' be curl'd up fix'd to fight,
But see dat you don' let him bite,
Den you hit w'en de time is right, Hoo-doo.

Ef you do, [its power] is dead, Hoo-doo;
'Cause it is all right in de head, Hoo-doo;
Save de head and de buttons, too,
Fer de work you'll have ter do,
You will need 'em till you're thru, Hoo-doo.

Ketch a live scorpen wid yo han', Hoo-doo;
Drown in mare's milk in a pan, Hoo-doo;
Den dry it on a pure lime rock,
Ninety-nine minutes by the clock, Hoo-doo.

Den git a hand which is a bag, Hoo-doo;
Made uv any sort of rag, Hoo-doo;
An' let de top be color'd blue,
Den git de hair from out de shoe, Hoo-doo.

Now w'en you find de folks ain't well, Hoo-doo;
An' dey wants you to move de spell, Hoo-doo;
Git your gedients together
Ster dem up wid a goose feather,
In sum dark an' cloudy weather, Hoo-doo.

Den put 'em in de hoo-doo bag, Hoo-doo;
In dat little blue top rag, Hoo-doo;
Den slip 'em in between de ticks,
Ef you want de conjure fixed,
Is de way you do de tricks, Hoo-doo.

Ef dey want you to git 'em well, Hoo-doo;
Dat is de han' dat moves de spell, Hoo-doo;
Take it out before der eyes,
An' you mus be awful surprised,
And dey will think dat you is wise, Hoo-doo.

Den lay right down on yo back, Hoo-doo;
Ef you hear de timbers crack, Hoo-doo;
Den yer kno's yer trick has won,
Den you'll ast er-bout de mon,
For you kno's yer work is don, Hoo-doo.

Now ef you want de conjure fixt, Hoo-doo;
All you do is run de tricks, Hoo-doo;
Jes git dat bottle what you had,
An' to make your patient glad,
Is but to make de conjurer mad, Hoo-doo.[125]

Recorded in Christian County, Kentucky, "Hoo-dooism" is remarkable simply for its existence despite years of oppression and calculated efforts to destroy Africans' spiritual resources. The weaving of this wealth of information into a coherent, unified, logical whole is just as fascinating. The lyrics of the text make it clear that Hoodoo is not a furtive art but a communal one, and "Hoo-dooism" is community property—a song meant to be shared and put to use.

While some rhyme and others seem impossible, each of Hoo-dooism's ritual instructions is directly linked to Continental spiritual practices. The rattlesnake recalls serpent Deities of Africa such as Damballah-Hwedo (Fon), Òṣùmàrè (Yoruba), and Mani (BaKongo). Far from a symbol of evil, as they are in the Judeo-Christian tradition, serpents and snakes recur as sources of mystery, regeneration, virility, and power in Africana spiritual works and orature. The lizard and the wily tortoise are staples of conjure and ritual semiotics.[126] In stanza eight, in addition to creative animal àṣẹ, the goose feather, symbolic of Ẹyẹ Ọrọ̀ and Maat, provides balance and coheres the various ritual elements. The emphasis on certain rituals being enacted during stormy, cloudy weather, indicative of Ọya, is an important aspect of Africana rituals and is mentioned twice in the orature. Ọya's number nine is also significant to the construction: the perfect number of rattlers, mentioned in stanza four, would be nine; and the preparation for the scorpion is "ninety-nine minutes by the clock." The hair and the shoe mentioned in the seventh stanza apparently refer to missing lines. However, given the importance of using such elements as hair, saliva, and nail parings to charge spiritual work, it is clear that spiritual DNA is being manipulated in the work.

The Hoodoo bag's construction and elements are similar to BaKongo *minkisi,* which are described as representations of the cosmos and hiding places for the soul. *Nkisi* (singular form of minkisi) is a constructed implement that includes a combination of spiritual objects (i.e., an egg, a black dog, and certain roots and herbs) which are all gathered and prepared according to nkisi's demands. Nkisi is a microcosmic encapsulation of all the àṣẹ and Àjẹ́ of the spiritual and material worlds, and it can be used for healing, protecting, and fighting oppression. Nsemi Isaki discusses nkisi with sincerity and affection: "It is . . . called nkisi because there is one to protect the human soul and guard it against illness. . . . Nkisi is also a chosen companion, in whom all people find confidence."[127] Stanzas nine to twelve describe the Hoodoo bag's effectiveness in sealing and removing conjure. In the latter capacity, the Hoodoo bag is not unlike the BaKongo *ngang'a ngombo,* the "searcher of causes," which is used to free someone of conjure; and the bag's wielder, depending upon the context, is the equivalent of *ngang'a mbuki,* the healer.[128]

"Hoo-dooism" and the various uses of the Hoodoo bag point to a sociospiritual shift that gave rise to a spiritual twin of Hoodoo.

Hoodoo's sibling and homophone is Whodo(?), whose origin can be placed circa 1880–1900. My father, born and raised in close proximity to practitioners, explained the orthographic and methodological difference between Hoodoo and Whodo(?) to me. He (jokingly?) stated that Whodo(?) implies a question: "Who's doing this shit to me?" Whodo(?) involves violent spiritual retribution that results in physical debilitation directed largely against Africana community members, and it can have numerous applications and impacts. Whodo(?) can work astrally, as does Àjẹ́, and it can be implanted in an object that is charged with one's àṣẹ, or spiritual DNA. "Hoo-dooism's" seventh stanza mentions using personal items such as hair, nail pairings, clothes, and shoes to charge the Hoodoo bag; however, conjurers can also use personal items of an intended victim to ensure exclusivity and direct effect. Whodo(?) can also infect the mind of a victim. The very idea that one has been Whodoed(?), whether or not it is the case, establishes a psychosomatic conjure that accelerates and can become its own rootwork.

While intracommunity conjuring occurred before emancipation, Whodo(?) reached epic proportions in the post-emancipation era. And both "victims" and "fixers" maintained extensive libraries of orature about their battles with and against Whodo(?). As two faces of one body, "Hoo-dooism" provides a clear example of the relationship between Hoodoo and Whodo(?). While stanza ten details ways to neutralize rootwork, stanza nine reveals ways to accelerate the conjure until the victim dies. Hoodoo and Whodo(?) and their practitioners are neutral; circumstances and communal politics dictate how the conjure is used and interpreted. Furthermore, traditional checks and balances remain intact, as Earth, the Mother of Us All remains the arbiter of justice, Àjẹ́, and Whodo(?).

"I'LL FLY AWAY"

One of the most well-documented Àjẹ́-induced abilities is the power to fly. As a Yoruba wisdom-keeper interviewed in the 1970s revealed, "If the 'powerfuls' want to travel to somewhere like Lagos, they will be making a lot of preparation [i.e., material-spiritual implements] in the afternoon. And when it is night time, they will tie all the medicine on their body. Then they will rise from the earth to the sky and they will be moving."[129] Other Yoruba transport devices include *egbé*, often translated as "carrier medicine," which is used for emergency travel; *kánàkò*, which shortens distances walked; and *ọfẹ*, which removes its bearer immediately from a site of harm.[130]

In *After God Is Dibia,* John A. Umeh describes *ekili,* a "mystic stick of flying light," which the adept Igbo *dibia* (diviner) can use for transportation. By holding the ekili, a stick of firewood burning at both ends, the dibia can transport himself or herself, other human beings, and goods in a beam of light that moves at "supersonic speed" without sound or emission. Umeh explains the metaphysical process of transportation as such: "The Dibia having burnt off the material body . . . or transformed it into pure light, achieved spiritual union with his *Chi* and the Universal Spirit while maintaining essential existence in this plane of existence encapsulated in the pure white light rod."[131]

The Àjẹ́-inspired knowledge of how to prepare tools of transport was carried in the minds of enslaved Africans and put to use in the Americas:

> African-born slaves were associated with conjure and magical powers exemplified in the frequently told stories of Africans who put up with the treatment accorded them by whites in America as long as they could and *then simply rose up and flew back to Africa. In some versions, they delayed their escape until they could teach their American-born relatives and friends the power of flight as well.*[132]

Historical studies are replete with testimonies about Africans flying throughout the ìtànkálẹ̀. Wallace Quarterman of Georgia described Africans uttering mystic words and using the tools of enslavement to promote mobility. After throwing a hoe to the ground, the Africans transformed into buzzards and took wing: "I knowd plenty wut did see em, plenty wut was right deah in duh fiel wid um and seen duh hoe wut dey lef stickin up attuh dey don fly away." Shad Hall of Georgia described a group of Africans who refused to be beaten and ran toward a river that became a runway for their flight back to Africa.[133] Group flight suggests the use of material-spiritual constructions, such as ekili, egbé, or kánàkò, or the spiritual charging of readily accessible tools. However, there is no single specific word or device used to facilitate flight. The methods are diverse—from spiritual medicine to spinning around to innate power—and may be related to specific ethnic groups.

In addition to echoing Jamaican testimonies about the prevalence of flight among the BaKongo and mentioning devices similar to Ọrẹamẹ's fan and Yoruba egbé that facilitated flight, Esteban Montejo, a Cuban of Kongo and Yoruba ancestry, stressed the fact that flight was not code for running away or a euphemism for suicide; it was literal:

> The Negroes did not do that [commit suicide as others did], they escaped by flying. They flew through the sky and returned to

their own lands. The Musundi Congolese were the ones that flew the most. They disappeared by means of witchcraft. They did the same as the Canary Island witches, but without making a sound. There are those who say the Negroes threw themselves into rivers. This is untrue. The truth was they fastened a chain to their waists which was full of magic. That was where the power came from.[134]

After reiterating the difference between myth and humanospiritual reality, Montejo also discusses the impact that African flight had on human traffickers: "Some people said that when a Negro died he went back to Africa, but this is a lie. How could a dead man go to Africa? *It was living men who flew there, from a tribe the Spanish stopped importing as slaves because so many of them flew away that it was bad for business.*"[135]

Flight was neither undertaken in secret nor limited to the African imagination. Priscilla McCullough of Georgia described how Africans, while working in a field, began running around in a circle with increasing speed until one by one, "Dey riz up an take wind an fly lak a bud. Duh obuhseeuh heah duh noise an he come out an he see duh slabes riz up in duh eah an fly back tuh Africa. He run an he ketch duh las one by duh foot jis as he was bout tuh fly off."[136]

Perhaps most telling is the fact that, much to their dismay, children watched as their parents flew away. Rosa Grant described how her great-grandmother Theresa, turned around, stretched out her arms, and rose in the sky, apparently headed toward Africa. Theresa left Ryna, Rosa's grandmother behind. After witnessing her mother's flight, Ryna "try an try doin duh same way but she ain nebuh fly. She say she guess she jis wuzn bawn wid duh powuh."[137]

While people might want to assume African flight was restricted to the era of slavery, that is not the case. James D. Suggs discussed a man in Jonesboro, Arkansas in the 1940s, who, when chased by the police, walked faster and faster until "he just spread his arms and sailed right off. And they never did catch him. Said he was faster than the planes. They told about him all through the South, in Alabama, Mississippi, Arkansas."[138]

Flight is also not restricted to persons fleeing oppression. In various African societies, hunters, who have to transport game from the forest to the town and spiritualists (i.e., priests and physicians) are known to use various transportation devices. Enslaved Africans opened the door of exclusivity so that the power of flight, if not in practice then in history and text, became community property. Communal empowerment is apparent in the accounts of flight given by those unable to make the journey and in the works of contemporary artists who encourage a modern community to re-member "ancient properties" to their contemporary collective consciousness.[139]

Physical flight reminded Africans of liberation's many paths, and Àjẹ́'s signature form of travel survived to exact justice for those left behind. Astral travel in African America parallels that in Africa. Astral travelers can be spirits (or "haints") forced to roam because of their hosts' untimely death.[140] Often they are living people, who, as Àjẹ́, can literally "step out" of their skins to go "riding." When they are ready to return to their physical form, they beckon their bodies with a ritual chant: "Skinny, skinny? Don't you know me?" Thus called, the body rises to receive its spirit. A woman who witnessed such a return said, "De skin jump up and dere she wuz again ez big ez life."[141] African and ìtànkálẹ̀an orature and contemporary literature are replete with texts of riding and methods to prevent such occurrences. Jamaican elders held that salt impeded BaKongo flight, and sprinkling a rider's abandoned skin with salt and pepper is said to prevent the spirit's return to the body.[142]

Most riding accounts involve women, but just as there are male Àjẹ́, there are also male riders. In the antebellum era, the majority of ridings were related to retribution. Levine recorded orature about a displaced male Àjẹ́ and his son who "ride the overseer an' his oldes' son." In their astral forms, the pair enters their oppressors' home through a keyhole, "turn the overseer into a bull and his son into a bull yearling, mount them, and spend the night riding and whipping them."[143]

Betty Brown asserted that, in addition to people who access spiritual and astral powers during their lives, "Wen people die angry with someone they usually come back after death in the form of a witch and then they ride the person that they were angry with."[144] Sophia Word recalled Hugh White, an oppressor whose cruelty drove two women to commit suicide. One woman was beaten "most to death" by White for "fergittin to put onions in the stew." The next morning the woman threw herself into the river and "fer nine days they searched fer her and her body finally washed upon the shore. The master could never live in that house again as when he would go to sleep he would see the nigger standing over his bed. Then he moved to Richmond and there he stayed until a little later when he hung himself."[145] Word offers a succinct example of the power of a rider to exact retribution beyond the grave.

The life of Rebecca Jackson of Philadelphia lends great insight into Àjẹ́'s various skills and its ability to revolutionize and restructure life and literature in the ìtànkálẹ̀.[146] From the 1830s to the 1850s, Jackson kept a diary which was published in 1981 as *Gifts of Power*. Indicative of a connection with Òrìṣà Oya, Jackson's power came to her during storms. During an especially terrifying electrical storm, Jackson's soul became fully empowered; she received gifts of literacy, prophecy, clairvoyance, healing, and the power to turn words into action. Jackson also gained the astral ability to fly through the air "like a bird," and she could converse with spirits and ancestors. In the material realm, she could levitate, control the elements (stop rain and thaw frozen rivers), walk through walls, and handle fire without getting burned. While walking at a normal pace, Jackson found she could cover city blocks in seconds. But Jackson did not have kánàkò; she simply had a multiply powerful gift of Àjẹ́.[147]

Jackson's remarkable spiritual and physical powers did not go unrecognized or unchallenged. In "A Dream of Slaughter," Jackson describes how two men attempted to kill her in the astral realm and, thereby, facilitate her physical death. After slicing her face with a lance, they disembowel her. Her spirit guide interceded and queried the astral antagonists about their "occupation." Recognizing a force greater than their own, the males fled. Jackson understood the reason that she continued to live astrally and physically: "He had not as yet taken out my heart, but my entrails were laying all this time by my right side on the floor."[148] While her persecutors employed the methodology of Àjẹ́ exactly, the Mother Earth and the rules that govern Àjẹ́ thwarted them. Jackson's guiding Àjẹ́ foiled numerous plots to kill her, brand her a witch, and undermine her credibility. Her spirit guide also thwarted attempts by her husband and brother and members of the African Methodist Episcopal Church and Shakers to "stop [her] spiritual useful influence among the people and destroy [her] spirit life."[149]

In addition to protecting, Jackson's guides educated her: "For all these years I have been under the tuition of invisible Spirits, who communicate to me from day to day the will of God concerning me and concerning various events that have taken place and those transpiring now and those that yet will occur in the earth."[150] Her guides imparted philosophical wisdom, knowledge of the earth's atmosphere and geographic regions, and skills to help her maneuver through an enslaving society. Most significant, Jackson described her "heavenly lead" as a Great Mother: "I saw that night, for the first time, a Mother in the deity.... I was obedient to the heavenly vision.... And was I ... glad when I found that I had a Mother! And that night She gave me a tongue to tell it!"[151] Jackson possessed a multitude of spiritual abilities, including Àjẹ́, and she used her skills for her community's benefit. Her life and her letters epitomize the cross-geographic, spiritual-aesthetic nature of Àjẹ́.

GRAND VERBALIZATION

One of the most significant manifestations of Àjẹ́ in the ìtànkálẹ̀, especially as it relates to orature and contemporary literature and the bridge that links them, is Ọ̀rọ̀, Power of the Word. Oduyoye translates the name Odùduwà as Oracular Utterance Created Existence. After using her power of the word to create the world, Odùduwà shared her Ọ̀rọ̀ with many daughters. Rebecca Jackson and Leonor de Isla offer stunning examples of Àjẹ́ Ọ̀rọ̀. Benedict M. Ibitokun discusses the force of another one of the Mother's daughters:

> In Ketu folk history, Ìyá Bọ̀kọ́lọ was a very powerful woman before whom the crown trembled. To show the king her mystic and medicinal superiority, she invited him to a duel: Who could kill with quicker means. By the time the king was trying to go into his room to take charms, Ìyá Bọ̀kọ́lọ *spoke* and down came the royal building on the chiefs. The king yelled out his fright, Ìyá Bọ̀kọ́lọ *spoke again,* the building rose up, so did the chiefs but covered with dust and looking otherworldly. Every year Alaketu sacrifices to the shrine of Ìyá Bọ̀kọ́lọ.[152]

"Iya Bọ̀kọ́lọ spoke" is the key phrase. We do not have access to Odùduwà's world-making words or Ìyá Bọ̀kọ́lọ's words of destruction and resurrection. We do not know Queen Makeda of Sheba's "goldmaking words."[153] However, word-power is generative and malleable. Enslaved African conjurers were able to induce flight back to Africa with power of the word.[154] Aunt Darkas of Georgia was noted as "saying something" as she waved her hand over a basin of water to create a healing elixir.[155] To cure thrush, my Great, Grand Mother, Donnie Harris, would take three leaves from a white oak tree, pass them through an ailing person's mouth, pass them through her mouth, "say something," and throw each leaf over a shoulder.[156]

While we may lament the loss of mystic phrases, some examples of Ọ̀rọ̀ are so potent that we may wish they were lost or at least encoded. The following is an example of what the Yoruba would call *aásàn*, the power to curse and drive insane; it is a curse/prayer/poem from the oral repository of Marie Leveau:

> To The Man God: O great One, I have been sorely tried by my enemies and have been blasphemed and lied against. My good thoughts and my honest actions have been turned to bad actions and dishonest ideas. My home has been disrespected, my children have been cursed and ill-treated. My dear ones have

been back-bitten and their virtue questioned. O Man God, I beg that this I ask for my enemies shall come to pass: That the South wind shall scorch their bodies and make them wither and shall not be tempered to them. That the North wind shall freeze their blood and numb their muscles. . . . That the West wind shall blow away their life's breath and will not leave their hair grow, and that their fingernails shall fall off and the bones shall crumble. That the East wind shall make their minds grow dark, their sight shall fail and their seed dry up so that they shall not multiply.

I ask that their fathers and mothers from their furtherest generation will not intercede for them before the great throne, and the wombs of their women shall not bear fruit except for strangers, and that they shall become extinct. . . . I pray . . . that the thunder and lightning shall find the innermost recesses of their home and that the foundation shall crumble and the floods tear it asunder. I pray that the sun shall beat down on them and burn them and destroy them. I pray that the moon shall not give them peace. . . . O Man God, I ask you for all these things because they have dragged me in the dust and destroyed my good name; broken my heart and caused me to curse the day that I was born. So be it.[157]

In its detail, description, and logic, the prayer/curse/poem mirrors that of Leonor de Isla. In its spiritual efficacy and aesthetics, one witnesses another dimension of the force that gave birth to "Hoo-dooism." However, Leveau's text is unlike any other in its precision, directed passion, and dispassionate force.

Leveau invokes Àájálayé, Òrìṣà Oya's Winds of the Earth, from each of their four directions. When these winds converge on the trespasser, Oya will lock him or her in an eternity of personal and well-specified torment. Not only are MawuLisa's astrological sentinels, the sun and moon, invoked to lend their unique forms of destruction but also the victim's own ancestors are asked to bear witness to the trespasses and withhold assistance. With little besides her words, Leveau could set to whirling the winds of Oya, summon cosmological forces, and, like Nana Bùrúkù and Ìyàmi Òṣòròngà kill with imperceptible means.

In addition to her Òrò, Leveau had a rattlesnake familiar and catalyst whose covenant with her, like Òṣùmàrè's covenant with human beings, ensured her supremacy. As do many African American rituals, Leveau's work relied heavily on Oya's sacred number nine, and nearly all her rituals included totems and symbols of Oya and Ìyá-Ayé. Indeed, as a representative of "Earth, the mother of the Great One and us all,"

Leveau's clients greeted her with the same reverence one would use in prayer: "Oh, Good Mother. I come to you with my heart bowed down and my shoulders drooping; for my enemy has sorely tried me." Marie Leveau's nephew, Luke Turner, said that Leveau received the ritual homage of Deities because "Marie Leveau is not a woman when she answer the one who ask. No. *She is a god, yes. Whatever she say, it will come so.*"[158] As did de Isla, Leveau melded African spiritual systems with Christianity, but the force of Àjẹ́ is not diluted with syncretism. Leveau's words became communal realities, and her curses, cures, and prayers took immediate effect. Furthermore, her Ọ̀rọ̀, which was recovered by literary Àjẹ́ Zora Neale Hurston and, later, Alice Walker, served as the foundation for the ìtànkálẹ̀an evolution of Àjẹ́ from life to orature to contemporary literature.

THE FOLKS OF THE TALES

Many Àjẹ́ manifestations in the ìtànkálẹ̀ have parallelisms to Yoruba forms, rituals, and figures. Prior to their transcription and publication in various texts and their infusions into contemporary literature, these experiences and rituals were shared orally among community members. Although they are often dismissed as hyperbole and devalued by the Western term "folktale," many African American oral texts are recastings of ẹsẹ Ifá, and some alleged "folktales" are revisions of actual events.

Many factors contribute to the merging of fact and fiction in African America. A primary contributing factor is that the Western dichotomy between sacred and secular does not exist in the traditional African worldview. As John S. Mbiti explains, "The spiritual universe is a unit with the physical, and these two intermingle and dovetail into each other so much that it is not easy, or even necessary, at times to draw the distinction or separate them."[159] The individual's trials and triumphs are as important as those of Òrìṣà, and all these experiences are communally shared for educational and entertainment purposes.[160] The way in which orature is delivered also contributes to the unification of genre. No matter what occurrence is being related—whether it is a recast ẹsẹ Ifá or the outwitting of an overseer—the telling itself becomes an event, complete with dramatic pauses, onomatopoeia, linguistic alteration, code-switching, signifying asides, repetition, assonance, rhyme, and interspersed proverbs. Most important, the fictionalization of reality protected and ensured the longevity of African ritual practices and practitioners in a society that ridiculed and sought to destroy them.

Zora Neale Hurston, whose literary craft has been described by Henry Louis Gates, Jr., as "speakerly," reveals the connection that orature and power of the word have to ritual performance and spirit work: "Belief in magic is older than writing. So nobody knows how it started. The way we tell it, hoodoo started way back there before everything. Six days of magic spells and mighty words and the world with its elements above and below was made." Following God's rest on the seventh day, which encompasses human existence, there will come an eighth day of re-creation.[161] As does the *Ìtàn-Oríkì Ìyàmi Òṣòròngà*, Hurston's description of creation melds lineal time and curvilinear spiritual time, and although many Westerners consider written communication and documentation to be superior to other forms, Hurston makes it clear that in the creation of the world and in transmission of knowledge, verbal communication, orature, and spirit work are supreme. Furthermore, that "magic spells" and "mighty words" are acknowledged as creative origin forces connects the oracular utterance of Odù and Àjẹ́ with African American cosmology and Hoodoo.

In Hurston's creation text, Hoodoo appears to be the elder of, if not a force indistinguishable from, God. Connections between mighty words and mighty spirits are also evident in African American praisenames for God, which are often translations of the oríkì of Mothers of Power. The African American God may be called Ole Maker, Who Sits High and Looks Low, just as Ìyàmi Òṣòròngà is Mother Who Climbs High and Looks Down on the Earth. The praisenames "Ole Maker" and "Earth, the Mother of the Great One and Us All," bring to mind Yewájọbí, The Mother of All Òrìṣà and Living Things, and Tamara of the Ijọ, The One Who Molded Us All. Another African American oríkì, Maker of the Rainbow, recalls Òṣùmàrè, who is the Rainbow Serpent Deity. African Americans did not have easy access to cowry shells or palmnuts, as did Ifá, Afa, and Fa diviners, so they used whatever spoke to their souls. Some people divined by reading clouds, others had àpo ikà or Hoodoo bags, others used common playing cards. Most significant, because individuals were unable to tote ritual objects through the Middle Passage, they carried ritual texts in their minds. Divination verses, especially those describing relationships among humans, spirits, flora, and fauna, became part of a large, open-ended, and constantly growing body of orature. Indeed, the centrality of Àjẹ́ to Ifá divination texts and Yoruba cosmology and ontology provided the foundation for Àjẹ́'s proliferation in African American written literature.

Numerous origin texts describe Àjẹ́ as a naturally occurring elemental power that is central to creation. There are also texts that describe how human women came to possess Àjẹ́ and how they use it to promote gender balance. The following orature concerns the human acquisition of Àjẹ́. Although it is relatively recent and contradicts more ancient origin texts, it provides insight into how the malleable nature of Àjẹ́ contributed to the retention and evolution of the force in the ìtànkálẹ̀.

> When coming from skyhome (Ikole Orun) to Aye [Earth]
> Women were endowed with no power by
> Olodumare when they arrived at Aye,
> Women asked themselves as to what special power they were endowed with
> Men were cheating the women
> They treated them as slaves and cruelly too.
> The women then went back to Olodumare to report to Him.
> Olodumare was moved and pitied them.
> He promised them a power that would be greater than that of men.
> Olodumare thus gave women power [Àjẹ́]
> He instructed the Witches not to use the power indiscriminately
> Olodumare endowed women with the power called [Àjẹ́]
> Which many of them now use.[162]

In her seminal study *Mules and Men,* Hurston records a revision of the foregoing ẹsẹ Ifá entitled "Why Women Always Take Advantage of Men."[163] Told by community member Mathilda Moseley, the orature concerns the first woman and the first man, who had equal strength but spent all of their time fighting.

Although the patriarchal shift contorted "harmonious dualism" into domestic violence, the original porous boundaries that linked the astral realm to earth, visually depicted in the diagram in chapter 1 and described by Mbiti (above), remained intact. Consequently, Man goes to heaven to ask God for more strength. But before he can make his request, he must, as God reminds him, "put [his] plea in de right form." God demands what African Americans would call *juba* and what the Yoruba would call *ìjúbà*, the ritual invocation that must precede spiritual works, and Man intones the praise that readies the soul and lubricates the ear:

> Ole Maker, wid de mawnin' stars glitterin' in yo' shinin' crown, wid de dust from yo' footsteps makin' world upon world, wid de blazin' bird we call de sun flyin' out of yo' right hand in de mawnin' and consumin' all day de flesh and blood of stumpblack darkness, and comes flyin' home every evenin' to

rest on yo' left hand, and never once in all yo' eternal years, mistood de left hand for de right, Ah ast you please to give me mo strength than dat woman you give me, so Ah kin make her mind.[164]

Similar examples of amply detailed praise orature can be found in Ifá and Vodun ceremonies and the African American Baptist church, as they are a prerequisite to prayer. After rendering the spoken song laden with praisenames detailing every aspect of Ole Maker's power, Man leaves heaven with more strength than Woman.

Having attained more power (and perhaps a bit of Oṣó), Man is able to beat Woman soundly. Believing a patriarchal shift has occurred, Woman goes directly to heaven, and "she didn't waste no words. She said, 'Lawd, Ah come befo' you mighty mad t'day. Ah want back my strength and power Ah uster have.'"[165] Thinking she has been "cheated" and treated "cruelly," Woman has no need to intone ìjúbà. Further, her curt manner of address, because she talks to God as an equal, recalls the superiority Àjẹ́ are said to have over Òrìṣà and the equality they are reputed to have with Olódùmarè. Indeed, this Africana God is one with Olódùmarè, who gave everyone and everything what he, she, or it requested when coming to earth; and as would Olódùmarè, God tells Woman, "Whut Ah give, Ah never take back." Man will always have the physical strength he requested.

As Henry Louis Gates, Jr., elucidates in *The Signifying Monkey*, African Americans rely heavily on tricksterian properties. And while the name "Èṣù" may have been lost in some circles, the cunning, mediating divine linguist's form and methodology remained inviolate. Europeans did not recognize Èṣù—a Deity with eyes like stilled lightning and an oversized penis and a fecund vagina who sits at the crossroads kindling fires of *munrun-munrun* wood with Àjẹ́[166]—so they called the Òrìṣà the devil. However, African cosmology does not include an inherently and irredeemably evil entity bedecked in red who sparks wickedness with a pitchfork. Consequently, when faced with the conundrum of a "devil," African Americans people expanded the multidimensional form of Èṣù and created—not a figure of evil—but the supreme trickster. In African American orature, the Devil character, who is a recasting of Èṣù is not at all evil. In fact, he can be just as helpful as God, often more so because he tests his charges' will and teaches them to make ways out of no way. As a case in point, Woman goes to Devil, who assures her that with his help, she will "come out mo' than conqueror." He instructs her to return to heaven and ask God for the keys hanging on his mantle. An exhausted Woman goes to heaven, intones ritual praise, obtains the keys, and returns to hell for instructions.

The keys control the doors of the "kitchen" (sustenance), the "bedroom" (sensuality and biological creativity), and the "cradle" (children). Devil tells Woman, "Go lock up everything and wait till he come to you. Then you don't unlock nothin' until he use his strength for yo' benefit and yo' desires." Finally, Devil reminds her to practice the reticence of Àjẹ́: "Don't talk too much."[167] Woman uses her power with discretion, and when Man comes home he finds all the doors locked. He goes to heaven to query God, only to find he has a new Òrìṣà. If he wants to eat, procreate, or know about his "generations," he has to "ast de woman." The Yoruba proverb about Àjẹ́—*Àwọn toni kọ́kọ́rọ́ ilẹ̀-àyé* (They have the keys of life)—takes on new resonance for the displaced but undiminished Àjẹ́ of the ìtànkálẹ̀. A Yoruba analysis of African American "folktales" also leads us to investigate the influence the folks had on the tales and vice versa, for there are living laughing humans (and Òrìṣà) behind these "characters."

The merger of the folks and the tales, of the real and seemingly fictional, is apparent in "How a Loving Couple Was Parted," an orature concerning an Àjẹ́ who surpasses both Devil's and Raw Head's cunning. Raw Head is a phenomenal two-headed doctor who "knowed all de words dat Moses used to make. God give 'im de power to bring de ten plagues and part de Red Sea. . . . And his head didn't have no hair on it, and it sweated blood all de time."[168] His physical head is literally raw with the weight and knowledge of his spiritual head. In addition to Raw Head's Christian/spiritual connections, he is "cousin" and kissing friend of the Devil. After discussing all the Whodo(?) they have been doing, Raw Head tells Devil about a couple whose bond he has been unable to destroy. The cousins bet that Devil cannot part the couple before Sunday. By Friday, he gives up. However, a poor woman who is "barefooted as a yard-dog" agrees to break up the couple for Devil in exchange for a pair of shoes. Before nightfall, she has divided the couple. Just as Èṣù and Àjẹ́ meet at the ìrókò tree, the woman meets the Devil at a sweetgum tree to claim her shoes:

> De devil come brought 'em but he took and cut a long sapling and tied de shoes to de end of it and held 'em out to de woman and told her, "You parted 'em all right. Here's de shoes I promised you. But anybody dat kin create mo' disturbance than me is too dangerous. Ah don't want 'em round me. Here, take yo' shoes." And soon as she took 'em he vanished.[169]

The significant difference between the barefoot woman and Raw Head and Devil is that the males are one part human, two parts spirit, and all parts powerful. The woman is "just" a woman. However, the barefoot, impoverished "sister in black" has her Àjẹ́ and its attendant ogbọ́n ayé (wisdom of the world). She breaks the couple up by simply exploiting their weak points. It is interesting that this barefoot woman has a historical progenitor who melded social and spiritual skills. Ellis Strickland of Georgia recalled a woman who worked her Àjẹ́ with a lodestone: "She could take men an' dere wives apart an' den put 'em back together again. She say dat she had killed so many folks dat she didn't know whether she would ever git fit fer forgiveness."[170]

When one reads *Mules and Men* from a Yoruba perspective, it appears that Òrìṣà, Àjẹ́, and àṣẹ, as well as folktales that recycle historical events and the orature of Àjẹ́ and Òrìṣà, influenced Hurston and her peers. The communities and work camps where Hurston undertook her research were filled with subtle Èṣùs, sensual and virile Ṣàngós, and sons of Ògún, the Òrìṣà of iron and technology, whose labors resulted in America's rails, roads, and technological advancements. Additionally, women such as Mathilda, the contributor of "Why Women Always Take Advantage of Men,"[171] exhibit their power of the word by sharing orature, and they subtly but consistently emphasize their personal "advantage" and firm grip on the keys of life. Indeed, it is in the lives of the women, including Hurston, that the resilience of the Òrìṣà is most clear. To understand the evolution of Àjẹ́ in African American life, orature, and literature, one need only imagine that Zora and Big Sweet are respective embodiments of Òṣun and Oya, that they are living and loving in the "hood," and that each woman is actualizing her own Àjẹ́ and enhancing that of her sister.

Zora Neale Hurston, as a stylish and sassy-sweet newcomer to the camps, consciously cultivates a friendship with Big Sweet. Zora feels as vulnerable as "an egg without a shell" in her new environment, so her friendship with the knife-hurling, good-loving master of specification is a shrewd move. However, Big Sweet derives little benefit from her affiliation with Hurston. She is already the established community "Big Momma" (the African American equivalent to Ìyánlá) and she is feared, revered, and respected in the work camps. Big Sweet neither understands nor cares about Hurston's anthropological mission, and her friendship with Hurston exacerbates her rivalry with Ella Wall. However, Big Sweet apparently sees in Hurston a grace, delicacy, and power that complements her own and is worth protecting. Just as Oya is the big sister of Òṣun, Big Sweet recognizes in Hurston both a little sister and a similar power. She gives Zora the pet name "Lil-Bit," which signifies personal intimacy and Hurston's acceptance in the community; Lil-Bit is often a term of endearment parents give to daughters, recalling the little bit of the tree in the independent sapling.

To ensure the growth of her sapling, Big Sweet tells Zora, "You just keep on writing down them lies. I'll take care of all the fighting. Dat'll make it more better, since we done made friends."[172] When Zora prepares to go to a jook (hall of dance, drink, game) without Big Sweet, she warns Zora against boisterous behavior and eating or drinking anything because she may be conjured. Other than this, Big Sweet tells Hurston simply to be her "Little Sweet" self because she will "back her falling."[173] In the words of Àjẹ́, one could say, "It is in [Big Sweet's] hands that [Zora's] life is placed," and Hurston's life is well-placed.

After Big Sweet proves her prowess in an altercation with Ella Wall, Joe Willard declares that she is "uh whole woman and half uh man!" The assertion that Big Sweet is *obìrin-kunrin,* a Yoruba expression meaning "a woman who is like a man," would be much more appropriate if there were a man who actually equals her force. That she has no peer of any gender is evident when she saves Hurston's life. In the course of her research, Hurston appears to be "Òṣuning" Slim. Lucy, Slim's former lover, cannot compete with Òṣun/Zora—an attractive, educated woman who not only blends into the community but also takes an exalted position therein—but she can try to kill her. Lucy enters the jook with her unsheathed knife and struts straight to Zora. Although she is standing next to Slim and surrounded by many men and women, Zora knows that no man will face death for her. "But a flash from the corner about ten feet off and Lucy had something else to think about besides me. Big Sweet was flying at her with an open blade."[174] Wearing her Àjẹ́ like an exquisite robe, a displaced Ọya comes to the aid of a neo-Òṣun; in doing so, Big Sweet ensures Zora's existence and her own textual immortality.

As Houston Baker argues in *Workings of the Spirit,* what Zora witnessed, and, thanks to Big Sweet, survived in the Florida work camps were community initiations that prepared her for spiritual enlightenment. *Mules and Men* is divided into Part I: Folktales and Part II: Hoodoo, but these sections are intimately connected; texts and events in Part I provide the foundation for initiation and application in Part II. The inherent unity of the realm that is commonly bifurcated as sacred and secular is apparent in the fact that many of the "folktales" told in Part I are actually revised divination verses.[175] The sociocultural import of knowledge and skills briefly mentioned in Part I—Joe Willard's information about how to see the wind, Big Sweet's plaiting/planting "Joe Moore" (mojo) in her hair and her advising Hurston to prepare her own food and drink because someone might "put a spider in [her] dumplin'"[176]—are recontextualized and practically applied in Part II. The most significant link between sections is understated. In Part I, at the Loughman camp, Zora finds a rattlesnake sleeping in her bedroom.

Rather than organize the typical Christian snake-killing party, Zora demands that her "lowly brother" be allowed to live.[177] This incident prepares the reader for Part II in a number of ways. Hurston foreshadows in literature and shadows in life Marie Leveau, who was also visited by a rattlesnake. The reptile bears the same message for Hurston as for Leveau: Study the work that is Voodoo.[178] Hurston doesn't kill her messenger in Part I and is rewarded in Part II with tutelage under Leveau's nephew, Luke Turner. And like Leveau, Hurston becomes the owner of the snakeskin crown.[179] With her graduate study in Part II with the "college of Hoodoo doctors," Hurston attains the spiritual-material skills of orature's "sister in black," and Georgia's "lodestone woman." She can break couples up and she can mend shattered unions; she can "feed the he" and she can "feed the she."

The comprehensive spiritual-material knowledge and skills of *Mules and Men* coalesce with Hurston's study with Kitty Brown. Like Yoruba market-women, who are respected for their business acumen and Àjẹ́, Brown is a Hoodoo entrepreneur. She keeps two-headed doctors stocked with necessary herbs and roots fresh from her huge garden. And while she has the means to harm and kill growing around her front door and awaiting activation in her mind, she prefers to "make marriages and put lovers together."[180] Depicted as the classic and fully evolved Àjẹ́, Brown, like Big Sweet, consecrates a spiritual union between herself and Hurston. They become complements, as the daughter dances for her mother and the mother suffers for her child. However, the Àjẹ́ shared and wielded by Brown and Hurston goes beyond spiritual skills and rituals. As Baker elucidates, their force is a holistic way of being and doing that forms the foundation for biological, spiritual, and artistic re-creation:

> And Kitty—in her squat black benignity—has the character of a deceptively droll African religious sculpture. Her tremendous powers among a congregation of vernacular believers [are] masked by her unremarkable posture. Surely it is because she, like Zora, is a carrier of the Black Cat Bone that she traverses the earth with powers unseen. A storyteller and uniter of lovers, a woman who has syncretized Western religion and African cultural traditions to ensure powers of retribution, redress, reward, and renewal. . . . She is the intimate home, the imagistic habitation or poetic space of the spirit in which works of mythomanic transmission can take place.[181]

As the progeny of the Òrìṣà, Kitty Brown and Hurston are at once the folks, the tellers, and the tales; the signs, the signified, and the signifiers;

the human and the divine. Although they use different means, Hurston and Brown use a shared power to enrich their communities, remind community members of their divinity, and offer them living and textual healing tools that can foment holistic wellness and individual and community evolution.

Through Hurston's efforts, many levels of neo-Africana Àjẹ́ are immortalized in one of the most unique textual constructions in literature. Just as *Ìtàn-Oríkì Ìyàmi Òṣòrònga* melds text with Òrìṣà with reciter with listener, the structure of *Mules and Men* blurs the line that divides the Òrìṣà from the folks from the tales and the folktales from Yoruba orature. Most important, rather than transcribing the orations of "informants," Hurston crafts interconnected community biographies. She necessarily humanizes the field of anthropology with her recognition that the contributors to *Mules and Men* were not objects to be studied but peers living myths and re-creating history—dislocated Africans remembering forgotten lives and critiquing their modern existence. It is important to note that in order to undertake her research, Hurston created a character for herself—a mask that would shield her researcher persona and allow her to participate in various ritual dramas. Once Hurston was welcomed into the sacred circle of conjure and cultural art, it is as difficult to tell the researching and writing Hurston from her efficacious creation as it is to distinguish where the "tales" end and "real life" begins. Hurston refused to offer up the folks, tales, and force for sacrifice into Western textual stasis. Instead, she fashioned a living text of immense healing properties so that those denied wellness and recognition could heal themselves while feasting on canonized fruit.

SIS CAT'S KITTENS

Hurston's artistic mastery has become a cornerstone of African American literary studies. However, to understand the origin of her power, it is helpful to turn, again, to Àjẹ́. While she was researching in Haiti, a houngan (babaláwo) named Dr. Holly introduced her to her birthright and the locus of creative power by demanding of her answers she had forgotten she possessed:

> "What is the truth?" Dr. Holly asked me, and knowing that I could not answer him he answered himself through a Voodoo ceremony in which the Mambo, that is the priestess, richly dressed, is asked this question ritualistically. She replies by throwing back her veil and revealing her sex organs. The

ceremony means that this is the infinite, the ultimate truth. There is no mystery beyond the mysterious sources of life.[182]

Dr. Holly and the Mambo lead Hurston on an excursion to the Truth of the Self, and there, Hurston learns where all powers originate and emanate.

It is important to note that when the Mambo reveals "the truth," only the outer encasement of power is visible: The inner sanctum, like Odù's sacred sealed calabash that contains all energies, all lives, all destructive and creative powers and can blind the uninitiated, is hidden from view. However, the Mambo, Hurston, and all Africana women have unlimited access to that inner sanctum. They are the Àjẹ́; they embody "the truth"; they are owners of the shrine of origins—the one that automatically libates, supplicates, and sacrifices to itself. And while Hurston, like Yẹ̀wà, Ọbà, and Rebecca Jackson, did not experience the "mysterious sources of life" through biological childbirth, the profundity of her artistic and cosmic issues is such that Hurston is African America's Ìyá-Iwé, or Mother of Letters.

In *Workings of the Spirit,* Baker heralds female analytical aesthetic-creative power. In addition to indirectly strengthening my assertions that Àjẹ́ has profoundly influenced Africana literatures, he also recognizes the significance of Hurston's *Mules and Men,* referring to it as a "*locus classicus* for Black women's creativity."[183] The infinite depths of Hurston's ink and the multitudinous reflective properties of the pages on which she signified became a spiritual-literary womb that gave birth to multitudinous "daughters" and "sons." It is important to briefly examine some of the ways Hurston's progeny went about reminding the folks of their tales and vice versa. Because I also refer to writers who were not aware of Hurston's work, the following discussion problematizes the concept of an African American *locus classicus* while strengthening my assertion that Àjẹ́ is *locus originalis* of Africana creativity and spirituality.

The matrix of Àjẹ́ that binds Òrìṣà to historical entity to character can occur through both unconscious and deliberate attempts to *remember* particular Great Mothers and powers. Moving beyond its lay definition, Carole Boyce Davies describes re-membering as a meta/physical process that involves the "bringing back together of the disparate members of the family in painful recall" by "crossing the boundaries of space, time, history, place, language, corporeality and restricted consciousness in order to make reconnections and mark or name gaps and absences."[184] Many writers make deliberate attempts to re-member their progenitors, but if one's Mothers have been dismembered from the collective conscience—if they or their works have become "unspeakable thoughts, unspoken"[185]—the Mothers may spark cognition from unconscious realms to force their progeny to re-member them. Furthermore, it is not unheard of for authors to be moved by a mélange of spiritual, historical, and community events.

From the sacred Seven Days and soaring ascension of *Song of Solomon* to an all-Africana *Paradise* to the tragically triumphant life of Margaret Garner, the soul of *Beloved*, Toni Morrison's novels are often born of overlooked or forgotten people, histories, and myths. Morrison employs the methodology of Odù and reconstructs time and tense, history and artistry to create literature that invokes, revises, and adds new dimensions to the "tales" and the "folks" that produced orature and history. Fittingly, Morrison gives historical progenitors and textual entities highest critical authority:

> My work bears witness and suggests who the outlaws were, who survived under what circumstances and why, what was legal in the community as opposed to what was legal outside it. . . . Whenever I feel uneasy about my writing, I think: what would be the response of the people in the book if they read the book? That's my way of staying on track. *Those are the people for whom I write.*[186]

As she writes, the ancestors relive their history and analyze Morrison's reconstruction of their reality. And through the text, author and ancestors speak to a contemporary community that may have ignored or forgotten ancient and historical truths.

Even in the conceptual stages of re-creation, Morrison relies on the words and experiences of the folks who bore witness as opposed to those who did research:

> When I first began to write, I would do no research in that area [African continuity in African America], because I distrusted the sources of research, that is, the books that were available, whether they were religion or philosophy. . . . *I would rely heavily and almost totally on my own recollections and, more important, on my own insight about those recollections and in so doing was able to imagine and to recreate cultural linkages that were identified for me by Africans who had a more familiar, an overt recognition (of them).*[187]

Morrison taps into her reservoir of re-memory and finds that the reality of the Ancestors—complex, pan-geographic, and resilient—is truth enough beyond what "science" can validate or philosophy can imagine.

Despite being dismembered from the word Àjẹ́, Morrison makes it clear that the gentle, resilient, and invisible force was instrumental in her life and the lives of Africana women.[188] Applying cosmic "rememory" and ritual to history, Morrison weaves the timeless words and deeds of "gathering women" who have the "kind of wisdom which is discredited in almost every corner of the civilized world" into her textual creations.[189] With both outer and ever-open spiritual inner eyes, she re-members the historical, mythical, and literal in her subtly critical art to help ancestral and contemporary audiences re-envision the past and better hone the potential of the future.

Nigerian author 'Zulu Sofola's writing process is similar to Morrison's. 'Zulu Sofola describes herself as a "research-oriented writer" who does not allow herself "artist's liberties": "I am always reproducing, as it were, from life."[190] Sofola's philosophy is indicative of a deep, abiding, and fully articulated relationship with history, spirituality, and creativity—a relationship from which Africans of the ìtànkálẹ̀ were often dismembered. Her statements also intimate that there is a certain level of creative freedom enjoyed by the African artist who lives in a largely homogeneous society.

During an interview with Sofola about her drama *Queen Omu*, which centers on the Nigerian civil war of 1967–1970, Adeola James remarks that *Queen Omu* is a "celebration of courageous women." "We see woman as nurse, priestess, mother, covered in the blood of childbirth, drawing attention to the unnecessary bloodshed of the foolish fratricidal war or woman as goddess of the river actively protecting her children." Sofola's elaboration of makes it clear that in both the conception of the play and in its production, women of Amusu (the Igbo equivalent of Àjẹ́) were essential:

> You know Omu is a priestess. *Some of the women you saw in the play were priestesses,* some were military people, some were heads of their various institutions. *Queen Omu, being the head of the women's arm of the government,* was on a par with the king who was the head of the government. So . . . when the king ran away during the Civil War, automatically, she stepped in. I had to do the research.[191]

In addition to faithfully documenting the Omu's political history, Sofola apparently felt it essential to artistic integrity that her drama include actual persons with Amusu as well as military and institutional leaders. As a result, *Queen Omu* is not merely a re-enactment of history. When staged as Sofola envisioned it, the "actors" relive the history of their progenitors. From their parallel contemporary positions, the actors become ritual dramatists who have the power to invoke spiritual forces (as Igbinola invoked Ìyàmi Òsòrònga[192]) who, unable to alter history, can reveal paths to evolution in the present.

Like Morrison, Sofola's connection to art, history, and spirituality begins with her personal relationship to Àjẹ́: "My own paternal grandmother was the last Omu before the one in the play, and I saw her place. *Her influence is still around.*"[193] Sofola experiences a relationship with the Mother that is personal to communal and flows from blood to ink. Furthermore, her spiritual impetus is not relegated to artistic expression. When asked if she "really believes" in the Igbo river Goddess whose spirit undergirded the struggle of the Biafrans and *Queen Omu,* the playwright allows history to tell its own truth:

> During the civil war, they said that the river goddess was at the war front. When the war was over they said she came back and they saw her foot-prints marked in white chalk on the road. That is a reality. The river goddess who was seen at Agbor and the one at Asaba about whose coming the prophet had pronounced years past are also historical facts.[194]

Sofola's personal and familial relationship with Africana female power results in an art that is for life's sake and for the Gods's sakes as well.

By contrast, Africans of the ìtànkálẹ̀ were often dismembered from their culture and language, and as a result of the caprices of the publishing industry, writers are often dismembered from their literary progenitors. However, perhaps as a result of epic or genetic residual memory, authors often create characters who mirror—in form, methodology, and characteristics—historical or spiritual entities that the author may have no knowledge of. Unconscious invocation validates my hypothesis that Àjẹ́ is timeless, multifaceted, and capable of exerting its creative and critical influence in a plethora of ways. As Toni Morrison makes clear, "The fact that I had never read Zora Neale Hurston and wrote *The Bluest Eye* and *Sula* anyway means that the tradition really exists. . . . [It] makes the cheese more binding, not less, because it means that the world as perceived by black women at certain times does exist, however they treat it and whatever they select out of it to record."[195]

Discussing the contemporary disavowal of ancient sources of knowledge, Morrison says, "It makes me wonder . . . if the knowledge we ignore is discredited because we have discredited it."[196] Disavowal of African cosmic reality has led to myopic analyses that are reluctant to acknowledge a text's spiritual center, and it encourages the use of culturally inappropriate theories, a reliance on Western dichotomy, and the use of unrepresentative terms such as "black magic" and "magical realism." Many contemporary scholars would discredit Sofola's revelation or define it in terms worse than "magical realism," but this would not change Idemilli's footsteps or the Deity's influence on Sofola's life and art. The spiritual and ancestral foundations from whence Sofola's and Morrison's artistry spring place them at the center of the ever-evolving matrix of Àjẹ́, and their access to this matrix is inherent and not dependent on a particular text or individual.

If Morrison is an unmothered daughter of Hurston who caught sense nonetheless, Alice Walker, who at one point masqueraded as Hurston's niece, is blood-ink kin. As is well known, Walker initiated the rebirth of a nearly-forgotten Hurston through a series of personal-textual tributes that culminated in Walker giving a poorly interred Hurston her proper burial rites. However, Walker's Àjẹ́-rich homage to Hurston began when she needed authentic information on Hoodoo to write a story based on actual events that befell her mother. Walker needed an effective and authentic Ọ̀rọ̀ to give her mother agency; but, similar to Toni Morrison, who "distrusted" published studies on Africana spiritwork, Walker described available expositions on the "*craft* of voodoo" as "all white, most racist."[197] A footnote led Walker to Hurston's *Mules and Men* and she found in Marie Leveau's prayer/curse/poem the means to reverse the humiliation that befell her mother when a Red Cross representative refused to give her government-issued food during the Depression.

In "The Revenge of Hannah Kemhuff," Kemhuff visits a two-headed doctor named Tante Rosie, and Kemhuff informs Rosie and Rosie's unnamed assistant of the humiliation she suffered at the hands of racist food-withholder Sarah Marie Sadler. In this short story there is an intriguing melding of entities and identities, for Kemhuff represents Walker's biological mother, Tante Rosie is a veiled recasting of Hurston, and Rosie's unnamed apprentice bears a striking resemblance to Alice Walker. With "The Revenge of Hannah Kemhuff," Walker does more than honor Hurston and her mother. As Kemhuff, Rosie, and the apprentice kneel and recite Leveau's "curse-prayer" against Sadler, Zora Neale Hurston, Marie Leveau, Walker's mother, and Walker herself are all present, reciting with "fervor" and demanding retribution.

In the evolutionary style of an Àjẹ́, Walker makes important revisions to the conjuring process. While Leveau summons the Man God for assistance, Tante Rosie prays to "the Supreme Mother of Us All, [who] could only be moved by the pleas of the Man-God."[198] Walker, as reorganizer and cultural critic, insists that the male and female components work in tandem. Furthermore, rather than let the Ọ̀rọ̀ work by itself or compound the power of the word with Whodo(?), Tante Rosie and her apprentice go directly to Sadler, remind her of her crime, and tell her what objects they need—her hair, fingernail parings, something she'd worn, and her urine and feces—to either Whodo(?) her or "prove" the impotence of rootwork. Rather than illustrate only behind-the-scenes machinations, Walker astutely redirects events to prove literarily the power of both material and psychosomatic conjure. Sadler drives herself insane and dies in a house reeking with her long-collected urine and feces; her stomach is filled not with conjure but her own dearly kept fingernail clippings.

To enact literary "revenge," Walker takes a buried text (*Mules and Men* was out of print at the time of Walker's writing) and uses Ìyá Leveau's forgotten Ọ̀rọ̀ verbatim. In the process of healing her mother, Walker expands the Ọ̀rọ̀ Àjẹ́ of Leveau that Hurston immortalized. Inspired by Hurston's proclivity to reinvent genre, Walker creates a curvilinear polyvocal text. The predisposition to open and conjure texts thought to be closed or those that have been forgotten may stem from an inheritance of the intimately connected woman-based powers of Àjẹ́ and Ọ̀rọ̀. In "Verbal and Visual Metaphors: Mythical Allusions in Yoruba Ritualistic Art of *Orí*," Rowland Abiodun informs us that in addition to being defined as Power of the Word, Ọ̀rọ̀ is the verbal and visual manifestation of wisdom, knowledge, and understanding.[199] Furthermore, Ọ̀rọ̀ is not static but exists to be expanded, revised, complicated, and demystified. Most important, Africana artists, as wielders of Ọ̀rọ̀, are obligated to create new and reconceive and critique established forms of Ọ̀rọ̀.

The Gẹlẹdẹ́ festival, staged to honor Àjẹ́, is an important site of amalgamated communal Ọ̀rọ̀ and Àjẹ́. Gẹlẹdẹ́ songs are called Ọ̀rọ̀ Ẹ̀fẹ̀, and, corresponding to the local, regional, national, and international meetings of Àwọn Ìyá Wa, the Ọ̀rọ̀ Ẹ̀fẹ̀ of Gẹlẹdẹ́ "cover virtually all the goings-on in the society, at the local, even at the regional, national, and international levels."[200] The Mothers pray for guidance and discernment as they undertake their work, and Ọ̀rọ̀ Ẹ̀fẹ̀ composers are just as careful with their artistry. To ensure propriety, relevance, and aesthetic appeal, Ọ̀rọ̀ Ẹ̀fẹ̀ are subjected to "pre-performance criticism," criticism during the performance, and "oral criticism of oral poetry . . . after performance."[201] These multiple levels of critique are important because while some Ọ̀rọ̀ Ẹ̀fẹ̀ are humorous and light-hearted, many are politically charged, as is apparent in the following example which critiques Ìdá Àlábá, the "official senior wife of Alákétu Ọ̀yẹngén (1894–1918)," who was appointed chef de Canton by French colonizers:[202]

> Father, if note were to be taken of Ìdá,
> Yam seed planted would germinate
> Into a maize plant! . . .
> Ìdá expelled us into the forest hideouts,

And brought small-pox epidemics on
The community,
And this led to the death of several persons.
Many were kidnapped and sold into
Slavery all in the reign of Òyèngén-Asákáiṣà
Life itself is rendered completely
Incomprehensible.[203]

When colonially appointed administrators' execution of imperialist orders results in social destruction and cultural upheaval, Òrọ̀ Èfè artists are prepared to critique, analyze, and educate in hopes of preventing future travesties and tragedies.

Gèlèdé artists' Òrọ̀ can also punish offenders: There are accounts of persons being struck blind for infringements and crimes against the earth after those trespasses were revealed by Òrọ̀ Èfè.[204] Additionally, because the composers/authors of Òrọ̀ Èfè are "the servant(s) of the [Àjẹ́]," Àwọn Ìyá Wa grant them immunity. A. I. Asiwaju notes that when an Èfè artist was jailed for one of his songs, he was set free because "the offending song was a message authorized by the 'ayé' [*ayé* is literally "world," a euphemism for Àjẹ́]."[205]

Sociocultural critique is inherent in Africana artistic creation and production, and it could be said that many contemporary authors create works that follow a Gèlèdé-esque model—replete with words of power, vindicating Àjẹ́, and astral-physical punishments. What befalls Sadler in "The Revenge of Hannah Kemhuff" is one example from Walker; another is found in *The Color Purple*. In the novel's famous rising action, the long-silenced Celie, as contemporary Òrọ̀ Èfè artist, broadcasts her husband's crimes against her humanity and condemns his destiny. She tells Albert, "I curse you. . . . Until you do right by me, everything you touch will crumble. . . . Until you do right by me . . . everything you even dream about will fail."[206] There is a definite African force empowering Celie's curse, and during her divine utterance, she acknowledges her cosmic assistance. Musing that the words first come to her from the trees, she tells Albert, "You better stop talking because all I'm telling you ain't coming just from me. *Look like when I open my mouth the air rush in and shape words.*"[207] With Ọya, the Deity of Transformation on the tip of her tongue, Celie's Òrọ̀ intensifies, and the wind and words take material form when Albert springs to attack her: "A dust devil flew up on the porch between us, fill my mouth with dirt. *The dirt say, Anything you do to me, already been done to you.*"[208] The speaking dirt is Onílẹ̀, the God and Mother of the Earth. As I discuss in *The Architects of Existence: Àjẹ́ in Yoruba Cosmology, Ontology, and Orature*, the Yoruba ingest a bit of ilẹ̀ (earth) to swear important and potent oaths because it contains the amalgamated powers of all who have gone before and all who will come to be as well as the all-seeing Àjẹ́ of Onílẹ̀, the Earth Deity.[209] With Onílẹ̀ sealing Celie's curse, Albert is literally listening to a promise made by his own grave.

Celie's stupendous act of verbal self-reclamation is facilitated by a host of Àjẹ́ including Onílẹ̀, Odùduwà, Ọya, and Ọ̀rọ̀. These Gods work with Celie and Shug to create a Gẹ̀lẹ̀dẹ́ that forces Albert to evaluate himself and modify his behavior modification, and more important, that vaults Celie in the realm divine self-actualization.

It is not necessary for human beings or literary characters to have an acknowledged relationship with African Deities and spiritual powers in order to access them. Celie is oppressed and silenced for three-quarters of the novel and has no evident links to African rituals or philosophy. She is not a two-headed doctor—she even has difficulty recognizing herself as human being worthy of respect—but when her spirit cycles toward evolution, historical truth and spiritual power flow from her soul and mouth through both Walker's and Celie's pens, as the novel is Celie's epistolary autobiography.

Celie's Ọ̀rọ̀ also has important antecedents and could have been inspired by Janie's curse on Joe Starks in Hurston's *Their Eyes Were Watching God* (see chapter 5) and/or Ajanapu's curse on Eneberi in Flora Nwapa's *Efuru*. When Eneberi accuses his wife, Efuru, of adultery, her friend Ajanapu curses him: "Nothing will be good for you henceforth. Eneberi, Ajanapu, the daughter of Uberife Nkemjika of Umuosuma village, says that from henceforth nothing good will come your way. Our ancestors will punish you. Our Uhamiri will drown you in the lake. . . . From henceforth evil will continue to visit you."[210] We will never be able to count all the actual and fictional women whose power to literally "cuss up a storm" flows through Celie. From a Yoruba perspective, *The Color Purple,* and many other novels that pay conscious and unconscious curvilinear tribute to Ọ̀rọ̀ and Àjẹ́, are multilayered intertextually-communicating literary Gẹ̀lẹ̀dẹ́s.

Where "The Revenge of Hannah Kemhuff" is a three-tiered intergenerational invocation for the healing of an individual's wounds, *The Color Purple* is a unique creative revision born of homage and invocation that is dedicated to acknowledging and healing the communal wounds few admit exist. A true literary Gẹ̀lẹ̀dẹ́, *The Color Purple* critiques patriarchy, misogyny, pedophilia, and all those who doubt and devalue the power of Africana women's relationships with and investments in each other. Most significant, in Ọ̀rọ̀'s open-ended fashion, *The Color Purple* inspires critique. With the publication of her novel, Walker joined and made firmer the foundation of such critical artists as Ntozake Shange and Michelle Wallace. And so bitingly truthful and painful were these women's literary Gèlèdés that they fell victim to a backlash that rocked the 1970s and 1980s. Led by Ishmael Reed and his novels *The Last Days of Louisiana Red* and *Reckless Eyeballing*, African American men (and women) wrote critiques/curses of Walker's political-spiritual art.

In 1995, the male R&B group After 7 interwove Celie's Ọ̀rọ̀ in their hit song "'Til You Do Me Right." This song helped heal the wounds that African American women and men had inflicted on one another and reminded us that, with an occupation of signification, Ọ̀rọ̀ doesn't discriminate.[211] Both men and women have the responsibility to create and critique Ọ̀rọ̀ in order to right actual or perceived social imbalance.

* * *

The *locus classicus* of Africana women's spirituality and creativity certainly includes Hurston, but in order to understand Hurston's creative impetus, we must investigate the myriad sources of African American spiritual expression and acknowledge the Yewájọbí, the Mother of All Living Things. And living things include texts. Yoruba elders interviewed by Barry Hallen and Olubi Sodipo describe *gbàgbọ́* (belief) as more than the *American Heritage Dictionary*'s "mental acceptance of the truth." Rather than being contingent upon individual will, indoctrination, or acceptance, gbàgbọ́ is semi-tangible and transferable. The wisdom-keepers reveal, "In the past, when they taught you oògùn [medicinal preparations] or when an ìtàn was told, they put it 'inside.' It lived 'inside.'"[212] Gbàgbọ́ is part of the text and the teller, and when told, it becomes a part of the listener. The orature need not be cognitively remembered because it is stamped into the DNA, psyche, and soul of the listener—just as it was once stamped upon the teller. We may even extend the foregoing and assert that the text is stamped into the universe. Perhaps these truly universal texts are those Ben Okri refers to as "invisible books of the spirit,"[213] those ancient, long-forgotten, poorly remembered, and never-heard oríkì (praisenames), ìtàn (historical accounts), and orin (songs) that actually bear the spiritual DNA of their owners and enhance that of their speakers and audience.

After describing the ancient composition and path of gbàgbọ́, the Yoruba elders quoted above went on to draw an important distinction between orature and literature. As opposed to the ìtàn living "inside" of the listener, something is lost with technological "advancements" because, "Whatever you are told as a story now, you put it 'inside' book. And it will appear there forever."[214] There is a difference between living and appearing, and once trapped in ink and caught on a page, gbàgbọ́ can become fossilized: Its influence on existence can be diminished once the act of verbalization is eliminated from the process of transmission. However, malleable Àjẹ́ loves a challenge, and Africana artists and artistry relish finding new ways to signify. The "invisible books of the spirit," the origin texts of Odù, and the Ọ̀rọ̀ of creation and creativity find new life but ancient purpose in wood-pulp progeny. The Àjẹ́ that inspires them and the gbàgbọ́ that runs through them speak, signify, specify, and magnify: These are the forces that live in the texts and breathe through the folks.

Part Two

ÀJẸ́ IN AFRICANA LITERATURE

> And she had nothing to fall back on: not maleness,
> not whiteness, not ladyhood, not anything.
> and out of the profound desolation
> of her reality, she may very
> well have invented
> herself.
>
> —Toni Morrison

3

Word Becoming Flesh and Text in Gloria Naylor's *Mama Day* and T. Obinkaram Echewa's *I Saw the Sky Catch Fire*

Gloria Naylor's *Mama Day* and T. Obinkaram Echewa's *I Saw the Sky Catch Fire* (*Fire*) examine the impacts of slavery and colonialism and the ways in which Àjẹ́ battles these forces in its attempts to reconsecrate the earth of origins. Both works demonstrate the curvilinear and intergenerational nature of Àjẹ́, and both are structured similarly to Yoruba and Igbo divination systems.

Odù is the Deity of Àjẹ́, and Odù is the spiritual writing of Ifá divination. Odù Ifá consists of sixteen primary figures called Olódù. Each Olódù contains sixteen ẹsẹ Ifá, making a total of 256 divination verses. Using palmnuts, the babaláwo casts divination to reveal the Olódù that is relevant to the client's dilemma. Following this, and depending upon the particular needs of the client, the babaláwo recites some or all of the sixteen corresponding ẹsẹ Ifá. Igbo dibia (diviners) are guided by Agwu, the Deity of Divination. Agwu also serves as "the intuitive impulse of divination—what you might call the creative genius in a diviner."[1] Agwu works with and through the dibia to reveal *Ogu*, Divine Truth and Moral Authority, and the path to Ọfọ, Infinite Justice. One method of Igbo divination involves the use of *ogu*, pieces from the central vein of the palm frond. A client brings four to six ogu to the dibia, who uses them to divine.[2] One might say the ogu (palm pieces) reveal Ogu (Truth).

As do many African peoples, the Igbo and Yoruba have many systems of divination. In addition to Afa divination, which is similar to Ifá, dibia may use the *akpa dibia*, the dibia bag, which is filled with ritual objects, not unlike the African American Hoodoo bag.[3] In Yoruba culture, divination by sixteen cowries is popular, and Igbo and Yoruba peoples both use the four-lobed kola nut to divine. However, sacred texts and ritual utterances (Odù and Ogu) are central to all these divination systems. Babaláwo and dibia have vast reserves of sacred texts, proverbs, "symbolic language[s]," analytical skills, and even "tricks" that they may use to aid their clients.[4]

Echewa and Naylor appear to have been inspired by Afa and Ifá; *Fire* and *Mama Day* are novels that consist of divine and intricately woven verses. In *Mama Day,* the term "Odù Ifá" could be translated as 1823, for this is the date, the code, the primary figure that contains all texts. 1823 is also synonymous with Sapphira, who is the novel's Odù, the Great Mother and the owner of all lives, texts, and subtexts. *Fire* is made up of numerous interrelated Ogu, texts of Divine Truth. However, these verses are not uttered by a dibia, which is an office that, in the past, has been largely restricted to males. These Ogu are those lived, chanted, and meted out by Ọha Ndom, the Solidarity of Women, as they undertake the comprehensive Ogu Umunwanye (Women's Wars) necessary to bring about Infinite Justice (Ọfọ). Nne-nne is the repository of history and truth in *Fire,* and with the utterance of one night, she oils the wheels of justice and reciprocity for innumerable lifetimes. Working through their spiritually adept protagonists, Naylor and Echewa, as literary diviners, use various skills, tricks, and powers to educate, plumb the analytical mettle, and gauge the evolutionary capacity of the textual characters and their actual audiences.

Part One of *Fire,* with which this analysis is concerned, details the exploits of Ọha Ndom who battled colonialism in the 1920s. Whether they are solos or choral efforts, each verse is an integral part of the unified Ogu that Ndom created during its quest to repair and restructure its society. Family matriarch and protagonist Nne-nne recounts and re-members Ndom's orature and historic struggles to her grandson Ajuziogu. Initially unmoved by the power of the Mothers, Ajuziogu is awakened in Part Two and adds the contemporary and personal wars of his wife Stella to the Ogu of Ndom. Issues of domesticity, survival, and re-creation link both sections, and both are united through Ajuziogu, who is the receptive ear of Nne-nne's orature and the vehicle through which her words become flesh and ultimately text.

Published in 1988, *Mama Day* spans from 1823 to 1999, with primary settings in New York City and the southeastern island of Willow Springs. Truly a curvilinear text, the novel's dominant action occurs at the crossroads of the spiritual and material realms—the Day family cemetery. *Mama Day* is a re-membering conversation between terrestrial wife Ophelia "Cocoa" Day and her deceased husband, George Andrews, who are trying, in curvilinear retrospect, to understand the events that altered their lives and the vast role of Àjẹ́ therein. George and Cocoa's trials, tribulations, and triumphs dominate the novel, and their exploits unify and give closure to events that began in 1823. Those events and their orchestrator, Sapphira Wade, are the true soul of *Mama Day* and the focus of the first part of this chapter.

1823 ODÙ OF SAPPHIRA WADE

The women creating mythistory in *Mama Day*—the community narrator, Sapphira Wade, and Mama Day—make up a trinity of Àjẹ́. The primary member of the trio is Miranda "Mama" Day. She is the backbone and Big Momma of her community. Like Yẹ̀wà, she has no biological issue, but she is mother of all of Willow Springs. A seer and healer who ushers new lives into existence and offers direction to all, this progeny of Yẹ̀wà can be Afìrìmáàkọ̀ and instantly kill those who violate her loved ones. However, with all her power and discernment, Mama Day is as human as any Àwọn Ìyá Wa; she makes mistakes, turns her back on signs she does not have the courage to interpret, and she misuses her Àjẹ́.

The first voice heard in the novel is that of a woman who knows the origin and intricacies of all of Willow Springs, the omniscient community narrator. With knowledge of the ancestral and the earthly realms, the unnamed narrator is the possessor of secrets, and she shares or withholds her knowledge according to her interpretation of the textual and extratextual communities' needs. She critiques the actions of Willow Springs's inhabitants orally for the reader. She also sympathizes, signifies, calls folks out, and helps the audience tie the threads Mama Day cannot. In addition to chastising community members and critiquing their actions, the neo-literary critic/community narrator also demands that the reading audience pay full mental and spiritual attention to the lives unfolding in the text. The book held in hand, like Odù Ifá, is scripted orature that is open-ended and ever in a state of re-vision. The seemingly fictitious lives have relevance beyond the page, and the full unification and pragmatic application of *Mama Day* occur only with active participation from the reading audience.

The Mother of Willow Springs and the motivator of the narrator's directives is Sapphira, the ancestral ordering member of the triad. As if foreseeing the confusion Sapphira will cause, the narrator opens *Mama Day* with the caveat that the Odù within "ain't about right or wrong, truth or lies; *it's about a slave woman who brought a whole new meaning to both them words,* soon as you cross over here from beyond the bridge."[5]

With the phrase "beyond the bridge," which refers to greater North America, the narrator makes it clear that in order to understand Sapphira's institutions of self and soul survival, Western concepts, Deities, and dichotomies must be exorcised from mind.

There are many provocative analyses of Naylor's novel, but few have elucidated Sapphira beyond referring to her as a Goddess or mother of "magic."[6] However, as Lindsey Tucker asserts in "Recovering the Conjure Woman: Text and Contexts in Gloria Naylor's *Mama Day*," African American spiritual works go far beyond "magic tricks": "Conjure addresses the undervaluation of African medicinal practices and belief systems, even as it comments on the subject of the power— not only in relation to medicine, but also to ancestry, religion, and finally to language and signifying practices."[7] Because Sapphira turns thought into deed, wish into word, because she is human and divine and reminds us of the African origin of many Western concepts, she has presented a conundrum to many theorists.

In "Matriarchal Mythopoesis," David Cowart addresses the inability of Western theoretical models to effectively elucidate Sapphira, and after offering a comedic list of possible but nonrepresentative European Goddesses, he concludes, "Still to be done is some definitive study of the Goddess in Africa"; until such a study exists, "any attempt to discuss Naylor's Black Goddess may seem to lean excessively on Eurocentric mythologies."[8] Cowart's concession is an important one, for Naylor seems, to me, to use European themes in *Mama Day* as decoys. Although there is syncretism at work in this novel, Westerners reading *Mama Day* may be tempted to latch on to the obvious references to Christianity, Shakespeare, and feminism. However, overmagnifying these themes while ignoring others leaves one, not unlike the character George, clutching desperately at beliefs, tools, and constructs that are useless for comprehending the whole of the text, the methodology of the characters, and the important role of the audience. Susan Meisenhelder recognizes the inability of "the white world" and "white artistic forms" to elucidate the lives of Willow Springs's inhabitants, Sapphira, and Africana woman-power. She argues that Naylor is "[investigating] ways of conceiving relationships, history, and reality that make it possible for black people to avoid replaying white dramas."[9] "Really listen[ing]," as the narrator directs the audience to do, is essential if one is to fully understand Sapphira and the Africana philosophical, cultural, and social beliefs and values that inform her ìwà (character).

Although her humanly existence ceased in the middle to late 1800s, Sapphira Wade is as present and potent a textual figure as Mama Day. She is the tutelary Òrìsà of Willow Springs and the center around which the text and textual lives revolve and evolve. Sapphira is the Great

Emancipator of Willow Springs; thanks to her, liberation came to the island more than thirty years before emancipation on the mainland. Embodying the "ancestry, religion, and language and . . . signifying practices" of Willow Springs, Sapphira is also the cosmic force that keeps the contemporary Willow Springs community rooted in the past and prepares it for an immediate future of temporary pain which will be soothed by the permanent establishment of peace.

Like the Òrìṣà, Sapphira boasts both historical and spiritual origins and texts. Terrestrially, she was born in 1799 and sold in 1819. However, the woman disguised as a "slave" is actually a self-existent entity like Odùduwà: Sapphira evolved spontaneously within the earth and emerged with the skills necessary to ensure her people's evolution. The spiritual properties she arrives on earth with are her "poor black hands" and "light." Bearing the elemental physical and metaphysical properties of Ọbàtálá and Odùduwà, Sapphira has all she and her people need. The importance of the attributes of Ọbàtálá and Odùduwà and their relationship to one another and Sapphira is explained by Awo Fatunmbi who states that, in Ifá cosmology, "[d]ark and light forces are not seen as forces of 'good' or 'evil.' Instead, they are seen as the essential polarity that generates life. It is the imbalance in either direction that causes the conflicts that are sometimes referred to as 'evil'."[10] The imbalance in *Mama Day* is the result of the European theft and enslavement of Africans and countless other Euro-patriarchal excesses.[11] As a unified spiritual-terrestrial force, Sapphira's orí, her destiny, is to correct cosmic and historic imbalances. And, as her origin text reveals, Sapphira begins her work at the beginning:

> The island [Willow Springs] got spit out from the mouth of God, and when it fell to earth it brought along an army of stars. He tried to reach down and scoop them back up, and found Himself shaking hands with the greatest conjure woman on earth. "Leave 'em here, Lord," she said. "I ain't got nothing but these poor black hands to guide my people, but I can lead on with light." (110)

Unlike Olódùmarè, who provides the tools necessary for the creation of life on earth, the Caucasian God is a mere bit player in the construction of Willow Springs, its text, and its architect. Willow Springs, when accidentally spit from God's mouth, took an army of stars on its own volition, and the land had Sapphira hidden in its soil.

Sapphira's origin mirrors that of a Central African original mother. According to BaKongo orature, "At the beginning of time there were no plants or trees, and nothing to eat just bare earth. Then Tule [a Zambi,

Divinity] arrived." However, on the barren earth, Tule met an old woman living in a house and harvesting yams!¹² Similarly, in the coming of Sapphira, Mother Earth knows what God does not. And when he attempts to snatch what is not his to take, he locks hands with always-already legendary Sapphira. Her "poor black hands" startle God with a firm, deal-making handshake, and with an army of stars magnifying her power, Sapphira, like a true Ìyánlá, "creates existence" in Willow Springs. Willow Springs's annual Candle Walks herald Sapphira's divinity and power. After the reciprocal sharing of gifts that are either products of the earth or fashioned by hand, gift givers and receivers alike cry "Lead on with light" and remember the onyx-hued Deity who created a free earth with a personal cadre of stars and left that earth—not unlike a dibia with ekili—"in a ball of fire."

Within the depths of blackness, every conceivable reality and possibility awaits. Light provides humanity with the means to comprehend, order, and interpret the immensity of black's "profound depths." Harmonizing the profundity of blackness and illuminating its myriad wealth, Sapphira's oríkì describe her as a mélange of Àjẹ́:

> A true conjure woman: satin black, biscuit cream, red as Georgia clay: depending upon which of us takes a mind to her. She could walk through a lightning storm without being touched; grab a bolt of lightning in the palm of her hand; use the heat of lightning to start the kindling going under her medicine pot: depending upon which of us takes a mind to her. She turned the moon into salve, the stars into a swaddling cloth, and healed the wounds of every creature walking on two or down on four. (3)

A sister of the Anlo Grandmother Deity, Sapphira is the Mama Dyumbo of Willow Springs. Sapphira, like Yemọja, is the controller of waters, the Mother of Waters, who protects her children with her fluid and lashes them with it when necessary. Sapphira harnesses Áàjálayé Ọya's winds of change, the force of regeneration, and she hurls lightning as if she had a Ṣàngó to match her force.

Sapphira is the literal and figurative Yewájọbí, Mother of all of Willow Springs. Similar to Ast, Sapphira is for Willow Springs "the Oldest of the Old . . . the Goddess from whom all becoming arose." She is Ntozake, She Who Comes With Her Own Things, and one of her possessions is a bottomless pot that brims with creativity and is always prepared to swallow "dubious people whole." Finally, just as birds of varying hues assisted Ọrúnmìlà and used white, black, and red objects to make a protective medicine for him, Sapphira's force shines through both individual hues ("satin black," "biscuit cream," and "red . . . clay") and the integrated Àjẹ́ of all. Daughter of Odù and Ọbàtálá, Sapphira embodies and reflects myriad roads and destinies, and she uses her multitudinous powers in many ways.

One of Odù's most significant gifts to humanity is Odù Ifá, the Way of Knowing. Correspondingly, Sapphira's gift to Willow Springs is the Odù of 18 & 23. As the signature spiritual-numerological text around which Willow Springs was created, the ẹsẹ Ifá of 1823 are as open ended as their Yoruba referents; and as is evident in the following, the community uses its minds and mouths to re-create and expand Sapphira's reality and constantly re-member the original and individual Self of Sapphira to the personal and communal self:

> And somehow, some way, it happened in 1823: she smothered Bascombe Wade in his very bed and lived to tell the story for a thousand days. 1823: married Bascombe Wade, bore him seven sons in just a thousand days, to put a dagger through his kidney and escape the hangman's noose, laughing in a burst of flames. 1823: persuaded Bascombe Wade in a thousand days to deed all his slaves every inch of the land in Willow Springs, poisoned him for his trouble, to go on and bear seven sons—by person or persons unknown. (3)

Sapphira reaches her apex in 1823. With a methodology similar to that of Nana Bùrúkù[13] and the abolitionist Àjẹ́ of the ìtànkálẹ̀, Sapphira cuts the life of Bascombe Wade with a knife/with poison; she spontaneously combusts/lives to tell her own orature; she has seven sons by Wade/ immaculately conceives her progeny. Not unlike Odù, Ìyàmi Òṣòròngà, and Yewájọbí, who have seemingly conflicting individual mythistories but also merge and flow into one another in such a way that the parts can be fully understood only as a whole, Sapphira's masterful "18 & 23ing" is complete and complex enough for the community to shape, historicize, mythologize, and re-member it in any and every necessary manner.

The 256 verses of the Odù, the ẹsẹ Ifá, are said to encompass all dilemmas, and the Odù of 18 & 23 is equally cyclic and ever relevant. Unlike the ritual Candle Walks held every December 22nd, 18 & 23 is not confined to a date but is a constantly recurring phenomenon. Just as Sapphira is always present in Willow Springs, patiently fomenting the peace she needs for ascension, so too are the island inhabitants constantly living out their own 1823s:

> But ain't a soul in Willow Springs don't know that little dark girls, hair all braided up with colored twine, got their "18 & 23's

coming down" when they lean too long over them back yard fences, laughing at the antics of little dark boys who got the nerve to be "breathing 18 & 23" with mother's milk still on their tongues. (4)

If these youngsters were to sneak off unattended, the product of their adolescent coupling would be an "early 18 & 23." In a different light, when the manager of a hotel offered Winky Browne $12 for a boatload of shrimp so that he could sell six boiled shrimp over crushed ice for $12, the community declares that the manager "tried to 18 & 23" Winky. 18 & 23 is also the curve in Cloris's spine that resulted from her pulling the reins of her plow when her mule broke its leg.

Paula Eckerd says that 18 & 23 is experienced through "intuitive, transcendent ways of listening and knowing."[14] 18 & 23 also abounds in a plethora of life experiences—from the extravagant to the mundane. As a malleable force, 18 & 23 is so relevant and present that it is part of an un/spoken orature of the past that becomes grafted into the un/spoken sources of power and pain of the present. And each ẹsẹ of 18 & 23 is a didactic affirmation of the timeless centrality of Sapphira.

The narrator makes it clear that Sapphira *is* 18 & 23—she is the embodiment of her Odù, and her community appropriates the Mother's multiplicity in the interpretation of their lives. 18 & 23 is also a handy signifier because Sapphira Wade is an unspeakable thought that is unspoken. The narrator informs us that "[e]verybody knows but nobody talks about the legend of Sapphira Wade." The silence could result from the phenomenal power of her 18 & 23ing, the fact that "everybody" is a spiritual and/or biological descendant of Sapphira and is at one with her mythistory, or the fact that nobody in Willow Springs remembers her name: Her people refer to her as Woman or God. Great irony surrounds Sapphira's name and her intriguing character, because women of her power and ethnicity are defined "beyond the bridge" as "Sapphires."

Sapphire, Hollywood's dehumanized depiction of the Africana woman as an overbearing, loud-mouthed, social castrator of the Black man, as depicted in *Amos 'n Andy,* became so popular a construct that any strong-willed, no-half-stepping Africana woman was labeled a "castrating bitch" or a "Sapphire." Sapphira's relationships with Bascombe Wade and God—her symbolically castrating hands and her ownership and application of Ọrọ̀—certainly place her in Sapphire's league.

In addition to Naylor's signifying on a pejorative Hollywood revision of the Mother in a way that reclaims and heralds the Mother's power and uses the castrating knife on the oppressor's phallus, it is interesting to note that the Yoruba Ìyánlá, Sapphira, and Sapphire have much in common. Sapphira inspires the same praise from her progeny as Ìyàmi Òṣòròngà. Sapphira came from Orífín, the cosmos, and, like Ìyánlá, her presence was greatly desired: "Ìyánlá come into the world, our mother / Kind one who will not die like the evil one." Sapphira and Ìyàmi are both beseeched, "Mother, Mother, child who brings peace to the world / Repair the world for us." Sapphira is also one with Ẹyẹ Òrò: "All powerful mother, mother of the night bird /. . . . / My mother kills quickly without a cry / To prick our memory suddenly." Like Ìyánlá, Sapphira "killed her husband in order to take a title," and she is "Mother whose vagina causes fear to all / Mother whose pubic hair bundles up in knots / Mother who set a trap."[15] Sapphira's trapping skills, possibly taught in Yorubaland, "spring" successful on an island of willows an ocean away.

As the literary manifestation of the women Toni Morrison refers to in the epigraph to Part Two, Sapphira created herself without assistance from anyone or anything. She is, quite simply, a God, and she is worshipped, heralded, and feared as such; and although she is the product of an ethos centered on gender balance, she is, for the most part, complete. When the Christian Deity meets her, he wisely gives the Unknown room. Having no spiritual complement, Sapphira can certainly have no terrestrial mate. Bascombe Wade, Sapphira's would-be owner, is merely the earthly representative of the spitting and mis/taking God. And both males, as reifications of European patriarchal power, are subordinate to Sapphira and her Àjẹ́.

While God is dispensed with immediately, Bascombe's relationship with Sapphira is a bit more complicated. He wants to own Sapphira, but not in the classic sense of slavery: He wants the incomprehensible whole of her to belong to him. No matter how one seeks to qualify it, Bascombe's and Sapphira's is not a "love" relationship. To purchase a woman and expect her to acquiesce in her enslavement and find peace under the lash, in the bed, and within the religion of the "master" is a relationship of oppression and systematic rape of various kinds. This is the antithesis of love.

Wade represents the negation of what Sapphira seeks most—balance, order, and peace. Thus, just as she took what she needed from God, Sapphira takes two necessary items from Wade: She uses his semen to create some of her progeny and she uses his ritually sacrificed body as a launching pad to propel herself into immortality. Sapphira's ritual use of Wade reaffirms the political power of Àjẹ́ and emphasizes the importance of the force's malleable and open-ended nature in the ìtànkálẹ̀. Just as God made way for Sapphira, she makes a way *through* Bascombe. Thanks to her 18 & 23ing, Bascombe, as would-be husband, probable father, and dubious M/master, chokes on the contentious bone of ownership. His figurative choking is followed by his literal insertion into the same bottomless pot that swallows buffaloes, elephants, and the progeny of oppressors. Further emphasizing the political import of Sapphira's Àjẹ́, Willow Springs is recognized as an autonomous member of the U.S. federation, thanks to her 18 & 23ing: its inhabitants are free, and they owe neither taxes nor allegiance to any state.

Sapphira's status as Yewájọbí is both literal and figurative. She is the Great Mother and liberator of the island's enslaved populace, and she creates seven spiritually endowed free Africana sons to continue the work she started. Sapphira bears Elijah and Elisha (twins), Joel, Daniel, Joshua, Amos, and Jonah, the seventh son. With the birth of Jonah, Sapphira frees herself and progeny from the alleged claims and names of master and Master through dual signification. The caption under the Day family tree simply states, "God rested on the seventh day and so would she." However, Sapphira's creations and labors surpass those of the Christian God. Her "seventh day" of creation is actually Jonah, and with his birth comes the surname Day. As Lindsey Tucker asserts, not only does Sapphira undertake profoundly important "labors" on the seventh day in giving birth, but she also names and claims her creations through Jonah, who is *the* Seventh Day and is magnificently "wrought of body and word."[16]

The naming of her sons is a spiritual act rather than a religious one, for by opening a closed text, the Bible, Sapphira names her sons her tricksterian own. The Great Mother does not give her sons Christian names as an act of appeasement (to a God) or assimilation (with Bascombe): She is creating a world in the way of Mawu, the Dahomean Great Mother, who also created the seven lives and solidified all human destiny through her Book of Fa. Sapphira also follows the path of Odù, whose sixteen sons became the principal divination verses of Ifá. The Bible, the text that Sapphira "Ifá-izes" or "Fa-izes," also happens to be revered by Zora Neale Hurston and two-headed doctors as "the greatest conjure book in the world." Sapphira uses her Àjẹ́ as an Ìyánlá steeped in the traditions, encoding, and orality of Ifá and Fa to conjure biblical pages and electrify them with her Testament of 1823.

Sapphira's seven sons are the Days of Creation, and they represent her microcosmic bettering of the Christian God's work. Seven more gifted sons, fathered by Jonah Day, follow the first seven. These Days are Matthew, Mark, Luke, Timothy, James, John, and when John dies, another son is born who bears his brother's name and his own, John-Paul. While Jonah expands his Mother's creations and institutes the New Testament of the Seven Days (solidified by John-Paul, the "seventh son of the seventh son"), it is the absence of peace that underscores the Days' creative efforts. To paraphrase Tucker's assertion, the fact that

Sapphira gives her progeny biblical names smacks of conjure's proclivity to signify, in both senses, or to comment on the subjects of power and language. Through her efforts, Sapphira also challenges the subjects of power and language—in this case, biblical and masculine/patriarchal forms—to necessarily critique, restructure, and revise themselves, for Sapphira's fourteen testament-bearing males are essential to the institution of peace. While the Wade era was easily transformed into the dawn of a new Day (and no one knows or cares which, if any, of the Days are Wade's offspring), his penchant for destroying peace in the name of love taints and shades the relationships of the Days.

In order to create the Testament of Peace,[17] the cycle of seven sons gives way to the triad of daughters. John-Paul and his wife Ophelia give birth to daughters who bear aspects of Sapphira's soul: Miranda, Abigail, and Peace. Peace, as an infant, drowns in a well. Ophelia's mind shatters at the loss of Peace, and she follows her daughter by jumping into the Sound. Peace's final home in the well represents reimmersion in the womb. Despite all the creative Àjẹ́ of her "poor black hands," peace is the only thing Sapphira could not conjure. So when Peace is born, Sapphira welcomes her gift, the spiritually significant third daughter, into the womb/devouring pot, the àpo ìkà.

Generations after 1823, the house Bascombe built for Sapphira is still riddled with the screaming silence of missing Peace and "unspeakable thoughts, unspoken." Born in John-Paul and Ophelia's matrix of loss, power, and pain, Miranda is quickly and necessarily recognized as a little "Mama." The power of her hands surpasses that of her father and sets her just under Ìyánlá Sapphira, but her hands alone are not enough to create unified peace. As familial and communal salve and stitching, Miranda is so busy bringing life into the world that she physically bears no child. Abigail is the literal mother who continues the Days, and she attempts to give Sapphira the solace she needs. Abigail gives birth to three daughters, Grace, Hope, and Peace. Peace's second àbíkú arrival becomes one with the first as Sapphira welcomes another gift into her wicked bag.

By the time Ophelia, one of the contemporary protagonists and Mama Day's grandniece, is born, Sapphira's name has been long forgotten and Peace has become a self-devouring àbíkú. Ophelia is the last hope for the continuation of the Days, and she is adorned with protective names to convince her to stay with her family and continue the Days. The African naming rituals in *Mama Day* echo those in Chinua Achebe's *Things Fall Apart*. The following passage describes how Ekwefi, who birthed a series of *ogbanje*, the Igbo term for àbíkú, named her ill-fated infants:

> She had borne ten children and nine of them had died in infancy. ... As she buried one child after another her sorrow gave way to despair and then to grim resignation. ... Her deepening despair found expression in the names she gave her children. One of them was a pathetic cry, Onwumbiko—"Death, I implore you." ... The next child was a girl, Ozoemena—"May it not happen again." ... Ekwefi then became defiant and called her next child Onwuma—"Death may please himself." And he did.[18]

Grace names her child Ophelia after her grandmother who lost her mind with the loss of Peace and shattered her husband's heart: "Let this be another, I told God, who could break a man's heart." Following this, Ophelia is given protective crib and pet names by her two "Big Mamas":

> At least Abigail had the presence of mind to give Grace's baby a proper crib name. Miranda would have done it herself and had fixed it in her mind to crib name her No—this was one girl they would *not* let get away. But it had to be the mama's mama. ... She was *the* baby girl. They dropped the "the" *when they were sure she was gonna stay,* and after Ophelia got to be five years old, she refused to answer to Baby Girl, thinking it meant just that. So they gave her the pet name Cocoa. "It'll put color on her somewhere." (39–40, italics added)

This is the first Odù of the child who survives to grow into the woman who will help unify the Days and inscribe the Testament of Peace in the Odù of 18 & 23. Cocoa is to work with her husband George Andrews, who is, in many respects, a reincarnation of Bascombe Wade.

According to Fatunmbi, "The search for spiritual transformation is never complete. Àshe must be continuously directed towards a deeper understanding of spirit and self."[19] This cycle of transformation is at the heart of *Mama Day*. Each community member takes up the chorus of another and adds her and his unique elements and experiences to create texts/works remarkably similar to those initially crafted by Sapphira. And the unifying Odù of 18 & 23, the ẹsẹ of Cocoa and George, is in many ways a recasting of the Odù of all their predecessors. However, complete harmonization and unification cannot be achieved until the male aspect unites with the female and the external audience receives and infuses into their lives the truth of the text.

THE OGU AND ỌGỤ OF ỌHA NDOM

Whereas all mouths of Willow Springs are filled with the glory of Sapphira, in *Fire,* one woman carries the entire Igbo nation of Nigeria on her tongue. Like the narrator of Willow Springs, Nne-nne is the living library of the many Ogu (Divine Verses) of Ndom that form the foundation for the Ogu Umunwanye (Women's War) against the British (1925–1931). Nne-nne is also an active participant in the Amusu-action that results in the earth-heaving ogu (war) for self-determination and societal reclamation. Unlike Sapphira, who created a safe evolutionary home for her progeny on appropriated territory, Ọha Ndom is fighting on land that has been theirs for millennia. The Igbo women are not creating a space in the way of Sapphira but are struggling to cleanse the earth; they are fighting the Igbo patriarchal shift and the witchcraft of Western imperialism, and Ani, Mother of Earth, is their guide. Just as no male force could complement Sapphira's Àjẹ́, the Igbo man is shown to be impotent, almost self-castrated, when juxtaposed with Ọha Ndom. As Bella Brodzki asserts, "Female ingenuity, courage, autonomy, and survival in the face of male impotence and unreliability are the dominant strands" in Nne-nne's recitation to Ajuziogu.[20] Like Sapphira, the women of Ọha Ndom must be everything to themselves and their community as they struggle to balance and restructure their skewed nation.

One of the things that makes Echewa's work especially compelling is that he uses fiction to contextualize and personalize the historical battles of the Igbo women. His work also makes it clear that Ndom's acts are not merely reactions to colonialism but contemporary manifestations of long-existent Amusu. Although the Igbo woman's power is undergirded by the Deities Ani, Idemilli, and Edoh, it is apparent that Ọha Ndom was battling an African patriarchal shift prior to European occupation and colonization. However, Nne-nne, signifying on her grandson and his male forebears, makes it clear that regardless of what the Igbo man posits about male superiority, it is the historical, biological, and natural force of Amusu that creates and orders existence.

As if setting the tone for her recitation, Nne-nne informs her progeny of ancient truths:

> Ajuziogu . . . men and women are like their organs. A woman's is mostly private, tucked away like a secret purse between her legs, with little to give away how big or deep it really is. A man's on the other hand, hangs loosely and swings freely about

for all to see. . . . A few years into old age, and men have to offer sacrifices and pour libations for their erections.[21]

In contrast to the male organ which grows limp with age, the woman's "secret purse," holding unfathomable power, becomes enriched: "Like palm wine, a woman gets stronger with age. The woman in a woman comes out as she gets older." Nne-nne's descriptions of the Igbo woman are one with oríkì of Àjẹ́. Just as Ìyàmi is "Mother whose vagina causes fear to all" and has "the vagina no penis must split," the Igbo woman attains "*awtu aligh-li*"—an organ that makes a mockery of a man's virility, the vagina that no limp or half-erect penis can enter—when she reaches her apex (5, 231).

The biological, political, and spiritual supremacy of Amusu underpins all the orature in *Fire*, making it clear that even in the face of complex African patriarchal power moves, the son cannot better the mother; the tributary cannot overpower the source. This reality is vividly elucidated in the "Crotch Song," an Ogu Ndom that is sung after a woman gives birth. As welcoming a new life turns into a celebration of women's eternal roles, the attending women squat and sway, mimicking childbirth and intercourse as the lead singer asks, "Where do they all come from?"

> Tall men?
> From the woman's crotch!
> Short men?
> From the woman's crotch!
> Hunters and warriors?
> From the woman's crotch!
> Chiefs and court clerks?
> From the woman's crotch!
> Even the White man?
> From the woman's crotch! (14)

In an interesting revision of Sapphira, who is both a poor Black slave (nothing) and Creator Mother God (Everything), the Igbo man may dismiss his mate as "nothing" outwardly, but he knows from his origin, that of his progeny, and his eventual death that she is "everything" and "is like a god!"

Nne-nne's elaboration on the power of women echoes the findings of Man in regard to the three keys of Woman and Zora Neale Hurston's discovery of the ultimate truth.[22] Nne-nne says, "A woman's crotch is a juju shrine before which men always kneel and worship. It is their door into this world" (14). Nne-nne's statements have great historical and spiritual resonance, especially in the light of some Igbo patriarchal assertions.

In a text that speaks volumes about the patriarchal shift and African male chauvinism, B. B. O. Emeh tries to negate the female role in the founding of Nnobi. In *Treasures of Nnobi*, Emeh offers an Igbo origin text: "Nnobi was founded by a man and a woman called *Obi* and *Nne* respectively, and [they] christened the town Nnobi (*Nneobi*)," but he dismisses it as implausible because "a man takes first place before a woman in Igboland."[23] In other words, given that men are first in every situation, no town could place a woman's name before a man's. According to Emeh, Nnobi should have been called "*Obinne*." Emeh goes on to deride the elders, probably male, who recounted this origin text: "The conclusion here is that *Nne and Obi* syndrome is a figment of the imagination of some early teachers who had no in-depth knowledge about local history."[24] Continuing his attempt to institute a patriarchal shift on ancient Igbo history, Emeh argues, "Another story which had it that Nnobi was founded by a woman, the mother of *Obi* . . . is also unacceptable, illogical and incomprehensible within the ethos of Igboland."[25] Given the emphasis on male-female balance in the origin texts Emeh discusses, it appears the Igbos originally had an ontology centered on "harmonious dualism." But harmony is not patriarchy's goal. From Emeh's postulations, it becomes clear that promoters of the patriarchal shift thought any type of female authority jeopardized their manhood.

The patriarchal order threw sharp jabs at spiritually empowered Igbo women. Amusu, the Igbo equivalent of Àjẹ́, and Ajalagba, the male equivalent of Oṣó, have become laden with hierarchical value. In *God and Man in African Religion*, Emefie Ikenga Metuh offers the following: "Ajalagba are by far more powerful and more dangerous than witches, hence the saying: *Amusu ada ebu ajalagba*, 'A witch cannot carry a wizard.'"[26] However, Metuh quickly adds that the foregoing proverb "has overtones of male chauvinism and is often used by men to remind women who appear to be very forward of their subordinate place in society."[27] With this disclaimer, Metuh complicates the theory that Igbo men are spiritually superior to Igbo women.

It is interesting to note that Igbo female Deities remained largely untouched by the patriarchal shift. Ala (or Ani) is the Earth Mother of the Igbos, and she is described in terms similar to Ẹdan and Odù as "the custodian of law and morality and guarantor of political stability."[28] Metuh finds that both Ani and Chukwu (the male Deity) "share responsibility for the universe"; others argue that Ani is "the most important deity in Igbo public and private cults."[29] While some researchers assert that Chukwu is superior to Ani, the Igbo patriarchy cannot dispute the following: "Earth Mother owns men / The Earth owns everybody."[30] Ani's "daughter" is the Goddess Idemilli. Like Òṣun in Oṣogbo and Sapphira in Willow Springs, Idemilli "is regarded as the mother of all in Idemilli, she protects her children [from] wars and pestilence."[31] She also gave life to many male and female Deities. Apparently, the primary targets of the patriarchy were not Deities but physical women—the wives, mothers, and daughters of the community—who might tap into their town-founding, life-giving divine natures. It seems that instead of bonding and using all their spiritual and social powers to confront and defeat slavery and colonialism, the men of *Fire* are more interested in instituting patriarchal supremacy. However, the Igbo women are empowered by Idemilli and Ani. And even if an Amusu can't carry an Ajalagba, she could lead her nation into battle against the British.

Nne-nne is well aware of the original truth and way, and in rendering her orature, she struggles to indirectly convince her selfish and myopic grandson of the maternal and communal truths his fathers tried to hide or neglected to share. Despite the fact that it is placed in a "novel," Nne-nne's orature is centered squarely in historical fact, and like the play *Queen Omu*, constitutes a matrix of Ogu, melding history, ritual praise, and re-memberings. Further, Nne-nne's critique of Ajuziogu and Igbo men is similar to the work of Òrò Èfè singers, who broadcast the ills of society and provide tools for restructuring society. Emeh seems to take the position that the word of a man—especially once written and published in a book—is sufficient to dismantle the mythistorical achievements of women. However, with one night's orature, Nne-nne unravels centuries of intricately woven lies and crushes the foundations of demigods.

Nne-nne's Ogu includes a blunt description of Igbo male impotence before colonialism: "When the White man came and took over our land, what did the men do? They fought here and there, heaved high and ho with threats of what they were getting ready to do, held long talks under the big trees and in the end handed over the land and all of us to him" (10). After seceding power to the racist vanguards of colonialism, the African man found he was victim of a new form of slavery:

> The White man had magic, which mesmerized our men. When the White man wanted slaves, our men left whatever else they were doing and began to hunt slaves to sell to him. They kidnapped strangers and children, women and weaklings, and sold them. They banded together and made wars and conducted raids for slaves. (32)

When the Euro-juju decreed that slavery-in-exile was out and enslavement on the Continent for cash crops was in, Igbo men complied with colonial dictates until "all of our lives had become pawned to palm fruit." After this, Nne-nne reveals, colonizers would "control our lives by yo-yoing the prices up and down."

Filling but nutritionally meager foods such as cassava were introduced to keep populations able-bodied enough to sow and reap cash crops for triangular economic "trade," while traditional wholesome foods were neglected nearly into extinction. Barter-and-trade and cowry economies were replaced with paper currency, which was controlled by the colonizers. New systems of colonially imparted "justice" resulted in numerous African victims; and prostitution became a popular style of life. The poison of economic oppression and the erection of alien institutions seeped slowly into and cracked the cohesive communal pot, and Igbo women devoted their energies to reclaiming, repairing, and cleansing that pot.

Historical attempts at righting and balancing society began in 1925 with the *nwaobiala* movement. Nina Mba's *Nigerian Women Mobilised* describes nwaobiala as a cultural and spiritual movement in which groups of women marched from village to village to pass on a message from Chineke (God). After invoking Ani and purifying the earth, the women ("the original dancing women were apparently elderly") performed the dance of nwaobiala. Following this, the women received a financial donation, a goat, and a promise from the village chief to pass the message on to four other villages.[32] The nwaobiala consortium made several demands. They wanted to return to the original Igbo form of currency for dowry payments, if not for all matters. The women demanded that there be no marriages between Christians and Traditionalists and that nakedness be reinstituted as the norm for maidens. Some sects of nwaobiala demanded that prostitution be eradicated, while others suggested that prostitutes not charge exorbitantly. Another point in their platform was that "married women should be allowed to commit adultery" as in the precolonial era, when adultery was not grounds for divorce. The women also demanded that all cassava-growing be stopped, that the safer "bush paths" be restored as opposed to the dangerous tarmac roads, and that the native court system be revised. Mba describes the movement as "a rejection of the new social system among the older women," who "saw their social and moral order threatened by the political, social, and economic innovations of colonialism."[33] As daughters of Ani and the guardians of society, these elders were fulfilling their duties. Just as the women of nwaobiala went to war against the system of depravity brought by colonialism, so too do the women of *Fire*.

Fire depicts a more personalized attempt at purification undertaken by a collective of women in the Ogu (Divine Text) and Ogu (War) of Oyoyo Love. When Orianu and Ekweredi learn that their daughter and daughter-in-law, respectively, is living in Agalaba Uzo as a prostitute under the name Oyoyo Love, they know they must reclaim her. The mothers go to their communal Ọha Ndom and explain their situation. Orianu and Ekweredi receive financial assistance, and when other mothers hear of the wayward daughter, they join the reclamation party. As the core group travels to Agalaba Uzo to reclaim Oyoyo Love, née Nwanyi-Nma, the Ndom of every village through which they travel contributes both money and additional mothers. The original group of 80 to 100 souls swells to nearly 200 and boasts ample financial support by the time the mothers, chanting and dancing, reach the abode of Love.

After the patriarchal shift and colonization, Nne-Nne describes Igbo men as positioning themselves as best they could within the colonial patriarchal order. Consequently, Igbo women were often faced with a potential foe in their men, many of whom had become clerks, officials, or "domesticated boys" (regardless of their ages) under the new order. As Ndom awaits the appearance of Oyoyo Love, the Igbo driver of a European woman slaps a member of Ndom. The battered woman replies, "You asked for it now, you ashy-bottom kitchen sweeper. . . . Get ready to receive me *because you just slapped your mother*" (53, italics added). Motherhood, like Amusu, is communal and comprehensive; any mother is a Mother. So when an elder woman tries to placate an arresting officer by calling him "son," she does so in respect to the four sons she has raised and the fact that the personal is communal. When this officer prepares to handcuff his "mother," whom he has verbally denied, all the mothers on hand send for those in the market for an impromptu group chastisement. They chant, "Rather than shame one of us, kill all of us," and inspire unity through lamentation: "The knot that holds the weaving together has unraveled!"

The incidents that occur in Agalaba Uzo reveal just how loose the knot of sociocultural continuity has become. Rather than offering the women welcome water to quench their thirst, Oyoyo's landlord threatens to have them arrested for trespassing. When Oyoyo finally greets the motherly multitude, she speaks "about her prostitution as if she were a *dibia*, an exalted high priestess, and her body a fetish that men paid a high price to come and consult" (61). Oyoyo even asserts that she is extending and revolutionizing the concepts of dowry and brideprice. Rather than being subjected to the will of a husband, any man with "One shilling for an hour. Ten shillings TDB (till day break)" can be her loyal subject. Nwanyi-Nma's pride and shamelessness astound her mothers. In response to her self-explication, the mothers spit at the abomination that was once a daughter.

After Oyoyo Love is publicly chastened, she returns home with her multitude of mothers to undergo "retraining," which includes taking care of her two children and being recircumcised. Following the recircumcision, Oyoyo disappears and is heard from again after having invoked the Euro-juju: She has issued a warrant against her mother, mother-in-law, and Ugbala, the circumciser, for attempted murder. Officers arrest the mother-in-law and mother, but Ugbala, possibly using ekili, disappears and escapes arrest. The battle of Oyoyo Love ends in a draw: Oyoyo is chastised and her mothers are vindicated, but she continues to practice prostitution, albeit half-heartedly. The Ogu of Oyoyo is representative of the cyclic nature of the struggles of Ndom, in life and in literature, as the struggle to purify the earth fouled by colonial economics continues today.[34]

It is interesting to note that Mba's queries about the nwaobiala movement, revolve around the seeming absence of a political agenda. However, it appears to be the case that the Igbo women were acting within the comprehensive scope of the African worldview in which the political, personal, spiritual, cultural, and socioeconomic are inextricably connected. Colonialism was not limited to select facets of life but ran the gamut; consequently, the Igbo women struck against the imperialists in a holistic political-spiritual manner. In many ways, the Ogu Ndom is an expansion of that of Sapphira Wade. Sapphira's struggle is that of an individual Creator working for the community. The women of Ndom are each "sapphires," who endure enough chipping and fragmentation to impel their fusion into a massive unbreakable stone of Ani. Because the Igbo women, like Sapphira, have few effective male counterparts, they rely on their Amusu and, at times, an Ajalagba. This is the case with Ahunze, "The Impossible Wife," who refuses to accept her allotment of patriarchal oppression.

The things that precipitate Ahunze's bid for freedom are the death of her husband, the fact that she bore him no male child, and Amusu and Ajalagba. When her husband's brothers rush to marry this handsome successful trader, Ahunze emerges from the mourning house and declares that she will marry no one. "Impossible, the men said. Something unheard of, that a woman, no less a widow without a son, could rebuff the entire manhood of a village" (124). These acts are unbelievable to the men only because they refuse to acknowledge their sociopolitical impotence. Ahunze's actions echo the diatribe that the grandmother of Zaynab Alkali's *The Stillborn* shouts, like the critical Ọrọ Èfè of Gẹlẹdẹ, from a rooftop perch:

> Men of this village . . . listen to my words. I was married fourteen times in the eastern part of this land. I left for this part because I could find no lion among them. The village was filled with red monkeys, black monkeys, jungle pigs, wild cats, toothless dogs and lame cocks. Did I know, gods of my fathers, that I was coming to meet a worse pack? This village is full of lizards, snakes, worms, and by the gods of my ancestors, cold slippery fish. . . . And the women? A pack of domestic donkeys with no shame. When they are not under the whip of their wizard husbands, they are busy plotting witchcraft.[35]

While their male counterparts might sacrifice themselves at civilization's altar, some African women choose not to join their men on the pedestal of oblivion. The grandmother quoted above is a former "priestess of the goddess of the hills," and like Queen Amina of Zaria, married or single, she will make manifest her Àjẹ́. Ahunze is not a priestess but a trader. While no one knows whether or not the shrine of Mami Wota (a Pan-African Water Deity known for giving wealth) is in Ahunze's bedroom, she has enough Amusu to refuse to marry Ozurumba, the feckless brother of her late husband, and to retain her property.

When Ozurumba and his rejected counterparts begin plotting Ahunze's demise, she summons her cousin Koon-Tiri, a two-headed doctor who syncretizes African and Western religious beliefs in the way of his ìtànkálẹ̀an kin. Ahunze is described as *uvuvu,* the "caterpillar that looked soft but stung fiercely when squeezed," and Koon-Tiri is reputed to have "a sting as painful as a centipede's." His spiritual backing is described in the following terms:

> Dibia of the highest possible order. . . . he had a statue of the Virgin Mary on a shrine at the back of his house, and next to it a collection of wooden agwus artfully carved by someone from the Ibibi area and arranged in a circle like a group of elders in conference. Then there was a third shrine, dedicated to Mami-Wota, wrapped in endless coils of river snakes. A candle and incense burner and frequent burial ground goer, Koon-Tiri was reputed to be in league with several occult powers—local spirits, Mami-Wota, and Dee Lawrence. (127)

The Amusu enlists the Ajalagba, and Koon-Tiri unleashes killer bees on all who molest his cousin. Likewise, Ahunze chastises all those who cross her, but she does so in the way of Ọ̀sun. When the people of Oṣogbo refused to honor Ọ̀sun as a God, she gave their children fever.[36]

Similarly, when the district officer leads the community in the appropriation and slaughter of one of her goats, Ahunze says nothing but places a plague of diarrhea on the community. Through the union of male and female power, The Impossible Wife lives alone, unhusbanded, without children, and free from molestation.

The sting of the uvuvu is even more painful in the Ogu of Akpa-Ego, the malnourished and oft-battered wife of Ozurumba. When Ahunze helps her abused friend respect her wealth of self, Akpa-Ego realizes her beauty, as does another. Akpa-Ego becomes pregnant, not for her sterile husband but for her lover. When Ozurumba is told what his sterility has whispered to him, he beats his heavily pregnant wife into an unrecognizable state. Seeing the mauled pregnant woman, Ahunze organizes Ndom, the communal arbiters of justice.

Having beaten one wife, Ozurumba becomes the husband of a grand serpent, an *iwi agwo* of 100 women who he has "married" by default. Ozurumba's "wives" begin the ritual courtship song and dance:

> *Ozurumba, Ozurumba, you like to beat your wife!*
> *You will beat all of us tonight,*
> *Until your arms fall off!*
> *Ozurumba, Ozurumba, you have the biggest prick in town*
> *You will fuck all of us tonight,*
> *Until your prick falls off!* (145, italics in the original)

Following this, Ndom administers to Ozurumba the classic West African punishment for outlandish men:

> The women pushed Ozurumba to the ground and spread him out, face up, holding his hands and legs so he could not struggle free. Then they took turns sitting on him, pulling up their cloths and kirtles to their bare buttocks and planting their nakedness on every exposed element of his body. (146)

A man who has been "sat on," slapped with a menstrual pad, or shown a woman's nakedness in derision is a man who has been cursed.

In "The Yoruba Image of the Witch," Raymond Prince recounts a group of Yoruba women who in the 1960s went to the home of the local chief to protest taxation. Like nwaobiala, the protest included "singing" and causing disturbances. "When the police were sent to disperse them the women brandished their menstruation cloths. This caused the police to take to their heels, for it is believed that if a man is struck by a woman's menstrual cloth he will have bad fortune for the rest of his days."[37] Akinwumi Isola's drama *Madam Tinubu* depicts a female collective, led by the legendary Tinubu, cursing colonial administrators with their nakedness.[38] Furthermore, *USA Today* reported the threat of vagina's vengeance in the 2002 takeover of Chevron-Texaco pipeline stations in the Nigerian Delta: "The women, ranging in age from 30 to 90, used a traditional and powerful shaming gesture to maintain control over the facility in Escravos after seizing it July 8—they threatened to remove their own clothing."[39]

The womb-lodged mysteries of woman are the locus point of Àjẹ́;[40] in fact, given its potency, one could say that menstrual blood is the "liquor" of the Pot of Origins.[41] For any mother—not necessarily one's biological mother—to threaten a man with her nakedness or menses is equivalent to showing him his entry into the world and promising him a timely exit for whatever trespass he has committed. To be sat on is equivalent to a death sentence.[42] Ransome-Kuti's threat that "vagina's head will seek vengeance" becomes powerfully literal in *Fire*, and after he is sat on, Ozurumba hangs himself.

In 1929, in the town of Oloko, Mark Emeruwa, a mission schoolteacher, went beyond his duties as a census-taker for the colonial administration and beat Nwanyeruwa, an impoverished woman who refused to be counted.[43] And Igbo women turned out to sit on Emeruwa. This was the historical start of Ogu Umunwanye (Women's War) in which "ten native courts were destroyed, a number of others damaged, houses of native court personnel were attacked, factories at Imo river, Aba, Mbawsi and Amaba were looted and fifty-five women were killed."[44] Melding the misogynistic abuses of the fictional Ozurumba with the historical Emeruwa, the Women's War begins in *Fire* when census-taker Sam-el kicks Akpa-Ego, causing her to miscarry.

What is compelling about the Women's War is that the tools with which they fight oppression are personal and domestic. These women wreaked serious havoc by brandishing their nakedness, pestles, and firewood. One is reminded here of the African American transformation of the pot of domesticity into a vehicle for prayer and retribution. Although condemned to eternal victimhood by some feminists, charities, and nongovernmental organizations, Africana women possess abundant revolutionary skills and abilities, and they have used them against slavers, colonizers, and other oppressors. The tools they brandish to obtain their goals, however, may vary depending on circumstance and locale. Ugbala is an example of a woman of great sociopolitical and spiritual import: She is a true daughter of the Mother of the Earth and the most respected and feared entity in the text. While she is not the leader of Ndom, because historically and in *Fire* Ndom neither has nor needs a leader, Ugbala is the heart of a network of women. Noting the deference she received during the case of Oyoyo Love, the colonial administration kidnaps and imprisons her. Ndom retaliates by taking the mate of the unwieldy beast ravaging the land; they kidnap Elizabeth Ashby-Jones, a British anthropologist traveling in Eastern Nigeria "studying" Igbo women. Ashby-Jones is inserted into the orature in an intriguing way. Prior to her introduction, the audience is privy to Nnenne's rapture and the fertilizing interjections of Ajuziogu. However, when Ndom kidnaps Ashby-Jones, it seizes her field notes. Ajuziogu, the final stitcher of Ndom's tapestry, secures Ashby-Jones's observations on Igbo women and adds her voice to the chorus.

Ashby-Jones is fascinated by the community's reverence for Ugbala, and a significant portion of her notes consists of interviews with Ugbala and observations of her work. The juxtaposition of these two women is compelling, for through comparison, one realizes that the social scales by which these women measure success are markedly different. Ugbala is widely renowned, generous, helpful, and remarkably influential. Although as a woman she cannot be a "full" dibia, Ugbala combined the techniques of her dibia father and husband to acquire skills that surpass every male dibia in her vicinity. Although Ashby-Jones, an academician and researcher, is successful in her society, Ndom considers her to be unevolved because she has no child, and she is recognized as impotent without her "writing stick."[45] She is considered a woman only by default, and nearly all of Igboland recognizes her physical presence and lack of melanin as the literal and figurative embodiment of death.

Brodzki has written an interesting analysis of *Fire*, its critique of translation, and the ethnocentricity in ethnography that includes a discussion of Sylvia Leith-Ross, who may very well be Ashby-Jones's myopic historical counterpart.[46] But what is compelling to me is the fact that in life, orature, and literature (through Ajuziogu's re-membering of Ndom), the Igbo women's critique of the European (woman and administration) is much more salient and valid than Eurocentric observations of the "natives." The figure of Ashby-Jones, pale, impotent, and deficient when juxtaposed with the lyrical, fecund, and politically savvy women of Ndom, is introduced to reveal the short-sightedness of European writers, researchers, and pseudo-scientists, whose inaccurate and often racist "findings" facilitated colonialism. Ashby-Jones's presence also forces the audience to fully appreciate the intricacies of cultural exchange and ethnic difference and bias from an African perspective. Furthermore, the European presence in *Fire,* like the references to Shakespeare and the Bible in *Mama Day,* acts as an obligatory nod to the "other." After textual insertion, the "other" is necessarily signified upon and reassigned. In an interesting correlation to the dialectics at work in Sapphira and Bascombe's relationship, the colonial government captures Ugbala, the soul of Ọha Ndom. In response, Ndom captures the antithetically significant Ashby-Jones. To conceal her within the collective, which has used indigo dye to disguise and unify themselves, Ọha Ndom "re-writes" the researcher. Ndom gives Ashby-Jones melanin, courtesy of indigo dye, crops her hair, and makes her an honorary woman.

After Ọha Ndom frees her from jail, Ugbala joins the core group that is holding Ashby-Jones. Ugbala decides that the researcher must be let go, and she leads Ọha Ndom in speaking the Ogu (Oath) which, along with menstrual blood wine, will temper Ashby-Jones's oral and written reports about Ndom with the threat of Ọfọ (Infinite Justice) and the force of Ogu (Divine Truth and Moral Authority):

> "This woman!"
> "*Iyah! Iyah!*"
> "This woman, whose skin is without color, hair is like corn tassels, and eyes are like shiny glass beads!"
> "*Iyah! Iyah!*" . . .
> "Dumb and speechless, but nevertheless a woman!"
> "Barren, but nevertheless a woman!"
> "Be the judge between us and her!"
> "She came to us, not we to her!"
> "We did not seek out to harm her!"
> "The war that now engulfs us has been made by her husband and her people!"
> "Ala, make a woman of her!"
> "*Iyah! Iyah!*" . . .
> "Let her feel our grief!"
> "Let her feel Woman's Grief!"
> "Let the burden of our grief sit before her eyes!"
> "And sit on her tongue!"
> "And make her fingers limp, so that she cannot pick up a writing stick and write with it!"
> "If she writes, let her write the truth about us!"
> "If she speaks, let her speak the truth about us!"
> "If she should fail to speak the truth about us, if she should fail to write the truth in her writing, let this wine that we all drink together, this wine of our joint womanhood, consecrated to Ala and Edoh and to Efanim, let it intoxicate her into a state of madness that no one can cure! Let this wine, which contains the blood of our wombs, seal her womb in this incarnation and in all her future incarnations." (216–217)

After uttering the Ogu, Ugbala drinks of the wine of womanhood and passes the multiply empowered concoction to Ashby-Jones, who drinks her share. "Then the rest of the women took turns *drinking the oath*" (217, italics added).

The Grandmother Deity of the Anlo, Red Substance That Is Always Present in a Women's Bathroom; the vengeance of vagina's head; and the pot liquor of origins unite all women. From the Earth to the womb to the tongue, all women become one Woman as Qha Ndom takes unified female power to its apex. During one of the inspirational ritual chants of Ndom, a caller asks, "How many are you?" The response is, "The White man wants to count us, but there is only one of us. Ndom is one, uncountable upon uncountable, but still one. Undivided." One can only imagine what the success of Ndom might have been if the male principle had been able to complement the female and recognize its privileged position within the dynamic whole.

Rather than stand beside their men on the earth ordained to them and battle their common foe, Ndom was forced to battle both their men and the European enslaver/colonizer. To initiate combat, Qha Ndom gives their oppressors their proper respect. Having turned their backs and bent over, Ndom "pulled their loin cloths, so as to expose their naked bottoms ... female bottoms, fat and lean, old and young, brown and black, and at every stage of the monthly cycle." Following this salute, called Ikpo Ololo, Ndom charges, crying, "Shoot your mothers! Shoot your mothers!" (208–209).

The night before Ajuziogu's journey, Nne-nne chants up a novel in order to ensure herself and her progeny of her ability to keep the compound's fire lit until he returns. Nne-nne is a grand elder warrior, more spirit than human and longing for rest, but the duration of Ajuziogu's academic program is unknown. Nne-nne's necessary act of re-membering gives her assurance, and because her memories are the family's inheritance, she places her wealth "inside" her progeny with full assurance of a return on her investment. Ajuziogu's name itself gives Nne-nne reassurance. As Anthonia Kalu reveals, *iju* is the Igbo word for ask. *Ijuzi* means to ask with clarity and return with clear answers. With the addition of Ogu, the Deity of Divine Truth and good intentions, Ajuziogu is "the one who asks with clarity and returns with clear answers" that have been Informed by Divine Truth.[47] Emphasizing the relationship of one's name to one's destiny in African cosmology, Kalu goes on to say that "it is hoped that one who is so named [Ajuziogu] is/will be the embodiment of this reality." The question that plagues Ajuziogu at the novel's onset is whether he can abandon the "collective past" of all his forebears for what he imagines is his "inevitable personal future" (5). Sensing his dilemma, Nne-nne responds with the Ogu (Divine Text and Truth) that is the first part of *Fire* and leaves her progeny to arrive at his own clear answers.

Ajuziogu, like his male progenitors, is initially so self-centered that he forgets Nne-nne, his wife and daughter, and all familial commitments as he chases academic degrees in America. When he finally returns, he finds that his wife is pregnant by another man (she attempts suicide on the night of his return), Nne-nne is dead, and his daughter only knows him from a picture. Distraught, Ajuziogu undergoes the process of rememory. He hears the chanting of Nne-nne and the Ogu of the Ogu of Ndom, and he also considers the battles his wife had to fight and continues to fight because of his neglect. Rather than return and take his Ph.D. qualifying examination, he literally lights the homefires. Ajuziogu, as fictive writer of *Fire*, not only immortalizes the life of his progenitor but also weaves the life and "wars" of his wife Stella and daughter W'Orima, as precipitated by himself, into the Ogu of Ndom, reaffirming the power of the word and the timelessness of Amusu.

By the conclusion of *Fire*, the babaláwo's assertion—"In the past, when they taught you oògùn or when an ìtàn was told, they put it 'inside.' *It lived 'inside.'* Whatever you are told as a story now, you put it 'inside' book. And it will appear there forever"[48]—is reversed and magnified. The Igbo would consider oògùn to be close kin to *ogwu*. Like oògùn, ogwu is not merely medicine; it is the comprehensive knowledge of the spiritual, verbal, and material implements necessary for holistic healing. John Umeh contends that ogwu is "the ultimate solution" to any and every problem.[49] Ajuziogu's dilemma—whether to abandon his people, culture, and traditions for assimilation in the Western world—appears to be a complicated one, and the verbal ogwu Nne-nne administers to her progeny seems largely irrelevant. In fact, the opposite is true. The Ogu of Ọha Ndom proves to be a time-released but potent capsule that works furtively "inside" Ajuziogu while he is abroad. Upon return to his homeland, Ajuziogu understands that true wisdom and the tools for humanospiritual evolution are not in Western academic institutions but in the collective that includes and embraces the self. Not only does Nne-nne's ogwu lead Ajuziogu to become one with his name and to take his position of honor beside the female principle but its force is so strong that her ogwu enacts its own Ọfọ (Infinite Justice) and finds modernized reincarnation "inside" a book, *I Saw the Sky Catch Fire*, where it lives and speaks its truths "forever."

* * *

Both Echewa and Naylor structure their texts around active and activated rememory and orality. Interweaving historical, spiritual, and mythical orature, the writers create unique yet historically grounded entities and art. The characters of Ndom are textual reincarnations of historical women. Sapphira seems wholly original, but her being is indebted to Odù, Ọya, Ṣàngó, Olódùmarè, Ọbàtálá, Ìyàmi Òṣòròngà, and the abolitionist Àjẹ́ of African America. Both *Fire* and *Mama Day* depend on the reading audience for textual cohesion and completion. The audience is asked to join Ajuziogu, Ashby-Jones, and Ugbala and enter into the solidarity of Ndom, to cross over from "beyond the bridge" and revise critical and historical interpretations of Africana life, culture, and history. In *Mama Day,* the communal voice of Willow Springs tells her listeners outright that they are obligated to place Eurocentric labels aside and "really listen" to Sapphira's Odù. Critics who forego her directives will end up like Reema's boy with the "pear-shaped head," whose academic training leads him to the following conclusion about Sapphira's Odù:

> 18 & 23 wasn't 18 & 23 at all—was really 81 & 32, which just so happened to be the lines of longitude and latitude marking off where Willow Springs sits on the map. And we were just so damned dumb that we turned the whole thing around.
> Not that he called it being dumb, mind you, called it "asserting our cultural identity," "inverting hostile social and political parameters." 'Cause see, being we was brought here as slaves, we had no choice but to look at everything upside-down. (8)

"Inverting hostile social parameters," if it is a reality, is only a secondary result of making manifest an inherent African consciousness. The Odù of Sapphira cannot be defined by alien concepts or limited anthropological tools. In order to fathom the full depth of her ìwà, the reader has to go to the Ìyánlá. In order to dig her roots, one cannot just read *Mama Day;* one must listen to its voices and feel its rhythms.

> He [Reema's son] coulda listened to them the way you been listening to us right now. Think about it: ain't nobody really talking to you. We're just sitting here in Willow Springs, and you're God-knows-where you are. . . . Uh, huh, listen. Really listen this time: the only voice is your own. But you done just heard about the legend of Sapphira Wade, though nobody here breathes her name. You done heard it the way we know it, sitting on our porches and shelling June peas . . . you done heard

it without a single living soul really saying a word. Pity though, Reema's boy couldn't listen, like you, to Cocoa and George down by them oaks—or he woulda left here with quite a story. (10)

The tree—cut, processed, and pulped into paper or painstakingly carved and assuaged with blood, gin, and prayer—has past lives as resonant and cyclic as the words and rhythms it produces in its new life. Oaks and ìrókò alike seek listeners to translate, interpret, and internalize their ancient and contemporary ring songs and sing them.

4

Initiations into the Self, the Conjured Space of Creation, and Prophetic Utterance in Ama Ata Aidoo's *Anowa* and Ntozake Shange's *Sassafrass, Cypress & Indigo*

Given the importance of Odù's "oracular utterance" in consecrating the earth and creating humanity, it is not surprising that prophets of Àjẹ́ arise periodically in life and literature to impart holistic guidance. Their spiritual power often recognized in adolescence, these emissaries of Odù are community wisdom-keepers and wisdom-sharers whose destiny is to offer their divine utterance and assistance in hopes of realigning misdirected communities and reinstilling the values that facilitate humanospiritual harmony. Because of the force of their message and spiritual affiliation, these prophets are often pushed off course by the very communities they seek to heal. However, no matter what the impediment is, the Ọ̀rọ̀ of Àjẹ́ will be manifest, even if it means the death of the prophet, and it will be heard and absorbed, textually if not extratextually.

Ayi Kwei Armah's *Two Thousand Seasons* is a spiritual-political-historical novel that reflects the impact that historical and ancient orature often have on contemporary Africana literature. The book depicts cycles of African oppression and enslavement as overseen by Arabs, African patriarchs, and Europeans. The primary source of hope and enlightenment for the Africans depicted in the novel is the wisdom and direction offered them by Àjẹ́-directed Prophets of the Anoa (also spelled Anowa). Anoa is a proper name and a title for a mythistorical line of female seers who arise cyclically and use their Ọ̀rọ̀ to enlighten, prepare, heal, and, facilitate their communities' evolution.

Reminiscent of "the one with two faces," one Anoa yields her prophecy in twin voices. The first voice lists a "terrifying catalogue of deaths" that will befall Africans at the hands of the Europeans, the "white destroyers." The utterance details what befalls both the survivors and the victims of the international enslavement of Africans—those who remained on the Continent, those taken away, and those pitched into the bloody waters of the Middle Passage. The voice reveals that this calamitous annihilation will have a span of "two thousand seasons."[1] Cognizant that many of the seeds of destruction were sown within, the second voice laments the disintegration of African unity, the loss of "the way." "The way" is one with Maat's keys of perfectibility and the sociopolitical impetus of Àjẹ́: It is centered on reciprocity, holistic connectedness, purposeful creation, and balance.[2] With the loss of "the way," disunity, discord, and selfishness prevail, ripping African social and moral bonds and leaving wide spaces for "predators" and "destroyers" to enter.

The Anoan prophecy that centers *Two Thousand Seasons* was rendered by a prophet who came of age just before the full Arab invasion of northern Africa. Because she was raised in a society still clinging to the threads of "harmonious dualism" where males and females followed vocations that suited their character as opposed to their gender, this particular Anoa becomes a master hunter. Her vocation is appropriate because Àjẹ́ are inclined to literally, figuratively, and spiritually "hunt" the dubious, traitorous, and deceitful—including and especially those who disregard "the way." Anoa exhibits the clarity of mind, voice, and purpose of a prophet from childhood, and the fact that her wisdom is greater than that of the elders is a respected fact in her community. However, because her destiny is one of struggle against any form of oppression, and because she sees present and future centuries of slavery awaiting her people, Anoa goes beyond prognosticating:

> She . . . brought the wrath of patriarchs on her head . . . by uttering a curse against any man, any woman who would press another human being into her service. This Anoa also cursed the takers of services proffered out of inculcated respect. It was said she was possessed by a spirit hating all servitude, so fierce in its hatred it was known to cause those it possessed to strangle those—so many now—whose joy it was to force the weaker into tools of their pleasure and their laziness, into creatures dependent upon their users.[3]

With an Ọ̀rọ̀ befitting her Àjẹ́, Anoa eternally condemns *all* enslavers—even and especially those styled as "benevolent"—and *all* forms of enslavement—even those routinely justified as benign. The only "good enslaver is a dead one. The only good form of enslavement is that which has been annihilated.

Armah's characterization of Anoa in *Two Thousand Seasons* owes a debt to Akan mythistory and to Ama Ata Aidoo's play *Anowa*, which is the first literary exposition of the prophet. Aidoo's drama is set in the late 1860s, after the close of *Two Thousand Seasons*, in a society that has lost "the way" and become so mystified by patriarchy it is not the men who ingrain into women the paths of subservience but the mothers. While not intentionally structured around the ancient prophecy of Anoa, Indigo, of Ntozake Shange's *Sassafrass, Cypress & Indigo* (*SCI*), is very much a daughter in the tradition of the Anowa. She is an active Àjẹ́, a healer and keeper of "the way," whose goal is to ensure the social and spiritual evolution of children of African ancestry displaced in America. Indicative of the acute psychological trauma of slavery that continues to impact Africans on all sides of the Ethiopic (also known as Atlantic) Ocean, both *Anowa* and *SCI*, though set about a century apart, are concerned with the holistic healing of multiply traumatized Africana peoples.

Lineage prophet Anowa is destined to reveal the shining wisdom of "the way" to a people lost in a wilderness of alien ideology. Unfortunately, her society is too tightly bound by the invisible ties of colonialism to permit space for spiritual and communal prophecy. What should be a safe and fertile space is nearly irreparably conjured. By contrast, the Africans of the ìtànkálẹ̀, those duped, deceived, victimized, and scattered (*tàn*) via the slave trade, as prophesied by Anoa, are also a people of an ironic shining (*tàn*).[3] That shining is a direct result of their collective trauma and their survival and furtive retention of "the way," both despite and because of that trauma. This resilient, shining collective consciousness (*tàn*) provides Indigo with a fertile prophetic space of creation that she can conjure to fit community needs.

Anowa is enmeshed in a web of conflict primarily because of the competing historical and literary traditions that inform her character. In addition to her cosmic genealogy, Anowa is a revision of the fickle young woman of African lore who refuses all the suitors her parents select for her. Trusting her vision and vanity, the young woman falls in love with a handsome man she meets in the market. Examples of this orature can be found in Flora Nwapa's *Efuru,* Amos Tutuola's *The Palm-Wine Drinkard,* and Zaynab Alkali's *The Stillborn*, and the text energizes countless storytelling sessions throughout Africa and the ìtànkálẹ̀. No matter what the variations, the maiden's marriage to the market-man is always disastrous.

Aidoo's incorporation of this popular text into her depiction of the returned prophet provides a deft diversion. Aidoo gives her textual and extratextual audiences the opportunity to conclude that Anowa's tragic life is the result of her being a fickle maiden and thus avoid translating Anowa's divine truth for both literary analysis and contemporary application. However, opportunities to avoid the issue are short-lived as it becomes clear in the course of the drama that the two primary morals of the socializing orature—that true beauty is found in character, not appearance, and that young women should trust the directives of their elders—are not relevant for Anowa. The protagonist is not superficial and selfish but misunderstood and misdirected; furthermore, her elders are either silent and unreliable or dishonest issue-avoiders.

The ways in which Anowa's elders describe and interpret her character reflect the two texts Aidoo offers for critical application. The Old Woman and the Old Man represent the community's wisdom-keepers, and they are engaged in a connected but external dialogue—or, more properly, retrospective analysis—of Anowa's life that mirrors the ruminations of Anowa's parents, Badua and Osam. The elders and parents do not directly interact with each other, and for the majority of the curvilinear drama, which begins with Anowa's death and retraces her fateful life, neither couple significantly interacts with Anowa. The only instance of interaction between the elders is brief and marked by distance. At the onset of the play, as the Old Man and the Old Woman reflect on the tragedy of Anowa, Badua, Anowa's mother, interrupts and indicts the elders while alluding to her complicity in Anowa's destruction:

> BADUA: Perhaps it was my fault too, but how could she come to any good when her name was always on the lips of every mouth that ate pepper and salt? . . .
> OLD WOMAN: And the gods will surely punish Abena Badua for refusing to let a born priestess dance![5]

Other than this isolated incident, there is no interaction between the elders. Furthermore, the statements of Badua and the Old Woman are made in third person, giving the impression of connected distance or mirroring. This exchange is also the only instance in which the Old Woman and Badua are shown to have discord. Actually, the women are as unified a force in their disgust toward Anowa as the Old Man and Osam are reflective and considerate of Anowa's divinity.

Initiations into Self, Conjured Space, Prophetic Utterance | 145

In *Anowa,* the males hold the knowledge of the past and the keys that can unlock the door of Anowa's self-awareness and actualization. The Old Man makes clear reference to the ancient curse of the original prophet Anoa, as discussed in *Two Thousand Seasons.* While Osam does not have the deep insight of the Old Man, he knows that Anowa is not following her true path. Although the men hold the keys and potential for understanding, they make no move to open the doors of revelation to Anowa during the course of her life. Their silence precipitates Anowa's fragmentation as much as the vociferous rantings of the Old Woman and Badua. A significant portion of the two couples' discussions are made after the destruction of Anowa and her husband, Kofi Ako; consequently, the elders are non/interactive critics whose curvilinear discussions are useless to Anowa because her fate is already sealed and resealed by cyclic breakdowns in communication.

At the onset of the drama, every elder is aware that Anowa should receive spiritual training. At the very least, she should be apprenticed to a priest until she can better understand her destiny. Her father says of Anowa, "From a very small age, she had the hot eyes and nimble feet of one born to dance for the gods" (80). The Old Man also refers to her as

> A child of several incarnations,
> She listens to her own tales
> Laughs at her own jokes and
> Follows her own advice. (67)

The Old Woman also recognizes Anowa's spiritual proclivities, but she refuses to overtly acknowledge them. Having two vastly different texts from which to choose, she undermines the seriousness of Anowa's dilemma by equating her with "all the beautiful maidens in the tales" who marry market/spirit husbands. She also negates Anowa's personal and political motivation, demanding "Where is she taking her 'I won't, I won't' to?" and dismisses her spiritual crisis of conscience: "No one knows what is wrong with her!" Badua, on the other hand, is fully aware of Anowa's power but refuses to allow her "only daughter" to become a "dancer priestess." In other words, she blocks the path that can help Anowa meet her destiny.

Indigo is also recognized from birth as spiritually inclined. The narrator introduces her with the following revelation:

> Where there is a woman, there is magic. If there is a moon falling from her mouth, she is a woman who knows her magic, who can share or not share her powers. A woman with a moon

falling from her mouth, roses between her legs and tiaras of Spanish moss, this woman is a consort of the spirits.[6]

Just as Anowa is the reincarnation of Ancient Mother Anoa, Indigo's name emphasizes her connection to communal Great Mother, Blue Sunday, whose name signifies her day of birth and her richly pigmented phenotype.[7] Blue Sunday manifests her force in the way of Yemọja. She controls the Ethiopic Ocean, and she can take the form of Yemọja's guardian, Crocodile Waaka (222–223).[8] Indeed, her control of the ocean and the crocodile totem are the means by which she liberated herself, her progeny, and the indigo plant from slavery and economic control. Descended from Blue Sunday and Yemọja, Indigo boasts as deep a spiritual lineage as Anowa.

Indigo's destiny is to facilitate the unification of various peoples, ages, places, spirits, and ancestors in her attempt to solidify and sanctify a safe place for African Americans. Her process of spiritual cognition and actualization involves many levels of initiation: stepping into her inner spiritual self, delving into the intricate blues of her community, tracing the footsteps of the enslaved ancestors, and, finally, spiritual tutelage under Blue Sunday, the African Òrìṣà/Ancestor who freed i/Indigo and "the Colored." Like Anowa, Indigo is destined to be a child of confusing crossroads, but she has a great deal of physical and spiritual assistance. Aunt Haydee, a powerful Àjẹ́ who is Indigo's mentor, guides the young healer. Additionally, Indigo is in constant communion with her Select Heads, Ọsanyìn and Yemọja, who provide spiritual and creative impetus. She also has an entire community of Àwọn Ìyá Wa, who lend their personal stories to the comprehensive text she weaves. Whereas Anowa only hears castigation and elders whispering behind her back, there is no division barring Indigo from her elders and Ancients; she has full terrestrial and spiritual mobility and she expresses her power of signification emphatically but respectfully to everyone.

Indigo's spiritual-political mission is complicated by the facts that she is an adolescent for the larger part of the novel, and her mother, Hilda Effania, cannot fully comprehend her daughter's complex motivations and character. Dismissing the cosmic realm, Hilda tries to prepare her child for existence in a brutal world of racism, sexism, rape, and pedophilia.

> Indigo, listen to me very seriously. This is Charleston, South Carolina. Stars don't fall from little colored girls' legs. Little boys don't come chasing after you for nothing good. White men roam these parts with evil in their blood, and every single thought they have about a colored woman is dangerous. You

have gotta stop living this make-believe. Please, do that for your mother. (22)

Hilda Effania's dismissal of Indigo's force as frivolous and potentially harmful "make-believe" and Badua's refusal to allow Anowa to become a "dancer priestess" are not uncommon reactions among Africana elders. Spiritualist Luisah Teish recalled that her grandfather's last words were "Don't let my grandchildren grow up to be no sanddancers." "Sanddancers" are Voodoo and Hoodoo worshippers who draw *ve ve,* spiritual insignias, on the ground in flour, brick dust, or sand and dance to invoke the Gods.[9] A common expression in the ìtànkálẹ̀ is, "White folks got all de money and Black folks got all de signs." The statement implies that while both peoples have definite and remarkable power, the dollar of the Western world is stronger and more valuable than the Africans' ability to interpret and control the spiritual and terrestrial realms of existence. While parents may recognize their children's spiritual depth and force, their goal for them is that they fully imbibe Eurocentric values.

The straitjacket of Western accomplishment for young women includes Christianity, a good job, and a husband. Explorations of the spiritual self are wholly unacceptable, nonlucrative, and dangerous. Armah's *Two Thousand Seasons* describes the fate of women who stood against the patriarchal shift:

> Those among them with a hearing too strong to be ignored were suppressed at once. Their bodies sometimes floated naked down the river in the beauty of the early morning, their genitals mutilated for the warning of docile multitudes. The weaker ones were given fondling treatment. For their individual selves, a small place was reserved among men so that it was usual to find one at a time even within the new male army itself, a mascot, or a simple honorary male. In the fullness of time these retired, to take on in the remainder of their lives the public character of barren women, stock for silent, easy laughter, living argument for the frivolity of their own best dreams.[10]

As if revealing the natural progression of female frivolity under patriarchy, Badua describes her "best" dream for her daughter:

> I want my child
> To be a *human* woman
> Marry a man
> Tend a farm

And be happy to see her
Peppers and onions grow.
A woman like her should bear children
Many children,
So she can afford to have
One or two die. (72, italics added)

With a few technological additions and a de-emphasis on children, Badua's dream can be translated into contemporary Western society. Badua assures Anowa that in addition to safe drudgery, she may eventually attain a "captainship" and become an "honorary male," but such dubious privileges can be bestowed only on women diminished enough to be deemed safe by the patriarchy.

Because the path of silent subjugation is precisely what the truncated mothers were made to trod, it is not surprising that they attempt to force their progeny into generic, linear, patriarchal dictates of womanhood. It is a common phenomenon for mothers to crush their daughters' souls for their own (assumed) good; it is manifest in any number of ways, from despicable marital arrangements to genital excision. The logic is that a socially and spiritually truncated daughter will be less likely to revolt, stand up, or stand out and become a dead daughter. Forced to be a "human woman," Anowa's nimble feet are stilled; her oracular mouth is locked. Indigo, by contrast, has an entire spiritual community guiding her. With multiple aides serving as an Ẹgbẹ́ Àjẹ́, Indigo is immersed in holistic humanospiritual wisdom and has unlimited access to a treasury of texts of triumph, pain, and transcendence. Indigo goes beyond absorbing the elders' wisdom for her personal enrichment; she creates shrines of holistic spiritual and physical healing to house the souls of psychologically and physically bruised women.

Although the term "rag dolls" is used to describe Indigo's first familiars and confidants, these dolls are not typical toys. Their compositions bespeak the seriousness of their functions; as they are fashioned not from discarded scraps but from the staples of her family's vocational, nutritional, and spiritual existence. They are fashioned with meticulous care to ensure each dolls' inner composition is compatible with her external appearance and her sociocultural experience. Consequently, each of Indigo's creations has soul, and each one also boasts soul-power:

> Indigo had made every kind of friend she wanted. African dolls filled with cotton root bark, so they'd have no more slave children. Jamaican dolls in red turbans, bodies formed with comfrey leaves because they'd had to work on Caribbean and

American plantations and their bodies must ache and be sore. Then there were the mammy dolls that Indigo labored over for months. They were almost four feet high, with big gold earrings made from dried sunflowers, and tits of uncleaned cotton. . . . She still crawled up into their arms when she was unavoidably lonely, anxious that no living Black folks would talk to her the way her dolls or Aunt Haydee did. (6)

With seamless symbiotic inversion, Indigo is the comforting, protecting Ìyánlá for the elder and ancestral Àwọn Ìyá Wa who bore the unbearable. As she creates, she gives birth to and holds mothers who lost their souls on plantations, prophets with locked mouths who were forced to be "human women," and sisters who fought with ferocity but were rarely held with equal intensity.

Indigo's dolls with their masterfully molded selves are an important part of the Africana spiritual-healing continuum. The dolls are offspring of the earthly manifestations of Òrìṣà Ọ̀sanyìn, the Crippled King, who holds in his calabash the elemental seeds of the earth which foment physical and spiritual healing. Ọ̀sanyìn's staffs are adorned with from one to sixteen birds that represent ascending voices of knowledge.[11] The number sixteen indicates Ifá's apex of spiritual knowledge: sixteen heads of power, sixteen styles, sixteen healing tongues. The birds also represent Ìyánlá herself, and her spiritual manifestation, the Ẹyẹ Ọ̀rọ̀ (Spirit Bird). If physical and spiritual healings are to occur, diviners of Ọ̀sanyìn must work with Ìyánlá Ẹyẹ Ọ̀rọ̀, who is the very owner of the earth's flora: She is the one who "makes our medicines [and charms] effective."[12] Ìyánlá, Ọ̀sanyìn, and diviners are interdependent, and human spiritual and physical healing is contingent upon the cosmic cooperation of these Deities.

While other Òrìṣà enter the heads of their devotees, Ọ̀sanyìn speaks to his divining healers through a doll. The doll, embodying Ọ̀sanyìn and his birds of wisdom, tells the human diviner what ails a particular person and how the person can be cured.[13] Ọ̀sanyìn's twin from the Kongo, nkisi, also exerts a powerful influence on Indigo and her work. As discussed in chapter 2, minkisi are "gifts from God." Their meticulous construction, which the God-nkisi directs, blends selected elements of kindoki (àṣẹ and Àjẹ́) such as kola, eggs, the head of a dog, soil, specific leaves, and chalk into a microcosm of the universe, which may take form in a pot[14] or a human figurine. Nsemi Iaski describes nkisi as

the name of the thing we use to help a person when that person is sick and from where we obtain health; the name refers to leaves and medicines combined together. . . . It is also called

> nkisi because there is one to protect the human soul and guard it against illness for whoever is sick and wishes to be healed. . . . An *nkisi* is also a *chosen companion. . . . It is a hiding place for people's souls, to keep and compose in order to preserve life.*[15]

Fashioned out of roots, herbs, swatches, and fibers that protect and heal, Indigo's dolls educate and soothe her spirit and invoke and assuage the troubled souls of ancestors. This is in keeping with the tradition of symbiosis manifest in Òsanyìn and minkisi and their architects and communities. The spiritual and material worlds are united in Indigo's room: Ancestral minkisi sit in Indigo's lap, and Òsanyìn's dolls speak through Indigo to the women of the community. This multigeographic and cross-generational linking of curative forces underscores the connectedness of West and Central African spiritual systems and the crucial role of divine healers in the African continuum.

In her nonfiction semi-autobiographical book *Jambalaya,* Luisah Teish teaches her audience how to make a "Little Soul Doll." Teish's painstaking and meticulous directions, if properly followed, will result in a doll that is as soul-filled as Indigo's creations. In fact, Teish warns would-be creators not to be surprised when the soul doll talks and moves. And if the doll "dies" in a natural disaster or is stolen, its creator should "do *everything* your head tells you to disassociate from that doll and to reclaim your little soul."[16] Describing her personal power to re-create and heal, African American visual artist Riua Akinshegun used the spirit she infused in her art to ease the chronic pain she suffered after being shot in the back. Like Teish's warnings and Indigo's experience, Akinshegun's dolls advise and comfort her and facilitate holistic healing: "It's been just recently that I've understood that one of my dolls, 'Wisdom Past and Future,' did all of my woeing, all of my nonverbal crying and mourning, for me. 'The High Priestess' was for protection, and 'Earth Mother' kept me grounded and in tune with nature."[17]

In addition to its Pan-African healing abilities, nkisi is also a force of war and retribution: "Kongo-Cubans of the nineteenth century made minkisi-figurines to mystically attack slaveholders and other enemies, and for spiritual reconnaissance."[18] Similarly, Indigo uses the skills of various minkisi to battle the enemy of her ancestral and modern communities—"white folks." In contrast to Anowa, who is stunted though born on the Continent, Indigo's power is not diminished by birth on alien soil. She improvises, as did her displaced ancestors: "There wasn't enough for Indigo in the world she'd been born to, so she made up what she needed. What she thought the Black people needed" (4). Just as Ifá, the medicinal healing of Òsanyìn, and the praise ceremonies of the Gèlèdé are used, so too does Indigo use her natural spiritual power for personal and communal evolution.

The narrator reveals that Indigo "only had colored dolls and only visited colored ladies." These ladies are the community's wisdom-keepers. They are elder women who have weathered all storms and have emerged, like Àgbàláàgbà Obìrin, with a "delicacy" in manner, "ritual . . . in daily undertakings," and the power to make "what is most ordinary . . . extraordinary . . . what is hard . . . simple" (8). Indigo seeks "to make herself a doll whose story that was, or who could have helped [these women] out" (8). Like diviners of Òsanyìn, who has sixteen styles of knowledge and sixteen tongues, each of Indigo's dolls tells a unique story, and each doll tells Indigo what the woman speaking the life-text needs and has needed. In the interactions between minkisi, Indigo, and Ìyá that spark rememory and orality, Indigo is educating and apprenticing herself to the Àgbàláàgbà of her community and building the foundation a young prophet needs.

Because the need for minkisi and holistic healing is not exclusive to Indigo's community, she shares self-healing conjure from her calabash of medicinal herbs and seeds with her extratextual audience. Indigo gives Shange's audience the means to cure spiritual wounds and celebrate the self. The burgeoning Àjẹ́ shares rituals to induce "moon journeys" (or achieve astral mobility), celebrate menstruation, "rid oneself of the scent of evil," and focus a lover's roaming eyes. Indigo's soul prescriptions are gleaned from her experiences with her Mother-elders. Described as "culture-specific markers"[19] by Arlene Elder, each prescription is designed to prevent or heal the spiritual and physical contusions of "Colored girls"—afflictions that cannot be cured with Tylenol, Pamprin, or Western psychiatry or psychology. By sharing rootwork that focuses on honoring the soul while nurturing and pampering the physical body, Indigo offers all her communities—extratextual, communal, and familial—the means to develop holistically.

The celebration of her first menstruation marks the end of Indigo's woman-exclusive spiritual tutelage. And as she makes her last public outing as a child with Miranda, her favorite minkisi, Indigo receives valuable lessons from and about males. Shining with new and undeveloped womanhood, Indigo ignores the rules of female discretion and is nearly raped by Mr. Lucas when she tries to purchase her Kotex menstrual pads at his store (28–29). However, she is able to put this experience beside a spiritual gift and tutorial from John Henderson, also known as Uncle John.

Indigo is an astute spiritual seer at a crossroads: She must put away "childish" things but is not yet a woman. She also doesn't "like real folks near as much" as she appreciates "unreal" or spiritually inclined people. Uncle John, an elder preparing for a wholly spiritual existence, is also at the crossroads. Both living unreal lives in a real world, Uncle John and Indigo are true complements. Like Èṣù, who has the power to facilitate all prayers, Uncle John has everything anyone needs in his wagon. But before he enters his wagon of healing, Uncle John's decree for the moon-mouthed child is that she's "gotta try to be mo' in this world." Having gained extensive knowledge of the spiritual realm, Indigo must translate that wisdom for a needy terrestrial community. To aid her, Uncle John gives Indigo a "new talkin' friend" that has vast experience in cosmic-to-physical and ancient-to-contemporary discourse. He also provides her with a proper historical context for her communicative tool:

> Them whites what owned slaves took everythin' was ourselves & didn't keep it fo' they ownselves. Just threw it on away, ya heah. Took them drums what they could, but they couldn't take our feet. Took them languages what we speak. Took off wit our spirits & left us wit they Son. *But the fiddle was the talkin' one. The fiddle be callin' our gods what left us* / *be givin' back some devilment & hope in our bodies worn down & lonely over these field & kitchens.* Why white folks so dumb, they was thinkin' that if we didn't have nothin' of our own, they could come controllin', meddlin', whippin' our sense on outta us. But the Colored smart, ya see. The Colored got some wits to em, you & me, we ain't the onliest ones be talkin' wit the unreal. What ya think music is, whatchu think the blues be, & them happy church musics is about, but talkin' wit the unreal what's mo' real than most folks ever gonna know. (27, italics added)

The ability to talk with the "unreal" is not limited to spiritualists. As they built America by force, enslaved African American men sang of their linguistic mastery and raw majesty:

> A col' frosty mo'nin'
> De niggers feelin' good
> Take yo' ax upon yo' shoulder
> Nigger, talk to de wood[20]

The brothers who laid the rails chided trees about their transformation from essential living entity to burden of industry:

> Come on cross tie-(*umph*)
> Git yo place-(*umph*)

....
Y' ain' no longuh-(*umph*)
A growin' tree-(*umph*)
Slip along-(*umph*)
Yuh ain't nothin now-(*umph*)
But a heavy log-(*umph*)[21]

For the community in Zora Neale Hurston's *Jonah's Gourd Vine*, the uprooted tree became the "drum wid the manskin." Like the drum of Ọbàtálá, honed from and beaten with the skin and limbs of his charges,[22] the ìtànkálẹ̀an referent is created from juba—blood, hope, sweat, tears, praise, and fears—the wealth of the Self:

> They called for the instrument that they had brought to America in their skins—the drum—and they played upon it. . . . The great drum that is made by priests and sits in majesty in the juju house. The drum with the man skin that is dressed with human blood, that is beaten with a human shin-bone and speaks to gods as a man and to men as a God.[23]

Despite being subjected to misnaming, being forced to shield spirits under someone's son, and having languages wrenched from tongue, displaced Africans retained and created signifying spaces for and within the Self. What was taken physically was held spiritually. What was considered trash was furtively crafted into tools for spiritual ascendancy. Feet, thighs, hands, and knees remained because they had to for the purposes of the oppressor, but even if people existed with only half-bodies, like Ọsanyìn,[24] full, filling spiritual rhythms would be coaxed out of that body. Indigo has a full body, an overflowing spirit, and now a talkin' fiddle to mediate her prophecy.

As a result of exile and enslavement, many instruments of African origin were introduced to the West, and these instruments all had spiritual roles that were overlooked in favor of their melody-making abilities. In "*Les Bambara*," Viviana Paques explicates the structural-spiritual significance of the *ngoni* harp, parent of Indigo's talkin' fiddle:

> The anthropomorphism of the *ngoni* harp is clear in the minds of its users.
> The rectangular box of the instrument represents the mask of Koumabana, the ancestor who received the word; the two lateral splits are his eyes; the hole, his nose and respiration; the *cordier*, his mouth and teeth; the 8 strings, his utterance. . . . The box represents also the face of the diviner and his tomb. . . . Each

sound yielded by each of the 8 strings is a prayer. The strings are plucked separately by the diviner according to their rank; and also depending both on the identity of the consultant and the questions he asks. . . .

[The harp] presides over the sacrifices, over catharsis or medication rites, over purifications, over apotropaic rites, over solitary meditations. Its higher notes are heavenly and are symbols of plenitude; the lower notes connote earthly things that are incomplete. Its play commands the arrivals and the departures, the proliferations and the scarcities, the calls to order; its presence on the edge of a pond where it has been placed secretly, is a pledge of appeasement.

The harpist, before beginning his divine service, puts his mouth on the hole of the box and whispers to the master of the Word: "Now, it is your turn, organize the world."[25]

Like the *ngoni* harp, the talkin' fiddle communicates with ancient spiritual rhythms. With her talkin' fiddle, Indigo has a tool as powerful as her minkisi to play, divine, heal, and help organize the world.

Anowa lacks the communal assistance that surrounds Indigo, and her community lacks the spirit of improvisation, resilience, and soul—the shining—so clearly evident in Indigo, her many "talkin'" friends. Even if only to play the "lower" "incomplete" notes, Anowa has no harp, no fiddle, no outlet. Unable to grasp her spiritual destiny, Anowa takes control of her material reality. Her first initiation into the self involves not the communal healing of Indigo's minkisi but marriage to Kofi Ako. Anowa's market-founded marriage deviates sharply from other texts in the tradition because of her intended purpose and destiny. Like Anoa, the hunter, Anowa and Kofi Ako become animal trappers. As the couple prospers, Kofi seeks to flaunt his status by trapping and owning human beings.

In a complex relationship of diametrically opposed forces, Anowa and Kofi Ako are locked in a struggle of "ways." Anowa's way of "harmonious dualism," reciprocity, and the inherent right to freedom is as forcefully directed as her husband's way of slavery and capitalism. Cognizant of her destiny and unalterable direction, Kofi Ako extends to her the "compliment" often given to Àjẹ́, that with her physical strength and mental acumen, she "ought to have been born a man." Fearing that her will may be jeopardizing their marriage, or at least impeding her from conceiving, Anowa suggests that Kofi take an additional wife. Kofi responds with a double entendre: "I cannot afford to lose you." The acquisition of another wife would mean a companion for Anowa. Most important, it would free her to delve deeper into her spiritual path. In his refusal to take another wife, Kofi superficially honors his wife's entrepreneurial skills, but he is also subtly praising himself on his first and most important acquisition. Anowa is actually Kofi Ako's most significant possession and the facilitator of his "way." Anowa's impetus to liberate her community is equal to and is "married" to Kofi Ako's desire to enslave human beings.

Like the exquisite market-man who clothed himself in human body parts to conceal his lack of humanity, Kofi Ako acquires human beings to conceal his deficit of soul. King Koranche of *Two Thousand Seasons,* who sells a young group of Anoa prophets into slavery, suffers from the same disease as Kofi Ako. Koranche muses that while he is constantly covered in ornate garb, the commoners "can walk naked and not be ashamed. . . . they give more than they receive. I, the king, I only know how to take. They are full vessels overflowing. I am empty. In place of a bottom I have a hole."[26] Kofi's ownership of a hole instead of a soul is evident in his impotence and lust to own human beings.

The Old Man describes Kofi Ako as a member of the "disparate breed" that uses human beings to camouflage their inhuman void, to prop up their dubious masculinity and humanity. The elder also makes it clear that because they actively enslave the souls of their own people, Africans such as Kofi and Koranche who mimic "white destroyers" are as much a part of African culture as European oppression, for they go hand in hand:

> OLD MAN: O my beloveds, let it not surprise us then
> That This-One and That-One
> Depend for their well-being on the presence of
> The pale stranger in our midst:
> Kofi was, is, and shall always be
> One of us. (67)

That Kofi Ako and his kind are inescapable realities, destroyers who must be destroyed, is the very reason Anowa is married to him. Anowa's spiritual mission is to begin with her husband, who is at once the closest person to her and the most cosmically distant and spiritually bankrupt.

Ama Ata Aidoo is a conscious artist with a Pan-African sensibility who recognizes the relevance of the past to the future and the great weight it places on activist-artists. Speaking of the world's most heinous tragedy, Aidoo says, "I think that the whole question of how it was that so many of our people could be enslaved and sold is very important. I've always thought that it is an area that must be probed. It probably holds one of the keys to our future." She goes on to assert, "Until we have actually sorted out this whole question of African people, both on the continent and in the diaspora, we may be joking, simply going round in circles."[27] Aidoo understands the poignant relevance of the fact that she has kinspeople, sold away, sunken into the sea, and exiled in the West, who are victims of greedy Kofi Akos, ineffective Anowas, and silent or victim-blaming elders, in addition to racist usurpers. In *Anowa* and *Dilemma of a Ghost*, Aidoo herself becomes a prophet of Anowa and takes her intended African audience through that painful journey of rememory, of crossing boundaries of time, space, place, and consciousness, so that the tragedies "the slaves who were ourselves" survived can be understood and avoided.

That Anowa's land of nativity, the birthplace of Ayen and the domain of Asase Yaa, is so stunted that she has no access to spiritual cognition testifies to the degree to which the land that Europeans called the "Gold Coast" was conjured. Conjured land affects all those who come into its sphere. For the spiritually and politically conscious indigenous person, living on conjured land is the equivalent to home exile. This is the weight of the original curse of Anoa. Anowa bears this burden literally, as she is one of the wealthiest women in her nation and is also a "wayfarer." Likening her situation to those Africans who were exiled and enslaved, she tells Kofi that "to call someone a wayfarer is a painless way of saying he does not belong. That he has no home, no family, no village, no stool of his own; has no feast days, no holidays, no state, no territory" (97). The irony is that Anowa has each of the things she mentions and more, but as gifts of a conjured land and people, they have no meaning for her. Badua is dumbfounded by her daughter's self-imposed exile: "I haven't heard the like of this before. A human being, and a woman too, preferring to remain a stranger in other peoples' lands?" (91). Anowa defines a "wayfarer" as a person who "belongs to other people" (97). As a communal prophet, she has no individual self. She "belongs" to Kofi Ako, her confused community, and communities across the ocean she has yet to meet. She is inextricably bound to all, but as a simultaneous "daughter of the Earth" and prophet in chains, she is unable to guide her people to evolution.

Recognizing Anowa's multifaceted dilemma, Osam says, "The children of women like Anowa and their children-after-them never find their way back. They get lost. For they often do not know the names of the founders of their houses.... No, they do not know what to tell you if you asked them for just the names of their clans" (94). Some of the children of Anoa are lost because they were captured and wrenched from their clans and houses. Others, like Anowa, left of their own accord because they were cognizant of the sham, shame, and impotence of those houses and the souls upon which they were erected. Some remain lost because when they return, they are not extended the honor of recognition. The latter is the case with Eulalie of Aidoo's *Dilemma of a Ghost*. Eulalie attempts the return Osam says is all but impossible and receives the following greeting from Nana:

> My spirit Mother ought to have come for me earlier.
> Now what shall I tell them who are gone? The daughter
> Of slaves who comes from the white man's land.
> Someone should advise me on how to tell my story.
> My children, I am dreading my arrival there
> Where they will ask me news of home.
> Shall I tell them or shall I not?
> Someone should lend me a tongue
> Light enough with which to tell
> My Royal Dead
> That one of their stock
> Has gone away and brought to their sacred precincts
> The wayfarer![28]

Dumfounded by and ashamed of Eulalie, her African American granddaughter-in-law, Nana implores, "She has no tribe? The story you are telling us is too sweet. . . . I have not heard of a human being born out of the womb of a woman who has no tribe. Are there trees which never have roots?"[29] Nanny of *Their Eyes Were Watching God* begins a sociological exposition to her granddaughter, stating, "You know, honey, us colored folks is branches without roots and that makes things come round in queer ways."[30] Despite their seeming ignorance, the Royal Dead, Nanny, and Nana all know the root, branch, and tree and the way in which they were poisoned and made to wither. These are the circles of stagnation that Aidoo describes as manifestations of disavowal and confusion. Aidoo's work gives voice to and subtly combats the disavowal of such elders as Nana and the Old Woman by juxtaposing their selective ignorance with knowledge.

It is not Anowa, whose prophecy lies mute in her mouth, but the Old Man who, shining with wisdom and Òrò, re-members the ancient curse of Anoa and compares the historical consequences to those of the present. He muses, "There must be something unwholesome about making slaves of other men, something that is against the natural state of man and the purity of his worship of the Gods. Those who have observed have remarked that every house is ruined where they take in slaves."

> One or two homes in Abura already show this;
> They are spilling over

With gold and silver
And no one knows the uttermost hedges of their lands.
But where are the people
Who are going to sit on these things?
Yes,
It is frightening.
But all at once, Girl-babies die
And the breasts of women in new motherhood
Run dry (100)

The resilience of the curse of Anoa is apparent in the opulent but sterile palace of Kofi Ako, who has become "the richest man, probably of the whole Guinea Coast." This palace, built and maintained on the backs of human beings, is also Anowa's home. The stymied prophet cannot articulate her own prophecy, and, becoming increasingly complicit in the very travesties she should be working against, Anowa loses weight and her sanity.

As she watches a bloated Kofi oil his corpulent limbs and survey his baroque surroundings, Anowa, wearing a tattered shift dress and a frayed mind, recalls her first abortive initiation into the self, during which she was introduced to conjured spaces of creation and the prophetic utterance that she bears but cannot successfully articulate. Anowa, becoming childlike in the throes of rememory, recalls when her grandmother sat her down and told her of her travels to the coast among people who owned houses wider than roads. Anowa asks who built the structures, and she learns of the "pale men" who look like humans who were free of skin and red like boiled or roasted lobsters. When her grandmother tells her that the big houses were used to house enslaved Africans, Anowa asks, "Did the men of the land sell other men of the land, and woman and children to pale men from beyond the horizon who looked like you or me peeled, like lobsters boiled or roasted?" Angry and ashamed, the Nana of *Anowa,* like the Nana of *Dilemma of a Ghost,* seeks recourse in selective amnesia: "All good men and women try to forget; / They have forgotten!" But her grandchild pushes the rememory, demanding of her elder, "What happened to those who were taken away? / Do people hear from them?" (106).

Following this, Anowa has a dream in which she is Mother Earth Asase Yaa and witnesses, first hand, the conjuring of her creative space.

I was a big, big woman. And from my insides were huge holes out of which poured men, women and children. And the sea was boiling hot and steaming. And as it boiled, it threw out many, many giant lobsters, boiled lobsters, each of whom as it fell turned into a man or woman, but keeping its lobster head and claws. And they rushed to where I sat and seized the men and woman as they poured out of me, and they tore them apart, and dashed them to the ground and stamped upon them . . . and everything went on and on and on. (106)

Within a conjured space, the Mother of Creation is a fecund-barren mother whose àbíkú issue is raped and killed regularly and repeatedly within her womb and doomed after birth. Following Anowa's rememory, the reality of Kofi's aberration and her stunted path become clear. She realizes that her husband has "exhausted," "eaten up," his "masculinity acquiring slaves and wealth." Not only did Kofi devour his own soul but he first dined on that of his wife, killing her prophetic potential. Anowa is unable to deter or help Kofi Ako or herself self-actualize. Perfect complements in an inherently and tragically flawed union, both Kofi Ako and Anowa commit suicide.

At one time, Zora Neale Hurston worried that she would be "in some lone, arctic wasteland with no one under the sound of [her] voice."[31] The "earless silences" Hurston feared condemn Anowa, a prophet who has no community to receive her utterance, help her achieve her goal, or allow her rejuvenating soul-expansion. Her earth of origins has been so corrupted that she has no foundation upon which to stand and no path upon which to walk. As a complicit although unwilling participant in her husband's "way" and acquisitions, Anowa falls victim to her progenitor's ancient curse. However, the Òrò is not dead: It thrives in the Old Man's soliloquy and in the opulent emptiness of enslavers. And as Aidoo's dramas are meant to transcend stage and text, the magnitude of Anowa's utterance surges in the mind of Aidoo's audience. The play's conclusion is a beginning; it is left to us to claim, mend, and apply the prophecy of Anowa.[32]

Aidoo, through Anowa, facilitates the re-membering of those Africans lost to exile and enslavement. Shange continues the work of cohesion, writing for "young girls of color, for girls who don't even exist yet so that there is something there for them when they arrive."[33] The curtain that falls on Anowa rises with the revelation of Indigo, who learns, as Hurston did, to trust "the geography . . . within" to lead her to fertile and receptive spaces for signification. In the course of her journey, Indigo answers Anowa's queries about those who were taken away, and she articulates the utterance lost in Anowa's throat.

Geechee refers to a Liberian society, the Gidzi or Kissi.[34] In African America, the term "Geechee" refers to Africans who refused to submit to Euro-American socialization and retained their spiritual and cultural traditions. Indigo heralds her Geechee blood, and the ancestors coursing in her veins move to juba as she fiddles. In addition to invoking all types of flora and fauna as she masters the strains of the keys of life, Indigo learns the chords of "Colored & Romance." And while playing the wicked strains, she conjures two Geechee boys, Spats and Crunch. Recognizing her power, the boys initiate her into the "Junior Geechee Cap-i-tans" (Junior G.C.) and rename her "Digo," because it means "I say" in Spanish. The name appears appropriate to her prophecy because "Digo was really sayin' somethin'" (41). With this initiation, adolescent Indigo secures the coveted "captainship" that Badua dangles before Anowa, and Indigo goes from playing the songs of the Colored to experiencing the full spectrum of Colored life.

Under Sneed's bakery are The Caverns, a maze of underground tunnels that leads to Charleston's underworld of numbers-running, cockfights, gambling, and the deepest blues; it is here that Indigo will hone her vast spiritual repertoire. Pretty Man, a full Geechee Capitan, initially places Indigo in the gaming room, and there she witnesses skin-trapping and life-selling similar to that enacted by Kofi Ako and Koranche. As Indigo watches a cockfight, her rage moves her to use her Àjẹ́ to place the "grown men laughing at [the] dying animals" in the places of the roosters: "The cocks stalked the ring quietly. The men round the ring leaped over one another, flailing their razored palms at throats, up & down backs, backsides, ankles" (44). Pretty Man recognizes the strength of Indigo's revisionist Àjẹ́, which has disrupted his gambling operation, and the two come to an unspoken agreement: Indigo and her fiddle will be relegated to the "social room." Indigo's organizational and healing powers, augmented by the talkin' fiddle, blossom in the social room, which is run by Pretty Man's woman, Mabel. The reproductions of nature, the snatches of rhythm and blues, and Indigo's social and spiritual lessons are put to use for a people desperately in need of peace. In the social room, Indigo and her fiddle channel the holistic power and relationship of the diviner and the ngoni harp:

> Indigo didn't change her style of playing. She still went after what she was feeling. But now she'd look at somebody. Say a brown-skinned man with a scar on his cheek, leathery hands, and a tiredness in his eyes. Then she'd bring her soul all up in his till she'd ferreted out the most lovely moment in that man's life. & she played that. (45)

Like the ngoni harpist, Indigo plucks and bows the strings that represent prayers according to their rank "and also depending both on the identity of the consultant and the questions [she or] he asks." Indigo uses the fiddle's sound holes the same way the ngoni harpist uses the harp's lateral splits, as spiritual eyes that reveal destinies. And "the slaves who were ourselves aided Indigo's mission, connecting soul & song, experience & unremembered rhythms."

Indigo plays soul music in its truest form, and soon the social room is full of rejoicings. Mabel is making good money, and the community experiences healing. The rhythm changes when Pretty Man takes it upon himself to direct Indigo's aesthetic; he decides that "[t]raining was what she wanted." Whereas *Indigo* acted as a conduit for the unheard melodies of spiritual forces awaiting recognition and brought joy to lives that had lived through too much pain, *Digo* ironically has no "say" in who, what, or how she plays. The mouth of her talkin' fiddle is eventually dammed with the compositions of Duke Ellington, Stephane Grappelli, and Svend Asmussen. From her truncated redefined name to her "place" as trainee and social entertainer to the changing of her aesthetic, Indigo attains a "captainship" and "honorary male" status; but, like the name "Digo," it is a mere fragment of her best dream.

Left to agree with what the patriarchy has decided, Digo submits. However, "Mabel was concerned, 'cause folks used to the child's fiddlin' till they souls spoke, were getting cantankerous, leaving early, not leaving tips, being genuinely unpleasant. Missing something" (47). When Spats and Crunch renamed Indigo "Digo," she resented it. She foresaw the changing of her name as having the potential to confuse the spirits and cause them to give her gifts to another person; or, angered at aberration, the spirits could "move with wrath instead of grace." What she feared occurs as Digo and her patriarchally signifying fiddle misname and ignore some and inspire violence in others.

Mabel ponders the misdirected force of Digo and her instrument: "Violins. Violins. Violins, white folks done come up from they grave to drive the Colored out of a nice spot, they spot. . . . All them empty tables. All them fiddles. It was better before, when the girl played her own mind" (47). Mabel cannot lash out at dead but string-pulling "white folks" or admit to Pretty Man's error in altering Indigo's aesthetic and destroying the bliss of the social room. Indigo and her fiddle are the most obvious and convenient targets, and Mabel moves with wrath to eradicate them from the social room and her life:

> Indigo moved quick, like moonlight. "Spats. Crunch. *G.C. in trouble. G.C. in trouble.*" Indigo let the force of her own style of fiddle-fightin' come to the fore. Such a war-cry bouncing in the social room where hips & bosoms used to shake. Mabel was overwhelmed by her mission to have things be the way they

used to be, not understanding that Indigo's existence made that possible. (48)

Hearing Indigo's war cry and summons, Spats and Crunch arrive and incur an avalanche of nails, heels, and teeth to protect Indigo and her fiddle from Mabel. Mabel screams for Pretty Man, and the Junior G.C.s flee into The Caverns, fearing he will attack them. When Pretty Man arrives, it is clear that he is also moved to wrath. But he is not enraged at the children; he metes out violence on Mabel.

Having been under attack as the pawn of the patriarchy, Indigo initially feels vindicated when she hears Pretty Man pummeling his lover. Hearing Mabel's screams, she tells Spats and Crunch, "We ain't the ones haveta run nowhere" (48). Directly following her selfish thought, Indigo feels the weight of centuries of violence inflicted upon her enslaved ancestors who were lodged in The Caverns prior to being sold. Indigo decides to return to help Mabel, whose screams have become one with those of the ancestors:

> Indigo felt The Caverns for the first time. The air was dark, heavy. . . . Her fiddle, as she let it fall over her side, weighed down her spirit. Shame crawled up her cheeks. She was going to see about Mabel. Mabel had gotten in trouble 'cause of Indigo's fiddle, 'cause Indigo was a Junior Geechee Capitan. Mabel was just some woman. One day Indigo would be a woman too. (49)

When Indigo sees Pretty Man emerge, she thinks she sees the "real enemy." Her nonchalance toward Mabel turns into wrath directed at Pretty Man, and she wishes that the decorative switchblade handles on her violin case were the knives themselves because "she'd have them all land in his back, but she didn't want to hurt anybody else. The Colored had been hurt enough already" (49).

The truncation of Indigo's name, Mabel's attack on Indigo, the training Indigo receives from Pretty Man, and the beating Pretty Man gives Mabel are all warped intracommunal reproductions of what the ancestors were forced to endure at the hands of oppressors. Back then, the slaves who were ourselves were misnamed Hilda, Cicero, or Circe and were stretched over barrels to receive beatings; their powers were either dismissed as heathen aberrations or contorted into an amusing diversion for a vapid "master." Sometimes survival meant submission to assimilation and spiritual death. Other times, insults against humanity were answered with the deaths of oppressors. With Indigo's wish to see Pretty Man dead, and the fact that she has the Àjẹ́ to fulfill this wish, she joins in the cycle of oppression. She is as complicit as Anowa in furthering the way of division and destruction. The fistwielding Pretty Man is a poor imitation of Eurocentria. His show of force is as pompous a display of impotence as the pageantry of Kofi Ako. However, Pretty Man is no more the source of Colored pain than Mabel or Indigo, who fully partakes in the twisted cycle that will lead to her spiritual evolution. The real enemy is not in The Caverns, and Indigo has the presence of mind to break the cycle of abuse and misdirected blame.

Indigo's prophetic epiphany marks her second initiation, and the ancestors welcome her:

> The Caverns began to moan, not with sorrow but in recognition of Indigo's revelation. The slaves who were ourselves had known terror intimately, confused sunrise with pain, & accepted indifference as kindness. Now they sang out from the walls, pulling Indigo toward them. Indigo ran her hands along the walls, to get the song, getta hold to the voices. Instead her fingers grazed cold, hard metal rings. Rust covered her palms & fingers. The Caverns revealed the plight of her people, but kept on singing. The tighter Indigo held the chains in her hands, the less shame was her familiar. Mabel's woeful voice hovered over the blood thick chorus of The Caverns. Indigo knew her calling. The Colored had hurt enough already. (49)

The Caverns are the North American equivalent of the Slave Castle and Slave Fort in Cape Coast and Elmina, Ghana. The Caverns, the Castle, and the Fort are all stationed on coasts of the Ethiopic, now misnamed Atlantic, Ocean, and they are all riddled with ancestral spiritual energy. The Castle and Fort in Ghana constitute a wide gateway for the multitudinous àbíkú children who spill out of Anowa's womb and into the claws of "lobsters." The Caverns is the womb that gave birth to tragic lives destined for triumph and the wisdom, knowledge, understanding that are the keys to evolution. Indigo completes the cycle of self-actualization that Anowa is unable to successfully navigate and de-riddles the conundrum that Nana and Anowa are unable to solve. The rusty rings of the Castle, Fort, and Caverns that held the necks and feet of countless Anowas, Mirandas, Osams, Uncle Johns, Indigos, Eulalies and Nanas in check with chains become tangible tools of re-membering and evolution in Indigo's hands.

Following her prophetic epiphany, Indigo shares with us ways to cure open wounds and treat psychic and genetic trauma. Healing for those who have been "hurt enough already" involves holding the victim and rocking her or him "in the manner of a quiet sea," humming "softly from your heart," and making her or him aware of the power to eventually heal herself or himself (50). Charging us to embrace the "treasures of black culture,"³⁵ Indigo utters the ancient prophecy and crafts a prescription for Pan-African healing as ancient and elemental as Yemoja's healing, cleansing, restorative waves lapping against the twin shores of Asase Yaa.

5

Un/Complementary Complements: Gender, Power, and Àjẹ́ in Selected Works by C. L. Adeoye, Octavia E. Butler, Zora Neale Hurston, Wole Soyinka, and Amos Tutuola

In *The Gẹ̀lẹ̀dẹ́ Spectacle,* Babatunde Lawal asserts that, "The Yoruba existential ethos is that all the creations in the universe will continue-in-being only when they remain in sociation (*àṣùwàdà*) and at peace with one another."[1] The patriarchal shift threatened gender àṣùwàdà and societal peace. However, Àjẹ́ have in their arsenal a plethora of harmonizing tools and skills and, as is detailed in the *Ìtàn-Oríkì Ìyàmi Òṣòròngà,* if necessary, they will use debilitation and painful didactics to institute gender balance and social harmony. Using texts of seemingly disparate genres—fiction, science fiction, drama, and ancient orature—by authors of different eras, geographical regions, and genders, I will examine the social and political methodology of Àjẹ́ who tap ancient roots to institute gender, and overall community, harmony.

The first part of this chapter will examine Àjẹ́, love, and gender balance in the lives of Òrìṣà Oya and Zora Neale Hurston's Janie Crawford. Using Octavia E. Butler's *Wild Seed* and Wole Soyinka's *Madmen and Specialists,* the second part of this chapter will examine gender balance from a sociopolitical perspective. To provide a proper context for this discussion, I begin with an analysis of Amos Tutuola's *The Palm-Wine Drinkard.* Tutuola's literature has been dismissed as childish and trivial in some circles; however, his fiction reveals the complex interweaving of myth, history, morality, spirituality, and critical analysis that characterizes traditional forms of African didactic entertainment. Tutuola's craft also emphasizes the interconnectedness of the spiritual and physical realms, and his work evinces the "harmonious dualism" between man and woman that Diop argued was central to the African ethos.

WINE, WORK, AND PLAY: TUTUOLA AND GENDER BALANCE

The protagonist of Tutuola's *The Palm-Wine Drinkard* is Father of the Gods Who Could Do Anything in this World, and he fittingly possesses a wealth of cosmic and terrestrial knowledge (or wicked bags) and countless spiritual powers, including the ability to fly. However, as Chinua Achebe astutely notes, "He always has to combine [spiritual] ability with honest-to-God work."[2] Tutuola's narrative is centered on the Father of the Gods's search for his dead palm-wine tapster and the spiritual, physical, and mental energies required to find him. In addition to revisiting various Yoruba oratures, *The Palm-Wine Drinkard* includes a revision of the tale of the marriage of the maiden and the exotic marketman. In fact, after Father of the Gods rescues the maiden, she marries him and joins him in his search for his dead palm-wine tapster. It is during their quest that the "harmonious dualism" of male and female principles is revealed as the couple shares in and fully plumbs the meaning of holistic and cooperative "work and play."[3]

The couple's cooperative existential ethos is central to the novel and the key to the pair's survival and success. For example, when they come to a large river with no way to ford it, Father of the Gods cuts down and carves a tree into a paddle and uses a "juju" to change himself into a canoe. His wife acts as ferrywoman. Charging three pence for adults and half of that for children, the couple does not just cross the river but works cooperatively to earn money; they spend one month ferrying persons across the river. As did Kofi Ako, Father of the Gods clearly understands the spiritual worth of his partner. Anowa is a figurative charm for her husband, Kofi Ako, but the wife of Father of the Gods literally becomes her husband's mojo when he transforms her into a doll for protection and mobility (108).

The couple has no squabbles about gender roles or gender-based duties. They work together to solve spiritual, physical, and metaphysical issues. If one member of the pair is stricken with a physical or spiritual ailment, the other becomes an oníṣègun (healer). When the husband is feeling trepidation, the wife lends cryptic words of knowledge and comfort. After the couple leaves the kind and generous Yéwà-like Faithful-Mother, they encounter a glamorous woman with a rich red skin tone. The wife muses, "This is not a human-being and she is not a spirit, but what is she?" As the couple follows the Red-lady to the Red-town, the wife prognosticates that what she and her husband are about to experience "is only fear for the heart but not dangerous to the heart" (73). Upon arrival in Red-town, the couple meets Red-king, who asks which member of the couple would sacrifice him or herself for the town's ritual. The wife cryptically tells her husband that the sacrifice "would be a brief loss of woman, but a shorter separation of man from lover." Her husband is confounded: "I did not understand the meaning of her words, because she was talking with parables or as a foreteller" (78). Once he successfully outmaneuvers the beasts waiting to devour him, he can fully appreciate the weight of his wife's prognostications. In a powerful series of spiritual, material, philosophical, and economic conflicts and resolutions, the wife's statements are revealed to be riddles that the husband must solve with her through experience.

It is significant that The Father of the Gods Who Can Do Anything in the World is partnered with a spouse whose power is the perfect balance and complement to his own. What is even more impressive is the Father of the Gods' lack of chest-thumping chauvinism and sneering recourse to unearned privilege. Tutuola created a couple that is effortlessly and organically harmonious. And rather than being motivated by a need to critique social gender bias, one gets the impression that Tutuola's gender dialectics are rooted in an appreciation of his social reality.

Tutuola's depictions of gender àṣùwàdà stand nearly alone in the literary world. Many works of Africana literature depict great animosity and struggle between the sexes. The struggle is rarely one of women attempting to regain lost power, for their inherent biological, spiritual, and political power cannot be usurped. Conflict often results when Africana men attempt to use culturally created concepts—ideology, chauvinism, sexism, Europhallogocentrics—to suppress Àjẹ́ politically and oppress women socially. Men's refusal to respect women's quests for personal actualization and soul-expansion also causes imbalance. As is evident in the relationship of Anowa and Kofi Ako, gender imbalance impacts personal, domestic, political, social, and romantic arenas. And as the discussion turns to male-female domestic relations, it becomes apparent that in the struggle of wills, romantic love may be phenomenal, but it is not a strong enough force to deter the evolutionary path of Àjẹ́.

ZORA AND ỌYA'S CURVILINEAR ARCHITEXTS

Zora Neale Hurston's great respect for and deep personal and professional relationship with Voodoo and Hoodoo are well known. Steeped from birth in the tenets and rituals of African American Hoodoo, Hurston was initiated into approximately twenty different Hoodoo/ Voodoo sects in America and studied traditional African spiritual systems in Haiti, Jamaica, the Bahamas, and Honduras. While it is clear that Hurston was a devoted scholar-practitioner of Africana spiritual systems, little mention has been made of Òrìṣà Ọya's influence on Hurston's life and art. That few scholars have made this connection is not surprising because Ọya's impact on Hurston, like her influence in the African American ethos, is ubiquitous but veiled.

The most obvious meeting between woman and Deity is recorded by Hurston in *Mules and Men* and her autobiography *Dust Tracks on a Road*. In 1927, Hurston met Luke Turner (aka Samuel Thompson[5]), the nephew of the legendary Marie Leveau. Turner and "other members of the college of hoodoo doctors" initiated Hurston into their sect. While in the seeking state of initiation, Hurston found herself in the spiritual company of Rebecca Jackson. Hurston saw herself striding "across the heavens with lightning flashing from under my feet, and grumbling thunder following in my wake.... I was to walk with the storm and hold my power, and get my answers to life and things in storms."[6] Turner named Hurston's *orí* (head, destiny): "I see her conquering and accomplishing with the lightning and making her road with thunder. She shall be called the Rain-Bringer."[7] He also painted a yellow and red lightning bolt down Hurston's back—the symbolic accompaniment to the cosmic revelation.

Turner recognizes Hurston as a child of Ọya. Ọya is the original Rain-Bringer. As Áájálayé, the Winds of the World, her awesome force is manifest in gale winds, tornadoes, hurricanes, and, less dramatically though more important, in the breath that sustains life and is essential to speech. Ọya is the brilliant lightning bolt, and she is found "making her road with thunder": Her lightning opens the path for her warrior-complement husband, Ṣàngó, Òrìṣà of Thunder, War, and Justice, and together they smite the wicked. Mother of Nine and guardian of the cemetery and ancestors, Ọya represents unlimited potential for humanospiritual development. She is an essential, ubiquitous, and ambiguous Àjẹ́; and while they are often overlooked, her manifestations are legion and they impact life and literature in compelling ways.

When Hurston was studying in New Orleans, Ọya marked her, and Hurston's flesh became the Deity's text. Through the lightning in her pen, Hurston returns the favor with *Their Eyes Were Watching God* (*Their Eyes*) and Janie Crawford, whose life-text is so similar to Ọya's it could be considered a contemporary revision. To reveal the similarities between Ọya and Janie, I include below, with your indulgence, a summary of a lesser-known biography of Ọya included in C. L. Adeoye's *Ìgbàgbọ́ àti Ẹ̀sìn Yorùbá* (*Yoruba Belief and Religion*).

Ọya's name in the cosmos and initially on earth was Àràká. She was married to Ògún while in heaven, and they were a highly honored couple. Both thought their union would continue on earth, but when

Àràká joined Ògún on earth, she was a young, energetic, and vibrant woman, whereas Ògún was old and taciturn. Grimy and sweaty from working at his forge all day, the Òrìṣà of Iron was aesthetically unappealing to the vivacious Àràká. Furthermore, her attachment to her "spiritual group" (or Ẹgbẹ́ Àjẹ́) was strong. She regularly sojourned with them, and because Ògún was not an initiate, she kept her whereabouts and actions secret from him; in fact, she would leave home furtively and return unceremoniously. Enraged at Àràká's independence, Ògún beat her. However, she did not invoke her deadly force, she simply left him.

After leaving Ògún, Àràká married Ṣàngó, who was both younger than Ògún and more aesthetically appealing, with flashy clothes, long braided hair, and jeweled ornamentation. Ṣàngó was also a renowned ruler and fearsome warrior. While both parties benefited from the compounded power of their union, the idea of his wife leaving furtively for undisclosed reasons did not sit well with the ruler of the Oyo Empire. For the second time, Àràká found domesticity and romantic love threatening her personal and spiritual needs. She left Ṣàngó, choosing to feed her spirit rather than his ego.

The divorce from Ṣàngó allowed Àràká the freedom to sojourn with Ẹgbẹ́ Àjẹ́ at her will and whim. The Àjẹ́ honored her with an Egúngún (ancestral) shroud that allowed her to take the form of a buffalo. Àràká kept her shroud at the base of an *ọbobọ* tree in a large *ọgán* (anthill). These were Àràká's portals to the spiritual realm. The shroud was used to galvanize and magnify her Àjẹ́. Unbeknown to Àràká, her spiritual portals were near the place Olúkòsì Ẹ̀pẹ́ set his traps. One day, while the hunter was furtively awaiting game,

> He saw a strange woman beneath the tree where he was hiding. . . . To his surprise, the woman threw her head-tie on the ground. Then she pulled a shroud from the base of the tree. The woman brought forth the dress of Egúngún [the Ancestors], and she was wearing it in the middle of the forest. . . . When she came to a large anthill, she removed the shroud, placed it inside the anthill, and continued moving into the forest where she joined her spiritual group. This frightened Olúkòsì Ẹ̀pẹ́. But because he was a great hunter he tried to contain his fear.[8]

Although Olúkòsì Ẹ̀pẹ́ was terrified by Àràká's powers, he removed her shroud from the anthill and took it home with him. The next day, when Àràká went to meet her group, she did not find her shroud, but she saw the tracks of the person who had taken it. She followed the footprints and met Olúkòsì Ẹ̀pẹ́. On the condition that he not reveal her secret to anyone, she became his wife, bore her noted nine children, and lived in harmony with him, his first wife, and his mother. Having witnessed Àràká's secret, Olúkòsì Èpè felt comfortable discussing his spiritual powers with her. Hunters are said to have many aspects of Àjé and access to a vast repertoire of spiritual skills, including shape-shifting.[9] Olúkòsì Èpé revealed that if he were in danger he could transform himself into ògán, eṣinṣin (a fly), or ìrò (a substance akin to dew or mist). Before he could divulge the details of ìrò, his mother interrupted and told him to never reveal all his secrets to a woman.[10]

The peace of Olúkòsì Èpé's home was shattered one day when his wives and mother argued vehemently over a female ram. During the argument, Olúkòsì Èpé's first wife and his mother, who had discovered that Àràká was a spirit-woman-buffalo, taunted and mocked her. Àràká was so devastated that her secret had been revealed and used to ridicule her that she took her shroud from the ceiling, softened it with her tears, and became the buffalo. After killing her antagonizers and their children, she went to find and kill Olúkòsì Èpé for revealing her secret. When she caught him, he transformed himself into ìrò and disappeared from sight. Àràká returned to the house, regained her human form, and gave her nine children her shroud and horns so they and Olúkòsì Èpé could worship her. From this point, Àràká would be known as Ọya, Àlàye, the Owner of the World or the Living One.[11]

Àjé is a force of reciprocity and social harmony, and these concepts are important to Ọya's life, relationships, and transformation. For example, rather than continue the path of destruction, Àràká and Olúkòsì Èpé reach a cosmic compromise: He was not at fault, and he was not punished. And after disciplining the appropriate bodies, Àràká transcends her terrestrial life and works and returns to the cosmos and a newly prepared space of immortal honor. Àràká becomes the first Egúngún (Ancestor) worshipped on Earth, and her husband is left to institute her worship. As the source of the argument that resulted in Ọya's deification, the female ram is honored and never eaten by devotees of Ọya. Àràká-Ọya's transformational power is cyclic and has multiple terrestrial and spiritual implications. It is especially important to note that Ọya ignores patriarchal edicts and chooses holistic personal and spiritual integrity over the nebulous concept of romantic love; Àjé validates her choice and rewards her with immortality.

Like Àràká-Ọya, Janie Crawford is a seeking woman. She dreams of being in a relationship with a man whose force and character complement her own, and, as the narrator of *Their Eyes* reveals, for women, "the dream is the truth." A pear tree in bloom symbolizes Janie, and although it is fervently fertilized by bees, the pear tree under which Janie envisions her truth is more than a sensual metaphor—it represents the cosmic tree of life. Rachel Stein notes that, as an avatar of profound significance in Africana spiritual systems, "The tree, like the waterfall, heals and re-affirms the black bodies so despised by the colonial order. . . . The tree . . . is a central Voodoo symbol and often signifies the sexual and spiritual union of the primary male and female deities."[12] Àràká had her galvanizing ọ̀bobọ̀ tree to charge her spiritual implements, and as the bees pollinate the tree, so too does the tree stimulate and prepare Janie for a cosmic, social, and sexual awakening. Additionally, both women encounter powerful male forces at their trees of life. However, unlike Àràká with Olúkòsì Ẹ̀pẹ́, Janie is not allowed to unite with her chosen male principle.

Their Eyes is set in the late 1800s and mid-1900s, when African American women were battling the oppressive hydra of neo-enslavement, racism, sexism, and serial rape. Caucasian men and women created and promulgated the myth of the sexually promiscuous and insatiable Africana woman to shield the fact that they had made the African American woman the most vulnerable and the most raped figure in the world. Janie's mother, Leafy, is evidence of this and so is Janie's grandmother, Nanny.

Hurston offers a compelling description of Nanny. She likens her to "the standing roots of some old tree that had been torn away by storm. Foundation of ancient power that no longer mattered."[13] Hurston may describe Nanny's Àjẹ́ as obsolete, but it is effective and protective. When Nanny catches Janie kissing Johnny Taylor under the pear tree, she is witnessing a logical and elemental biological force that, in a heinous American society, can leave her progeny irreparably broken.

Nanny uses orature to educate Janie about realities of Africana womanhood and American oppression:

> Honey, de white man is de ruler of everything as fur as Ah been able to find out. Maybe it's some place way off in de ocean where de black man is in power, but we don't know nothin' but what we see. So de white man throw down de load and tell de nigger man tuh pick it up. He pick it up because he have to, but he don't tote it. He hand it to his womenfolks. De nigger woman is de mule uh de world so fur as Ah can see. (14)

What Nanny describes as a visually verifiable truth is actually a text so often told it has come to take on the *appearance* of reality for the Africana woman. No longer one with the buffalo, one of the strongest forces in the forest, a symbol of spiritual transcendence and the unfathomable bounty of Àjẹ́, the displaced daughters of Ọya became the denigrated "mule[s] uh de world." However, the ìtàn of the woman-who-would-be-mule has not so completely obfuscated Nanny's vision that she is unable to draft her own living text for her progeny and her self.

She tells Janie of her personal ìtàn and her dream of an intergenerational revival of Àjẹ́:

> Ah wanted to preach a great sermon about colored women sittin' on high, but they wasn't no pulpit for me. Freedom found me wid a baby daughter in mah arms, so Ah said Ah'd take a broom and a cook-pot and throw up a highway through de wilderness for her. *She would expound on what Ah felt.* But somehow she got lost offa de highway and next thing Ah knowed here you was in de world. So whilst Ah was tendin' you of nights Ah said *Ah'd save de text for you.* (15–16, italics added)

Nanny envisioned herself as the leader of a neo-Ẹgbẹ́ Àjẹ́ and sharing Ọ̀rọ̀ and Àjẹ́ with her sisters, but extenuating circumstances forced her to direct her power inside the home as opposed to outside in the community. Using the tools of Earth Mothers, Odù's pot and Nana Bùrúkù's broom, Nanny cleared a path through the world for her daughter, Leafy. Attesting to the malleability of Àjẹ́, Nanny transformed her material and textual Àjẹ́ in even more practical ways when Leafy was raped and thrown off the path. The sermon she sought to deliver to her sisters becomes Janie's legacy, her personal text of potential power. However, having experienced the disintegration of her and her daughter's dreams through rape, Nanny errs on the side of caution and revises her text. The final alteration yields not a gift of holistic creation but one of immediate destruction. Having prearranged the union (in the African tradition, perhaps), Nanny marries Janie to Logan Killicks.

Killicks strongly resembles Àràká's first husband. Like Ògún, Killicks is uncommunicative, uncouth, and harsh. He does not bathe regularly, and he "look like some old skullhead in de grave yard." What makes Killicks appealing to Nanny is his sixty acres of land and relative prosperity. She thinks marrying Janie to a father figure will provide her progeny with stability and allow her to die in peace. However, she realizes she has stunted Janie's development. Praying over her miscalculation, Nanny seeks refuge in the "basin in the mind where words float around on thought and thought on sound and sight. Then there is a depth of thought untouched by words, and deeper still a gulf of formless feelings untouched by thought. Nanny entered this infinity of conscious pain again on her old knees" (23). Like the enslaved ancestors who gathered around the pot of water and invoked the Spirits, Nanny kneels in front of her own pot of rememory and laments the fact that the only protection she can offer Janie is destructive. Nanny weakens physically and spiritually and is driven to the grave by generations of alteration and deferral of the texts, lives, and dreams of herself, Leafy, and now Janie.

Janie soon learns what Nanny experienced—that it is not marriage, menstruation, sexual intercourse, or love that makes the Africana female a woman but the death of her dream (24). Killicks is prepared to fully enmesh Janie in a perverted concept of womanhood. He even purchases an actual mule for the "mule uh de world," so that she can plow alongside him.

Ọya glories in her ability to cut her own path through any wilderness and to level any obstacle—indeed, that is the meaning and orí of "Ọya." Janie is not aware of her inherent gifts of Àjẹ́ or autonomy, so she is delighted to be led from Killicks' cottage of constriction by a shining neo-Ṣàngó. Joe Starks is "citified, stylish," and "dazzling," with his rakishly tilted hat and silk sleeveholders. When Janie sees him strutting down the road, she sees the same brilliant, expansive road to freedom that Àràká thought she had found in Ṣàngó. Unlike Killicks, who sows and reaps monotonously on his cherished land, Starks represents mobility, action, prosperity, and the ever-distant horizon.

When the Ògúnian Killicks returns home to bridle his mule, Janie bucks at him verbally, and he threatens to take his axe and kill her, as a master of iron would. At this point, the first hint of Àjẹ́'s cosmic knowledge, duality, and power surface in Janie: "She turned wrong-side out just standing there and feeling. When the throbbing calmed a little she gave Logan's speech a hard thought and placed it beside other things she had seen and heard" (30–31). Àjẹ́ rínú ròde: They see the inside, they see the outside. The outside relates to the material realm; the inside to the spiritual realm and the internal organs that can be attacked if necessary. The phrase arínú ròde also intimates a power of perception that includes foresight of thought and action. Reminiscent of Àràká's silent judgment of Ògún, Janie measures the weight of Killicks's threats and finds insecurity and impotence in the balance. She makes no physical strike against Killicks because, like Àràká knew, her absence is punishment enough.

Joe (also Jody) Starks and Janie marry and move to Eatonville, an all-Black town, and Starks takes the fledgling community by storm. He demands to see the mayor; and when the community members declare that they govern themselves, Starks begins molding the town in such a way that he is the only logical choice for mayor. He also becomes postmaster, landowner, and sole shopkeeper. Ṣàngó was the Aláàfin (King) of the Oyo Empire; Starks becomes the "Little Emperor" of Eatonville. Citizens describe Starks as "uh whirlwind among breezes," "he's de wind and we's de grass. We bend whichever way he blows" (46). Logically, his favorite expression is "I god almighty!"

The antithesis of Àràká, who with a toss of her headtie could become spirit, buffalo, or woman, free to move when, where, and how she desires, Janie is confined to the store: Her hair and ability to self-actualize are bound under her scarves. Oya embodied the whirlwind, surpassed Ṣàngó in warring, equaled him in ruling, and refused to bow before patriarchal decrees. Conversely, Janie is Joe's silent subordinate. Rather than moving closer to her truth, Janie occupies the same position with Joe that she did with Logan; the only change is in scenery and terminology. Killicks considered Janie a mule that had "no particular place" except where he needed its labor; Starks turns Janie into an elegant window dressing whose "place is in de home." Janie's horizon has gone from being marred by dead-end domesticity with Killicks to being clouded by Starks's pseudo-presidential profile.

The depth of Janie's dilemma is even more poignant when juxtaposed, as it is textually, to the life, liberation, and death of Matt Boner's yellow mule. Unlike the stately buffalo, Bonner's mule is ritually underfed and brutalized and, as a result, is fractious and ornery. Very much enslaved by Bonner, the mule occasionally frees itself and goes on rampages through town. The community engages in "mule-baiting" and a bit of Bonner-baiting to pass the time. Janie says nothing and even enjoys the fun until the men physically abuse the animal. When Janie shows her disgust at men who antagonize an old mule, Starks buys the animal from Bonner and frees it. While the town applauds Starks's move, Janie laces appreciation with signification:

> Jody, dat wuz uh mighty fine thing fuh yuh tuh do. 'Tain' everybody would have thought of it, 'cause it ain't no everyday thought. Freein' dat mule makes uh mighty big man outa you. Something like George Washington and Lincoln. Abraham Lincoln, he had the whole United States tuh rule so he freed de Negroes. You got uh whole town so you freed uh mule. Yuh have tuh have power tuh free things and dat makes you lak uh king uh something. (55)

Because Janie has not spoken freely in public before, her words are taken at face value. The community marvels at her oratorical power without hearing the signification in every line. Despite his possessions and power, Janie makes it clear that Eatonville's "Little Emperor" is actually small-time and petty: He frees a mule, but as an oppressor would, he keeps the human being enslaved. While Janie languishes in a brass prison of Starks's design, the mule becomes fat from the hands of the community; it becomes healthy, stately, more like the Oya's buffalo. The mule gains so much respect that when it dies the entire community, save Janie, attends its "dragging out." Freed first through ego-economics and then in death, the mule enjoys liberty on multiple levels while "de mule of de world" remains bridled.

There are important similarities in the relationships of Janie and Jody and Kofi Ako and Anowa. Like Kofi Ako, Starks is a member of the "disparate breed" that adorns itself in material trappings and props itself up on the spirits of subjugated human beings. Janie, as Joe's trophy wife and prized possession, brings to mind Anowa's becoming Kofi Ako's humanospiritual mojo. Additionally, it appears that like Kofi Ako, Starks attains power at the expense of his "birth-seeds." As the narrator of *Their Eyes* reveals, "The spirit of the marriage left the bedroom and took to living in the parlor" (67), and neither couple bears a child.

Outwardly, Janie resigns herself to a life of external graces for Joe's sake, but just as Àjẹ́ are *abáàra méjì,* the ones with two bodies, Janie's second self, her inside, frolics freely. Inside, pear trees bloom and a whole man waits. However, when Starks slaps her because of a poorly cooked meal, Janie enters her inside for critical evaluation:

> She stood where he left her for unmeasured time and thought. She stood there until something fell off the shelf inside her. Then she went inside to see what it was. It was her image of Jody tumbled down and shattered. But looking at it she saw that it never was the flesh and blood figure of her dreams. Just something she had grabbed up to drape her dreams over. (68)

Janie realizes, "She had an *inside* and an *outside* now and suddenly she knew how not to mix them" (68, italics added). A deeper version of the same process of spiritual-realization that overtook Janie after Killicks threatens her occurs when Starks slaps her. The comprehension of her duality and her naming that phenomenon, albeit subtly, in terms of Àjẹ́, is essential to the process of self-realization that precedes self-actualization.

Janie's spiritual vision is not restricted to herself; she also witnesses her husband's thoughts, fears, and desires:

> For the first time she could see a man's head naked of its skull. Saw the cunning thoughts race in and out through the caves and promontories of his mind long before they darted out of the tunnel of his mouth. She saw he was hurting inside so she let it pass without talking. She just measured out a little time for him and set it aside to wait. (73)

Janie's inner vision is far deeper than marital sensitivity. Similar to Àjẹ́, Janie's ability to *rínú ròde* (see the inside and the outside) includes seeing and knowing the inside of the other. Most important, when Joe slaps Janie, he awakens a lethal aspect of Àjẹ́, the inner Spirit Bird. The orin Àjẹ́ warns, "I have a bird inside / I have a bird outside / Give me my proper respect." Having been physically abused and disrespected, Janie's inner bird begins its journey outside in search of retribution.

After listening to the men casually discuss the need to beat, break, and, if necessary, kill their wives, Janie offers them her cosmic insight:

> Sometimes God gits familiar wid us womenfolks too and talks His inside business. He told me how surprised He was 'bout y'all turning out so smart after Him makin' yuh different, and how surprised y'all is goin' tuh be if you ever find out you don't know half as much 'bout us as you think you do. It's easy to make yo'self out God Almighty when you ain't got nothin' tuh strain against but women and chickens. (70–71)

As Henry Louis Gates, Jr., notes in *The Signifying Monkey,* "Janie reveals God's 'inside business' to the superficial store-talkers, warning all who can hear her voice that a 'surprise' lay in waiting for those who see only appearances and never penetrate to the tenor of things."[14]

In addition to giving an encoded warning about impending acts of Àjẹ́, it appears that Janie is questioning not only patriarchal supremacy but also the supposition that God is male: Why else would "He" be surprised that men, in being made different from women, turned out "so smart"? Unlike men who use gender to claim connection to the divine and speak for Ole Maker, Janie and God's relationship is apparently as intimate as that of Ọ̀sun and Olódùmarè. Apparently, she and those of her gender need not use "God" for verbal emphasis because they embody the divine.

Janie's relationship with Joe parallels her relationship with God in other intriguing ways. She has knowledge of both entities' "inside business," and she knows that the existence of both entities is predicated upon her Ọ̀rọ̀. First she opens her mouth to share God's truths; later she comes to the following conclusion about Joe, "Maybe he ain't nothin' . . . *but he is something in my mouth*" (72, italics added). Janie know realizes that her Ọ̀rọ̀ can bolster, empower, revivify, or kill. Janie is even careful with the force of her thoughts and doesn't disclose to herself the "something" that Joe actually is. It is as if Janie is aware that even deeply pondering Jody's truth could be sufficient to bring about his death.

Even with enlightenment and burgeoning power ripening within her, Janie practices the discretion of Àjẹ́ and she lets the "inside" dictate her external actions: "She saw he was hurting inside so she let it pass without talking" (73). It is ironic that when Janie is physically at her nadir, her spiritual perspicacity is on the rise. Just as she *chose* to signify during the mule-freeing, Janie *chose* the path of reticence after she'd been assaulted. That she recognizes and uses her power when and how she sees fit is as important as the fact that she begins recognizing and appreciating her duality and power during her marriage to Killicks.

Janie gives her husband a reprieve of "measured" time, and he spends it like found money. During one of the busy and convivial hours when the store is filled with patrons, he decides to publicly humiliate his wife: "I god amighty! A woman stay round uh store till she get old as Methusalem and still can't cut a little thing like a plug of tobacco! Don't stand dere rollin' yo' pop eyes at me wid yo' rump hangin' nearly to yo' knees!" (74). Although couched in the "harmless" dozens contest that involves playful verbal abuse, Joe's insults are described by the narrator as being as powerful as Janie's thoughts: "It was like somebody snatched off part of a woman's clothes while she wasn't looking and the streets were crowded."

Having been stripped and displayed for public inspection, Janie decides it is time to return the favor. Janie, however, is not playing a game. When she calls out Starks the second time, she employs what the Yoruba would call *aásàn,* the power to curse and drive insane:

> Naw, Ah ain't no young gal no mo' but den Ah ain't no old woman either. Ah reckon Ah looks mah age too. But Ah'm uh woman every inch of me, and Ah know it. Dat's uh whole lot more'n *you* kin say. You big-bellies round here and put out a lot of brag, but 'tain't nothin' to it but yo' big voice. Humph! Talkin' 'bout *me* lookin' old! When you pull down yo' britches, you look like de change uh life. (75, italics in original)

Janie opens her mouth and unleashes Oya's wind of destruction. Janie strips away Joe's regal façade and reveals her husband to be a flabby hermaphrodite struggling through menopause. Joe attempts to reclaim his masculinity by hitting Janie, but his action costs him the dozens battle and his life.

When Starks falls ill with kidney failure, he accuses Janie of being a "witch" and conjuring his food. The more astute township attributes Starks's illness to Janie's Ọ̀rọ̀: "It's been singin' round here ever since de big fuss in de store dat Joe was 'fixed' and you wuz de one dat did it" (78). Janie has not consciously Hoodooed Starks; she has simply named his inside and outside. But with words flowing from a spiritual reservoir of Àjẹ́, when she names his void, she unconsciously curses his destiny.

Janie's act has any number of Yoruba referents. In "The Performance of Yorùbá Oral Poetry," Oyin Ogunba describes the myriad forms and uses of Yoruba incantatory poetry. In addition to effectively summoning and invoking the spiritual world to bless the community, the cantor can also use her or his Ọ̀rọ̀ to verbally-*cum*-psychically destroy an adversary. The technique involves the

> piling up of attributes in mounting speed building up to a crescendo. . . . The idea is that the reciter of incantation must overawe his opponent not only by sheer eloquence but also by the "multitude" of examples called up, each one delivered a shade faster than the preceding one. . . . The sum-total of this is that the cantor in this medium tries to destroy the psychological balance of the adversary and if the latter is impressionable. . . . He may indeed become a victim of the "magic" in the utterances.[15]

Tejumola Olaniyan also finds Yoruba methodology in Janie's speech: "What Janie has just done is to speak a 'kengbe oro' to Joe. Kengbe oro . . . is a speech with profound metaphorical depth, complex multiple significations and deep, fearful implications."[16] From this perspective, the phrase "change uh life" is on the outside a joke about a man in menopause, but on the inside it is a man's death sentence. Furthermore, while Starks recognizes the power of Janie's *kèngbe Ọ̀rọ̀*, which, paraphrasing Ogunba, he calls "tearin down talk," he refuses to admit that his outside actions (verbal and physical) have internal (kidney failure) and eternal (death) consequences.

Olúkòsì Ẹpẹ́ witnessed Àràká hurl her headtie to the ground to catalyze her Àjẹ́. After Starks's death, Janie burns all her headties. Free of domestic scarves and patriarchal bridles, Janie's inner paradise coalesces with the outside world, and she meets Verigible Woods, also known as Tea Cake.

Approximately fifteen years her junior, Tea Cake is Johnny Taylor revisited; he is Janie's Olúkòsì Ẹpẹ́. The pair leaves pseudo-bourgeois Eatonville and heads for the agrarian proletarian "muck" of the Florida Everglades. Although they work side by side, planting and harvesting for the gain of an unseen Caucasian landowner, with her inheritance and his gambling "hands," Janie and Tea Cake actually need not work at all.[17] Leisure, relative wealth, and passion motivate Janie and Tea Cake to form a harmonious gender-balanced union, and they go in search of a community that will welcome them.

The fertile muck of the Florida Everglades foments the growth of their union. According to Claire Crabtree, "In the environment of the migrant camp, life is reduced to the simple functions of work and play. Play in fact is a part of the work routine."[18] Crabtree's assessment of the Woods's life on the muck is similar to Achebe's analysis of the protagonists of *The Palm-Wine Drinkard*. Tutuola's couple is perhaps the most perfectly balanced pair in Africana literature. But with Tea Cake making a gambling mojo from nine of Janie's hairs (120) and the two of them bending over rows of beans and sharing in domestic chores and communal joy, Hurston's couple matches the balance of Tutuola's for a while. However, unlike Tutuola's couple, Janie and Tea Cake are not united against external forces, and one of the most petty but problematic issues in the Africana community easily creates dissension for them.

Mrs. Turner, a pale African American who is attracted to Janie's "Caucasian characteristics," suggests that she and Janie "class off" from the richly pigmented—including and especially Tea Cake. Turner's dream of instituting a color caste system on the muck would reach its apex if Janie would leave Tea Cake for her equally blanched brother who bears the dubious glory of "dead straight" hair. Janie is uninterested in all Turner proposes because she is incapable of seeing beauty in any form or visage other than Tea Cake's. However, rather than relax in Janie's devotion, when Turner's brother comes to town, "Tea Cake had a brainstorm. Before the week was over he had whipped Janie. Not because her behavior justified his jealousy, but it relieved that awful fear inside him. Being able to whip her reassured him of possession" (140). Although Janie and Tea Cake pet and coo over one another as her bruises heal, like Starks, Tea Cake has crossed a line from whence there is no return.

Tea Cake's physical abuse of Janie and her reaction to it have been the subject of much debate. Mary Helen Washington interpreted the incident as an "uncritical depiction of violence toward women."[19] From a Western point of view this is correct. Janie does not seek out a Western justice system (which may very well delight in her tragedy), she does not turn to a girlfriend and share her woes, she does not turn violently upon Tea Cake, and she does not leave him. Janie doesn't seek out any Western model of redress. As when Starks slaps her, she adheres to the model of an Àjẹ́, who when offended will "just look at you and beg you. Then some time later another thing will happen."[20] In the African ethos, justice, as human rights, cannot be doled out by government agencies.[21] Justice is Janie's birthright and Àjẹ́ ensures she will have it.

The cosmic forces of reciprocity at work in Janie and Tea Cake's relationship are alluded to in *Their Eyes,* as the narrator distinguishes between the rituals that appease religious constructs and the mandates of Àjẹ́, The Gods of Society, who are often described as the very embodiment of justice:

> All gods who receive homage are cruel. All gods dispense suffering without reason. Otherwise they would not be worshipped. Through indiscriminate suffering men know fear and fear is the most divine emotion. It is the stones for altars and the beginning of wisdom. Half gods are worshipped in wine and flowers. Real gods require blood. (138–139)

A truthful acknowledgment of the Gods to whom Hurston refers is important. She wrote *Their Eyes* while healing from a tumultuous relationship and while researching Voodoo in Haiti: The Loa were swirling through and about her. She even had a terrifying physical experience that may have been a warning from a Petro (fire, destructive) Loa.[22] Just as *Their Eyes* confounds the concept of fiction, providing Hurston with the means to better understand her husbands and her father, her spiritual studies went far beyond academic forays: Hurston knows personally the "real gods" to whom she refers. And if the eyes of her loving couple and their friend are "watching God" when the hurricane descends, the eye of the hurricane that watches Janie and Tea Cake belongs to Ọya.

Ọya's primary symbols are the tornado and the hurricane, and her praisename is Áàjálayé, the Winds of the World. Elucidating the various degrees of Ọya's spiritual and physical power, Luisah Teish states that Ọya "brings about sudden structural change in people and things,"[23] and John Mason contends that Ọya's "wrath [is] so devastating that it must be absolutely avoided."[24] As a hurricane approaches the muck, all humans and animals flee. Trusting the Caucasian planters, Tea Cake, Janie, and a few of their friends remain behind. The couple's decision to ride out and bear witness to Ọya's wrath is as central to the novel as the title implies. And as Hurston gives Òrìṣà Ọya room to "work and play," the Deity of Transformation enters the novel to ensure retribution and reciprocity, collect her debt of blood from Tea Cake, and facilitate Janie's evolution.

Just as Ọya inscribed her truth on Hurston's back, she marks Tea Cake in such a way that Janie might see his inner truth and later realize her limitless potential. When Janie is submerged in rushing floodwaters, she encounters a cow that is being ridden by a massive dog. Tea Cake tells her to grab the cow's tail and drift to safety. When she does, she adds an extra burden to the cow. Sensing a threat on its privileged (albeit unearned) position, the dog turns to attack Janie. Tea Cake intervenes and kills the beast, but not before it "managed to bite Tea Cake high up on his cheek-bone once" (157). The cow's relationship to the dog provides a visual complement to Nanny's philosophy. As another manifestation of "de mule uh de world," it follows that as the cow struggles resolutely and methodically to make her own path through the storm (of life), a mad dog has jumped on her back for a free ride. This dog, a carrier of rabies, symbolizes Tea Cake's leech-like violent possessiveness of Janie. Tea Cake kills the dog, but his canine twin marks him, and the position of the bite mirrors the bruises he strategically placed on Janie. Janie signified on Starks and verbally marked him; stepping in to assist her forgiving daughter, Ọya enlists forces to signify on Tea Cake's body and soul.

The Igbo of Eastern Nigeria describe the Ajalagba, in the same manner as African Americans describe haints, as "one who kills by smothering."[25] In the grip of rabies, Tea Cake wakes up screaming, "Something got after me in mah sleep. . . . Tried to choke me tuh death." Thinking it may have been "uh witch ridin,'" Janie uses mustard seed to prevent the ridings from recurring, and she gets a medical doctor to tend to Tea Cake. However, Tea Cake is being ridden by the inner bird that soars to avenge Janie's transgressors.

Upon realizing that her lover will die from rabies and may kill her too, Janie turns to God: "Her arms went up in a desperate supplication for a minute. It wasn't exactly pleading, it was asking questions. The sky stayed hard looking and quiet so she went inside the house. God would do less than He had in His heart" (169). Janie does not fully comprehend the difference between the God of wine and flowers and the Gods of Àjẹ́. The latter oversee harmonization, gender balance, and retributive justice; their eyes see all, and their dispensation of justice is swift. Ẹdan has summoned Tea Cake's skull for a conference, and, unable to justify his infringement, Tea Cake is welcomed into Odù's pot.

Janie and Àràká were both threatened three times by romantic love, but both had a spiritual inheritance rich enough to ensure their survival and evolution. Àràká traveled from the cosmos to the earth and back, magnifying her divinity with each relationship. She refused to allow the fragility of the male ego to imperil her soul-expanding sojourns with her "spiritual group." She used her Àjẹ́ to ensure herself freedom from domestic/patriarchal oppression and attain full transcendence. Janie's life is in many ways a journey in and to and into herself. The equivalent of Àràká's "spiritual group" is Janie's "inside," and she constantly travels to and nourishes the space where her Àjẹ́ resides. Her Àjẹ́ responds with profound emotional, spiritual, and psychological assistance and answers each abuse given Janie. After his threat, Killicks is left to continue his life of social death. Starks's kidneys fail, filling his body with offal. Tea Cake is marked, bitten, and smothered by the embodiment of the figurative dog that slapped Janie's jaw. And like Hurston's pen-gripping fingers, Janie's ability to fully signify, name, and claim (for) herself is evident in the rifle's report that is born of her trigger-pulling finger. After slaying the beast in her lover, Janie commiserates with Tea Cake's truest soul "and wept and thanked him wordlessly for giving her the chance for loving service" (175). In the manner of Olúkòsì Èpẹ́, and in the most paradoxical of ways, Tea Cake gives Janie the gifts of self-love, self-actualization, and ultimate vindication. And while much ado has been made about the trial in *Their Eyes*, the Western "justice" system's formalities and pronouncements are less than irrelevant.

To better understand Janie Woods's participation, or lack thereof, in her trial, we need only turn to the book of "John," for Hurston establishes the foundation for Janie's vindication, discernment, and political discretion with *Jonah's Gourd Vine*. Hurston's first novel explores the lives, loves, and cosmic struggles of a couple based loosely on her parents and focuses on the father. In the novel, John Pearson refuses to defend himself at his divorce trial or have his confidants divulge certain truths before the court because American justice would only find amusement in the intricacies of Africana love, life, and Àjẹ́. Hurston, as observant narrator, captures the mood of the court perfectly: "Now listen close. You're going to hear something rich. These niggers."[26] The eloquent John practices silence because, "Dey's some strings on our harp fuh us tuh play on and sing all tuh ourselves."[27] Similarly, if Janie doesn't feel the need to plead to God on behalf of herself or Tea Cake, she has no reason to beg for the mercy of people who have less power than any deity and who know nothing about her or her man. Janie embraces her vindication when she holds and thanks a dying Tea Cake, who had already been sentenced. So while she takes the stand, she has no need to beg, explain, or weep; the most meaningful trial in the most important of courts had already occurred.[28]

In addition to the lessons Janie and Àràká learned by and through males, their soulful ascensions could not have occurred without the problematic assistance of the community. Whether they are well-meaning elders, nosey neighbors, jealous co-wives, or racist judges, community members play major roles in these women's lives and are central to their quests. Jealous of Àràká's unfettered freedom, Olúkòsì Èpẹ́'s mother and first wife signify on Àràká, saying she could "continue her eating and continue her drinking [but her spirit/shroud was] hanging on the ceiling."[29] In actuality, the co-wife and mother sing of their spiritual infertility and cosmic barrenness. The beginning of Janie's life mirrors the end of Àràká's terrestrial existence, as Nanny has hung her spirit so high on the ceiling of the patriarchy that it is nearly unattainable except in the form of a noose (85). However, just as Nanny gave Janie twisted gifts of neo-enslavement, she also gave her *the text,* the implement to clear her own road to freedom. Janie's efforts to loosen the noose and control her own living narrative are indeed successful until Mrs. Turner places a psychological wedge between the pair that Tea Cake tries to remove with his fists.

Following her humiliation, Àràká shifts from buffalo to honored Òrìṣà, leaving her husband and progeny to voice her praise, invoke her force, and articulate her text. *Their Eyes* takes a line from Àràká's verse but "flips the script," so to speak. Tea Cake, the male principle, is removed from the terrestrial sphere. His memory is wholly dependent upon Janie, and, most significant, he is removed from the realm of articulation of events. Janie becomes the "living one" who is left to comprehend and order her existence on her own terms with all forms of spiritual and terrestrial cognition as her determiners. With her choice to live, Janie earns a praisename of Àjẹ́; she becomes Apọkọdoṣù, the One Who Killed Her Husband in Order to Take a Title.[30]

Crabtree finds that "[t]he three marriages and the three communities in which Janie moves represent increasingly wide circles of experience and opportunities for expression of personal choice."[31] This is true for Janie, Hurston, and the author's intended Africana female reading audience. The novel commences with Janie returning to Eatonville after Tea Cake's death. When her "kissing friend" Pheoby comes to her with a gift of sustenance, Janie speaks the orature that becomes the novel. Sitting on the porch near the earth and sharing her text with Pheoby, Janie delivers Nanny's "great sermon about colored women sittin' on high." Her recitation of her life is so powerful that it becomes Òrò, the word actualized and, more important, transferred. Listening to Janie's text, Pheoby critiques her own one-dimensional life and experiences growing pains: "Ah done growed ten feet higher jus' listenin' tuh you, Janie. Ah ain't satisfied wid mahself no mo'" (182–183). But Janie makes it clear that the metaphorical and the metaphysical of the inside must be developed externally. Hearing of Janie's transformation is insufficient; the word and text must be manifest in personal experience, in and with the flesh. Just as Janie "[goes] tuh God" inside and returns rich, whole, and shining, so too must Pheoby and all Hurston's listeners/readers "*go* there" and "*know* there" for themselves, return, and add their texts to Ọya's ìtàn and Nanny's great sermon.

EARTH MOTHERS VERSUS SYNTHETIC FATHERS

The male force has an indispensable role in communal evolution; however, as is evident in life and literature, many men do not accept their position beside women. Some give in to wanderlust. Others may see the powerful woman as a foundation upon which to erect many poorly built polygamous houses of male cyclic enjoyment. Others may seek to enter a quasi-competitive space against Àjẹ́ and, aligning with Eurocentria or subverting their masculine gifts (Oṣó, or male Àjẹ́), attempt to destroy the forces of nature (Àjẹ́).

Such conflicts are brilliantly depicted in Octavia E. Butler's novel *Wild Seed* and Wole Soyinka's drama *Madmen and Specialists*. Although separated by gender, geographic location, and literary genres, Soyinka and Butler have written works that address similar issues. Both their texts are set in Nigeria during the nation's most trying periods. *Wild Seed* opens in Igboland during the 1600s, the height of the theft, murder, and exile of Africans; after a speedy trip through the Atlantic, the characters settle in the United States. *Madmen and Specialists* is set in the late 1960s after the failed Biafran War for secession that resulted in a million deaths. Although set in different eras, these works are motivated by similarly horrific events, and both Butler and Soyinka rely on the force of Àjẹ́ to reinstitute gender balance and lay a foundation for holistic communal growth and development.

The force of Àjẹ́ in *Wild Seed* and *Madmen and Specialists* is most apparent in the female protagonists of these works. In *Madmen and Specialists,* Ìyá Agba, Ìyá Mate, and Si Bero comprise a trinity of Àjẹ́. As the name Àgba (Elder) indicates, Ìyá Agba is the wise and fully evolved elder mother. Although subordinate to Ìyá Agba, Ìyá Mate is, as her name implies, Agba's companion. True to the Yoruba conceptualization of Àjẹ́, these Ìyá are stately, reserved, reticent, and powerful. Si Bero is the young initiate who apprentices herself to the elder Mothers and becomes part of their microcosmic Ẹgbẹ́ Àjẹ́. Ìyá Agba and Mate share all their wisdom and knowledge about the properties of flora with Si Bero, who painstakingly collects the plants and absorbs the knowledge that can bring their entire community physical and spiritual health and a more perfect state of being.

The work of the women of *Madmen and Specialists* is in accord with the historic vocation of Àjẹ́ who are healers par excellence as a result of their ownership of all life forms, including flora. As the daughters of Ìyá-Ayé, Àjẹ́ are obligated to foment the growth and protect and utilize the medicinal and spiritual properties of the Earth Mother's plants. A Gèlèdé praisesong elucidates Àjẹ́'s relationship to flora:

> It is you who make our medicines effective
> Oh Mother, the Primate (Owner) of Birds
> We have never had any leaves of our own before, oh ye elders!
> I affirm that it's you who make our charms effective
> . . . .
> Ye weaver birds, make a crowd round me, oh
> Ye with one hundred and forty Deities[32]

Of great import is that fact that the knowledge Ìyá Agba and Mate share with Si Bero is contingent upon male-female harmonization and unification. Before he left for the war front and was promoted from surgeon to intelligence specialist, Si Bero's brother was an esteemed oníṣègùn. When he enlisted, Dr. Bero asked his sister to collect potent plants for him so that at the war's end, when his services would be needed most, he would be fully prepared to heal his community. In preparation for his return, Si Bero and the Ìyá transplant the most important and potent herbs from the forest to a communal shrine/pharmacy that is overseen by the Ìyá.

Anyanwu of *Wild Seed* is also a life-sustaining healer, but her force is far beyond that of Ìyá Agba. Anyanwu means sun in Igbo, and in addition to being a master Amusu and daughter of Ani, the Igbo Earth Mother, Anyanwu is the product of Igbo mythistory. In an interview with Randall Keenan, Butler discussed her protagonist's progenitor:

> I used in particular, the myth of Atagbusi, who was an Onitsha Ibo woman. She was a shape-shifter who benefited her people while she was alive and when she died a market-gate was named after her, a gate at the Onitsha market [one of the largest markets in Nigeria]. It was believed that whoever used this market-gate was under her protection.[33]

Anyanwu boasts many of Atagbusi's powers and quite a few of her own. Anyanwu is over 300 years old, and she cannot die or be killed. She has the strength to crush stones with her bare hands. She can take the anatomically correct forms of other human beings and animals, such as Royal Pythons, dolphins, and leopards, by simply tasting their flesh.

When Janie's dream died, she learned to sojourn inside herself, visit her "truth," and gain knowledge and insight. African American artist Riua Akinshegun mastered Àjẹ́'s astral mobility and learned to travel deeply into and completely out of her body to cope with chronic pain.[34] By going inside herself, Anyanwu can inspect and alter her body's chemical composition, produce cures for illnesses, and completely alter her physical shape and internal structure.

Àjẹ́ are revered as the Gods of Society; they are also heralded as Our Mothers. Anyanwu is a classic Àjẹ́ who uses her power to heal, protect, and guide her community, and she keeps clay figures in her home that she calls "my mothers," but they are window-dressing, as she reveals, "For my people . . . I respect the gods. I speak as the voice of a god. . . . In my recent years, I have seen that people must be their own gods and make their own good fortune."[35] Anyanwu is the only God she needs.

Unlike Anyanwu, who is the product of African legend, Doro was conceived in Butler's imagination. Her creation melds personal "fantasy" with history and patriarchal domination. A walking immortality without blood kin, Doro is a spirit who changes bodies like people change clothes. Of Nubian origin, Doro's name means "the east," which would be the perfect complement to Anyanwu/Sun. However, Doro is the antithesis of the hopeful dawn his name signifies.

Born millennia ago, Doro was the only one of his parents' children to survive; they had given birth to eleven *ogbanje* (Igbo) or *àbíkú* (Yoruba) children. Perhaps Doro carried the cosmic strength of all his siblings and some ancestors when he continued to live, because with adolescence it became clear that Doro was unlike other children; he had painfully acute sensory perception and was subject to convulsions. When he was thirteen he went through a violent "transition," which is a delicate period of marked instability when dormant or fledgling power can become full-force Àjẹ́:

> He transferred to the living human body nearest to him. This was the body of his mother in whose lap his head had rested.
> He found himself looking down at himself—at his own body—and he did not understand. He screamed. Terrified, he tried to run away. His father stopped him, held him, demanded to know what had happened. He could not answer. He looked down, saw his woman's breasts, his woman's body, and he panicked. Without knowing how or what he did, he transferred again—this time to his father. (178)

While the Ajalagba falls upon a sleeping person's spirit, Doro is a purely mobile soul and need not wait for sleep to slay. With fear, pain, need of a fresh body, greed, or boredom as catalysts, he can push his soul from one human body to another effortlessly. He cannot die; and just as Anyanwu is a healer, Doro must kill. He comes to realize that persons with high levels of Àjẹ́ make more pleasurable and empowering "kills" than average persons. In a macabre blend of family/feeding ground, Doro seeks out his spiritual kin and collects them:

> He learned to gather reserves of them, breed them, see that they were protected and cared for. They, in turn, learned to worship him. After a single generation, they were his. He had not understood this, but he had accepted it. A few of them seemed to sense him as clearly as he sensed them. Their witch-power warned them but never seemed to make them flee sensibly. Instead, they came to him, competed for his attention, loved him as a god, parent, mate, friend. (179)

Doro perverts the traditional role of Àjẹ́: instead of hunting down the dubious to bring them to justice, he tracks down all spiritually inclined individuals and warehouses, protects, and/or feeds on them. Gẹ̀lẹ̀dẹ́ is called the "ultimate spectacle," and Doro, who left his true face in his mother's lap, is a constant one-man masquerade. However, rather than wearing the mask and dancing in honor of The Mothers, Doro's power is such that, until he meets Anyanwu, he has no need to worship any entity, and for centuries after he meets her, he resists recognizing the Womb of Origins. In other words, he has all the force of Àjẹ́ but none of its balance or temperance. Doro creates multiple colonies of Àjẹ́-inclined individuals, and, in addition to saving them from persecution, he breeds them for his amusement and the thrill of manufacturing Àjẹ́. While many of his breeding projects are aberrations, if any develop a power that may equal or surpass his or if they seem inclined to challenge him, he kills them immediately.

When Anyanwu and Doro meet, she is living alone, wearing the mask of an elderly mother of power isolated from but charged to heal and defend her community. Anyanwu has been married thirteen times and has countless descendants. Although she joins Doro on the strength of veiled threats and the dubious promise of immortal children, when in America she makes the decision to become a sedentary biological mother, which heightens the sexual, political, and spiritual tension between her and Doro and places her firmly in his control. In addition to this, Anyanwu fails to recognize the fact that her powers equip her with a natural Doro-defense system: When she morphs fully into another life form, Doro cannot "track" her—cannot sense her existence.

Anyanwu reads flesh as human beings read books. She tells Isaac that the "messages" revealed to her when she bites the flesh of an animal "are as clear and fine as those in your books":

> Privately she thought her flesh messages even more specific than the books [he] had introduced her to, read to her from. But the books were the only example she could think of that he might understand. "It seems that you could misunderstand your

> books," she said. "Other men made them. Other men can lie or make mistakes. But the flesh can only tell me what it is. It has no other story." (80)

Anyanwu's ability to read animal flesh is absolute; but, like the books they produce, human beings can be read in numerous ways. Anyanwu often seems unable or unwilling to "read" and fully interpret human emotions or the text of her own supremacy. But her misreadings and myopia are textual necessities that propel the narrative and complicate any attempt at developing a "good" Earth Mother/"bad" Father dichotomy.

The Old Man of Soyinka's drama creates an ideologically based Oṣó that is as destructive as Doro's spiritual-physical force. Old Man creates an Ẹgbẹ́ Oṣó out of four devotees/beggars and his son, Dr. Bero. The Old Man amassed his following when he suggested that cannibalism be legalized to reduce of the amount of "meat" going to "waste" as a result of the war. Unable to make physically and psychologically maimed soldiers whole again, the Old Man offered them succor in transcendent cuisine. His son recalls the initiation:

> Does it sound that bad? It was no brain-child of mine. We thought it was a joke. I'll bless the meat, he said. And then—As Was the Beginning, As is Now, As Ever shall be . . . world without world. . . . We said amen with a straight face and sat down to eat. . . . Afterwards . . . I said why not? What is one flesh from another? So I tried it again, just to be sure of myself. It was the first step to power you understand. Power in the purest sense. The end of inhibitions. The conquest of the weakness of your too human flesh with all its sentiment. So again, all to myself I said Amen to his grace.[36]

The elder buttressed the ingestion of power with an ideological component: "As. The new god and the old—As." The concept of fighting a war that resulted in a million deaths and countless atrocities is senseless; perhaps to his credit, the Old Man creates an appropriate Deity, with attendant rituals and myths, to make the concept of war logical: "All intelligent animals kill only for food, you know, and you are intelligent animals. Eat-eat-eat-eat-eat-Eat!" (267). Truly his father's son, Bero admits that he "prefers the balls."

I refer to the work of Doro and the Bero men as neo-Oṣó because of their wanton disregard for laws that traditionally are upheld by men and women in African societies. The mendicants, Aafaa, Cripple, Goyi, and Blindman, describe themselves as completing the cycle of As by consuming and integrating into their bodies the flesh of other human beings (255). They also compare themselves to vultures, cleaning up the "mess made by others" (227). In addition to the depravity inherent in human beings consuming human flesh, the role of Ìyá-Ayé, the Mother of the Earth and tutelary Deity of Àjẹ́, is omitted. What comes from the earth must there return. Furthermore, the vulture is respected for its discernment, and it is a key totemic bird of Àjẹ́.[37] In usurping the vulture's role, the work of the Bero men is a direct affront to Àjẹ́, who own the cycle of creativity, destruction, and regeneration.

Dr. Bero has taken an ecological and cosmic stand against the laws of the Earth Mother. He is also enmeshed in a Lacan-inspired struggle with his father, and he finds himself isolated from his complement and sister. The intelligence specialist and Si Bero are biologically linked as brother and sister sharing the same blood and the Bero siblings have made a cosmic pact with the guardians of the Mother of the Earth, Àjẹ́. Because of the link between onísẹ̀gun and Ọ̀sanyìn and Àjẹ́, Dr. Bero's connection to Àjẹ́ predates the war and the pact Si Bero made while constructing the herbal shrine. As are Doro and Anyanwu, Si and Dr. Bero are linked but diametrically opposed. Their paradoxical connectedness is alluded to when Si Bero returns from an expedition with what she thinks is a rare healing plant. She has actually brought the plant's more prevalent "poison twin." Rather than destroy the plant, Ìyá Agba emphasizes connectedness: "You don't learn good things unless you learn evil." And she tells Si Bero that "[p]oison has its uses too. You can cure with poison if you use it right. Or kill" (233). With one sibling devoted to healing and the other to killing, the link between the rare healing plant and its poison twin is an appropriate metaphor for the Bero siblings. It is interesting to note that the only plant Dr. Bero immediately recognizes is the poison twin (277).

John Mason describes Ọbàtálá and Odùduwà as two halves of one calabash and as manifest in flora as two plants that grow one on top of the other in a symbiotic/parasitic relationship.[38] Ọbàtálá and Odùduwà's relationship, as that of the twin healing and poisonous plants, is analogous to the relationships of Doro and Anyanwu and Si Bero and Dr. Bero. From a Yoruba perspective, no plant, person, or power is inherently evil: Actions and uses are determined by ìwà, necessity, and desire and are subject to multiple interpretations. Many empowered Oṣó and Àjẹ́ recognize their interconnectedness and work together to maintain balance and harmony. However, plants and powers can be used variously. The exercise of free will and recognition of individual character and destiny are important aspects of the Yoruba ethos. However, when a person or group threatens social order, spiritual forces must reconstitute balance.

Like Doro, Dr. Bero must decide whether he will enter into the female-authored force of origins he does not understand or respect or unite fully with a male force that is an aberration. The members of his community ensure that Dr. Bero's decision will be an informed one. Blindman, the mendicant Si Bero trusts above all, tries to inform Dr. Bero about the nature of his sister's and Mothers' work: "I can only tell you what I felt—in that room where I stood with her. There is more love in there than you'll ever find in the arms of a hundred women" (240). Blindman offers a most resonant and succinct description of the truth of Àjẹ́ that lends insight into why women with such dedication and power were branded witches. Their love is not romantically inclined, nor is it patriarchally defined and approved—it is a love guided by holistic healing and positive evolution.

Reflecting the love of Àjẹ́, Ìyá Agba attempts to educate Dr. Bero and offers to help heal the Old Man. He rejects her offer, calls her a "hag," and demands to know what "cult" she is affiliated with. Ìyá Agba, unperturbed, reveals that she and Ìyá Mate cannot be destroyed by the likes of man because they "move as the Earth moves, nothing more. We age as the Earth ages." When Bero demands that Ìyá Agba name her power, she defines Àjẹ́ in contrast to the neo-Oṣó of the Beros:

> Don't look for the sign of broken bodies or wandering souls. Don't look for the sound of fear or the smell of hate. Don't take a bloodhound with you; we don't mutilate bodies. . . . If you do, you may find him circle back to your door. . . . You want the name? But how much would it tell you, young man? We put back what we take, in one form or another. Or more than we take. It's the only law. What laws do you obey? (274)

Àjẹ́ have been stereotyped as evil, flesh-eating witches, but Soyinka offers the reader a wonderful opportunity to compare the ancient methodology and justice of Àjẹ́ to the destructive cultural creations of patriarchy. Moving and aging "as the Earth," and embodying social, spiritual, and cultural reciprocity, Àjẹ́ is a far cry from the megalomania and cannibalistic sorcery of the creators and followers of As.

Their society's culture has rendered the Bero men and mendicants oblivious to the power of holistic love and their role in its evolution; they shun "women's work" and appear to be incapable of doing anything that doesn't reflect patriarchal excess. Even the work the mendicants do for Si Bero morphs into a fragmented ritual of martial destruction:

> GOYI. First the roots.

CRIPPLE. Then peel the barks.
AAFAA. Slice the stalks.
CRIPPLE. Squeeze out the pulps.
GOYI. Pick the seeds.
AAFAA. Break the pods. Crack the plaster.
CRIPPLE. Probe the wound or it will never heal.
AAFAA. Cauterize.
CRIPPLE. Quick-quick-quick-quick, amputate. (236)

The mendicants' regression continues, moving from herbalism to orthodox medicine to torture: "Rip out his vocal chords." Finally, alluding to the cult of As, they conclude, "We don't want you in this fraternity." The mendicants continue their revelry in exclusivity and torture until they begin to fight among themselves.

The phrase "We don't want you in this fraternity" seems directed toward Dr. Bero, who is a key member of the fraternity of As but is confused by the synthetic deity. In his quest for answers, the intelligence specialist turns from interrogating the Earth Mothers to querying his biological father, who is also *the* Father, the High Priest of As, the "transcendental signifier." Pulling a Freudian trump card, the Old Man tells his son, "I am the last proof of the human in you. The last shadow" (265). With his shadow obscured by a deified adverb, Bero queries, "Why As?" The Old Man replies, "Because Was—Is—Now." His attempts to decode As only yield intricate linguistic riffs. When prodded for clarification, the Old Man intimates that by feeding the sons the flesh of the fathers and the fathers the flesh of the sons, the transcendental signifier became fully signified "As" an unending cycle of oblivion: "So you see, I put you all beyond salvation" (266). As sign, signifier, and signified that yields only grammatical flights of fancy, As signifies everything but means nothing. Dr. Bero demands admittance into and full disclosure about the fraternity of As, but as the orchestrator of the killings that become the sacraments of As, he is the literal sergeant at arms of the cult. The Old Man heightens his son's frustrations by appearing to deny him verbal access to the oblivion he helped create, but as an ephemeral theoretical construction, As has no entry or exit. The Bero men, with the help of As, become their own complements. In looking at and speaking to each other, one reflects the other's void as well as that in the self. They are twin "HOLE[S] IN THE ZERO of NOTHING" (292).

Soyinka's drama critiques the Biafran War of Nigeria specifically and war in general. The dramatist forces the reader to acknowledge the depravity that wars foster on the warfront and the impact of that depravity and destruction on all societies, especially those attempting to reintegrate physically maimed and psychologically ravished warriors into the community. Wars constitute the ultimate in destructive Oṣó—patriarchal excess and wanton disregard for the laws of Earth and humanity. Blindman's speech elucidates how through linguistic manipulation myth becomes reified to justify war and genocide:

> It was our duty and a historical necessity. It was our duty and a historical beauty. . . . What we have, we hold. What though the wind of change is blowing over this entire continent, our principles and traditions—yes, must be maintained. For we are threatened, yes, we are indeed threatened. Excuse me please, but we are entitled to match you history for history to the nearest half-million souls. Look at the hordes, I implore you. They stink. They eat garlic. What on earth have we in common with *them*? . . . The black menace is no figment of my father's imagination. Look here . . . have you had the experience of watching them—breed? (286)

Rather than rousing Nigerians against Biafrans, Blindman's oration employs the rhetoric and dehumanization through stereotype customary of Caucasian leaders and political pundits such as Thomas Jefferson, Lord Lugard, Cecil Rhodes, P. W. Botha, Hitler, Mussolini, and George ("axis of evil") Bush.

Perhaps *Madmen and Specialists,* in juxtaposing Àjẹ́ to neo-Oṣó, is asking us to re-examine the concept of evil and its characteristics. Let us consider the following assertion from Fatunmbi:

> With Ifa theology, there are no forces that are regarded as inherently "evil." But there are spirits known as *elenini* that set up barriers to the full expression of freedom, enlightenment, and environment balance. The forces of *elenini* are closely associated with sorcery, which is defined as the attempt to alter nature without regard to ethical principles. In the category of sorcery, I would include the development of nuclear weapons, the "Star Wars" defense system and the destruction of the Brazilian rainforest.[39]

Fatunmbi could have added the decimation of Native Americans, attempts at global colonization, the bombings of Hiroshima and Nagasaki, the Holocaust, the decimation of Congolese people and the cutting off and collection of their hands, and "shock and awe" crusades to his list ad infinitum. Clearly the terms "evil," "witchcraft," and "wizardry" signify the acts of the creators of these terms best.

In more ways than one, *Madmen and Specialists* signifies, and that the psyches of the Old Man and his mendicants have been deeply affected, if not irreparably damaged, by Eurocentric ideology is evident in their rhetoric. As symbolizes mastery of European language, theory, and ideology. And just as imperialistic, As demands that its devotees deconstruct and disavow all other ideologies and systems of beliefs:

> The dog of dogma, tick of a heretic, the tick in politics, the mock of democracy, the mar of marxism, a tic of the fanatic, the boo of buddhism, the ham in Mohammed, the dash in the criss-cross of Christ, a dot on the I of ego[,] an ass in the mass, the ash in ashram, a boot in kibbutz, the pee of priesthood, the peepee of perfect priesthood, oh how dare you raise your hindquarters you dog of dogma and cast the scent of your existence on the lamppost of Destiny you HOLE IN THE ZERO of NOTHING! (292)

The Old Man's rant, his semantical "Practise . . . on the cyst in the system," encompasses the mandated world religions and philosophies, those who follow them, those who have the audacity to question their veracity, and those who have been slaughtered (metaphorically or physically) by them.

While it is apparent throughout the drama that As is nourished by verbosity, puns, signifying, and pontification, the pervasive linguistic riffing intimates an ongoing battle in another, more covert, war. The Old Man's linguistic "practise" could easily be interpreted as Soyinka's veiled attack on his colonial forebears and their "system" of education and indoctrination.

There appears to be a metaphysical juncture at which the African student (read: Soyinka/Old Man) both sees and "reads" through his teacher (read: "colonial master") in life, language, and literature. In a 1973 interview with Biodun Jeyifous, Soyinka asserted, "Ideology, once it departs from humanistic ends, is no longer worthy of the name. The ultimate purpose of human striving is humanity. The moment we deny this, we grant equal seriousness and acceptability to *any* and *all* ideology. We become victims of dogma and verbalisation for their own sake."[40] Using the Old Man's phraseology, we become the running dogs of dogma, the lies of verbalization. Having seen through the masquerade posing as knowledge, the African student asks his European mentor in the words of T. S. Eliot, "After such knowledge, what forgiveness?"[41] And he sings with Fela, "Teacher, Don't Teach Me Nonsense."[42] To his credit, the Old Man logically extends ideological and cultural cannibalism to actual cannibalism. Anything less would be hypocritical.

Butler's commentary on European patriarchal political imperatives and theories and their destructive aspects is also subtle. In fact, Anyanwu and Doro's simple assertion that "it is better to be a master than to be a slave" rings rather hollow (9), especially given the depth of that centuries-long crime against humanity and the fact that, together, Doro and Anyanwu have the spiritual and physical power to exterminate every living enslaver. At the very least, the reader is left to wonder why Anyanwu, who is supposedly dedicated to the preservation and protection of humanity, doesn't encourage Doro—who *must* kill—to find his victims among those raping the African continent.

In a 1984 interview, Butler admitted to Sandra Govan that reading about those who "endured and escaped slavery" was "very grim reading! It convinced me that (among other things) I was going to have to present a cleaned up, somewhat gentler version of slavery. There's not much entertainment in the real thing."[43] Her "cleaned up" version of slavery has glaring oversights, but Butler seems to be writing with a goal that transcends gender, time, and text. Govan states that Butler's "didactic" Pan-African setting and foundation "are important because they illustrate the longevity, continuity, and richness of African civilization; they also give us a present context, and they form the structural basis of the Patternist society to come."[44] Perhaps, having written other novels in the Patternist series before *Wild Seed*[45], Butler had to narrow Anyanwu and Doro's political consciousness in order to frame her ethnically melded, gender-bending series.

Wild Seed's exploration of Àjẹ́ and Oṣó does, in fact, contextualize previously published Patternist novels, and it may very well have influenced Butler's Pan-African and pan-human consciousness. Indeed the re-membering at work in *Wild Seed* so moved Randall Keenan, who interviewed Butler in 1991, that he proclaimed, "Such rich etymological and cultural resonance. *It's almost as if the African lore itself is using you as a medium.*"[46] Butler's concentration on the spiritual dimension of African society also sets an important tone for novels that followed *Wild Seed*. With *Parable of the Sower* (1997) and *Parable of the Talents* (1998), it becomes evident that Butler realizes the social death that continued use of neo-Oṣó will bring and that a collective of dedicated Àjẹ́-inspired people (often boasting Yoruba names and traditional ideologies) holds the keys to holistic evolution.

Butler found the realities of slavery so "grim" she had to revise them. Doro is a fascinating revision. He cannot be categorized as a slaver—his "kin" do not work for him, he doesn't auction them off or brand them, and they love and revere him. However, in many ways, Doro takes on the attributes of American oppressors: He has no respect for others' religious beliefs; monogamy and fidelity have no meaning for him, as he enjoys practicing eugenics as much as having sex, and he kills casually. Systematically perverting the natural cycle of life has the same effect on Doro as it has on the Old Man, as he sacrifices his humanity to nourish a soul that begins to take on the attributes of a devouring hole.

However, Doro is no more inherently "evil" than Anyanwu is intrinsically "good," and living in a society structured upon dichotomy and predicated upon racism profoundly affects Anyanwu, making her character as complicated as Doro's. Upon arrival to New England, Anyanwu immediately realizes the power of the Eurocentric racial hierarchy. In addition to learning the difference between a "real lady" and an uncivilized "savage," she ponders the benefits of appearing white. After escaping Doro and relocating to Louisiana, Anyanwu creates and lives as European American plantation owner Edward Warrick. She wears this mask with such ease that she forgets that the "slaves" surrounding her are human beings until a countryman calls her out telepathically: "Anyanwu! Does that white skin cover your eyes too?" The "protective" African Earth Mother admits, "I had been white too long" (211). It is interesting to note that it appears to be the case that Anyanwu's personal ethnocentricity prepares her for immersion into the upper echelon of the Eurocentric racial caste system. When she arrives at the English factory of enslavement on the African coast she is stunned by the magnitude of the brutality: "Doro, this is an evil place" (37). However she saves only two people, both her direct kin, from the horrors of slavery. While Doro can appreciate Anyanwu's being the mother-source of the concept of communality—"The land must be full of your descendants"—her vision is disturbingly narrow.

In addition to adding lessons of European American oppressors to her somewhat elitist worldview, Anyanwu also integrates Doro's lessons into her evolving self. On one of her first nights in the New England village of Wheatley, Anyanwu watches as Doro logs journal entries in Nubian hieroglyphics. However, when he finds her in Louisiana, it is Anyanwu who is the master of letters and finance. Doro marvels, "You are a better businesswoman than I thought with your views on slavery" (242). Furthermore, Anyanwu is practicing humane eugenics on a plantation that boasts the "harmonious dualism" of old. Having mastered, melded, and revised various texts of oppression and power, Anyanwu gains the ability to truly "read" and decode and encode the text of human immortality. And although Doro is nearly 4,000 years old—"when Christ, the Son of God of most white people in these colonies, was born, Doro was already impossibly old" (129)—Anyanwu applies her learned wisdom and critical skills to the errant elder and other who is inherently the self.

After reading the "messages" in his soul's text, the Earth Mother tells the demigod, "Everything is temporary but you and me. You are all I have, perhaps all I would ever have. . . . And you are an obscenity" (269). Anyanwu also informs Doro of her decision to shut her body and soul down. She tells him, "Everything truly alive dies sooner or later." When the "human part" of Doro dies completely, he will be a pure unstoppable force of unalterable wickedness, a synthetic god. Realizing that without Anyanwu he will be truly alone, a god cursed to live among mortals, forced to write a text without living ink, Doro weeps like a newborn. His tears provide the libation of life for Anyanwu and himself, as they reveal his human potential. With Doro's evolution, he and Anyanwu can coexist as the complements they are with the East embracing the Sun.

There is another compelling site of confluence linking Butler's and Soyinka's works. Early on in *Wild Seed,* Anyanwu asks Doro what Gods he respects, and he replies that he respects none because he helps (and is worshipped as a God) himself. However, at the conclusion of *Wild Seed,* Doro is confronted with the Igbo man's dilemma, as the saying *Nwanyi abugh ihie* ("A woman is nothing") meets the spiritual assertion articulated by Nne-Nne in *I Saw the Sky Catch Fire:* "A woman's crotch is a juju shrine before which men always kneel and worship. It is their door into this world."[47] By *Wild Seed's* conclusion, Doro, understanding where his help and origin lie, removes his mask of supremacy and kneels before the shrine.

During their first encounter, Ìyá Agba asks Bero what laws he obeys. The question is rhetorical because she knows his law is the system that created and empowered him and consecrated As. Even though Bero refuses to acknowledge it, the Old Man articulates the relationship between god and demigod: "As Is and the System is its mainstay though it wear a hundred masks and a thousand outward forms" (287). With linguistic dexterity, As, the system, and its devotees all share in the mask-wearing, divinity, and authority of neo-Oṣó. But for all its linguistic morphing and troping, As is rigid, static: "As doesn't change" (278). Conversely, in *Parable of the Talents,* Butler's protagonist, who is named after Oya, the Òrìṣà of Transformation, teaches her flock that "God is Change." The Bero men and mendicants, in omitting the juju shrine of Àjẹ́ from their lives and trapped by ephemeral but stagnating dogma, have truly robbed themselves of psychological flexibility and spiritual salvation.

Near the end of the play, the Old Man's "practise on the cyst of the system" leads to frenzied ritual for As that will include "sacrificing" and eating the Cripple. Armah's *Two Thousand Seasons* depicts a similar instance of destructive neo-Oṣó during an ancient era of patriarchal rule:

Below the powerful the ordinary multitudes, in their turn seized by the fever of jealous ownership, turned our people into a confused competition of warring gangs, each gang under its red-eyed champion seeking force or ruse to force its will against the others. In the end it was this hot greed itself that destroyed the power of the men. They had smashed up everything, and in their festival of annihilation they had forgotten to spare each other and themselves.[48]

Recognizing the Bero men and their minions to be owners of broken and degenerate destinies, Ìyá Agba does not take their lives: They are already spiritually and socially dead. Leaving the men to "earth's rejection," she sets fire to the shrine of herbs, reclaiming the knowledge and power of her lineage and soul that can be used only in a negation of the way of Àjẹ́ in the hands of the Bero men and their mendicants. Simultaneous with Ìyá Agba's reclamation, the intelligence specialist succeeds in killing the Old Man and destroying "the last proof" of his dubious humanity. Like the women who watched the "festival of annihilation" depicted in *Two Thousand Seasons,* the women of *Madmen and Specialists* are left "to begin the work of healing."

Octavia Butler and Wole Soyinka both rely on Africa's ancient history to articulate empowered women's historical and contemporary social roles. Those with a Western mentality might describe Anyanwu and the Ìyás as representing "a passive acceptance of an apparently nature-based order of things,"[49] but they are active in important spiritual and historical ways that Western and feminist theory and practice may be unable to appreciate. *Wild Seed* and *Madmen and Specialists* do not depict dominating or abusive shrews who seek to flip the dichotomous male/female hierarchy. These women do not invest energy in trying to kill or proselytize their "way" to males. These characters' use of Àjẹ́ to re-establish "harmonious dualism" may be understated, but their labors of realignment are almost as quiet and certainly as sure as the Earth's rotations. In the words of Ruth Salvaggio, the women of *Wild Seed* and *Madmen and Specialists* "are heroines not because they conquer the world, but because they conquer the very notion of tyranny."[50] The conquest of tyranny can take many forms, and rather than enforcing a particular order, Àjẹ́ engage in the quiet consecration of forces that open the path for harmony to naturally reconstitute itself. In the realm of contemporary literature's gender relations, Àjẹ́ are evidently always and already prepared to perfect and manifest their selves and souls for the communal good, and this is the work they undertake whether or not their male counterparts are ready.

6

The Relativity of Negativity: Àjẹ́ in Jean Pliya's "The Watch-Night," Zora Neale Hurston's *Jonah's Gourd Vine*, and Gloria Naylor's *Mama Day*

This chapter is devoted to depictions of the most feared and reviled aspects of Àjẹ́: Àjẹ́ dúdú and Àjẹ́ pupa, which are supposedly distinguished by their respective black and red colors and wanton killing and maiming. Under the Western color hierarchy, the Yoruba word for the color black, dúdú, is associated with evil; however, the word connotes "great depth." To fully understand certain acts of Àjẹ́, such as violent retribution, it is necessary to eschew the convenient and superficial and investigate underlying terrestrial and cosmic issues, for close readings of works imbued with Àjẹ́ dúdú reveal balance, reciprocity, and compelling didactics at work. In my attempt to elucidate the cosmic depth of Àjẹ́ dúdú and Àjẹ́ pupa, I begin with brief analyses of Jean Pliya's short story "The Watch-Night" and Zora Neale Hurston's novel *Jonah's Gourd Vine*. These works both typify and complicate stereotypical views of Àjẹ́. The bulk of this chapter focuses on Ruby in Naylor's *Mama Day* and the way in which Sapphira uses Ruby's Àjẹ́ dúdú to right ancient wrongs and finally institute peace.

Pliya is a native of Benin Republic, and there are many cultural and spiritual similarities between the Fon and Yoruba peoples. These similarities are evident in Pliya's short story. For example, the fact that all Africana women possess some degree of Àjẹ́ elucidates the character of Aunt Gussi, who is not a fully evolved Àjẹ́ but shares important information about the spiritual realm with her nephew. Aunt Gussi is the primary spiritual reference for and aunt of the young narrator, and the story opens with her admonishing her nephew for whistling at night, because he could summon "poisonous snakes . . . that . . . embody dangerous spirits or jinn."[1] Shedding light on the acquisition of such abilities as shape-shifting and invisibility, Gussi goes on to inform her nephew that spirits "called *aziza* can even become friendly. They may, for example, tell us the secret of plants which make you invisible or change a man into a snake or lion" (84).

In addition to her spiritual knowledge, Gussi divulges that Zannu, the watch-night, or guard, of the small community, owns a vast collection of powerful spiritual implements that lend him protection against the spirits of the night. In addition to a plethora of wicked bags, Zannu keeps his watch over the community from the base of a silk cotton tree. Ìrókò and silk cotton trees are known to be meeting places of Àjẹ́, Oṣó, and other spiritual forces. Zannu's choice of post and his wicked bags make it clear that he has Àjẹ́. In fact, the narrative centers on his battle against Ayele, the community food-seller, and her Ẹyẹ Àjẹ́.

Owls are commonly thought to be the birds of Àjẹ́ on the Continent, and in the ìtànkálẹ̀, the screech owl's cry is considered an omen of death. In "The Watch-Night," spiritual and physical violence begin when Zannu finds that an owl has given birth in the narrator's attic. Zannu tells the narrator's father that the bird and its offspring are harbingers of evil. The father scoffs at what he considers superstition but orders Zannu to kill the infant owls. As soon as they are tossed into a pit latrine, David, the protagonist's little brother, is stricken with a debilitating headache. Aunt Gussi, against the wishes of the patriarch, furtively consults a diviner. The home of the *bokono* (babaláwo) is replete with "wicked bags," including a red feather of Àjẹ́ crowning a black bottle circled by white cowry shells. Using Afa divination, which is similar to Ifá, the diviner reveals that a "spell" had been cast on David as "revenge for a wrong suffered" at the hands of his family. At the end of the consultation, the bokono gives Aunt Gussie medicine that cures David.

Three weeks later, an owl, ostensibly a parent of the baby owls, is spotted near the narrator's home. The owl is simply perching in a mango tree, but the father insists that Zannu kill it. As Zannu prepares to burn the owl carcass, Gussi suggests collecting its scattered feathers "because it's dangerous to let them lie around." However, the straitlaced father reproaches her, saying, "One would think you'd turned into a sorceress yourself" (92). Following this, Ayele, the respected community food-seller, asks for one of the owl's feathers so that she can use it as protection against harm. Gussi protests, but the father silences her again, and Ayele and a farmer are both given feathers. After burning the bird, Zannu ritually bonds the community: "Zannu scattered part of it in the compound. Each of the persons present put a pinch of it on the tip of his tongue. Aunt Gussi powdered her face with it" (93).

While ritual bonding through owl ash provides an excellent example of the transference of spiritual power, Zannu's killing of the elder owl has destroyed balance. Just as David fell ill following the death of the infant owls, Zannu finds his daughter, Cicavi, writhing in agony after the death of the elder owl. The entire community attributes the illness to the slain owl's revenge. The diviner confirms, "A witch wants to kill your daughter. She's marked you down too. Beware" (95). After deep cogitation, Zannu realizes that Ayele is his antagonist and opens his wicked bags to combat her. He calls for "twin gongs, a fresh egg, and a black horse tail"; builds a fire in a freshly dug pit; and summons the messenger-bird, a third owl, of Ayele. Drawn over the spiritually charged pit, the bird careens into the fire and dies.

Zannu goes to Ayele's home to continue his quest for vengeance and finds her debilitated and suffocating. She promises to "send [her] messenger to release Cicavi" once Zannu reverses his spiritual work. When Zannu reveals that he has killed the messenger-bird, Ayele, in a final burst of strength, tries to attack Zannu and curses him, "You too will die. . . . You've eaten the soup. . . . By the power of voodoo, by all that flies by night or crawls with its mouth full of poison, you'll die" (99). Ayele, whose name means Power of the Earth, swears by the same spiritual forces the narrator had been initially warned against invoking. Although it seems to be a minor detail, it appears to be the case that the young narrator attracted the owls by whistling at night.

At the story's onset, both Ayele and Zannu are respected members of the community: one providing protection, the other sustenance. And during the text's spiritual-terrestrial battle, Ayele and Zannu both harness the neutral power of Àjẹ́ for their desired ends. However, it is obvious that we should consider Ayele "evil" and Zannu "good." Ayele is depicted as the classic terroristic Àjẹ́ dúdú or Àjẹ́ pupa. However, at the beginning of the story, she is respected as a benevolent industrious woman: She cooks for the entire community, including Zannu and Cicavi. When Zannu accuses her of witchcraft, the diviner and the narrator's father defend her (96). The death of the baby owls, instead of releasing the community from evil, for there is no "evil" in the community at the onset of the story, sparks a chain of reciprocal events. This chain includes David's tormenting headache; at approximately four years of age, he is a perfect substitute for the baby owls. When David is cured and balance restored, Zannu spins the wheel of reciprocity and kills the elder owl, which results in his daughter's illness. In killing the third owl, Zannu assumes he is ending the revolutions of Àjẹ́. However, the cycle in which he participates must make a complete revolution: Ayele dies, but so does Cicavi, whose destiny was carried in the owl.

Zannu avoids death because he was engrossed in killing owls and forgot to eat the food she prepared for him.

"The Watch-Night" also offers an interesting, albeit indirect, examination of the roles patriarchal authority and reason play in contemporary African society. The narrator's father represents reason, logic, and the debunking of superstition. However, he is revealed to be an enabler whose dictates are as instrumental to destruction as the actions of Zannu and Ayele. The narrator's father carries considerable weight in his community. The strength of his words is sufficient to make Zannu suspend his judgment and give Ayele one of the owl's feathers. Simultaneous to his ridiculing or disavowing nearly everything that Aunt Gussi and Zannu suggest with regard to the neutralization of spiritual forces, including the consultation that heals David, the patriarch passively and actively participates in spiritual works. However, his rational Western-science-based mandates along with his disavowal of spirit work lead to Cicavi's death. Zannu even admits that his error was in relaxing his judgment and giving Ayele a feather, but he refuses to admit his or the father's role in the events. Before Cicavi dies, rather than take any personal responsibility or acknowledge the power of Ayele, Zannu, who has purchased medicine from Nigeria that "can raise a person from the dead" says, "If it fails, it means that my dead wife wishes to take back her daughter and that it had to happen" (100). While the acknowledged power of Nigerian medicine is significant, it is Zannu, not his wife, who has helped set these events in motion.

In "The Watch-Night," interconnected male-female relationships underpinned by Àjẹ́ and reciprocity problematize attempts to define Àjẹ́ dúdú as intrinsically evil and inherently malicious. The story also debunks the theory that disbelief in spiritual realities removes one from their sphere of influence.[2] In this text, Western religious beliefs and linear reason, factors thought to place one out of the reach of Àjẹ́, actually precipitate disaster.

Hurston's first novel also depicts interactions between the religious linear and the spiritual curvilinear realms as mediated by spiritual animals and the overarching force of reciprocity. *Jonah's Gourd Vine* chronicles the life of John Pearson, who goes from barefoot fieldhand to being the most influential man in two small all-Black towns in Florida. John becomes a renowned reverend, a "Battle-Axe"[3] who rolls "his African drum up to the altar, and [calls] his Congo Gods by Christian Names."[4] However, community members joke that John is a "wife-made man" because his wife Lucy is a dynamic ordering force in his life.

In addition to personal attributes, an intriguing blend of traditional and modern cosmological symbols informs John and Lucy's lives and destinies. The Select Heads of the couple are the male-female spiritual serpents of Dahomey cosmology, Damballah and Aido Hwedo. Depicted as conjugally entwined on the tree of life and regarded as a unit, Damballah-Hwedo, in the form of serpents, trains, and the penis, exerts a powerful influence throughout *Jonah's Gourd Vine*. Embodying power, virility, and regeneration, Damballah-Hwedo perfectly symbolizes the protagonist, John Pearson. However, Damballah-Hwedo also represents spiritual laws—monogamy, cosmic union, and covenant-keeping—that John and Lucy, in different ways, both ignore.

When John leaves his dysfunctional home for life across the creek, he encounters a rumbling, hypnotizing, one-eyed snakelike beast. The train, new industrial deity of America, is a technological cousin of Aido Hwedo, who toured the earth with Mawu in her mouth, creating curves, valleys, and mountains.[5] Like the serpent who "lives in a hole right under God's foot-rest" and speaks words of power to Moses,[6] the machine speaks to John. But unlike Moses, John does not have the interpretive ability to understand Damballah-Hwedo's message. He muses, "Ah lakted dat. It say something but Ah ain't heered it 'nough tuh tell what it say yit" (36). Even as he ages, John remains unable to comprehend and differentiate exoteric aspects of the train/serpent—sensuality, virility, and terrestrial power—from esoteric aspects—harmonious duality with one's terrestrial and spiritual complement and the promise of immortality. To heighten the serpentine connections, John's lack of development is directly related to his personal snake, his penis. Damballah-Hwedo will repeatedly attempt to enlighten John, but the messages are encoded, and John will pick only the meaning suitable to his quest for sexual satisfaction.

Before his introduction to the steel snake, John has his first encounter with the sassy and intelligent Lucy Potts, and the two spend many months kindling their young love. One day while crossing the creek to her home, Lucy spies the water moccasin that has lived in the creek since before she was born. She claims she is deathly afraid of the snake, who has left his perch on the foot-log during their conversation and retreated into his hole to let the couple pass freely. Seizing the opportunity to impress Lucy, valiant John kills the serpent and carries Lucy across the creek not once, but a spiritually binding three times (66–69).[7]

Slaying the snake is seemingly indicative of John killing the oppression, abuse, and torment of his old life. However, John's encounter with the snake, having been foreshadowed by the train and his initial creek-crossing, represents another spiritual crossroads. In traditional African spiritual systems, certain serpents and snakes are considered divine. These earthy representatives of Òṣùmàrè, Dan, Damballah-Hwedo, and Mani are protected and revered, and their appearance before a person or in a community is considered auspicious. A divine serpent passed between Olaudah Equiano's legs and prepared him for his remarkable future.[8] Camera Laye opens his autobiography with a discussion of his father's and the Malinke peoples' "guiding spirit," a small black snake with brilliant markings. After the father recovered from his fear of the reptile, it visited him regularly and granted him authority, prosperity, and the gift of foreknowledge.[9] Similarly, Hurston's encounter with a rattlesnake and her demand to her would-be snake-slayers to allow her reptilian brother to live is directly related to her being adorned and crowned with rattlesnake skins and becoming a spiritual daughter of Marie Leveau.[10] Hurston's connection to Damballah-Hwedo and the Tree of Life is evident to her adolescent intimacy with "the loving pine" and her lifelong respect for and fascination with snakes.[11] Fittingly, Hurston employs the "ole cottonmouf" to enter into cosmic discourse with Lucy and John; but Lucy's Christian interpretation of the reptile and John's ego lead them to slay their messenger.

Relationships in the animal kingdom are just as complex and intimate as those humans enjoy. As is depicted in Toni Cade Bambara's "Blues Ain't No Mocking Bird," Tina McElroy Ansa's *Baby of the Family,* and "The Watch-Night," certain animals will mourn the loss of a slain companion and, if possible, avenge the death of their mate.[12] Appropriately, Lucy asks John, "Reckon his mate ain't gonna follow us and try tuh bite us for killin' dis one?" John reassures her that the mate cannot get them if they don't take the same path (68). While the couple does not take the same way home on that particular day, they are bonded by their ritual crossing of water, the invocation of the number three, the murder of their spiritual guardian, and their marriage. In addition to their destiny being textured by the killing of the cottonmouth, the snake's symbolic mates—John's penis and the train—play significant roles in the couples' relationship.

Once wedded, Lucy's love for John is unswerving. She endures abuse and trauma throughout their relationship and waits patiently for him to send for her when his transgressions force him to run away and take his first train ride from Alabama to Florida. Once Lucy joins John in Florida, her perspicacity catapults John to success. Yet John's concubines nearly outnumber the seven children Lucy bears. Had it not been for his liaison with Hattie Tyson, the couple probably would have continued looking in opposite directions for decades. Hattie, however, is not satisfied with weekend love; she desires the same ownership of John that he has over Lucy. In order to achieve her aim, she seeks out An' Dangie Dewoe, two-headed doctor extraordinaire.

Under Dewoe's direction, Hattie has been "feeding" John "out of her body"—feeding him tomato-based stews laced with her menstrual blood[13] and undertaking other harmless acts to bind love. However, Hattie is impatient and demands that An' Dangie Whodo(?) Lucy in addition to Hoodooing John. An' Dangie instructs Hattie to chew "wish beans" while standing over the Pearsons' gate and meditating on her desire. Hattie's ritual acts complement An' Dangie's woe inducing works:

> An' Dangie crept to her altar in the back room and began to dress candles with war water. When the altar had been set, she dressed the coffin in red, lit the inverted candles on the altar, saying as she did so, "Now fight! Fight and fuss 'til you part." When all was done at the altar she rubbed her hands and forehead with war powder, put the catbone in her mouth, and laid herself down in the red coffin facing the altar and went into the spirit. (201)

Dewoe asserts, "Jes' you pay me whut Ah ast and 'tain't nothin' built up dat Ah can't tear down" (200). She is sister of the lodestone woman who could break up and put couples back together at her wish and whim, the barefoot woman who breaks up a couple for the Devil for a pair of shoes; and she is as much an Àjẹ́ as Ayele. It is not that these women are committed to destruction; Àjẹ́ is a neutral force and could have been accessed by Lucy as readily as Hattie. However, Lucy places no stock in Hoodoo, and her earlier participation in the killing of the snake augments Dewoe's works.

Lucy quickly succumbs to Whodo(?), and when John, who has been out for days, returns to find Lucy in her sickbed, he shouts, "Oh you sick, sick, sick! Ah hates tuh be 'round folks always complainin' and then agin you always doggin' me 'bout sumptin'" (203). With this, the fussing and fighting begin. Blinded by Whodo(?), John berates his wife until Lucy checks her marital docility to engage in some necessary truth-telling: "Tain't nobody so slick but whut they kin stand un'nother greasin'. Ah done told yuh time and time uhgin dat ignorance is de hawse dat wisdom rides. Don't git miss-put on yo' road. God don't eat okra" (204). Lucy's proverb-rich statements to John mirror Ìyá Agba's "reading" of Dr. Bero. Rather than be humbled, John lies about his transgressions. When Lucy tells her husband, "You can't clean yo'self wid yo' tongue lak uh cat," John reveals himself to be the progenitor of Jody Starks and Tea Cake; he stuns his debilitated wife with a blow across the face.

Through her Whodoed(?) illness and her husband's absences and actions, Lucy has learned some esoteric truths, and she shares them with her daughter, Isis, who is Hurston's depiction of herself. Lucy points out a spider to Isis, and Isis asks if she should kill him. Lucy seems to have progressed since her snake-killing days; she says, "Naw, Isie, let 'im be. You didn't put 'im dere. De one dat put 'im dere will move 'im in his own time" (206). Lucy, on the way to Odù's pot, now understands the spiritual significance and messages of certain animals such as the serpent and the Akan trickster spider, Anansi. She continues her exposition, giving her daughter the gift of wisdom earned through experience:

> Don't you love nobody better'n you do yo'self. Do you'll be dying befo' yo' time is out. And, Isie, uh person kin be killed 'thout being struck uh blow. Some uh dese things Ahm tellin' yuh, you won't understand 'em fuh years tuh come, but de time will come when you'll know. (207)

Lucy's death can be attributed as much to Whodo(?) as to her myopic concept of love and her disavowal of the spiritual realm. Lucy adamantly insists that "last breath" rituals not be performed on her. When a person dies while in sickbed, certain rituals are performed to ease the spirit out of the body and prevent the spirit, angered by the end of life, from engaging in wrathful destruction. The rituals include covering up mirrors to prevent one from seeing the deceased's spirit therein, which could result in crossing or death; clocks are covered or they will not work again; the pillow will be removed from the dying person's head; and he or she will be turned to face the east so that the spirit's transition will be smooth.[14] Even as she acknowledges the weight of the terrestrial and cosmic Àjẹ́ that has killed her, Lucy refuses the rituals of that same tradition that will help her make her transition.

When Dewoe dies, the wheel of reciprocity that has undergone a full revolution in the life of Lucy cycles toward Hattie, who has married John. One day John has a "peculiar feeling" and asks Hattie, "Whut am Ah doin' married tuh you?" (223). After seven years of marriage, John feels as if he has awakened from sleep. Hattie attempts to soothe John back into a Hoodooed slumber, but he is resolved to find the "bug under dis chip." With his mind clear of conjure, Deacon Hambo urges John to scour his home:

> "John, youse in boilin' water and tuh you—look lak 'tain't no help fuh it. Dat damn 'oman you got b'lieves in all kinds uh roots and conjures. She been feedin' you outa her body fuh

years. Go home now whilst she's off syndicatin' wid her gang—
and rip open de mattress on yo' bed, de pillow ticks, de bolsters,
dig 'round de door-steps in front de gate and look and see ain't
some uh yo' draws and shirt-tails got pieces cut offa 'em. Hurry
now and come back and let us know whut you find out." . . .
John Pearson went and returned with a miscellany of weird
objects in bottles, in red flannel and toadskin. . . .

Hattie saw the hole at the gate and the larger one at the front
steps before she entered the yard. Inside, the upturned rugs, the
ripped-up beds, all had fearful messages for her. Who had done
this thing? Had her husband hired a two-headed doctor to
checkmate her? How long had he been suspecting her? Where
was he now? (251–252)

The number of roots Hattie has planted attests to the addictive nature of Hoodoo. Dewoe warned her, "You done started dis and it's got tuh be kep' up do hit'll turn back on yuh" (201); One root is never enough. Not only will the force eventually weaken but it will also revert. Constructing relationships in this manner can only lead to destruction. After an ugly trial, the couple is granted a divorce. Following this chastening, Damballah-Hwedo offers John a final opportunity for redemption.

Relocated in Plant City, John meets the widow Sally Lovelace, who is Lucy reincarnated. With Sally, John attains a new pastorship, property, a Cadillac, and love. He prays to God and Lucy that Sally will never "look at him out of the eyes of Lucy." She never does. John leaves Sally in Plant City, at her behest, to visit his home. He meets Ora, who is as "fresh as dishwater" and the re-embodiment of Hattie. In spite of everything he should have learned, John listens to his personal serpent rather than the covenant of Damballah-Hwedo and copulates with Ora. The final transgression being enough, the mate of the slain serpent, in the form of the powerful sleek train that first speaks to John, kills him as he tries to sneak through the crossroads of life.

In Ayele one sees the Owner of the Birds, Ẹléyẹ, in exact form. An' Dangie Dewoe is a definite sister to Ayele. She is a clear example of the Àjẹ́ of African America. She is the one who could cause the master's wife to feel every stroke the slave was dealt; she is the one who could make the ship sail backward. Ruby of Gloria Naylor's *Mama Day* is a blend of Ayele and Dangie. She has the power to kill and drive insane, and just as Hattie exercises her personal knowledge of Whodo(?) to get and recharge her hold on John, Ruby uses Àjẹ́ to obtain and retain men.

This is fitting, for Whodo(?), whether administered by a man or woman, is often a staple of love triangles.[15]

Having killed her first husband manually when "all them roots she had working on him wasn't doing the job fast enough,"[16] Ruby's primary love interest in *Mama Day* is a sloth of a man named Junior Lee who makes his living off of older women who cook for him, give him money, and generally "keep him up." When Ruby becomes interested in Junior Lee, he is the common-law husband of Frances. For unknown reasons, Frances desperately wants her man and asks Mama Day to help her outdo Ruby's Whodo(?). Mama Day sends her away, refusing to acknowledge the power of Whodo(?):

> The mind is everything. She can dig all the holes she wants around Ruby's door. Put in all the bits of glass and black pepper, every silver pin and lodestone she'll find some fool to sell her. Make as many trips to the graveyard she wants with his hair, her hair, his pee, her pee. Walk naked in the moonlight stinking with Van-Van oil—and it won't do her a bit of good. 'Cause the mind is everything. (90)

Mama Day has an interesting philosophy about Hoodoo and Whodo(?). She has and uses Àjé, but she distinguishes herself from Whodoers(?) like Ruby and Hoodooers like Dr. Buzzard. Unlike Ruby, her works are "good" in a Western sense—she is a midwife and healer—and they are "real," as opposed to the works of Dr. Buzzard. Also, as a peer of the only orthodox medical doctor to service Willow Springs, Mama Day's work is "approved" by Western sources.

After Mama Day's refusal, Frances employs Dr. Buzzard to combat Ruby. Following his prescriptions, she sprinkles salt on Ruby's doorsteps and breaks eggs on her porch. "But the last straw was when Ruby came out one morning and found a *hog's* head swinging from the limb of her peach tree—had a red onion stuffed in its mouth and nine little bits of paper with Ruby's name written on 'em" (93). Frances's works to regain her man are typical of Whodo(?). The salt is supposed to remove Ruby's "evil" presence, the broken eggs should shatter Junior Lee and Ruby's union, and with the nine petitions, Frances has taken her plea and death request to Ọya. But Frances's actions are useless and damning. Not only does Ruby shrewdly indict Frances on charges of attempted Whodo(?)ing before Reverend Hooper and the deacon board and thereby cement her appearance as a meritorious woman but she also has a spiritual repertoire so vast that Buzzard's directives are laughable:

> It ain't no secret what she done to Frances, no, ain't no secret at all. Frances went clear out of her mind, wouldn't wash or comb her hair. Her city folks had to come shut down her house and take her to one of them mental hospitals beyond the bridge. But Ruby had warned her . . . deacons or no deacons, come the next full moon she'd stop her from hanging them hogs' heads on her peach tree. (112)

Just as Hattie Whodoed(?) Lucy to get her out of the way, so too does Ruby unhinge Frances's mind and later kill May Ellen, whose crime was clam-digging with Junior Lee. Concerning May Ellen's demise, the narrator recalls "night's rest broken by them piercing screams echoing from that brick house on the edge of the south woods. Uh, uh, them that believes in roots and them that don't, all know that child died a painful death. And that is fact enough to leave anything Ruby says is hers alone" (163). In other words, one may not believe in Àjẹ́ or traditional African spiritual systems, but one has to believe in Ruby.

In addition to respecting her considerable spiritual power, the community realizes Ruby has Whodoed(?) herself over Junior Lee: "Folks think Ruby is close to losing her mind over Junior Lee. What goes around comes around, some say. Didn't she run Frances crazy? Where is all her roots now that Junior Lee won't stay home nights?" (162). Ruby has the same dilemma Hattie had when her roots wore out. The difference is that Hattie could walk away from the relationship, whereas Ruby takes greater pains to resecure her man. Although she earlier told Frances "the mind is everything," after Frances's insanity and May Ellen's murder, Mama Day lies and tells the trio that Cocoa has a migraine when Junior Lee, Dr. Buzzard, and Ambush come to pick up her grandniece to attend a concert. Abigail thinks her sister's fear unreasonable, but Mama Day knows if the last woman of child-bearing age in their family sits innocently in a vehicle with Junior Lee it would signal the end of the Days.

Assertions of overreaction to Ruby's power are put to rest when she materializes at the Day's home: "One moment she wasn't there. One moment she was. The smoke clears on the silent figure, staring up at the porch from the gate. A mountain. Huge and still. But the voice could be a light breeze, whispering from its summit" (156). Whether Ruby has traveled via Black Cat Bone, egbé (carrier medicine), or her Ẹyẹ (Spirit Bird) or has a relationship with aziza is unknown, but she refuses to leave until she has verified that Cocoa has not gone with the men. Mama Day sees clearly the Whodo(?) Ruby has worked on herself. She has become "a jealous woman. Creeping through the woods picking up nightshade and gathering castor beans . . . the full moon shining on twisted handfuls of snakeroot. May Ellen's twisted body. Ain't no hoodoo anywhere as powerful as hate" (157).

As is the case with Zannu, it is tempting to classify Mama Day as the force of "good" in the novel, but her flaws are evident. Miranda (as opposed to an evolved Mama) Day takes the high road and refuses outright to help Frances in any way, including providing patient wisdom and guidance. Even more detrimental, Miranda's attempt to give the infertile Bernice peace results in two women creating life without the male principle (139–140). From this audacious act of "giving" life, only death can result. Prior to the death of her and Bernice's child and Cocoa and George's arrival, Miranda begs not for clarity but to be blinded from her own transgressions and important historical and cosmic issues (138, 174). Having hierarchically positioned herself above Ruby and Dr. Buzzard, Mama Day has a higher perch from which to fall.

Miranda's blinders and her misuse of her own and lack of respect for others' powers lead indirectly to Ruby's conjuring of Cocoa. However, Ruby is good enough to give Miranda a clear sign, a message from one Àjẹ́ to another:

> [Miranda] gets on her knees, shoos the chicken away with the rake, and drags out what looks like a dirty piece of cloth. The hen had ripped the flannel covering, so when Miranda pries it from the end of her rake it falls apart in her hand. The flannel bag was holding about a tablespoon of dirt mixed up with a few white specks of something, little purplish flowers and a dried sprig. . . . Frowning behind Clarissa she wonders if there was anything to them old wives' tales about chickens after all. (171)

Examining the root that was planted under her trailer, Miranda finds salt, a spiritual staple used to keep harmful spirits at bay; goober or goofer dust, or soil from a graveyard which is infused with the power of the dead; and verbena, which is called "herb of grace." Cocoa's mother is named Grace, and "what better concoction to use if you have singled out the child of Grace?" (172).

Despite receiving Ruby's clear warning, Miranda relaxes her vigilance, and when Cocoa and George come to Willow Springs, Ruby plants a root directly on Cocoa's scalp:

> A straight part down the middle, north to south. The teeth of the comb dig in just short of hurting as she scratches the scalp showing through the parted hair before she dips her fingers into the round jar and massages the warm solution down its length.

The second big part crosses the first, going east to west, and this time she dips her fingers into the square jar, massaging hard. North to south, east to west, round to square. (246)

These jars hold enough nightshade, snakeroot, and Whodo(?) to seep through Cocoa's scalp, infest her, and kill her. Bringing her own comb and burning the loose hair that has been collected, common practices to ward against Whodoing(?), are useless.

Perhaps recognizing Naylor's signifying on and with Shakespeare, Susan Meisenhelder argues that Africana people using Western models to establish relationships leads, in *Mama Day,* to "madness" and, eventually, "suicide."[17] This may be true in the cases of Cocoa's mother and grandmother. But Frances and Ruby use a uniquely African force to establish their relationships and destroy others' unions. An elder in Georgia who had been conjured and saw her family members die of conjure went on to research Whodo(?). Echoing Lucy's deathbed revelation, the elder elucidated the truth of the overlooked and unbelievable:

> T'aint no need talking'; folks can do anythin' to you they wants to. They can run you crazy or they can kill you. Don't you one time believe that every pore pusson they has in the 'sylum is just natchelly crazy. Some was run crazy on account of people not likin' em, some 'cause they was getting' 'long a little too good. Every time a pusson jumps in the river don't think he was just tryin' to kill hisself, most times he just didn't know what he was doin'.[18]

Naylor and her character Sapphira make it difficult to ignore the interconnectedness of seemingly disparate spiritual powers and entities. Sapphira orchestrates events that will level the Western hierarchies held dear by Miranda and George, and Ruby's Whodo(?) is so important to her goals of peace and unification that Sapphira could easily be standing over Ruby's shoulder advising her on the proper methodology to use in planting the roots on Cocoa.

Sapphira's force is also evident in the hurricane that strikes Willow Springs, takes the life of Bernice's child, and destroys the bridge that links the island to the United States. This hurricane is the literary offspring of the one that slams into the Florida muck in *Their Eyes Were Watching God* and opens the space for Janie's climactic transformation and self-actualization.[19] The hurricane of *Mama Day,* born on "the shores of Africa," is none other than a second literary visitation from the all-transforming Áàjálayé, Òrìṣà Oya. Sapphira, working through Ruby and the hurricane, brings Mama Day to a necessary state of evolution.

With her inner eyes opened to Ruby's power and her personal misuse of power and Sapphira's larger agenda, Mama Day checks her ego, nurses her niece, and, in the way of Afírìmáàkọ̀, The Greatest, Strongest Elder Who if Touched Kills (the Sacrilegious One) by Magic, visits her adversary. The unifying properties of the number three, manifest in *Jonah's Gourd Vine* and the killing of owls in "The Watch-Night," resurface when Mama Day seeks vengeance against Ruby. She ritually calls Ruby's name three times: "That'll be her defense at Judgment: Lord, I called out three times." Miranda uses a powder charged with electromagnetic àṣẹ and John-Paul's hand-carved walking stick to invoke the ancestors and mark Ruby's house. Entwined on this walking stick are two serpents. With an intertextual nod to *Jonah's Gourd Vine*, Mama Day summons Damballah-Hwedo, the covenant-making unified female-male serpent Deity who graces the Tree of Life, to judge Ruby's case:

> She don't say another word as she brings that cane shoulder level and slams it into the left side of the house. The wood on wood sounds like thunder. The silvery powder is thrown into the bushes. She strikes the house in the back. Powder. She strikes it on the left. Powder. She brings the cane over her head and strikes it so hard against the front door, the window panes rattle. . . . The door don't open when she leaves, and the winds don't stir the circle of silvery powder. (270)

Luisah Teish says that Oya "brings about sudden structural change in people and things. Oya does not just rearrange the furniture in the house—She knocks the building to the ground and blows away the floor tiles."[20] Answering Damballah-Hwedo's summons, Oya's lightning strikes Ruby's house twice, and it explodes. Although horribly burned, Ruby survives, and, thanks to Sapphira's agenda, so does Ruby's Whodo(?).

As discussed in chapter 3, Sapphira seeks a peace that can be attained only through the unification of male and female forces and, on a covert level, holistic acknowledgment of Africana spiritual forces. Sapphira is aware that Cocoa's husband George, twinning Bascombe Wade, is the male principle who must unite with the spiritually adept female, in this case, Mama Day. The only way George can be brought into the curvilinear intergenerational fold of Àjẹ́ is if his wife's life is threatened by the most unbelievable and debilitating of Africana powers.

Dr. Buzzard, stationed between Ruby and Mama Day, is the most balanced and consistent entity in the novel. Although he is often positioned as Mama Day's foil and described as a jackleg conjurer, Dr. Buzzard boasts an important spiritual heritage. His birth name is Dan Simpson, and Dan is not short for Daniel but complete for Dan. The progenitor of Damballah-Hwedo, Dan is depicted as a serpent biting its tail, recalling the ravage-renewal motif of Àjẹ́. And as the rainbow that encircles, supports, and unifies the earth and all its elements, Dan is the Deity who literally holds the world together. Given Dr. Buzzard's gender and cosmic affiliation, his stage name is "Rainbow Dan" (188); he is a perfect messenger for George. Albeit through a haze of liquor, George saw Dr. Buzzard become one with his tutelary Deity (215). However, rather than remind him of this or blow his mind with information about his role in Sapphira's humanospiritual covenant, Dr. Buzzard simply tells George that his wife has been Whodoed(?). Recalling the exchange from the spiritual realm, George asks his wife

> What do you do when someone starts telling you something that you just cannot believe? You can walk away. You can stand there and challenge him. Or in my case, you can fight the urge to laugh if it wasn't so pathetic: the grizzled old man with his hat of rooster feathers and his necklace of bones, shifting his feet and clearing his throat as he struggled to provide me with the minute details. . . . Snakeroot. Powdered ashes. Loose hair. Chicken blood. I would work until I dropped to get you out of there. (287)

Rather than open his nonspiritual, individualistic, and linear worldview to include a timeless force of origin, sustenance, creation, and evolution, George places his confidence in European constructs, mirroring Lucy's denial of the import of Africana spirit-work. Rather than join Mama Day in spiritual recognition and actualization, he struggles to repair Willow Springs's bridge/connection to North America so that he can find a "real" doctor.

While George is relying on the rational and echoing Mama Day's earlier sentiments concerning the ridiculousness of spirit work, Cocoa enters the second phase of Ruby's Whodo(?). She is hallucinating and her body is covered in red welts. Coming home from a futile day of bridge-building, George sees the physical ravaging of Cocoa, but he refuses to recognize the cause or the cure. In order to truly see, he must suspend his reliance on reason for submergence in the spirit. At Abigail's insistence, George goes to "the other place," the Day's spiritual powerhouse, to meet Mama Day. Attempting to open George's *ojú inú,* his inner eyes, Mama Day gives him, as Ruby gave her, a cosmological sign to interpret:

> I can do more things with these hands than most folks dream of—no less believe—but this time they ain't no good alone. I had to stay in this place and reach back to the beginning for us to find the chains to pull her out of this here trouble. Now, I got all that in this hand but it ain't gonna be complete unless I can reach out with the other hand and take yours. (294)

Miranda recites an Odù that melds revelation with riddles. George refuses to "really listen" to or decode Sapphira's latest Odù of 18 & 23, dismissing it as "a lot of metaphors." When Mama Day prescribes a cure that involves him going to her henhouse, reaching under the red hen in the northwest corner who is setting her last batch of eggs, and bringing her whatever he finds, George snatches his hands from hers and castigates her for talking "mumbo jumbo" about hens and eggs when her niece is sick.

Rootless and raised in an orphanage, George relies only on the power of his hands. They pulled him up by his bootstraps, grasped a Columbia education, yanked out an engineering degree, and carved out ownership of his own company. But George must join hands with the progeny of the Woman who also had nothing but her poor Black hands and light and used them to create a free society. George is asked to acknowledge the unifying covenant of and his inherent position within the gender-melded force of Damballah-Hwedo. He is asked to expand the immense belief he has in himself to include belief in a Woman and Force that defies Western definition. If George could put his hands into Mama Day's in a gesture of faith, all the bifurcation that made Sapphira's 18 & 23ing necessary, all of the divisions that meet on Cocoa's scalp—individuality/communality, objectivity/subjectivity, spirit/science, belief/disbelief, and man/woman—would be united through peace.

While George is denying spiritual realities, Cocoa, in the Whodo(?)'s final stages, is noticing that the strange welts that covered her skin have submerged themselves into her body. These welts are the larvae of worms, and her body is their host. Cocoa is the victim of one of the most oft-recounted works of Whodo(?), infestation of vermin. Stephen Farrow found that among the Yoruba, "Various forms of disease are described as 'snakes inside' (*ejo-inu*), 'an insect,' (*kokoro*), etc., and it is supposed that these have been introduced by a foe through the agency of witchcraft."[21] De Isla of Mexico was reputed to have spoken to three live salamanders before parching and grinding them and sprinkling the dust in a potential victim's drink.[22] And an African

American woman recalled the Whodo(?) put in her sister's water that resulted in an infestation of carnivorous spiders. The woman noticed that her sister's caregiver continuously wiped at her debilitated sister's mouth: "I had got very anxious to know [what she was wiping] so I stood by her head myself. Finally I seed what it was. Small spiders came crawlin' out of her mouth and nose."[23] With these we get a clearer understanding of the significance of Big Sweet's advice to Zora to avoid getting "uh spider in [her] dumplin'."

Contemporary author Gloria Naylor has listened closely to the elders; the Whodo(?) put on Cocoa is similar to historical infestations:

> It was no illusion that the welts had left the surface of my skin— it was smooth. And George, it was no illusion that they had begun to crawl within my body. I didn't need a mirror to feel the slight itching as they curled and stretched themselves, multiplying as they burrowed deeper into my flesh. . . . [T]hey were actually feeding on me, the putrid odor of decaying matter . . . I could taste on my tongue and smell with every breath I took. (287)

During his third and final call, George does not have to decode spiritual riddles because he experiences the 18 & 23ing of Cocoa first hand. After showering and copulating with a clear worm-infested Cocoa and telling her that the worms are only water, he finds a worm clinging to the head of his penis. The Yoruba elders state that gbàgbọ́ (belief) is "placed inside" a human being through spiritually charged medicinal preparations and power of the word. George is so resistant to African realities gbàgbọ́ must literally bite him to make him believe.

On his final visit to Mama Day, George does not snatch away his briefly held hands but embraces the gifts of the progenitors he has yet to know. Bearing Bascombe Wade's ledger (European patriarchal power) and John-Paul's walking stick (African male power) George makes his way to the henhouse. In a moment of simple brilliance, he decodes the Odù that recalls Sapphira's founding of Willow Springs and the covenant of Damballah-Hwedo: "Could it be that she wanted nothing but my hands?" But after distinguishing the Mama Dyumbo from mere mumbo-jumbo he insists, "There was nothing that old woman could do with a pair of empty hands." Like the males before him, George decides that "[t]here was no way [he] was going to let her go" in peace (301). Refusing to acknowledge the spiritual power of Willow Springs's women, George 18 & 23s himself. Grace named her daughter after a heartbreaker; and fittingly, George's heart explodes as soon as he steps on the road toward Ophelia. George and Cocoa's relationship in *Mama*

Day borrows an overlooked theme from Hurston's *Their Eyes Were Watching God*: "Real gods require blood." Because, as Bascombe, George would not become one with and acknowledge the power of Woman, his physical life becomes a sacrifice that saves Cocoa's, assures the Day's continuity, and finally brings Sapphira peace.

* * *

At the novel's onset, Mama Day contends that "the mind is everything." Truly, Whodo(?) and Hoodoo can have profound psychological impacts that accompany and act independent of material agents. However, Pliya's, Hurston's, and Naylor's works confound the assertion that Whodo(?) is all in the mind, and this is done in compelling ways. George's disbelief in Whodo(?), Hoodoo, and Àjẹ́ is as powerful as Zannu's slaying of Ayele's messenger birds and John and Lucy's killing of the serpent. Zannu loses his daughter as a result of his actions against Ayele, and Lucy dies as a result of Whodo(?) and her breeching of a cosmic covenant. John dies because of his inability or refusal to interpret and adhere to any covenant other than what his penis decrees. George Andrews was given full disclosure and a path to healing: He dies because he rejects the truth and the path. With his disbelief, like Lucy, George actually Whodos(?) himself, but he continues the search for wisdom, knowledge, and understanding in the afterlife. It is interesting to note that in the cases of the father of "The Watch-Night," Lucy, and George, Western reason, logic, and high-mindedness fail to thwart the overarching and furtive cosmic forces at work in these texts. And as it relates to the "wicked witches" of these texts, it is important to note that Ayele is the only Àjẹ́ killed for her actions. An' Dangie Dewoe dies an unremarkable death unrelated to any form of spirit-work. Hattie loses her husband, and Ruby is punished by fire. Rather than leaving us with the impression that these women are eternally condemned, the authors seem to ask us to continue probing the textual causes and effects.

A comprehensive analysis of Whodo(?)/Àjẹ́ dúdú in *Jonah's Gourd Vine*, "The Watch-Night," and *Mama Day* nullifies Western valuations of "good" and "innocent" and "evil" and "guilty." In *Death and the Invisible Powers*, Simon Bockie describes the context-based communal interpretation of Kindoki: "Any ndoki suspected of harming others is disliked or hated at the time he is harming. But when he is at peace . . . the community more or less forgets his wrongdoing and welcomes him into the family."[24] Bockie goes on to make an important point: "Harmful kindoki is allowed a well-defined place in the community so it can be subjected to the checks and balances that keep the group unified."[25] Acceptance of multidimensionality surfaces in early African American discussions of Whodo(?). Most elders, whether named or anonymous, are nonjudgmental about conjure that struck themselves and family members; many even speak with pride about their struggles with and against conjure.[26] Perhaps literary criticism could learn from those who, by acknowledging a spectrum of possibilities, ensured themselves unlimited potential to evolve.

7

The Womb of Life Is a Wicked Bag: Cycles of Power, Passion, and Pain in the Mother-Daughter Àjẹ́ Relationship

Àwọn Ìyá Wa control reproductive organs and are bonded through the power of menstrual blood and the lives it promises. Because the locus of Àjẹ́ is the womb, children can inherit the force as they inherit genes or particular traits. However, while a Yoruba proverb asserts, "Instead of the Àjẹ́ changing for the better, she continues to have more daughters, producing more and more 'birds,'"[1] Africana literature is not overly reflective of the mother-daughter Àjẹ́ relationship.

Most writers depict two types of Àjẹ́. One is the controlling matriarch, who forcefully or gently uses her Àjẹ́ to guide her family and, often, the community. The other is the young Àjẹ́ who is misunderstood by her mother, who denies or is unaware of her daughter's latent force. In the case of the latter, it is often a surrogate mother Àjẹ́ who guides the young woman to self-actualization. To avoid potential conflict, some works depict a mother who is nearing death or whose force is waning while the daughter's power is still latent. This is the case with Janie and Nanny in *Their Eyes Were Watching God*. If both women are simultaneously active, they often immediately find separate spaces for existence and expression. This is apparent in Amos Tutuola's *My Life in the Bush of Ghosts*, in which an uninitiated Àjẹ́ daughter flees her initiated Àjẹ́ parents and lives alone, honing her own force.[2]

In Toni Morrison's *Sula*, concurrent mother-daughter Àjẹ́ interaction is briefly evident. Eva Peace is the ambiguous one-legged matriarch of Medallion, Ohio, who exercises supreme control over her community. Eva renames and protects community children with the same intensity she uses to kill her own son. Her granddaughter, emergent Àjẹ́ Sula Peace, truncates Eva's reign. Sula, whose bold indifferent Àjẹ́ bonds her entire community by shattering its ego, returns from college and years of roaming to immediately send her grandmother to a nursing home. By doing so, Sula initiates a changing of the guard of Àjẹ́ and removes Eva's dominating influence from the sphere of interaction and from interfering with her personal textual climax. Like other settings, Medallion is not large enough for two simultaneously active Àjẹ́, but some texts give opposing powers space to interact. And when Àjẹ́ amalgamates genetically and artistically, the result is the enmeshment of mothers and daughters in a web of creation and destruction, love and hate, isolation and expression.

The works analyzed in this chapter are all from the ìtànkálẹ̀: *Zami: A New Spelling of My Name,* by first-generation Grenada American Audre Lorde; the short story "My Mother," by Antiguan Jamaica Kincaid; and *Beloved,* by African American Toni Morrison. Morrison's novel will constitute the bulk of this chapter's analysis, but all three works share compelling features that accentuate and facilitate the development and interaction of lineage Àjẹ́. Each of these texts is centered on a physical-cosmic space that alternately represents a void and a creative palate. In *Zami,* the free space is transformed from American nooses to Linda Lorde's perception-changing Àjẹ́ survival tactics to the spiritual and re-creative tablet that immortalizes Audre Lorde's power of the word in ink. In "My Mother," the space morphs from brackish pond to blinding blackness to a sea, and the mother uses these media to initiate her daughter ever deeper into the force of Àjẹ́. In the relationship of Sethe and Beloved, the mother and daughter, respectively, of *Beloved,* the space is an arena filled with profound sacrifices, "savings," re-embodiments, futility, and a fragile hope.

Another theme that connects the three texts is the fact that the male principle is deemed irrelevant to the mother-daughter Àjẹ́ relationship. In each text, fathers are dead, are not mentioned, or have been moved out of the sphere of interaction. Audre Lorde, who describes her father's print on her psyche as "a distant lightning" when compared to the singeing and illuminating, "kind and cruel," ever-relevant presence of mothers, gives the clearest articulation of the role of the father in the mother-daughter Àjẹ́ relationship. She testifies, "I have felt the age-old triangle of mother father and child, with the 'I' at its eternal core, elongate and flatten out into the elegantly strong triad of grandmother mother and daughter, with the 'I' moving back and forth flowing in either or both directions as needed."[3] As Lorde defines movement from the monodimensional to unity within a multidimensional spiritual consortium, the "elegantly strong triad" names, claims, and is shared holistically by a spiritual-material gathering of women.

It is not that the father has no place. He occupies a position of indisputable relevance, even in his absence. However, as mothers and daughters struggle to attain their rightful positions within an expansive and complex female spiritual power matrix, the father is relegated to the outside. This is evident throughout Lorde's exposition and in the concept of Zami. In "My Mother," no father is ever mentioned. In *Beloved,* Halle, Sethe's husband, is last seen with a lost mind and a face covered with butter. Even if father figures are present, they are pushed out of the sphere of interaction so that the lineage Àjẹ́ can define themselves for and against each other.

Another similarity among the works that feature lineage Àjẹ́ is the narrative style. Kincaid's writing style is often haunting, rhythmic, and spatial; her style infuses the page with spirit and the spiritual with texture. Her technique forces her audience to grope for and grasp meanings beyond the written text. Morrison also conjures ink to create a cosmically open text that welcomes and demands the participation of many entities. In all the voices of *Beloved*'s characters are nearly bottomless silences that are given texture by Morrison and textual and extratextual communities, making critical analysis of life and literature a multicommunity endeavor. As Morrison informs us, "My language has to have holes and spaces so the reader can come into it. . . . Then we (you, the reader, and I, the author) come together to make this book, to feel this experience."[4] Such intratextual and extratextual unification is also precisely what occurs at the close of Lorde's "biomythography," which ultimately invites all Africana women into the healing Ẹgbẹ́ Àjẹ́ of Zami. Linked by the exclusivity of womanhood, linguistic stylings, and the theme of mother-daughter power, the works of Morrison, Kincaid, and Lorde reflect lineage Àjẹ́ literarily. The transmission of Àjẹ́ occurs on multiple levels: genetic, cosmic, and via movement from an authorial creative pot to textual, extratextual, and spiritual communities that are alternately prepared, horrified, accepting, and oblivious.

ỌRỌ̀ ÀJẸ́: GENETIC ACQUISITION AND LINGUISTIC REVISION

Audre Lorde blends history, autobiography, spirituality, and myth to create a biomythography through which she can relate the philosophical, spiritual, and sensual peaks, nadirs, and cornerstones of her life. Lorde's relationship with her mother Linda dominates the first part of the biomythography. Linda's Àjẹ́ extends from altering perceptions of reality to obvious spurts of spiritual power, but most significant are the soul-stifling strictures she uses to raise a family in the midst of America's racist brutality and the myriad effects motherly Àjẹ́ and American oppression have on Audre Lorde.

Audre describes her mother Linda as "a very powerful woman" who exercises Àjẹ́ in a society that defines her as a mere mule. She not only shares equal household power with her husband, she is very much the head of the home (16). Like Anyanwu's mother in *Wild Seed*, Linda is a seer who aids community members with her spiritual perception, whether the situation is as mundane as bargaining or as dire as death. However, in retrospect, Audre wonders how much of her mother's power is spirit and how much is spiritual mystique:

> Strangers counted upon my mother and I never knew why, but as a child it made me think she had a great deal more power than in fact she really had. My mother was invested in this image of herself also, and took pains, I realize now, to hide from us as children the many instances of her powerlessness. (17)

Linda controls her surroundings by altering others' perceptions of her and cushioning her children against America's assaults. This is not a simple feat for a Caribbean woman who looks European who is married to a melanin-rich man and gives birth to three richly pigmented daughters.

Constantly in a position of battle, Linda becomes a "commander" capable of silencing racist entities with a glance. What she cannot control she twists into the impotent, the accidental, or the wonderful. Linda makes it easy for young Audre to overlook Caucasians "spit[ting] into the wind" and on her and Linda's disowning of Audre in public. The meager hand-to-mouth meals that materialize from these public disavowals always seem the most exquisite. Like Indigo's communal Mothers, Linda "knew how to make virtues out of necessities" (11), but such re-creation comes at great cost.

Audre has a difficult time navigating the uniquely charged and often-brutal world Linda creates, especially because stultified mother love is often unpredictable and violent. In a passage that highlights the generational impact of the Àjẹ́, Lorde reveals the nature of the weaponry she inherited from her mother:

> My mother's words teaching me all manner of wily and diversionary defenses learned from the white man's tongue, from out of the mouth of her father. She had to use these defenses, and had survived by them, and had also died by them a little. . . . All the colors change and become each other, merge and separate, flow into rainbows and nooses. (58)

Linda's lessons, as described by her pupil, illustrate the struggles, losses, and gains of being divine and displaced, of having Òrò in a neo-slave society that attempts to deny Àjẹ́ voice. Linda's gifts do not involve initiation into the covenant of Òṣùmàrè, witnessing the union of Odùduwà and Ọbàtálá on the horizon, or letting the rhythms of Damballah-Hwedo possess one's spine. The mother's lessons are those of surviving in spite of the fact that the Loa and Òrìṣà have been contorted into tools by which the devotee should hang. It is often the case that flawed jewels or noose-like rainbows are the only gifts of survival the Africana mother in America can offer her daughter. In *Their Eyes Were Watching God,* the narrator likens Nanny's lessons of survival for her granddaughter to taking the infinity of the horizon and turning it into a noose: This is the intertextual cross-generational noose that chokes both Audre and Linda.[5]

While Audre's testimony is a mourning of what her mothers lost, it is also a reclaiming and a reissuing of words so that the daughters can unbind the mothers' tongues and find their true birthright. Linda Lorde's hood-eyed observations, once understood, become the creative impetus for her daughter's pen. Audre reinterprets the paradoxical gift of her mother's Àjẹ́ and finds a force of signification and creativity that predates racism, slavery, and the land known as America. Prior to learning how to manipulate and create in America, Linda learned spiritual lessons from the neo-Ẹgbẹ́ Àjẹ́ of the "Belmar women." These Carriacou women carried African skills inside their breasts and passed them on to their daughters. Inspired by her mothers, Lorde's search for the source of her power leads her to Africa and her Mother: "I grew Black as my need for life, for affirmation, for love, for sharing—copying from my mother what was in her, unfulfilled. I grew Black as *Seboulisa,* who I was to find in the cool mud halls of Abomey several lifetimes later—and, as alone" (58, italics in original). Linda's seemingly blank pages bear the invisible ink of the Book of Destiny (Fa), as penned by Seboulisa, Creator Mother and Great Determiner of Destiny.

As she interweaves her critique and observations of life in America with African rhythms and signification techniques and fills those "unfulfilled" spaces in her mother, the Belmar women, and herself, Audre—Black as ink and filled with all signifying properties—massages choking ropes and fleeting rainbows until she consecrates a curvilinear space of juba born of spirit, flesh, and text.

> Ma-Liz, DeLois, Louise Briscoe, Aunt Anni, Linda, and Genevieve; MawuLisa, thunder, sky, sun, the great mother of us all; and Afrekete, her youngest daughter, the mischievous linguist, trickster, best-beloved, whom we must all become. (255, italics in the original)

This is the vibrantly scripted "elegantly strong triad" of the "I" of Àjẹ́. Similar to Àwọn Ìyá Wa within Ìyàmi Òṣòròngà, the matrix Lorde describes melds individual, familial, communal, and spiritual forces. Eschewing the master's tools for the Mother's Text and recognizing her position in the circle of power, Lorde turns blood into ink and scripts an Odù of salvation for the struggling self and a needy audience.

Zami details Lorde's romantic relationships, primarily with women, and the pain, joy, and sorrow that accompany these relationships and the inherent racism that pervades interracial relationships in the lesbian arena. However, the word Zami is a Carriacou term that defines a community of women who live and work together as friends and/or lovers.[6] Afrekete is Lorde's last lover in *Zami,* and it is she who guides Lorde to full self-realization and initiation and welcomes her home—into the Zami.[7]

> Afrekete Afrekete ride me to the crossroads where we shall sleep, coated in the woman's power. The sound of our bodies meeting is the prayer of all strangers and sisters, that the discarded evils, abandoned at all crossroads, will not follow us upon our journeys. (252)

When Lorde finds Afrekete, she finds her lover, spiritual head, community, and her patiently waiting, fully defined Self. Lorde informs her sisters that they also have a prepared space in the Ẹgbẹ́ Àjẹ́, the Womb of Mawu, where the Gods speak to their daughters, make love to them, and stand before them so that the Africana woman sees in herself not an American anomaly but the true reflection of her "ancient properties."

TRANSFORMING ÀJẸ́ FROM M/OTHER TO SELF

Kincaid's evocative work revisits the concerns, divisions, and fragile unity apparent in Lorde's early relationship with her mother. However, with no characters save a mother and her daughter, "My Mother" magnifies the intensity and paradox at work in the mother-daughter Àjẹ́ relationship. With the characters unnamed, except for their fully representative titles, and set in a quasi-spiritual realm, "My Mother" seems more cosmic allegory than short story, and this text's lessons are multitiered.

The first words of the story, which are the daughter's, reveal an intense conflict that has origins beyond the page: "Immediately on wishing my mother dead and seeing the pain it caused her, I was sorry and cried so many tears that all the earth around me was drenched."[8] The daughter is so confounded by the existence of her mother and her self that she weeps a pond into existence. This brackish, stagnant water represents the space of potential that will demarcate the parameters of this mother-daughter relationship, and it is a space as malleable and variable as the daughter herself.

Following the daughter's murderous thought, which is as powerful as an act, and her effusive remorse, the mother opens her wicked bag for her child. She showers her daughter with kisses and draws her close to her bosom, but this motherly embrace becomes a death grip. She suffocates the daughter, who dies, yet is conscious of her death and mothered resurrection: "She shook me out and stood me under a tree and I started to breathe again" (53). Revived under the Tree of Life, the daughter learns that while she can cause her pain, she cannot better her mother, who is creator and orderer: This is the daughter's first mother-administered lesson in the cosmic order of Àjẹ́.

Creating, destroying, and re-creating, the mother navigates the rage, delight, and passion of her daughter with a mature force that affirms who is elder in years, knowledge, and power. The women's cognizance of mutually shared, dense, and unlimited Àjẹ́ sets the boundaries for a relationship that is actually boundless. But just as the mother and daughter share vast creative abilities, they also are separated by the brackish pond, a space that simultaneously represents death and destruction, division and creativity, unification and cohesion. The mother shows her daughter how to shape, name, and claim the space that signifies their Àjẹ́.

Significant examples of educational and transformational Àjẹ́ occur when the daughter sits on her mother's bed, "trying to get a good look" at herself in a completely dark room. It is solid Blackness, the full depth of dúdú, that the daughter uses as a mirror. To aid her daughter's desire to distinguish her uniqueness from the blackness of everything, her mother lights candles. Rather than illuminating the singular self, a divided unity is revealed. Just as Janie Crawford recognized her astral and physical selves and the power of each, so too do Kincaid's mother and daughter witness the singularity of their indivisible material and spiritual forms: "We sat mesmerized because our shadows had made a place between themselves, as if they were making room for someone else. Nothing filled up the space between them, and the shadow of my mother sighed" (54).

The profundity and possibility within blackness move the mother first to sigh and later to juba. The daughter's shadow joins the mother's in texturing free space with rhythm, vibration, and expression. The women sing each other's oríkì and pay homage in the way of a community performing Gẹ̀lẹ̀dẹ́ for Ìyàmi Òṣòròngà: "The shadow of my mother danced around the room to a tune that my own shadow sang, and then they stopped" (54). Just as light made their shadow-spirits visible, their shadows reciprocate and impart existence to the space, in the light, and between the shadows. The mother reveals the space between her and daughter to be not a void but a tangible astral realm—a spiritual playground and classroom. Extending lessons in the transformational capabilities of Àjẹ́ from shadows to Select Head, with her third lesson, the mother gives her daughter the gift of immortality.

The significance of Serpent Deities across Africa and their covenants with humanity have been extensively discussed in previous chapters. In the ẹsẹ Ifá, women become serpents and receive immortality through Òṣùmàrè, who represents the ability of human beings to "become transformed and experience rebirth" or attain everlasting life.[9] The Alur people of Central Africa recall the power of serpentine women and immortality in "Why People Die." The text concerns an elder Ndoki who asks her granddaughter not to disturb her as she sloughs her skin. The child's curiosity moves her to interrupt the elder. Just like a snake, the grandmother has sloughed half her skin when her progeny disturbs her, and the interruption ruins the entire sloughing process. The elder castigates her granddaughter, saying, "If you had not called me, I could have shown you the secret of renewing the skin," which would have yielded eternal life. Instead, the young woman and her progeny (humanity) are cursed with hard work, struggle, and death.[10] In "My Mother," the millennia-old secret is revealed and revised, unifying Kongo, Yoruba, and Fon ways of knowing in the ìtànkálẹ̀.

> My mother removed her clothes and covered thoroughly her skin with a thick gold-colored oil, which had recently been rendered in a hot pan from the livers of reptiles with pouched throats. She grew plates of metal-colored scales on her back, and light, when it collided with this surface would shatter and collapse into tiny points. Her teeth now arranged themselves into rows that reached all the way back to her long white throat. She uncoiled her hair from her head and then removed her hair altogether. Taking her head into her large palms, she flattened it so that her eyes, which were by now ablaze, sat on top of her head and spun like two revolving balls. Then, making two lines on the soles of each foot, she divided her feet into crossroads. (55)

In the way of Anyanwu, the mother undoes body, time, and space to welcome the eternal. She instructs her daughter to follow her example, and the pair becomes one in Damballah-Hwedo. Just as Mawu and Aido Hwedo undertook a tour of the earth and fashioned mountains, valleys, riches, and rivers along the way, so too do mother and daughter step through the crossroads of the mother's feet and undulate into the realm of the origin of existence.

The mother's phenomenal tutorials in power provide brief respite for the daughter, whose desire for destruction counterbalances the force of unification. At one point, she stands beside her mother with her arms around her waist and her head on her shoulder in order to make her mother believe she is frail and weak. In actuality, the daughter feels she's "invincible." She leans heavily on her mother, either to prove the elder's weakness or crush her. However, the more weight the daughter presses on her, the stronger her elder becomes. Enraged by the mother's superior Àjẹ́, the daughter yearns to see her mother "permanently cemented to the seabed." She roars to frighten her mother and whines when she is ineffective. Finally, she resigns herself to the fact that she "had grown big, but my mother was bigger, and that would always be so" (56).

The twinning and unification of self and other that perplexes the daughter is the same unified relationship of the individual Àjẹ́ within the Ẹgbẹ́ who work under the auspices of Ìyàmi Òṣòróngà and are subject to Ìyá-Ayé and Odù. Each of these entities is distinguishable from the other, having unique traits and inclinations, and yet all are aspects of Àjẹ́. The daughter attempts to establish her individuality apart from her mother but instead discovers the immortal promise of unified Àjẹ́. When she sits on an island and adorns eight full moons with the expressions of her mother, she recognizes her own perfection and resemblance in those reflections. The bliss of oneness is short-lived, as later, the daughter weeps at her mother's daily absence, only to become enraged by her elder's return: "At the end of each day when I saw her return to her house, incredible and great deeds in her wake, each of them singing loudly her praises, I glowed and glowed again, red with anger" (59). The daughter's dilemma is not that mother is "other" but that mother is the *self*—an ancient self—that she, in spite of her Àjẹ́, did not create, cannot destroy, and refuses to find peace within.

Realizing her daughter's paradoxical impasse, the mother invokes Yemọja, Owner of Waters, to seal the fact of their immortality and cool her child's rage. She stretches the brackish pond into an ocean that can provide unity through distance and sends her progeny on a boat ride to her Self. Having crossed the void she created only to find the architect of her existence reflecting her Self as always, the daughter finally enters into a "complete union" with her mother. Their union is metaphysical: "I could not see where she left off and I began, or where I left off and she began." It is also physical: "I fit perfectly in the crook of my mother's arm, on the curve of her back, in the hollow of her stomach." Instead of straining for the individuality of "I," the narrating daughter speaks in plural possessive pronouns: "Our white muslin skirts billow up around our ankles, our hair hangs straight down our backs as our arms hang straight at our sides" (60). The daughter anticipates reaching the same spiritual apex of amalgamated Àjẹ́ that Lorde attained: "As we walk through the rooms, we merge and separate, merge and separate; *soon we shall enter the final stage of our evolution*" (60–61, italics added).

MY MOTHER'S WOMB HAS INFINITE RICHES

"My Mother" is a text woven on a largely ahistorical tapestry, and liberated in that free space, the protagonists themselves constitute their only barriers to expansion. *Beloved* also revolves around a mother and daughter's desire to enjoy such a unity. However, as the narrator poignantly reveals, enslaved Africans were struggling for existence in lands in which they could list more relatives, especially children, who had "run off or been hanged, got rented out, loaned out, bought up, brought back, stored up, mortgaged, won, stolen or seized" than loved.[11] Rather than subject their progeny to the financially based, sexually depraved, and morally bankrupt whims of their oppressors, some mothers of Àjẹ́ returned the creations of their wombs to the tomb-like "wicked bag." Although many critical analyses of these acts of lineage Àjẹ́ describe the mother killing (mentally, spiritually, or physically) her daughter, Morrison's work forces us to re-evaluate this simplistic assessment. Tormented mothers of Àjẹ́ might not be destroying their progeny; they might be *saving* them. As Sethe says, "I took and put my babies where they'd be safe" (166).

Having a safe sacred space has always been of paramount importance to displaced African peoples, and under circumstances only Odù could have imagined, her enslaved progeny attempted to recreate her consecrated space of creation. The Ancestors called such spaces the Arbor Church, the Conjuring Lodge, the Crossroads, and the Praying Ground. What occurred in these spaces took many forms, but it was all juba. In the African American lexicon, juba acts as both a noun and a verb, and it signifies the confluence of song, dance, prayer, lamentation, and exultation—*juba*lation. In *Zami,* Lorde transforms the linguistic tools and silences of her mother into a juba of Àjẹ́. The comprehensiveness of juba pervades every line of "My Mother." In *Beloved,* various types of juba are discussed in relation to the sacred spaces and times that galvanize them: As a child, Sethe witnessed shape-shifting juba (31); Baby Suggs's Calls to the Clearing are juba; and Sixo structures his entire liberated, empowered, immortal existence on the inviolable force of juba (21, 25, 225–226). The juba created by Sethe and Beloved twice in the novel is a phenomenal melding of spiritual and material Àjẹ́, and both jubas occur at 124.

The primary setting of *Beloved* is the home at 124 Bluestone Road in Cincinnati, Ohio. From the opening of the work it is apparent that 124 so enshrines soul-power, juba, and Àjẹ́ that it can be considered a character. Morrison emphasizes 124's humanity at the beginning of each of the novel's three sections, which respectively describe 124 as "spiteful," "loud," and "quiet." Sethe's daughter Denver regards 124 as "a person rather than a structure. A person that wept, sighed, trembled and fell into fits" (23). While these descriptions of 124's vitality are due to Beloved's spiritual presence, the domicile had long been an arena for cosmic and terrestrial interrelations, and this may be the result of its spiritual and numerological stationing. Bluestone Road is apparently named after the fungicide copper sulfate. A highly toxic staple of conjure, bluestone "burns like hell" when applied to a cut but heals instantly.[12] In numerology, 124 can be condensed to seven, which is the number of Òrìṣà Ògún, owner of iron, weaponry, and technology. Ògún's role in protecting and empowering enslaved Africans and complementing Sethe's Àjẹ́ is profoundly important. The sequence 1-2-4 also unconsciously represents the unseen number three.[13] Three is a number of spiritual unity, and it is also the number of the alternately silent and signifying Yoruba trickster Èṣù, who, like the *concept* of Beloved (discussed below), is omnipresent and omniscient.

Located on the "free side" of the Ohio River, 124 is where runaways and the officially free go to find succor, connect with lost relatives, and rebalance shattered equilibria. However, when Baby Suggs realizes and actualizes her Ọ̀rọ̀ Àjẹ́, 124 becomes a gateway for the transformational force of the Clearing. Located just outside 124, the Clearing is the equivalent of the sacred African groves where initiations and rituals, including sacrifice, take place. Baby Suggs uses the complementary spiritual forces of 124 and the Clearing to enact a two-tiered communal initiation. After she mends, as well as she can, the torn lives of the newly freed and those still seeking freedom, she "Calls" them to the Clearing to mend their spirits:

> They knew she was ready when she put her stick down. Then she shouted, "Let the children come!" and they ran from the trees toward her. . . .
> "Let your mothers hear you laugh." . . .
> Then "Let the grown men come," she shouted. . . .

"Let your wives and your children see you dance." . . .
Finally she called the women to her. "Cry," she told them. "For the living and the dead. Just cry." . . .
It started that way: laughing children, dancing men, crying women and then it got mixed up. Women stopped crying and danced, men sat down and cried; children danced, women laughed, children cried until, exhausted and riven, all and each lay about the Clearing damp and gasping for breath. (87–88)

Like the Anlo Ewe diviners, Baby Suggs recognizes the àṣẹ of the Clearing, and she uses its power to help her community determine its destiny.[14] Initially, Suggs specifies roles for gender and age groups. As these roles become transformed through her Àjẹ́, they are holistically melded until such divisions are rendered meaningless because of their interdependence. The Àjẹ́ of Africana women, the Oṣó of Africana men, and the àṣẹ of both, as manifest in the promise of their children, are united in the Clearing through the juba of Baby Suggs, holy.

The text that accompanies the juba is not a religious sermon or catechism but a spiritual charge to embrace the few things the Clearing participants dare lay claim to—their bodies, their spirits, and, most fragile, their ability to love.

Here . . . in this here place, we flesh; flesh that weeps, laughs, flesh that dances on bare feet in grass. Love it. Love it hard. Yonder they do not love your flesh. They despise it. They don't love your eyes; they'd just as soon pick em out. No more do they love the skin on your back. Yonder they flay it. And O my people they do not love your hands. Those they only use, tie, bind, chop off and leave empty. Love your hands! Love them. Raise them up and kiss them. Touch others with them . . . stroke them on your face 'cause they don't love that either. *You* got to love it, *you*! (88)

Suggs transforms gender roles and individual and anatomical character until everything is merged and shared holistically. Revising the concept of human sacrifice, Baby Suggs leads each community member to submit every element of the self—section by section, entity by entity—to re-establish connection with the communal Self and the Ground of All Being.

As the "caress" after her name indicates, Baby Suggs, holy is the Ìyánlá, the quintessential Àjẹ́ who galvanizes the powers of the earth with her staff of àṣẹ. But as the governing heart of her community, Suggs is subject to critique and correction for improper actions. Twenty-eight days, one monthly moon after the arrival of Sethe and the newborn Denver, Suggs celebrates the arrival and life of her progeny by turning two buckets of blackberries and a few chickens into a feast to feed the entire community. The celebration commemorates a unity that is false, and the feast calls Suggs's application of Àjẹ́ into question. Just as the Ketu community used Gẹ̀lẹ̀dẹ́ to critique Ìdá Àlábá, who nearly destroyed the community with war-mongering, slavery, and excess, so too does Baby Suggs's community critique her actions. However, rather than publicly sing her infractions, the community critiques Suggs through perfect silence and, as punishment, allows riders to enter her yard. However, because she is the community's soul, the censure of Suggs destabilizes the entire community and sends Àjẹ́ soaring.

Spirit Birds of Àjẹ́ manifest themselves in many of Toni Morrison's novels. In *Paradise*, buzzards circle over and signify at a wedding; in *Sula*, sparrows signal the changing of a guard.[15] In *Jazz*, Violet is introduced as living with and later releasing her flock of birds, and Wild, Violet's seeming mother-in-law and re-embodiment of Beloved, is signified by "blue-black birds with the bolt of red on their wings."[16]

The Spirit Bird regularly assists Morrison's literary Àjẹ́ with their confounding actions. In *Sula*, matriarch Eva Peace is described in terms of Àjẹ́. Swooping like a "giant heron," Eva extends her arm in the manner of "the great wing of an eagle" as she douses her son in kerosene before setting him ablaze.[17] This mother creator-destroyer-protector, who "held [her son] real close" before baptizing him in fire, also takes wing and jumps out of her window in an attempt to save her daughter, who sets herself on fire.[18] Sethe follows Eva's path. When she sees the hat of her former oppressor, schoolteacher, Sethe sees a life she will not tolerate. The Ẹyẹ Òrò snatches up her children "like a hawk on the wing . . . face beaked . . . hands work[ing] like claws," to put them in a "safe" place.

> She was squatting in the garden and when she saw them coming and recognized schoolteacher's hat, *she heard wings. Little hummingbirds stuck their needle beaks right through her headcloth into her hair and beat their wings.* And if she thought anything it was No. No. Nono. Nonono. Simple. *She just flew.* Collected every bit of life she had made, all the parts of her that were precious and fine and beautiful, and carried pushed, dragged them through the veil, out, away, over there where no one could hurt them. Over there. Outside this place, where they would be safe. *And the hummingbird wings beat on.* (163, italics added)

Guided by an Àjẹ́ collective of hummingbirds whose wings spark Ọya's winds of change, Sethe secretes her children in the woodshed of 124. Melding her Àjẹ́ with the power of the Clearing and 124, she creates in the woodshed an *ojúbọ*, a sanctuary where Òrìṣà are kept and worshipped with libation and sacrifice. Sethe takes her children, who she defines as minor Òrìṣà—her "precious," "fine," and "beautiful" creations, or re-embodiments of herself—inside the ojúbọ/woodshed. There, the mother Àjẹ́ begins the work of transformation—placing her children back into Odù's pot of origins. Under the institution of slavery, this may well be the most profound expression of devotion. Using a handsaw, one of the iron implements of Ògún, as a tool of facilitation, Sethe returns the living Deities of her self to the Mother, aware that Àjẹ́ and Ìyánlá are the only forces that can ensure her children's safety.

It is well-known that *Beloved* is a re-membering and reordering of the life, actions, and Àjẹ́ of a woman named Margaret Garner. In "The Negro Woman," Herbert Aptheker discusses Garner's saving work, which occurred in 1856, and her philosophy and resolve:

> One may better understand now a Margaret Garner, fugitive slave, who, when trapped near Cincinnati, killed her own daughter and tried to kill herself. She rejoiced that the girl was dead—"now she would never know what a woman suffers as a slave."—and pleaded to be tried for murder. "I shall go singing to the gallows rather than be returned to slavery."[19]

Garner ordered her existence and that of her progeny with the only means available to her—her Àjẹ́. Using the same maternal, retributive, protective Àjẹ́ as Garner, Sethe successfully sent her oldest daughter to the other side.

Sethe and Garner's actions are not rare or unique. Fannie of Eden, Tennessee, is another saving mother. Cornelia, who was interviewed in the 1920s, described her mother Fannie as "the smartest black woman in Eden" and a woman with an Àjẹ́-esque duality. Fannie "could do anything": "She was as quick as a flash of lightning, and whatever she did could not be done better." But she was also "a demon." As her daughter recalls, "Ma fussed, fought, and kicked all the time. . . . She said that she wouldn't be whipped. She was loud and boisterous. . . . She was too high-spirited and independent" to be a slave. "I tell you, she was a captain."[20] An enslaved captain, Fannie ingrained Àjẹ́ survival tactics into Cornelia from childhood, telling her, "*I'll kill you, gal, if you don't stand up for yourself.* . . . fight, and if you can't fight, kick; if you can't kick, then bite."[21]

As a living example of Àjé resistance, Fannie beat the plantation mistress when she struck her, chased her into the street, and ripped off her clothes, revealing female equality and Àjé's superiority.[22] Fannie declared, "Why, I'll kill her dead if she ever strikes me again." In *Beloved,* the utterly self-possessed Sixo grabs his captors' gun to provoke a standoff, but Fannie is his historical progenitor. Below is Cornelia's description of her mother's reaction to the county whippers who had been employed to chastise her for beating Mrs. Jennings:

> She knew what they were coming for, and she intended to meet them halfway. She swooped upon them like a hawk on chickens. I believe they were afraid of her or thought she was crazy. One man had a long beard which she grabbed with one hand, and the lash with the other.
> . . . She was a good match for them. Mr. Jennings came and pulled her away. I don't know what would have happened if he hadn't come at that moment, for one man had already pulled his gun out. Ma did not see the gun until Mr. Jennings came up. On catching sight of it, she said, "Use your gun, use it and blow my brains out if you will."[23]

When Fannie declared, as would Brer Rabbit, "I'll go to hell or anywhere else, but I won't be whipped," Jennings decided to send his unbeatable slave out of his Eden, but he told Fannie she could not take her infant, his "property," with her. Truly Garner's (and, literarily, Sethe's) sister of the struggle, Fannie, on the day of departure, took her infant, held her by her feet, and, weeping, "vowed to smash its brains out before she'd leave it." Cornelia concluded, "Ma took her baby with her."[24]

And yet Fannie was not exiled. She and her husband returned from Memphis to Eden and their children with "new clothes, and a pair of beautiful earrings."[25] Fannie lived the rest of her life in as much peace as her Àjé and an oppressive society could afford her. Indicative of biological acquisition of Àjé, Cornelia grew to be just as Àjé-influenced as her mother.

Cornelia's testimony is included in a volume titled *The Unwritten History of Slavery.* Toni Morrison corrects this oversight and writes the lessons and sprinkles the spirit of Fannie—from swooping vengeance to whip-grabbing standoff to beautiful earrings—throughout *Beloved.* Fannie's commandment to her daughter to use every means, from fighting to kicking to biting, to defend herself also wells up in Sethe in an intriguing manner during her escape from Sweet Home and schoolteacher and his breast-raping nephews. A nine month and painfully pregnant Sethe, with blasted feet and a freshly whipped bloody back, stretches out on a dirt path. Unable to walk, she contemplates death and wonders how long her unborn child will keep kicking in her womb after she passes. Prostrate with compounded misery, Sethe groans and attracts the attention of a traveler, who begins to investigate the source of the grieving. The voice, the smell, and the memory of schoolteacher's nephews raping her breasts of milk trigger cosmic assistance for and within Sethe:

> She told Denver that a *something* came up out of the earth into her—like a freezing, but moving too, like jaws inside. "Look like I was just cold jaws grinding," she said. Suddenly she was eager for his eyes, to bite into them; to gnaw his cheek.
> "I was hungry," she told Denver, "just as hungry as I could be for his eyes. I couldn't wait." (31)

Sethe does not know who is calling out from the other side of a stand of trees—the nephews, a new rapist, riders, or lynchers—but with the help of Ìyàmi Òṣòròngà, who swallows dubious people whole, she is prepared to devour any adversary: "I wasn't just set to do it. I was hungry to do it. Like a snake. All jaws and hungry" (31).

From the Yoruba cosmological view, Ìyá-Ayé enters Sethe— "something came up out of the earth into her"—and provides space for Erè, the woman who became the àṣẹ-filled python known as Òṣùmàrè, to possess and protect Sethe. Indicative of the covenant Odù, Òṣùmàrè, and Olódùmarè extend to human beings, what happens to Sethe as she lies on the path gives Fatunmbi's translation of Olódùmarè—"The light of the Rainbow comes from the Primal Womb"—new depth. The light of Òṣùmàrè enters Sethe's womb and magnifies and compounds her and her child's ability to "become transformed and experience rebirth."

With much more rapidity and without any ritual accompaniment, Sethe shows herself to be as much a daughter of Damballah-Hwedo as Kincaid's mother. In "My Mother," the women become the Serpent Loa and embody their promises of protection, power, and immortality. In *Beloved*, the Òrìṣà enter Sethe so that she can share the covenant of immorality with her progeny—when they are in the womb and while they are in the world.

Sethe's saving Beloved is the focal point of the novel, but cosmic assistants and literary and historical progenitors are protecting and guiding her long before she sees the hat that is symbolic of hell. Her protection is also evident in that fact that the entity Sethe is prepared to eat—feet first if necessary—is a Caucasian girl named Amy Denver. Whether she is human, spirit, or haintly human, Amy saves Sethe, and

Sethe names her newborn daughter Denver so that her child will always be one with her multiply miraculous life-text.

The manner in which Sethe saves Beloved, and her entire family, from slavery is also miraculous and divinely guided. Using the methodology of the traditional Yoruba Ẹyẹ Ọ̀rọ̀, Sethe's juba in her sacred space blends the actions of both Garner and Fannie. Sethe, like Margaret Garner, is able to make safe her oldest girl. When schoolteacher and his men enter the woodshed, Sethe, like Fanny, is holding Denver by her feet and is about to save her by bashing her newly born head against the rafters. It is apparently important to Sethe, Margaret, and Fannie that the daughters be made safe first and foremost: They are the ones who can grow to have their milk stolen, their wombs defiled, their womanhood mocked. Sethe saved a womb-lodged Denver and made the child synonymous with her text. But circumstances force Sethe to send her oldest daughter to the other side without her ìtàn. It is fitting, then, that Beloved becomes both the family's text and an ìtàn for all times.

When *Beloved* opens, nearly eighteen years after Sethe's saving act, the home that was a sanctuary for her and countless other displaced Africans in America is the desolate stomping ground for a wrathful "baby ghost," who is the daughter successfully sent to the other side. Sethe and Denver live alone with the "ghost," exiled from the community not because of fear but because the community finds Sethe's show of love, similar to that of Suggs, too prideful and selfish. From the outset, condemnation on the grounds of pride seems a stretch in Sethe's case. She is remembered as holding her head too high and carrying her neck too stiffly as the police led her away. It seems that either the community is too judgmental or that the author is too heavy-handed in directing events. However, from a Yoruba perspective, Sethe and Baby Suggs trespass the law of Àjẹ́ that "one must not display wealth."

The community, acting very much as a society of traditional African elders would, punishes Baby Suggs with silence after she celebrates her spiritual and material wealth with a magnificent feast. Sethe, a mere runaway, did not even own herself, let alone her children, by America's standards. However, she dares to love and protect them and claim them fully. Because Sethe does what no other community member would conceive of doing to protect his or her wealth, her private work of protection is interpreted as a grandiose display. Her knowledge of her wealth and power is evident in her refusal to weep or beg forgiveness. Showing no remorse and exuding an air of "serenity and tranquility" after her act, she loses the respect and consideration of her community.

Sethe's crime of displaying wealth, her "outrageous claim" to love and protect her children, speaks volumes about the complexities of the Africana ethos. In an interview with Elsie B. Washington, Morrison elaborates on the centrality of self-worth to enslaved Africans in America: "Those people could not live without value. They had prices, but no value in the white world, so they made their own, and they decided what was valuable. It was usually eleemosynary, usually something they were doing for somebody else."[26] Sethe clearly values her children, as is evident in her descriptions of them, and she does for them what no other person can do. But her trespass is better understood in the light of Morrison's next statement: "Nobody in the novel, no adult Black person, survives by self-regard, narcissism, selfishness." This is the imperceptible line Sethe crosses. The community doesn't punish her for saving her daughter; they punish the individualistic narcissism precipitating that act.

The goal of slavery and racist oppression is the complete destruction of the magnificence that Nikki Giovanni calls "Black wealth." This goal is evident in the fact

> [t]hat anybody white could take your whole self for anything that comes to mind. Not just work, kill, or maim you, but dirty you. Dirty you so bad you couldn't like yourself anymore. Dirty you so bad you forgot who you were and could think it up. And though she and others lived through and got over it, she could never let it happen to her own. The best thing she was, was her children. Whites might dirty *her* alright, but not her best thing, her beautiful, magical best thing. (251)

Although the divine part of Sethe was maimed, dirtied, and twisted nearly beyond repair, her children emerged from her womb as whole, perfect, and brilliant as she once was. The statement "The best thing she was, was her children" makes it clear that Sethe was not just saving the deified progeny that she created, she was also claiming and making "safe" the "magical," priceless, and most exquisite aspect of her divine original Self.

Abandoned by nearly every living person except the daughter who almost became a recipient of her saving love, Sethe and her daughters exist in a perfect trinity of Mother, Daughter, and Spirit that is broken only when Sethe goes out to work. 124's isolation from the larger Africana community emphasizes Morrison's point about Sethe choosing individuality over communality, and it facilitates unification of this Àjẹ́-rich trio. Sethe's desire to help her "best thing" understand her actions and Denver's loneliness and frustration move the women to summon their spiritual third for a terrestrial meeting. Denver and Sethe use Òrò—"come on, come on, you may as well just come on"—to unite spiritual, physical, and geographic planes of existence at 124. They invite the hidden number three, the unifying spiritual member, to share their material space. Just as Oyeronke Igbinola used power of the word to invoke Ìyàmi Òṣòròngà, who arrived to take part in her praise, so too does Beloved, having received her ritual invitation, begin crossing all boundaries to enter the sacred realm prepared by her mother.

However, the brutality of America imparts a new dimension on transformational juba: Beloved was sent to a "safe" place through the violent protective Àjẹ́ of a handsaw. In cosmic reciprocity, it is violence that precipitates her revivification. In Chinua Achebe's *Things Fall Apart*, Okagbue slashes the corpse of an ogbanje (àbíkú) infant named Onwumbiko, holds it by one foot, and drags it into the forest for burial. Similarly, Paul D takes a chair and beats Beloved's spirit without mercy as soon as he enters 124 (19). The Igbo dibia and Paul D seem to have the same thing on their minds: "After such treatment it [the spirit child] would think twice before coming again." However, to quote Okagbue's musings, Beloved is "one of the stubborn ones who returned, carrying the stamp of their mutilation—a missing finger or perhaps a dark line where the medicine-man's razor had cut them."[27] Paul D's seemingly successful exorcism actually forces Beloved from the spiritual to the material realm. She arrives, and Sethe takes her in as she would any other young orphaned African American woman.

Great debate continues over who Beloved is and what she represents. The common theory that Beloved is a ghost is dubious because she eats, makes vicious love, dribbles, and washes and folds clothes on request. Beloved could be defined as ghost prior to Paul D's arrival, but the woman who reveals his Red Heart is no ghost. Morrison describes Beloved as a multifaceted entity: Beloved is "a spirit on one hand, literally she is what Sethe thinks she is, her child returned to her from the dead. And she must function like that in the text. She is also another kind of dead which is not spiritual but flesh, which is, a survivor from the true, factual slave ship. She speaks the language, a traumatized language of her own experience."[28] Beloved is each of these things, and as a confluence of all, she is infinitely more.

Beloved reflects and represents all manner of Àjẹ́'s ravage and renewal for a people seeking to forget the atrocities that have befallen them. As a spiritual force of sufficient tangibility to impregnate, Beloved is a girl recently escaped from a defiler's prison, and because she is too weak to walk, she glides or two-steps over the earth. Beloved is the marked child in African American culture who is affected, in vitro, by the horrors the mother witnessed.[29] She is also the àbíkú—the one-born-to-die—who is slashed and scarred to prevent return, but who re-enters, from the spirit realm, the traumatized womb for rebirth and perhaps a chance at terrestrial longevity. A child of countless sacrifices and as many Mothers, Beloved bears on her neck the scar of the one for whom she vows to bite away the choking "iron circle."

Each of Àjẹ́'s signature colors shine in Beloved: She left in a river of blood; her spirit kneels beside Sethe in white, and she arrives physically at 124 Bluestone Road clothed in the living power of black. Seated on the stump of Pan-African cultural and ethnic awareness, the Blackness of Beloved unites the deeply buried ancestral roots and painfully pruned modern branches of the African family tree—and her blood increases the mineral content of undeserving lands and the volume of the Ethiopic.

When she describes her journey on a ship of death, Beloved is the walking recollection of atrocities too horrible to remember, and she is the sacrifice that endows us with the abysmal luxury of forgetting. The Mother enslaved Africans first thanked for surviving the Middle Passage of death was Yemọja: No matter what immediate atrocities life held, the eternal covenant of Mother of Waters—of peace, evolution, and rebirth—would not be broken. Yemọja is the "universal principle of the survival of the species,"[30] and Beloved is her strolling promise. Indeed, when Beloved is spotted in the forest at the end of the text, it is not surprising that she bears the Great Mother's fish on her Select/ed Head (267). Occupying various identities and positions—including protagonist/antagonist, author, and intended Africana audience—Beloved is Ọbàtálá, everything and nothing. She defies any and encompasses all definitions.

In her full multidimensionality, Beloved travels through the sixteen crossroads to return home to 124. When she arrives, she opens Sethe's "restricted consciousness" and demands the naming and claiming of her dis-membered self therein. In the initial stages of her arrival, Sethe is too close to the truth of Beloved to recognize her as her daughter. However, Denver, who took mother's milk and sister's blood in one swallow, realizes what one will not reveal and the other cannot see. It is through the slow process of rememory that Sethe understands who Beloved is. Rememory is an unalterable, unforeseeable, and frightening process that is related to material and spiritual spaces and books.[31] Beloved initiates the process by which she will be re-membered gently. Watching Sethe comb Denver's hair, she asks, "Your woman she never fix up your hair?" That question takes Sethe to the plantation upon which she grew up and to the mother with whom she had few encounters. Sethe verbally rememories her mother showing her the mark burned into her breast and that her mother was so brutally lynched that "[b]y the time they cut her down nobody could tell whether she had a circle and a cross or not" (61).

Before the force of rememory can overwhelm her, the telling of the narrative is transferred. It is Sethe's "restricted consciousness" that rememories her being taught an African language by her mother and her caregiver, Nan. Sethe's rememory enlightens the reader to the fact that her Àjé and its methodology are products of genetic transmission. Memories—of Nan telling Sethe that her mother named her after a man she loved, one she "put her arms around" and of Nan telling her that her mother killed the products of rape and projects of breeding forced into her womb—well up in Sethe's consciousness but do not cross her lips. While Sethe's verbal rememory clearly helps Beloved cement her transitory spiritual self in the material world, the unspoken orature provides a doorway for other dis-membered selves to enter.

The subconscious rememories the narrator recounts are "spaces" that the author and historical, textual, and extratextual community members fill. Beloved inquires about Sethe's "diamonds." Her request—"Tell me your earrings"—places Cornelia, who had been briefly abandoned in "Eden"; Sethe, who had chosen to forget a gift from "Sweet Home"; Morrison; and all other seeking survivors at the Mother's knee. Additionally, because of free indirect discourse, in the passage where Sethe's concept of value is defined, the "you" that can be dirtied, shamed, egregiously used, and fouled is at once Ella, Stamp Paid, Paul D, Baby Suggs, Sethe and her children, Margaret Garner and her children, and the entire Pan-African world. And while the passage begins with Denver's ruminations, it is the narrator of *Beloved* who articulates Sethe's assessment of worth and value and opens the discourse and pronouns to include textual and extratextual communities. For another example, the question "How did she know?" follows Beloved's first spate of inquires (63). Although the reader might assume that Sethe is thinking to herself, the space within the unspecified pronoun is wide. "She" can refer as easily to Morrison as to Beloved. Furthermore, the query seems subtly directed at the audience—as a question *we* must answer, a space *we* are charged to fill.

Toni Morrison is clearly the medium of rememory. When the coalescence of history and tragedy are too much for her characters to bear, Morrison writes the unwritten and verbalizes the unspoken. It is not Paul D who recounts a flooded wooden cage, the Hi-Man, and a breakfast of horror. He had placed these atrocities "one by one, into the tobacco tin lodged in his chest [and] nothing in this world could pry it open" (113). It is Morrison, as other-worldly "Beloved" Self, who, at the three-road junction of history, the spirit realm, and the present, can share Paul D's rememory comprehensively. Expanding Lorde's Afrekete-centered matrix of Àjẹ́ in a multidimensional manner, the holistic aesthetic of Morrison, the mediating Ìyá-Ìwé (Mother of the Text) makes the act of reading *Beloved* an initiation into the Beloved Self, the Beloved Spirit, and the ever-present past for spiritual, historical, and contemporary audiences. As the novel's biblical epigraph makes clear, Beloved is a divine Pan-African paradox: She is human and spirit; recognized and dis/re/membered; other and self; novel, character, historical entity; and, as is stated in the dedication, she is one of "Sixty Million and more" lost-found Africans. The very existence of *Beloved*, let alone reading the work, becomes a cosmic application of a necessarily stinging bluestone for every Africana person who bears but has ignored the genetic scars of slavery in order to survive but must re-member every fragmented affliction in order to fully heal and evolve.

Although Sethe, like most Africana people, cannot safely re-member without sliding into an abyss of pain, she can and does articulate the terrifying uncontrollable process of rememory to Denver and explains why she had to open her pot of creativity and place her best, most exquisite, and magical creations safely inside it—away from the ever-threatening force of rememory and the more terrifying threat of repetition:

> Someday you be walking down the road and you hear something or see something going on. So clear. And you think it's you thinking it up. A thought picture. But no. It's when you bump into a rememory that belongs to somebody else. Where I was before I came here, that place is real. It's never going away. Even if the whole farm—every tree and grass blade of it dies. The picture is still there and what's more, if you go there—you who never was there—if you go there and stand in the place where it was, it will happen again; it will be there for you, waiting for you. So Denver, you can't never go there. Never. Because even though it's all over—over and done with—it's going to always be there waiting for you. That's how come I had to get all my children out. No matter what. (36)

Sethe, like so many Africana people, attempts to escape a past that cannot be outrun, a past that follows, taints, and tickles. By using her Àjẹ́ to save her daughter and exorcise the memory and reality of Sweet Home from her and her progeny's realm of existence, Sethe consecrates an infinitely more turbulent space of rememory. With the invocation and arrival of Beloved there is anti-creation, because the daughter returns with an Àjẹ́ equal to the love, intensity, and killing pain of her mother.

Morrison explains the doubling at work between Sethe and Beloved as what occurs when a "good woman" displaces "the self, her self." She describes that dislocated "self" as the Igbo describe the *chi,* the personal spirit who guides one to one's destiny, and as Yoruba describe the *ẹnikejì,* the twin soul with whom one makes agreements before birth. With *Beloved* and *Jazz,* Morrison said she tried to "put a space between [the] words ['your' and 'self'], as though the self were really a *twin* or a thirst or something that sits right next to you and watches you."[32] Most relevant to *Beloved,* Babatunde Lawal and Emefie Metuh make it clear that the ẹnikejì and chi can become offended and angered by their earthly representative's actions. Just as the spirit twin can protect its human complement from harm, "Offending one's spirit double or heavenly comrade may cause it to withdraw its spiritual protection," leaving one susceptible to death.[33] Beloved is more than a daughter; she is the "self" and "best thing" of Sethe. Just like the *chi,* she is the Deity of Sethe and all Africana peoples. Sethe's "best thing" also revises African cosmology; she withdraws her dubious spiritual protection only to go directly to her mother, at her request no less, for full re-membering.

Beloved and her life, death, and return represent the juncture between the rememory/reality of Sweet Home, the bonding and bloody jubas of 124, and the cycles of tragically dislocated Africana peoples, who are doomed to repeat past lessons because of a failure to re-member, heal, and evolve. As the women navigate this immense matrix of love and pain, shades of the daughter Àjẹ́'s desire to kill her mother, which is prevalent in Kincaid's work, surface in *Beloved.* Overwhelmed by rememories and the knowledge that her husband lost his mind as he helplessly watched her be raped, Sethe seeks solace in the Clearing. She prays to feel Baby Suggs's "holy" touch, and she is rewarded: "Sure enough—they were there. Lighter now, no more than the strokes of a bird feather, but unmistakably caressing fingers" (95). It is not Suggs, but Sethe's "self," her personal Ẹyẹ Ọrọ̀ in the form of Beloved, who massages away the psychological trauma. But, as if in repayment for the scar on her neck, Beloved follows Kincaid's mother and turns her soothing touch into a death grip. Immediately after she chokes her mother, Beloved caresses and kisses Sethe's bruises with more intensity and tenderness than any lover could muster (97). Like Ìyàmi Òṣòròngà, Beloved is the one who devastates her mother, and she is the one who delivers her mother from devastation. And deliverance becomes an important concept, because Beloved does not want to destroy Sethe. She wants the two of them to "join" and return fully unified to the "other side."

In addition to complete re-memberment, Beloved desires free uninterrupted discourse with the fascinating entity who placed her in a safe place of confusion. To achieve her aim, she uses her Àjẹ́ to force Paul D, with his distracting "love" for Sethe, out of 124, and Paul D facilitates the process. Having found out about Sethe's saving work, he demands that she explain what to her is elementary. Rather than answer him directly, Sethe circles—the kitchen, the topic, the answer. She circles, as would a buzzard, that spiritual messenger; she moves in the manner of the spirit-hummingbirds that wait over her head. Within Sethe's circles is definite avoidance of the issue, and for many reasons: (1) explaining her actions to Paul D would be akin to explicating the esoteric to the uninitiated; (2) her actions are beyond the justification his silent query seeks; (3) Morrison makes it clear that no human being, including the "last of the Sweet Home men," can judge Sethe.[34] Paul D's questions can only rightfully be asked by Beloved. However, Sethe's circular response to Paul D is also what Ama Ata Aidoo would describe as useless perambulation. Until the issues concerning the events that forced millions out of Africa to alien lands, the bones bleaching in the Ethiopic Ocean,[35] and the warriors on auction blocks are addressed, Africana people will run to, circle about, and seek out safe havens but will always bump into that silently waiting and watching Self.

Paul D is the primary male force in the novel, and it is in his Westernized masculinity—his acts of violence, his audacious attempts to query and judge, and his refusal to respect the integrity of Sethe's love—that his unpreparedness is apparent. These along with his newspaper inquiry and counting of Sethe's feet make it clear, long before Beloved moves him, that Paul D is simply not ready, and he does not become prepared until the novel's end—after the mother-daughter "join" has been thwarted—to be the complement Sethe needs. Consequently, he is moved out of the sphere and cannot move anything in it. With the male aspect exorcised, Sethe and Denver harness all their power to re-member Beloved, and with the latter's physical-spiritual reality, the women become a trinity of Mother, Daughter, and Daughter-Divinity similar to the cosmic union Lorde entered in *Zami* and the holistic unification experienced by the characters of "My Mother." But rather than a shared "I" or a unified "our," a possessive "mine" flows among the women: "Beloved, she my daughter. She mine"; "Beloved is my sister"; "I am Beloved and she [Sethe] is mine" (200, 205, 211). Instead of the customary narrative style, Morrison uses open-ended lyric free verse to accommodate the space and the unspoken language of love of this trinity of Àjẹ́:

You are my face; I am you. Why did you leave me who am you?
I will never leave you again
Don't ever leave me again
You will never leave me again
You went in the water
I drank your blood
I brought your milk
You forgot to smile
I loved you
You hurt me
You came back to me
You left me
I waited for you
You are mine
You are mine
You are mine (216–217)

Morrison expands English syntax to accommodate Beloved and provide space for lost-found souls and intended audience members to enter.[36] With the first line of the passage, *Beloved* becomes a mirror. The fathomless depths of the black ink encompass, absorb, and reflect every community member, the pages provide reflection and refraction, the margins radiate with impending revelations. But the glimpse of eternity Morrison offers her reader glints with a different light for Sethe.

Within the rhythms, de-riddling, and reunion of Beloved, Sethe, and Denver are accusations, gatherings-up of pain, demands of ownership, and reminders of debts impossible to pay. Sethe's ẹnikejì would ordinarily texture her existence and consciousness from the sacred realm. But because she equated her best self with her children, made the decision to save that precious self, and summoned the self for a discussion, Sethe comes face to face with her spirit, her embodied conscience, and her and all her people's past. As any good mother would, Sethe is resolved to nourish her (and our own) "best thing."

> The bigger Beloved got, the smaller Sethe became; the brighter Beloved's eyes, the more those eyes that used never to look away became slits of sleeplessness. Sethe no longer combed her hair or splashed her face with water. She sat in the chair licking her lips like a chastised child while *Beloved ate up her life, took it, swelled up with it, grew taller on it. And the older woman yielded it up without a murmur.* (250, italics added)

The Beloved/Sethe-Self has returned for what she was denied: recognition, what Brother J of the Dark Sun Riders calls "verbal milk," and cohesion. With no other means to appease her physical (spiritual guide), Sethe gives herself to her Self.

Denver realizes that Beloved and Sethe's "join" will mean the end of Sethe, so she steps out of 124's spiritually charged haven and into the world. Although Denver has been isolated from the community for over a decade, the displaced Àwọn Ìyá Wa of the Cincinnati respond and offer sustenance and covert support to Denver and Sethe. For Beloved, the community mothers make plans. Although the community women believe Beloved to be Sethe's daughter, she also represents Sethe's best Self, that of each of the community's women, and through Morrison's efforts, the best Self of all Africana people. Given the all-encompassing totality of Beloved, Sethe's sacrifice in the ojúbọ is far from selfish. She saves the entity whose destiny is to remind, confound, and facilitate the healing of textual and extratextual Africana communities. However, by community standards, Beloved as an all-in-one Deity is too complex, too brilliant, and far too painful to exist. Embracing the most reductive and the least agonizing aspect of Beloved's multitudinous Self, the community women gather to destroy the "devil-child."

The overwhelming paradoxical truth of Beloved and the grief undergirding their collective un/conscious move the women to take "a step back to the beginning." In the beginning, there were no whippings, no bits to suck, no lynching, no lessons in the racist brutality that tutored Hitler. There was only Ọ̀rọ̀. In "Verbal and Visual Metaphors: Mythical Allusions in Yoruba Ritualistic Art of Orí," Rowland Abiodun reveals the cosmic etymology of the word Ọ̀rọ̀. Stating that "words" is a lay translation, Ọ̀rọ̀ is also "a matter, that is, something that is the subject of discussion, concern, or action," and it is the "power of the word."[37] An important "matter" and serious subject of concern, Beloved embodies and attracts Ọ̀rọ̀. And just as in the beginning of creation Ọ̀rọ̀ opened the path for wisdom (ọgbọ́n), knowledge (ìmọ̀), and understanding (òye) to enter the world,[38] so too does the community women's Ọ̀rọ̀ partially catalyze their creative, destructive, and interpretive abilities.

As the Àwọn Ìyá Wa hum, sing, and harmonize, the vibrations of Ọ̀rọ̀ Àjẹ́—identical to those Odù made when she pulled existence out of her pot and those Sethe groaned to invoke Ìyá-Ayé and Òṣùmàrè—interrupt Sethe and Beloved's joining and invite them into the Clearing juba that has been brought to their front lawn. Sethe's carefully nurtured "best thing" emerges as a surviving àbíkú about to give birth:

> The singing women recognized Sethe at once and surprised themselves by their absence of fear when they saw what stood

next to her. The devil-child was clever, they thought. And beautiful. It had taken the shape of a pregnant woman, naked and smiling in the heat of the afternoon sun. Thunderblack and glistening, she stood on long straight legs, her belly big and tight. Vines of hair twisted all over her head. Jesus. Her smile was dazzling. (261)

The beauty of Sethe's Beloved-Self helps us better understand the mother's rapture, devotion, and vanity. What is more, although they condemn her with Western terminology, the women have no fear of Beloved, for they know her well. She is, like Denver, "everybody's child." These women do not bond to exorcise Beloved because she is a "devil"; they move to destroy her because her presence and their acknowledgment of her reality, which is also their own reality and the totality of the power, pain, glory, gore, and divinity of themselves, would quite simply break their hearts.

Sethe, for all her seeming vanity and pride, is the text's most progressive entity. Having conferred with Odù, she knows what has the ultimate value and how to protect what is priceless—not just for her personal satisfaction but for the evolution of the community. Sethe also turns the community's gifts of sustenance for her into sacrifices that nourish Beloved's pregnancy. It is possible that this unborn child holds the keys to the complete healing and evolution of Africana peoples, provided we can survive the labor and growing pains.

On another level, and despite the fact that the act results from a case of mistaken identity, Sethe's personal development is evident in her decision to kill Edward Bodwin, the Euro-American abolitionist owner of 124, employer of Denver, and owner of a Sambo figurine. In this community, still reeling from the horrors of slavery and outraged by the sick reality of neo-enslavement, it is the external factor, that of Euro-America—that which seeks to make a commodity of what is priceless and make dirty the best thing—that acts as a catalyst. The arrival of Bodwin expedites the convergence of the twin circles of Àjẹ́. Bodwin is ignorant of two orbs of Àjẹ́ and his role in unifying them, but when Sethe sees him approaching, she thinks the defiler, schoolteacher, has returned, again, to enslave, steal, and sully her "best thing," and she becomes one with her Spirit Bird:

> She hears wings. Little hummingbirds stick their needle beaks right through her headcloth into her hair and beat their wings. And if she thinks anything, it is no. No. Nonono. She flies. The ice pick is not in her hand; it is her hand. (263)

When Sethe mounts on wings of Ìyàmi to attack, the community women thwart her, and, again, through violence there is partial peace, as the women simultaneously save Bodwin and reintegrate Sethe. Still in the throes of their joining, Beloved misinterprets Sethe's updated saving act as abandonment. With the "join" compromised by a re-unified community, Beloved explodes, leaving "precious," "fine" vestiges of her unspeakable Self to take root in the soil, float on the waters, make darker and more defined the ink of the text, and burrow into the recesses of and tickle all-too-forgetful minds.

* * *

With an intricate profusion of pain, power, and potential, Kincaid, Lorde, and Morrison use the text as a palate to re-create and navigate a labyrinthine love of epic proportions. No matter what the magnitude of destruction, sorrow, and loss faced by these writers' characters, the writers themselves, or the reading audience, there is a fragile hope in each of these works—a whispered promise that the trauma of healing will indeed bring wholeness. In these texts there is neither beginning nor end: The circular covenant of Damballah-Hwedo, the promising embrace of Afrekete, and the infinitude of Odù are always-already waiting. Like these literary mothers and daughters, we readers must have the courage to enter the charged spaces, claim our priceless and often unwieldy inheritance, and resuscitate it, revise it, and pass it on.

8

Twinning across the Ocean: The Neo-Political Àjẹ́ of Ben Okri's Madame Koto and Mary Monroe's Mama Ruby

One of Àjẹ́'s most significant jobs is enforcement of the laws of the earth. Given the stunning, astounding, and daring works of historical women such as Olufunmilayo Ransome-Kuti, Madame Tinubu, and the Igbo women warriors, who battled patriarchal tyranny, slavery, and colonialism, it is logical that contemporary African literature reflects Àjẹ́'s political acumen. As a result of segregation, economic deprivation, and choice, African Americans often find themselves living in self-governed societies that are nearly or fully autonomous. In addition to all-Africana towns such as Eatonville, Florida; Mound Bayou, Mississippi; and Princeville, North Carolina; there are scores of inner-city urban and rural communities where the Africana population is high and a non-Africana presence of authority is rare. Parliament's song "Chocolate City" paid homage to such cities and communities, especially the U.S. capital, saying, "God bless Chocolate City and its vanilla suburbs!"[1] The unrecognized mayors and administrators of those towns and communities are often Africana women. And just as African life and literature inspire one another, historical women such as Rebecca Jackson, Harriet Tubman, Mary Ellen Pleasant, Barbara Lee, and Maxine Waters boast kinship with such literary figures as Baby Suggs, Aunt Haydee, Sapphira, and Mama Day. This chapter will examine literature's most impressive and perplexing wielders of neopolitical Àjẹ́: Mama Ruby of Mary Monroe's *The Upper Room* and Madame Koto of Ben Okri's *The Famished Road* and *Songs of Enchantment*.

Although each woman's place of origin and application of Àjẹ́ is unique, Ruby and Koto have many similarities. Both women are born Àjẹ́, and this force is manifest in their actions and their physical appearances. Ruby and Koto are both obese and can be hideous:

Madame Koto is likened to a rhinoceros without a horn; Mama Ruby is said to resemble "Godzilla in a half-slip." However, juxtaposed to descriptions of their unsightliness are elaborations on their magnetizing sensuality. In addition to alternately evoking feelings of disgust and desire, both are charismatic leaders who attain unquestionable supremacy in their communities by successfully applying their Àjẹ́ and bending alien political agendas to fit their needs. Using their Àjẹ́ to ensure community stability, leisure, and enjoyment, Ruby and Koto are respected political powerhouses and feared "elders of the night." However, both women are held in check, if only partially, by spiritual children who are at once their totems and holders of their life energies.

THE MAMA'S MAMA

In the Africana worldview, spiritually endowed children are often marked as such at birth. Cauls, the placement of the umbilical cord, tooth and hair growth, and multiple births all portend specific spiritual destinies. Ruby Jean Upshaw is perhaps the most marked figure in literary history:

> Lightning struck the house that night and I was born, premature. I had a full set of teeth . . . scales on my hands and feet like a serpent. I had webbed toes up until I was five and Mama got me operated on. They say when I got old enough to talk, I had the voice of a man. . . . I was marked by [a] stole Bible. That conflicted with me bein a seventh daughter of a seventh daughter and havin healin hands. When I was two, I told Papa to his face I was the devil.[2]

With a pilfered Christian "good book" foretelling her destiny, Ruby burst into the world with a blink from Ṣàngó, wriggled from the womb like Damballah, and when she spoke, she did so as Àjẹ́: "Mother who speaks out with the voice of a man."[3] As the novel progresses, she takes on nearly all oríkì Àjẹ́, including "Mother who kills her husband and yet pities him."[4] Weighing from 300 to more than 500 pounds, Mama Ruby is also large enough to hold the power of many Òrìṣà in her frame. She takes on the attributes of Ọ̀ṣun, giving life with healing hands, and she protects her children in the way of Yemọja.

In addition to her birthmarks, the order of her coming is also important to Ruby's vast power and her composition. In Mama Ruby, we find a reconstitution of the "seventh son of the seventh son" motif. This important motif recurs in African American literature and culture, as is evident in the trickster figure that Ralph Ellison's protagonist meets in New York. In *Invisible Man,* the eccentric character who calls himself Peter Wheatstraw, in the tradition of the "shit, grit and mother wit"– steeped folk hero who is "the devil's only son in law,"[5] informs the protagonist of his remarkable origin: "Iamaseventhsonofaseventhsonba wnwithacauloverbotheyesandraisedonblackcatboneshighjohntheconquer orandgreasygreens."[6]

In addition to Wheatstraw's catalyzing diet of Black Cat Bones and John the Conqueror roots, the fact that he is the "seventhsonofaseventh son" is of the utmost importance. Focus on the "sons" has led people to ignore empowered mothers. But with Sapphira of *Mama Day,* Gloria Naylor reminds the sons of their stupendous origin, and Toni Morrison does the same in *Sula* with her description of Mrs. Jacks:

> She was an evil conjure woman, blessed with seven adoring children whose joy it was to bring her the plants, hair, underclothing, fingernail parings, white hens, blood, camphor, pictures, kerosene and footstep dust that she needed, as well as to order Van Van, High John the Conqueror, Little John to Chew, Devil's Shoe String, Chinese Wash, Mustard Seed and the Nine Herbs from Cincinnati. She knew about weather, omens, the living, the dead, dreams and all illnesses and made a modest living with her skills. Had she any teeth or ever straightened her back, she would have been the most gorgeous thing alive, worthy of her sons' worship for her beauty alone, if not for the absolute freedom she allowed them . . . and the weight of her hoary knowledge.[7]

With Morrison conflating such adjectives as evil, blessed, and adored, Mrs. Jacks emerges as yet another paradoxical Mother of Power who hones a "discredited" force for members of her community and recycles aspects of that force in her seven sons.

Long before African American mothers began giving birth to power, Great Mother Mawu gave guidance and a central position to Legba, the seventh and most precocious of her offspring:

> "You are my youngest child, and as you are spoiled, and have never known punishment, I cannot turn you over to your brothers, I will keep you with me always. Your work shall be to visit all the kingdoms ruled over by your brothers, and to give me an account of what happens." So Legba knows all the languages known to his brothers, and he knows the language Mawu speaks, too. Legba is Mawu's linguist. If one of the

brothers wishes to speak, he must give the message to Legba, for none knows any longer how to address himself to Mawu-Lisa. That is why Legba is everywhere.[8]

Both Legba of the Fon and Ẹlẹ́gbára of the Yoruba are commonly misgendered male (or assigned that gender by default) and mislabeled devil, but they are "everywhere," take on both genders, hold àṣẹ and manipulate Àjẹ́, and have multitudinous offspring. Corresponding to the multiplicity of Legba is his Fon sister, Afrekete, MawuLisa's seventh *daughter* and divine linguist whose sphere of influence encompasses the land and, significantly, the sea upon which Africans rode to the ìtànkálẹ̀.

Monroe reopens the text of the seventh sons to include a forgotten daughter of Afrekete who grew up to become communal Big Momma, or Ìyánlá. And when the spiritual forces inherent in those doubly magnified sevens are fortified by Àjẹ́, the result is a confluence of all powers. Mama Ruby, the seventh daughter of the seventh daughter, is gifted with healing hands and power of the word, and as a descendant of Ìyàmi Òṣòròngà, she boasts control of material and astral realms. She is the cross of the sixteen crossroads, and her power has both cosmic and terrestrial origins. Ruby describes her lineage as such, "Papa say his papa told him and his papa told him that his mama told him our folks come from one of the most warlike tribes in Africa. Say durin slavery couldn't nobody do nothin with us. Shoot. *I ain't scared of nothin*" (88, italics in original). Because her great, great, grand Mother and patriarchal forebears have provided the historical foundation for her self-conceptualization, Mama Ruby knows she has nothing to fear—not even the Western God and Devil.

Mama Ruby is, in fact, both Lord and Lucifer, and she is the level ground upon which these seemingly disparate entities meet. The embodiment of divine paradox, Ruby says of herself, "Though I am filled with the Holy Ghost, I am also the doorway of darkness" (127). The melding of God and Devil in Ruby reflects the African expansion of Western religious beliefs. As is apparent in African American orature, the Devil is not inherently evil, and such a figure does not exist in the vast majority of African societies. Cursory readings of African American orature reveal the Devil to be as helpful as God—even more so—because he tests will and skill and gives sound advice. He doesn't give one what one wants but what one needs—character-building trials from which all eventually learn (as the orature are shared communally). In marrying God and the Devil in one form, Monroe doesn't just complicate the two entities, she renders them void. Although too humble to admit it, as a true Àjẹ́, Ruby is "superior to . . . the gods"—and the devils!

As "the Lord's pet nigger" and "the devil's walking stick," Ruby defies categorization in any terms other than Àjẹ́. However, her potential is initially overshadowed by her companionship with Othella. Her best friend since childhood, Othella is an African American of mixed ethnicity. While Othella is lauded in a racist society for her Caucasian features and her "white folks' sense," Ruby has the more enduring qualities of "spunk," charisma, and charm, and these characteristics are augmented by her "power" and "glory." Even Othella recognizes the significance of Ruby's ìwà, saying, "Ruby Jean, I got too much good sense for my own good, true enough, but you the one with all the glory. Yep . . . you got the power and the glory" (15).

The novel opens in Silo, an isolated community in the bayou-rich alligator-ridden Florida Everglades, and although they complement one another, Othella's "white folks' sense" and Ruby's "power" and "glory" have not served them particularly well. Othella earns her living with occasional crop work and by giving sexual favors to proprietors to whom she is indebted. As proof of payment, Othella has eight children of various skin tones. Ruby augments her meager Social Security check with theft and illegal business ventures. When anyone comes to inquire about her activities, she "chastizes" or kills them as she feels Lord-Lucifer would have her do. For example, an impoverished Ruby steals an income tax check and justifies her killing of "ole meddlin government [men]" who come to inquire about the theft by stating that she is living a life dedicated "to the Lord" and doing "nothing Jesus wouldn't do."

Ruby's primary accomplice is her son Virgil, who aids in the killing and disposal of bodies. Virgil is also unique in being one of the few people who can query Mama Ruby. Despite having little contact with larger society, Virgil knows that his mother's actions are not representative of those of most people. He recalls dubious reprobates, such as a Hispanic man Ruby killed because he "looked like" he wanted to rape her, and asks, "Mama Ruby . . . you ever . . . I mean . . . well what I'm tryin to say is, you ever think about them folks we done chastized? I mean, sometimes at night I be layin in the bed thinkin about it" (31). When Virgil probes too deeply, Ruby weeps and pleads righteousness from the perch of her newfangled Christianity.

The Christian religion is replete with gaps that displaced Africans in America, coming from all-encompassing political, cultural, and spiritual systems, must fill. Contradictions such as slavery, racism, lynching, and violent subjugation in a nation that calls itself Christian need to be accounted for. In subtle ways, and throughout the text, Monroe challenges her readers to analyze the role reification plays in hierarchical categorization and dichotomy. Mama Ruby is the ultimate dichotomy-buster, being both Lord and Lucifer; furthermore, members of her communities also undertake the work of self and cultural analysis and religious re/appropriation. The characters in *The Upper Room,* having weathered unimaginable storms, are ultra-Christians. They have more "glory" than average people, and given the nebulous concept of sin, they backslide freely and get "saved" many times a year. Just as enslaved African Americans did before her, and as is apparent in the encoded prayer of Leonor de Isla (see chapter 2), Monroe's characters necessarily open and fill the mandated Christian religion to fit their needs.

De Isla was accused of worshipping the Devil but uttered prayers rich with pleas to "Our Lord" and "Jesus." Similarly, Ole Scratch's tricksterian capacities are important to Ruby's self-conceptualization as Jesus; both figures motivate and provide justification for her actions: "My bosom is a battleground for good and evil. . . . All my life I been straddlin that thin line what divides good and evil. I got Jesus in front of me and in the back of me but I got Lucifer on my right . . . and on my left" (285). Mama Ruby is the holiest of unholies and above reproach. While the Devil silently motivates her quick-to-kill actions, Jesus is her overall sanctioning agent: "My switchblade and my shotgun and Jesus done settled a lot of disputes around here" (183). In addition to chastising, Ruby heals and renews community members and performs various wondrous feats, as Othella reveals in the following passage:

> Folks say you can raise everything but hell with your healin hands. I seen you myself rub the croup out of my boy Joe. . . . You straightened out Brother Hamilton's crooked leg. . . . *You delivered my soul.* You growed a rose bush on a bed of rocks. I seen you do it. (24, italics added)

Jesus and the Devil, for all the lip service they are granted, are so completely regrafted and seamlessly recrafted in Ruby that they are irrelevant. They are empty hangers upon which her glory, or Àjẹ́, is draped.

Her power over religious forms and figures is apparent in her Òrò. Even her prayers are demands, as is evident in the following example of rhetorical eloquence:

> "Lord, I went up to Satan last Sunday and slapped him down where he stood with my powerful prayer. Now, I ax you, will you let this woman here be in peace? Will you help us birth her baby when the time come? In Jesus' name I pray . . . amen." When Ruby left Othella's house, she did so with tears in her eyes. For she felt she had delivered Othella from evil. (19)

Mama Ruby does not commence her prayer with the classic ritual praise of the Lord but with praise of herself! She reminds the Lord of the work she has done in his service and demands reciprocity—or else! With rhetorical questions, she signifies on the "Lord," verbally whipping him into submission as a mother would chastise and direct a child. Furthermore, the Lord answers Ruby's prayer for Othella in a way that thanks Ruby for her hard work and bolsters her power and glory.

Àjẹ́ is manifest in the ability to make desires realities. Ruby had always wanted a baby girl, but at thirty, with no man in sight, she begins to lose hope. After Ruby prays for her, Othella gives birth to a beautiful but stillborn daughter, and Ruby's healing hands are ineffective. Seizing the moment, Ruby demands of Othella, "[L]et me name this baby and make out like she was mine" (27), and Othella reluctantly assents. Ruby names the infant Maureen after the New Orleans madam she and Othella once prostituted for, and Ruby immediately constructs an ìtàn about having a beautiful daughter who died. While she is carrying Maureen's corpse home in a shoebox, Ruby rejoices, "You is my very own little girl. I prayed to get you and I got you" (28). Filled with adoration and humming a spiritual, Ruby wraps the corpse in newspaper so that it can be buried immediately and not burst in the summer heat. Perhaps Ruby's great love and desire unite with her Àjẹ́ and Othella's approval, because after Virgil unwraps the corpse to better view an advertisement for a kite, Maureen moves.

Ruby is terrified that Othella will learn of the resurrection and demand that her infant be returned, so she and Virgil secrete themselves in their home with Maureen. After few days, the trio leaves Silo in the middle of the night. Once she gets situated in Goons, Florida, Ruby enshrines her divine gift in the Upper Room and massages her Àjẹ́ into its fullest form.

Like Afaro, the "mother of the clan and daughter of Oziara" who was so revered she was considered a Deity and engaged in no manual labor,[9] Ruby, as mother of the clan of Goons and embodiment of power and glory, has no need to work. Her duties are restricted to healing, chastising, and bonding her community through many means, including entertainment. Ruby installs a record player in her living room and sells watered-down bootleg beer to her friends and neighbors. But when her poor-man's Gẹ̀lẹ̀dẹ́ is disturbed, her entire community witnesses the power of the woman who has taken up residence among them. When he realizes that his beer is mostly water, a visitor bashes Ruby across the mouth with an iron tool, ruining her false teeth. "Ruby grabbed the man and slammed him against the wall repeatedly until he was dead, his brains oozing onto the floor" (45). She tells her remaining guests, "Ain't nobody seen nothing." Ruby's first show of Àjẹ́ in Goons is followed by Virgil's observation that she resembles "a fat, old, no-teeth witch." Despite her actions and appearance, Ruby inspires not fear or disgust but admiration. Her friends procure a new set of teeth for her, and she is soon boasting both a fiancé and a "fancy man."

In her second show of force, Mama Ruby extends her authority and legend to West Miami. Out dancing with Slim, her fancy man, Ruby accidentally knocks over the table of Mack Pruitt, who signifies not only on her—"I say you is a big, black cow"—but also on her mother—"and your mama one too!" (48). Although the community warns Mack, "That ain't no regular lady—that's Mama Ruby!" he shoots Ruby in the chest. In retaliation, she shakes the gun out of his hand and then shakes off his entire arm. Days later, when she realizes she has been shot, she performs surgery on herself and removes the bullet with her fingernail and a butcher knife. Learning that Mack has also survived, she puts everyone on notice: "Somewhere in this world is a one-armed *dead* man" (52, italics in original). At this point, Ruby's Àjẹ́ is at its apex and will remain so for years. It is important to note that the community forms the foundation of her force. They befriend her, shore her up, egg her on, and participate in the necessary chastisements that create a political enclave controlled by Àjẹ́ in Goons and surrounding towns.

Ruby's sphere of power is comparable to Sapphira Wade's solidification of Willow Springs. The island's inhabitants pay no state tax and are under the jurisdiction of no state agency. Goons is also autonomous, albeit on a smaller scale. Ruby's fiancé Roscoe owns a provisions store; Zeus is the communal seer who "runs cards," or divines by playing cards; itinerant crop work is available for those who need to work; and Reverend Tiggs keeps the sinners in a constant state of salvation and re-salvation. Like Sapphira Wade, Mama Ruby is the soul of the community. She initiates and ends all action. She is the center of good times. Manifestation of the Spirit Bird, Mama Ruby is "the one who brings festival." However, the Spirit Bird waits with a blood-reddened beak for those who seek to wreck the festivities.

Using her power with much less discretion than traditional Àjẹ́, Ruby reshapes African conventions to fit her gargantuan form and her community's needs. As Àwọn Ìyá Wa, she is a multiform construction: She is the singular Àjẹ́, she is the Ẹgbẹ́ Àjẹ́, and she is also Ilẹ̀ Ọgẹ́rẹ́: Anyone who "steps on [Ruby] wrongly," "where it may cause [her] injury," is disposed of quickly and efficiently. Fancy men, bill collectors, and would-be rapists all "die on the farm," and Ruby places them in her ever-devouring pot. Just as "no one ever sees the remains of an Òrò victim,"[10] no one sees the remains of enemies of Goons and Ruby. Furthermore, as Àwọn Ìyá Wa, Ruby is reticent about her work.

When Maureen asks about Abdullah, who was "settin on his front porch yestiddy mornin, yestiddy afternoon, and yestiddy evenin," Mama Ruby laconically replies, "He ain't settin there no more . . ." (207).

Ruby's political power cuts also across the lines of state, race, gender, ethnicity, and American law. Zora Neale Hurston jokingly (?) asserted that in the early 1900s, African American women were charged for murder of African American men only if they went over an unknown "quota."[11] African Americans, in most cases, were governing themselves in small towns and migrant labor camps. Therefore, Mama Ruby-esque self-appointed governors were common. If external non-Africana governing occurred, it was not done by a federally recognized authority in most cases, but by the Ku Klux Klan and other hatemongers. However, the Klan stirs no fear in Ruby. She modernizes the quota Hurston describes and makes no ethnic distinction among those she kills for breaking her laws. When she and Maureen go to New Orleans, Maureen encounters a Klan rally. Her playmate Debbie informs her that what she thinks is a parade is a rally of racism—a rally of grown men who recently killed a schoolboy, a rally of men so proud in their impotent fear they must cloak themselves in sheets—and Maureen hits a parading Klan member in the head with a stone. The Klansman chases Maureen and Debbie and bashes them with his flagpole. However, like Legba and Afrekete, Mama Ruby is "everywhere." She hurls her switchblade with the accuracy of a true African warrior and stabs the Klansman in the base of his neck. Declaring she will spend no time in prison and that the "law ain't got nothin to do with me," she and Maureen head back to Goons (143–147).

Big Red is a Caucasian Miami policeman who is Ruby's friend and ally; through him, Ruby extends her sphere of power beyond Goons. Big Red is also one of the common anomalies in the African American community: the Caucasian with a taste for African American energy and a lust for African American women. Ruby supplies him with women, and in return, in a quasi-official capacity, he shields Ruby's crimes but not Ruby, for she needs and will have no shielding. The success of their relationship lies in reciprocity: neither Big Red nor his employers care who or how many people Mama Ruby "chastizes," and their relationship satisfies Red's lusts and expands Ruby's sphere of power.

Given her relationship with Big Red and the fact that she has the power to kill a Klansman and not be tried or lynched, Mama Ruby has no need to concern herself with issues regarding Mack Pruitt. In fact, Ruby is genuinely surprised when Big Red questions her about the missing one-armed Pruitt and offers to protect her. Ruby, who killed Pruitt by plunging a pitchfork through his body, inquires of Red, "Since when was it up to you to keep them laws off my tail?" (85). When Big

Red continues to interrogate her, Ruby threatens *him* with a killing. Ruby is well aware that her protection is assured by the very society that never acknowledged her humanity and that her Àjẹ́ lends her diplomatic immunity. While Big Red has the law emblazoned on his badge, Mama Ruby is the law.

In *Mules and Men,* after her run-in with the assumed force of "law," Lucy re-enters the juke declaring, "Ah got de law in mah mouth."[12] One could argue that Sethe's unspoken statement to schoolteacher is that she has the law in her hands. Women like these, who created a phenomenal existence from the great pit of nothingness America offered them, are guardians of ancient laws, and they recognize and exercise their prerogative to fashion new laws that will facilitate personal and communal evolution. Although the laws of Àjẹ́ and those of America rarely mesh, Big Red recognizes Ruby's authority and does not mention Pruitt again. Red also remains a key member of her enforcement team: an quasi Oṣó pupa, if you will. Big Red, Loomis, No Talk, and Fast Black constitute Mama Ruby's Ẹgbẹ́ Àjẹ́. When anyone trespasses against a member of the community, Ruby and her posse "chastize" the offending party: the justice of Àjẹ́ with an American twist!

Mama Ruby can exclaim with Ọrẹamẹ, "I am she that surpasses a city."[13] Her influence orders the community's evolution, sustenance, joy, and longevity. Mama Ruby is Ìyàmi Àbèní, The Mysterious Mother We Beg to Have, and she is "the one in whose hands" communal lives are placed. Any slight, breach, or violation is taken to her with confidence, because the living Òrìṣà of Goons will not allow a member of her communal family to suffer. For example, at Catty and Yellow Jack's wedding reception, Willie Boatwright dies from liquor poisoning, and Ruby resurrects him:

> Boatwright, I say, oh, Boatwright, I'm fixin to haul you up off this floor. With the help of the Lord I am fixin to bring you back to life! . . . RAISE THIS MAN! LOOK-A-HERE, LORD, YOU RAISE BOATWRIGHT LIKE I JUST SAID! HE'S A CHRISTIAN FROM HIS HEART AND YOUR FAITHFUL SERVANT TO THE END. WALKIN IN YOUR LIGHT! HE JUST HAD A LITTLE TOO MUCH TO DRINK, LORD— BUT YOU CHASTIZE HIM FOR THAT LATER ON . . . PUT IT ON THE REGISTRAR. GET UP BOATWRIGHT! (174)

After her Òrò and laying on of hands, the Lord and Boatwright have no choice but to comply with her demands.

Ruby has everything. She is the adored arbitrator of a vast sphere of influence, and she amassed this power with nothing but the Àjẹ́ and Òrò with which she was born. No matter how many backsliders find in her a pitchfork-throwing Ìyá-Ayé prepared to introduce them to the wicked bag of death, Ruby is heralded and lauded as indispensable. But she is human and has weaknesses. The only thing that can ruin her is the absence of Maureen, her immaculately reconceived savior. As she explains it, Ruby experienced rebirth in Maureen's resurrection:

> I axed God for me a second chance, to be born all over. He answered my prayer by giving me you, you is me all over again. You is my second chance. I axed him to make me beautiful the next time. Lord knows you is sharp as a tack. Havin you with me, I feel like I'm the beauty queen myself. . . . You is sort of like a special delivery to me from the Lord. Ain't no way I can let you go. If you ever do leave me, you'll be takin' away a part of me . . . the part that keeps me alive. (285–286)

Maureen listens patiently to Mama Ruby's revelry; her only query is, "What about me? . . . What I get out of this deal? I don't like bein you."

Mama Ruby enthralls her constituency with her force, but the ever-growing number of corpses that fills the bayous sickens her children. Virgil escapes by fighting in Vietnam and becoming a prisoner of war for the majority of the text, but Maureen is trapped as Ruby's messiah, and she is also the only community member who rejects her divinity. Bishop attempts to explain to Maureen the necessity of Mama Ruby to Goons:

> Mama Ruby just like a mama to them folks. She just like a mama to everybody. Why you think we all call Mama Ruby *Mama* Ruby. Shoot. I'd have to be weaned if Ruby—MAMA Ruby was to ever leave Goons. Mama Ruby done opened all our eyes our here in these swamps. She was sent here to us by the Lord, I sho nuff believe. Healin hands and all. (181)

When Maureen asks if the community would die without Ruby, the response is the same as always, "Ruby ain't no regular woman, Mo'reen. She got an answer for everything. Ain't nothin you can't ax her, she can't answer." She is the Ìyánlá of Goons, the savior and mother to everyone with answers to everyone's dilemmas, except her daughter's.

After Maureen endures a series of tragedies—being raped and impregnated by a Euro-American delinquent, being attacked by her insane biological mother, and having one of her twin daughters drown in a lake—she summons the courage to leave. Ruby curtails her political activities to concentrate on riding her daughter. After mysteriously losing her job, Maureen finds herself the victim of constant brazen vandalism. She finds piles of manure in her living room; someone devours her chickens and leaves nothing but bones and dirty dishes. She finds her phone ripped out of the wall, and she is generally living in a frightening hilarity as Ruby gently but methodically directs all of her Àjẹ́ against her daughter.

Ruby does not contain her persecution to the physical realm; Maureen feels entities standing over her bed as she is sleeping and wakes to find that nothing is out of order, except that her Bible, which is as thick as a New York City telephone book, is ripped in half. It is clear that the woman riding Maureen "ain't no regular lady":

> Ruby was constantly on her mind. It was not long before Maureen started seeing her everywhere she looked. Fat women, thin women, all began to look like Ruby. She saw her in stores where she shopped, peeking in windows at places where she had job interviews, loitering around outside her apartment building. (296)

With the psychological effects of Ruby's riding augmenting her astral force, her goal is to drive Maureen crazy and force her back into the sanctity of the Upper Room. However, Maureen's courage is stronger than Ruby's ability to live without her Òrìṣà.

When Ruby dies, all of Goons mourns and tries to imagine living without their Ìyánlá. With Ruby's healing hands, there had been no need for physicians; she was the only police force, judge, jury, and executioner Goons needed. She was also sexually otherworldly, as Zeus reveals, "Roscoe told me to my face he ain't never had a woman what had what Ruby had between her legs. Said she had a pocketbook shaped like a guitar. And not a snap of hair on it" (307). Apparently, for those brave enough to witness the vagina of an Àjẹ́, oddities and ecstasies await, if one can survive the unveiling. With Ruby firmly tucked into the wicked bag of earth, the vulnerable, motherless Goonsians plan to leave the city en masse.

THE MADAME OF MADAMES

Ruby attributed her power to her African ancestry. Interestingly enough, in Nigerian literature there is a woman who reached her Àjẹ́-inspired peak concurrent with Ruby in the 1950s–1960s. Truly Ìbejì (twins), Mama Ruby and Madame Koto grow fatter and more dominating in the course of these novels, and both stand as the sole arbiters of law and justice in the societies they govern. However, their successes are debatable. As Ruby's power and weight increase, so does the security and unity of Goons, but her works are impermanent and end with her death. Madame Koto appears to be immortal, and her growth is physical and spiritual and spans three novels. But her expansion occurs at the expense of her community, and her application of Àjẹ́ often precipitates community setbacks. As does Ìyàmi Òṣòròngà, Koto both devastates her community and delivers community members from devastation; her acts inspire community critique, bonding, and restructuring in Okri's textual and extratextual communities.

Mama Ruby and Madame Koto have much in common including the way they make their initial marks on their communities. Like Ruby, Koto's Àjẹ́ reaches full maturity in stages. However, with her textual introduction, it is apparent that she is a powerful woman. Just as Ruby was abused in her home/lounge and slew her offender, so too does Madame Koto refuse to be taken advantage of by a patron who declines to pay for the drinks he has consumed in her bar. After she gives the man a gentle chastising, Koto has no other choice than to introduce the rogue to Ọlọ́run, the sky Òrìṣà, and Ìyá-Ayé, Mother Earth.

> Then, suddenly, to our astonishment, the woman lifted him up by the pants and threw him to the ground. The crowd yelled. The man flailed, got up, shouted and huffed. Then he pounced on her, lashing at her face. . . . The madame grabbed the bad loser's crotch and he screamed so loud that the crowd fell silent. Then, with a practised grunt, she lifted him on her shoulders, turned him round once, showing his mightiness to the sky, and dumped him savagely on the hard earth.[14]

Àjẹ́ control reproductive organs, including semen. Madame Koto gives a painful example of one form such control can take. After showing him his origin and end, Koto turns the man upside-down, shakes all the money from his pockets, takes what belongs to her, and "nakeds"[15] him—publicly exhibiting his genitals and impotence. Koto and Ruby prove, first and foremost, that they will not be subject to the caprices of patriarchy. Their public displays of power also educate the community about the stock these women have in themselves and the seriousness with which they approach life and personal and communal injustice.

Madame Koto's power is not relegated to violent retribution; she also has the power to heal and bless. At protagonist Azaro's celebration of life, Koto reveals her gift of àfọ́ṣẹ́, the power to pray effectively, as she intones over him:

> The road will never swallow you. The river of your destiny will always overcome evil. May you understand your fate. Suffering will never destroy you but will make you stronger. Success will never confuse you or scatter your spirit, but will make you fly higher into the good sunlight. Your life will always surprise you. (*The Famished Road*, 47)

Just as Ruby did, Madame Koto gains respect with her Ọ̀rọ̀, especially because it is used for the benefit of a community member. Furthermore, in blessing Azaro, she strengthens herself.

There is a significant connection between Azaro and Koto that is in many ways analogous to that of Ruby and Maureen. Azaro is an àbíkú. And àbíkú, along with children who cut their upper teeth first, those born with cauls covering their faces, and twins, are *ará'gbó*, spirits who are thought to be masquerading in human bodies. Ará'gbó, àbíkú and ẹlẹ́gbẹ́ children are thought to be more spirit than human, and Àjẹ́ give these children to human women who are having difficulty conceiving.[16] Accordingly, Ruby heralds Maureen as a "special delivery . . . from the Lord." Azaro's mother hails her son as "a child of miracles" with "many powers" on his side (*The Famished Road*, 9). Just as Maureen is the humanospiritual powerforce of Ruby and Goons, so too does Azaro represent his community's hope. Additionally, both these children experience death and resurrection. Maureen is stillborn but comes to life a few hours after her birth. Young Azaro slips into a coma (and the spiritual realm), is given up for dead, and is placed in a coffin, where he is discovered weeping.

The Yoruba say the ọkẹ́ (amnion) links M/mother to child and can never be untied. That link is cosmically represented in Àjẹ́ holding sixteen long livers at the sixteen crossroads of heaven and earth. As a gift from Àwọn Ìyá Wa to his biological mother, Azaro is cosmically bound to his mother and the Mothers, and this binding is visually depicted in *The Famished Road*. When Azaro is lost and kidnapped by a police chief, his mother enters into many spiritual rituals until she arrives at the terrestrial house of spirits in which her son is imprisoned. Azaro sees clearly the chord of Àjẹ́ binding mother to Mothers: "I saw a rope round her neck, connecting her to the sky. The rope transformed into a thread of lightning. For a moment I thought I had known her in another life or in the world of spirits" (*The Famished Road*, 27). Later in *The Famished Road*, when Mum awakens from a feverish sickness, she tells Azaro she saw him in "the land of death." Mum goes on to describe her encounter with her son's ẹnikejì: "There was a white rope round you and it went up to the sky. I pulled the rope and it pulled me. I couldn't cut it. And then the rope jumped from your feet to my neck. The rope pulled me up to the sky" (*The Famished Road*, 57–58). This rope is the cosmic twin of the umbilical cord upon which members of Ọha Ndom swear in *I Saw The Sky Catch Fire:*

> If I should ever betray the secrets of Ndom, may I be strangled to death by the umbilical cord of the babies I am birthing. In this incarnation and in all my future incarnations . . .
> I have performed my part of the oath, *taken the noose from around my neck, and placed it around yours.* If you wear it honorably, it is a garland for a parade. If you do dishonor to Ndom, it becomes a hanging noose.[17]

Just as Ndom is tied to both the spiritual realm and its children, Azaro's cosmic cord ties him to the spiritual realm, Mum, and the Mothers. But by refusing to honor his obligations and return to his cosmic àbíkú companions, Azaro's humanospiritual tie to his mother becomes more intricately entwined, as is evident in the inextricable rope that links mother to son to the cosmos. The bond between mother and son is so strong, Azaro sees his mother's sad face before he is born, and he decides to live in the hope that he can bring her happiness. The spirit child's birthmarks also foretell his destiny, for, unlike other infants, Azaro is born smiling (*The Famished Road*, 6).

"A child of miracles," boasting a dual human-spiritual existence, Azaro is obligated to these realms and all the entities therein by choosing life, and throughout Okri's texts we witness Azaro's deft navigation of entwined spiritual material realms. But he also has a special tie to the Àjẹ́. While Koto serves as his literal and figurative terrestrial "God Mother," Azaro's link to Àjẹ́ is not exclusive to her. Following a catastrophe that separates Azaro from his family, he is captured by a group of Àwọn Ìyá Wa. The women's leader takes him to a room where he is bathed and oiled in preparation to meet the Ìyánlá. Awaking in the shrine house, Azaro finds the women staring at him as if "it were in my power to save their lives" (*The Famished Road*, 13). He is fed rich foods, clothed in the "immaculate white" cloths of Àjẹ́, and then he meets his Maker:

> She was an image with a beautiful face and eyes of marble that glittered in the sun. All around her feet were metal gongs, kola nuts, kaoline, feathers of eagles and peacocks, bones of animals and bones too big to belong to animals. In a complete circle round her were white eggs on black saucers. Her mighty and wondrous pregnancy faced the sea. . . . Her magnificent

pregnancy was so startling against the immense sea that she could have been giving birth to a god or a new world. (*The Famished Road*, 13)

Maureen is sanctified by the sanctity of the Upper Room; Azaro is a gifted gift of the Mother who holds the keys to all roads, possibilities, and evolution. Because of his vast wealth, Azaro, the gift of Àjẹ́, can also be used to charge Àjẹ́. Like Sethe with Beloved, he is so enamored with and enraptured by the Ìyánlá that he is unaware that he is being made ready for the "join."

Although he escapes becoming The Child the Mother Would Birth at this point, his inextricable bond with the Ìyánlá is illustrated later in the novel. After wandering in a circle, Azaro arrives, dazed and confused, at Madame Koto's bar. Before he faints he sees Koto and describes her as "the elephantine figure of an ancient mother"; the fact that he makes no distinction between woman and icon reinforces the fact that Àjẹ́ are the women, are the Deities, are the Mothers, are one. His seeing the Àjẹ́ in Koto foreshadows his encounter with Koto's personal shrine to the Ìyánlá. The rituals and symbols are the same as before: Azaro is carefully bathed, assuaged, and fed prior to the meeting. Adorned with feathers, constantly libated by snails and with snail excretion, and surrounded by the sacrificial elements of Odù and Ọbàtálá, the Ìyánlá is depicted as having the eyes of Ẹdan and the knowledge of all times:

> I could feel the intense gaze of an ancient mother who had been turned into wood. She knew who I was. Her eyes were pitiless in their scrutiny. She knew my destiny in advance. She sat in her cobwebbed niche, a mighty statue in mahogany, powerful with the aroma of fertility. Her breasts exuded a shameless libidinous potency. A saffron-coloured cloth had been worn round her gentle pregnancy. Behind her dark glasses, she seemed to regard everything with equal serenity. (*The Famished Road*, 290)

During his first encounter, Azaro is spellbound by the beauty and gentle majesty of the Mother, but his meeting with Koto's Ìyá is suffused with symbiotic power. The ancient mother speaks to Azaro directly and through all the objects in Koto's room. Mesmerized by her heartbeat and indecipherable language and entranced by her shaded eyes, Azaro initiates the "join":

> I climbed the body of the goddess and took off her glasses. In the deep hollow of her sockets she had eyes of red stone, precious stones the exact colour of blood. My breathing seized.

Her eyes fixed on me with such heat that I hurriedly put her glasses back on. . . . I found myself caught in a strange immobility. Then to my greatest horror, she moved—as if she were about to crush me into her pregnancy. (*The Famished Road,* 291)

So closely related are the pair that the immobility of one sparks the mobility of the other; the inhalation of one is the exhalation of the other. Azaro soon recognizes his interconnectedness with all the sacrifices, shrine implements, ritual decorations of the room, and Koto and the Mother. He is the child climbing the pregnancy and he is the Mother's pregnant promise.

As a result of the cosmic ties that bind them and the human consideration that exists in this community despite rampant corruption, Madame Koto proves herself to be a devoted surrogate mother to Azaro and his family and taps many sources of power to provide for their needs. When Azaro's mother becomes deathly ill, Koto proves her worth as an oníṣègun and master of Òrò. First she prepares an herbal distillate, and after Mum takes the medicine and coughs the cough of life, Madame Koto, aided by her inner Spirit Bird, whips that cough into a summons to live. Similar to Mama Ruby's resurrection of Boatwright, "Madame Koto called her name with such violence it sounded like a whip. She went on whipping Mum with her name, calling back her spirit, in a very peculiar birdlike voice" (*The Famished Road,* 57). Later in *The Famished Road,* Madame Koto, a female oníṣègun who flies "as if the wind were her ally," and a featureless Àjẹ́ work in concert to save Azaro's father from death (405). The family's indebtedness to and inextricable link with Koto is repeatedly emphasized, especially in her gifts which keep the family just above the poverty line, but for remuneration all Koto asks is that Azaro sit in her bar and "attract customers."

Ruby magnifies her power through Maureen and by stationing her in the Upper Room, also known as heaven.[18] Similarly, the presence of àbíkú Azaro brings a bit of heaven to Koto's bar. Just as Anowa became Kofi Ako's mojo, Koto uses Azaro's spiritual energy for economic gain and to solidify her "way."

In addition to harnessing Azaro's power, she is also observed doing what African Americans call "working roots." The spiritual importance of dirt obtained from graves recurs in many Africana ritual works. Indeed, the term "goofer" dust, which is graveyard dirt, comes from the KiKongo word "kufua," meaning to die.[19] This earth contains the àṣẹ, the life essence, of the buried person and is a potent spiritual implement. Additionally, African shopkeepers may take dirt from a popular footpath and use the àṣẹ of all those who have trod that earth to construct a root that will draw those and other customers to their place of business. Constantly "digging in the earth, planting a secret, or taking one out," Koto creates a phenomenally powerful root that summons rowdy spirits, who feast, drink, create commotion, and simply vanish (*The Famished Road*, 75, 105–111).

After Azaro absconds with and buries this root, Koto is seen sacrificing with fervor at a crossroads. This time she is successful, and it is not spirits she conjures but Politics. With mouths filled with lies and a van full of free poison milk, Politics, in the form of the Party of the Rich—adversaries of, but indistinguishable from, the Party of the Poor—arrives in the township. A peculiar bond was born of Sethe's feeding Denver with breast milk laced with her sister's blood; similarly, politics melds sustenance with violence in the community. As the people pummel one another to receive free milk, "blood mixed with milk on the earth." Just outside the mêlée, Madame Koto is seen conferring with politicians and, later, "leaving the scene of confusion with the utmost dignity" (*The Famished Road*, 125). She has initiated the courtship ritual with Politics and begins to revise the holistic evolutionary properties of Àjẹ́, Ọ̀rọ̀, and àṣẹ to fashion a force of neo-Àjẹ́ whose power lies in "selfishness, money and politics."

Divisions are immediately drawn, as Politics threatens the community: Join our particular party or (and) perish. The only people who benefit from political fraternization are Madame Koto and the landlord. The rest of the community becomes political refugees in their land of origin. Despite promises of wealth and rejuvenation, the community begins its three-novel-long slide into abject poverty.[20] As the Party of the Rich becomes, nearly exclusively, her clientele, Madame Koto does what Mama Ruby would never dream of doing; she grovels and becomes unctuous in pursuit of political power.

Both Ruby and Koto have moments when their humanity and vulnerability bubble forth. Mama Ruby weeps, gnashes her false teeth, and wails on numerous occasions. Madame Koto also reveals her humanity, but under compromised circumstances. After one of the drunken sprees of the politicians, inebriated more on power than Koto's palmwine and more outlandish than her former spirit patrons, Koto finds her bar nearly destroyed. When she sees the destruction of her economic investment, she weeps. Azaro, who witnesses this moment, realizes that with her tears, Koto "crossed the divide between past and future. She must have known that a new cycle had begun" (*The Famished Road*, 225). Like the mingled blood and milk seeping into the earth, Koto's weeping is not unlike a most efficacious libation poured on the shiny domed head of a new synthetic Òrìṣà. In the paradoxical manner of Àjẹ́, her tears ensure that she is on the most economically advantageous side of Politics: Her bar is repaired; money and wine flow. However, Politics, under the guise of technology and modernization, begins the destruction of the spiritual and terrestrial foundation of the community. Europeans arrive to install electricity and build a macadam road that will kill the living road of the community and turn the neighboring forest into a "graveyard of trees." The purpose of the road is purely colonial: It is not built to connect peoples but to transfer raw materials from the hinterland to the shore for export. Its purpose is so heinous that the "famished" road takes as a sacrifice those who initiate its killing.

Mama Ruby had a lackadaisical fiancé and a trophy lover. Neither Roscoe nor Slim are Ruby's equals; they are status symbols who provide occasional sensual enjoyment. Mama Ruby is very much an Ìyá; she is enigmatic, gargantuan, and sensually desirable, but she courts no man. However, when Politics anoints itself a Neo-God, Madame Koto recognizes its virility and courts, dates, and finally becomes its quasi-fiancée. She is the owner of numerous contracts with the Party of the Rich, and the ever-forecast, never-to-materialize political rally is to be held in her bar. Because Politics is literally everywhere, Madame Koto begins the multiplication and division of herself so as to accompany her mate as they ravage the community. It is interesting to note that Koto's relationship with Politics can be considered a complementary gender-balanced union!

Madame Koto offers up the community to Politics, and her betrothed showers her with gifts. Olufunmilayo Ransome-Kuti was celebrated for her political prowess and her Àjẹ́, and she was the first Nigerian woman to own a car. Koto literally follows Ransome-Kuti's path; her bar is the first place in the community to enjoy electricity, and she owns her community's first car. However, Koto is not praised for her pace-setting but is denounced as the "GREAT WHORE OF THE APOCALYPSE." The community competes for space with party thugs and jumps into gutters as the "mad tortoise" (Koto's car) speeds by. The community is "living just enough for the city," to quote Stevie Wonder, or just enough to continue to feed the desires of the political parties and Koto.

The community's descent into squalor is directly related to the material wealth and political ascent of Koto: Their rags become the silk boubous on her back; the hairs they lose carrying gargantuan loads are reincarnated in her wigs. Additionally, Koto becomes the inspiration for the creation of myths and the recipient of the power born of myths' mystique:

> People came to believe that Madame Koto had exceeded herself in witchcraft. People glared at her hatefully when she went past.

> They said she wore the hair of animals and human beings on her head. The rumours got so wild that it was hinted that her cult made sacrifices of human beings and that she ate children. They said she had been drinking human blood to lengthen her life and that she was more than a hundred years old. They said the teeth in her mouth were not hers, that her eyes belonged to the jackal, and that her foot was getting rotten because it belonged to someone who was trying to dance in their grave. She became, in the collective eyes of the people, a fabulous and monstrous creation. It did not matter that some people insisted that it was her political enemies who put out all these stories. The stories distorted our perception of her reality for ever. (*The Famished Road*, 374)

Revising the title Owner of the Night, Koto is "Queen of the Ghetto Night," the controller of all political dreams, destinies, and roads. Her power takes many forms, including a long-overdue triplet àbíkú pregnancy of bearded, full-set-of-teeth-bearing, wicked-eyed children who are not borne to be born (*The Famished Road*, 464).

Near the end of *The Famished Road*, Azaro has an important revelation about Koto and her ability to transform the community's individual and collective dreams, fears, and myths into her personal spiritual smorgasbord:

> At night when she slept, she stole the people's energies. (She was not the only one; they were legion.) The night became her ally.... Madame Koto sucked in the powers of our area.... Her colossal form took wings at night and she flew over the city, drawing power from our sleeping bodies.... Her dreams were livid rashes of parties and orgies, of squander and sprees, of corruption and disintegration, of innocent women and weak men.... Slowly while the people of the area grew weaker, more accepting, more afraid, she grew stronger. That is when I understood that conflicting forces were fighting for the future of our country in the air, at night, in our dreams, riding invisible white horses and whipping us, sapping our will while we slept. (495)

Azaro's understanding of the depth of the struggles of the various spiritual forces and entities in his community is remarkably similar to Simon Bockie's discussion of "eating" and "protecting" bandoki who patrol, deliberate, attack, and avenge in the astral realm, sparking repercussions in the material realm.[21]

Literature mirrors life in Okri's Nigerian community, as it eventually becomes impossible and unnecessary to distinguish "real" from astral acts and figures. Fueled by her neo-political Àjẹ́ and additional male assistance, Madame Koto continues her struggle for complete control of her society in *Songs of Enchantment*. Compounding her sociopolitical relationship with Politics, she forms a spiritual alliance with the blind old man. True to the assertions of the elders, he, as neo-political Ọṣó, performs the acts Koto decrees. Furthermore, he is depicted, anatomically and in action, as twin of Èṣù: "He had two sexual organs, his prick was monstrous and erect, his vagina was tiny, like a comma."[22] While the blind old man, henchman of the astral realm and mercurial social thug, has a "pact" with Koto, he is not the sole owner of her triplet àbíkú pregnancy.

As Koto becomes a masterpiece of inscrutable and uncontrollable spiritual and political dominance through the course of the novels, the historic texts of Àjẹ́ are not adequate to define her force. New myths must be created. The Egúngún, Orò, and Gẹ̀lẹ̀dẹ́ masquerades are obsolete; the just vigilance of Ẹdan's eyes is insufficient. Consequently, a new Òrìṣà of political control is born:

> It was a gigantic red Masquerade, bristling with raffia and rags and nails. It had long stilts for legs and two twisted horns at the sides of a wild jackal's head. The red Masquerade held aloft a shining machete in one hand and a white flag, emblem of their party, in the other. (*Songs of Enchantment*, 98)

Like the coming of Nana Bùrúkù, Politics arrives spontaneously, giving no inkling of its origin. Keeping an unceasing vigil over the community, the Masquerade sees all with impossibly human eyes, but it punishes subjectively. Koto's relationship to a concept, Politics, becomes reified reality with the jackal Masquerade, who is both the personification of Politics and the primary owner of Koto's àbíkú trinity. Like Beloved's pregnancy, if the àbíkú triplets are brought to term, they could seal the socioeconomic, political, and spiritual destruction of this society—or they could force the community to evolve into its truest Self. However, the community's protecting bandoki do not wait for the arrival of the indefinable trinity. They make two bids for freedom, but on both occasions, Madame Koto brings them to their collective knees.

During the apex of Koto's political-spiritual reign in *Songs of Enchantment*, the community is serenaded by melodic voices from the nearby forest. Soon, community women join the forest spirits. As a child, Sethe witnessed a juba so empowering that her elders danced, "shifted shapes," became the antelope, and became freer than any enslaver could fathom.²³ Similarly, the women of *Songs of Enchantment* transform into white antelopes and enter into a cosmic arena of spiritual enlightenment and sociopolitical empowerment. The Spirit Bird of the Mother is the leader of this cult, and her motivation reflects the ancient work of Àwọn Ìyá Wa:

> Some said she [the women's leader] was an owl. Others maintained that the women, seduced by the spirit of the forest, were against Madame Koto and her ascendant cult. *And mum surprised me one night by telling me that the women were singing of the forgotten ways of our ancestors.* They were warning us not to change too much, *not to disregard the earth.* (*Songs of Enchantment*, 79, italics added)

Political sorcerers quickly crush Àjẹ́'s peaceful attempt at reclamation. Slain antelopes are soon littering the ghetto, and it appears that even the Great Mother is impotent before the power of "selfishness, money and politics."

It is not often that Koto speaks at length, as Àwọn Ìyá Wa are known for their reticence. And with conceptual (Politics), reified (Masquerade), and cosmic-terrestrial (the blind old man) husbands on ground to take over some of her responsibilities, Madame Koto is rarely seen, let alone heard from. However, when a luminous white snake, possibly a warning messenger from Òṣùmàrè, stations itself on the bonnet of her car, Koto acts swiftly. After unflinchingly absorbing several bites, Koto kills the reptile. Following the altercation, she decides her recalcitrant constituency needs a lecture on the futility of using any means, spiritual, physical, or political, to end her reign:

> What does it take to make you people fear me eh? Heaven knows that I am good to you. When you are in trouble I send you provisions, I get our party to bring you help, I give you food, I take care of your damages, I protect you, and yet you people still want to poison me, to kill me. (*Songs of Enchantment*, 190)

Unlike Mama Ruby, who enjoyed unmitigated community support, Koto must coerce community backing.

While elaborating on her supremacy during a verbal tirade, Madame Koto details her spectacular origin and her birthmarks of divinity:

> I am too strong for you all. My father was an iroko tree. My mother was a rock. The tree grew on the rock. It still stands deep

in the country. The rock itself has grown. Now it is a hill where people worship at the shrine of the great mother. My enemies sent thunder, but the rock swallowed the thunder. They sent lightning, but the rock seized the lightning. Now, when the people of the shrine touch the hill with iron, electric sparks fly in the air. Our enemies sent rain, but the water made the rock grow even bigger. Now, flowers and plants that cure blindness and cancer can be found on the rock. Then our enemies tried to cut down the iroko tree, but their instruments were destroyed. And when they tried to blow up the rock the explosives failed and the rock started to bleed. Then one by one our enemies died or went mad. And when the worshippers of the shrine saw the blood they made a great sacrifice and the oracle told them that the blood of the rock saves lives, cures palsy and madness, it cures leukaemia, epilepsy and impotence.... A new god will be born for our age from the blood of the rock and the trunk of the great tree. I am only a servant. Friends of mine are friends of great forces. My enemies will turn to stone, will go mad, go blind, lose their legs and hands, forget who they are. They will tremble from dawn to dusk, their wives will give birth to children who torment them, and some will give birth to goats and rats and snakes. The rock is my power. The sea never dies. (*Songs of Enchantment*, 191)

Koto has birthmarks as spectacular as Mama Ruby's, her origin text commingles the powers of key Òrìṣà of Àjẹ́, and she reveals herself to be the spiritual sister of Ìyá Bọ̀kọ́lọ, Sapphira Wade, Marie Leveau, and Leonor de Isla. But Koto hones her force through inversion and usurpation. Even the healing blood born of the rock and ìrókò will be of dubious assistance, as Koto will hoard, share, or withhold her salves as she sees fit.

Madame Koto is a daughter of Odù, whose "oracular utterance created existence," but in choosing to promote neo-political Àjẹ́, she inverts and subverts her ability to create and sustain. She becomes an indirect killer, a Doro with a twist: "Anyone who tries to kill me will kill someone else in my place, will kill their best friends, their child, an innocent bystander, a servant, but they won't touch me" (*Songs of Enchantment*, 191).

Directly following Koto's lecture/curse, Ade, Azaro's companion in the fight against the forces of synthetic Àjẹ́, stands up to her. This second spirit-child verbally challenges Koto and stabs her in the arm. In *The Upper Room*, when Othella found that Maureen was alive and living as Ruby's daughter, she tried to kill Ruby and stabbed her numerous times, but Ruby killed her former best friend with ease. Likewise, Madame Koto does not feel the wound Ade delivers, but the entire community witnesses the truth of her inverted protection. After he stabs her, Ade is accidentally run over by Koto's driver. When Koto weeps this time, her tears bear salt. For with Ade's death, her façade, meticulously constructed on the life-energies of the spiritually endowed, cracks, and her reality bleeds through: "Madame Koto's face collapsed into its true visage of a woman hundreds of years old" (*Songs of Enchantment,* 199). Aware that her physical form is contradicting her astral life and placing both in jeopardy, Koto takes a page from Doro's early text and reduces her humanity for submergence into the synthetic astral realm of uncompromised political power.

Madame Koto's neo-political Àjẹ́ is a destructive synthetic blend that can best be described as "government magic," to quote legendary musician Fela Anikulapo-Kuti, also known simply as Fela, the son of Olufunmilayo Ransome-Kuti. In his classic song "Unknown Soldier," Fela, not unlike the politically astute Òrò Èfè composers of Gẹlẹdẹ, sings the historical counterpart of what Okri depicts in fiction:

> Government magic
> Dem go dabaru [scatter, destroy] everything
> Government magic
> Dem go turn green to white
> Government magic
> Dem go turn red into blue
> Government magic
> Water dey go, water dey come
> . . . .
> Government magic
> Dem go turn electric to candle[24]

For the rich, all amenities are guaranteed, but for the poor, electricity is reduced to candlelight; water becomes the dust of Harmattan.

Art mirrors life as the verdant fertility of Nigeria becomes barren whiteness as its resources fuel the West. To emphasize the multicultural components of "government magic," Fela melds classic sacrificial elements of Àjẹ́ with the staples of Western magicians:

> Dem start magic
> Dem bring flame
> Dem bring hat
> Dem come jump
> Dem bring rabbit

Dem bring egg
Dem bring smoke
Dem dey scream
Dem dey fuck
Dem dey jump
Spirit catch dem

In contrast to Ransome-Kuti's use of Àjẹ́ to cow colonial administrators, neo-political Àjẹ́, melded with Western political values, results in greed, depravity, rape, and murder. Indeed, the most notable victim that Nigeria's "unknown soldier" claimed was Fela's own mother, Madame Ransome-Kuti. Fela documented the attack on his mother in song:

Dem throw my Mama
78 year old Mama
Political Mama
Ideological Mama
Influential Mama
. . . .
Dem throw my Mama
Out of window
Dem kill my Mama

That such a remarkable woman could be maliciously tossed from a window is a clear indication of the seriousness of Àjẹ́'s battle with its neo-political twin.

* * *

Mama Ruby and Madame Koto have vastly different effects on their communities, and their communities' reactions to their existences are as varied as the forces of Ọya, Ọ̀sun, and Ìyàmi Òṣòròngà. But these characters, Deities, and seemingly disparate forms of Àjẹ́ are siblings—many heads of one body connected by one umbilical cord. Furthermore, these African and African American communities are connected. Although *The Upper Room* is a humorous text, Monroe is careful to remind her audience of the curvilinear trauma that America promises Africans. By conflating numerous opposing Western ideological concepts in and through Mama Ruby, Monroe forces her audience to examine their own religiosity, ideologically structured dichotomy, and national and international political hypocrisy: Mama Ruby's casual killings of would-be rapists are perhaps a subtle signification on America's recent national pastime of lynching and raping African

American men and women. Using the shifting concept of American justice to fit her needs, Ruby, riffing with Blindman of *Madmen and Specialists*, does her best to match America "history for history to the nearest half-million souls." By acquiring and revising knowledge and devastating skills from both cultures, Ruby becomes more than the line that divides the dichotomous concepts of good and evil; she becomes the signifying space that unifies and divides the term "African American." That space is filled with "unspeakable thoughts," unimaginable cruelty, and profound potential.

The characters in *The Famished Road* bear witness to one of the signs that hide in that space when Jeremiah the photographer, who becomes a walking martyr for visually documenting the rapings of the community by Politics, extends his lens across the ocean:

> And then I came upon the strangest photograph of them all, which the photographer said he had got from another planet. It was of a man hanging by his neck from a tree. I couldn't see the rope that he hung from. A white bird was settling on his head and was in a blurred attitude of landing when the photograph was taken. The man's face was strange, almost familiar. His eyes were bursting open, they were wide open, as if had seen too much; his mouth was twisted, his legs were crossed and crooked. (263)

With all the spiritual revelations and terrestrial tragedies Azaro and his community have witnessed and endured, they have not beheld acts so barbaric and despicably inhumane that they defy spiritual and linguistic definition. And yet the otherworldly subject of the photo boasts both a familiar face and a familiar of African origins: The Spirit Bird is caught witnessing the crime and, like the Kemetic Ba, guiding the victim's soul to transcendence.

It bears repeating that with all the glitter and technology adorning Madame Koto's Àjẹ́, her true visage is described as hundreds of years old. Although she reaches her apex as colonialism and neocolonialism merge and converge, Koto's birth is concurrent with the height of the international exile and enslavement of Africans: There is no telling what types of "government magic" led to the creation of a "Slave Coast" in West Africa. Through Jeremiah's camera, Okri offers a window on the world of terror created by racism, dehumanization, and exile, and he probes the complex nature of women such as Koto and Ruby, who in struggling to manifest their divinity despite oppression may end up fomenting communal subjugation. Okri's personal feelings about Koto are similar to those Ruby inspires, "Madame Koto is actually an ambiguous figure. I feel a great compassion for her. But at the same time I think she's quite terrifying."[25] It is impossible to neatly define and categorize these paradoxical wielders of neo-political Àjẹ́; similarly, it is nearly impossible for humanity to come to a full realization and appreciation of the historic and ongoing psychological, sociological, and spiritual effects of that exile and enslavement have on Africans. At times it seems improbable that Africana peoples will clear a path to the evolved Self through a hegemonic and often pathological Western wilderness.

However Okri, as neo-Gẹ̀lẹ̀dẹ́ composer, uses ancient forms and methodologies to encourage a restructuring of priorities, values, and, ultimately, society. Olatubosun Ogunsanwo contends, "Okri's neo-traditional art is not merely making a nostalgic return to the African folktale. It is actually a re-writing of the socio-cultural past in the present in a way that demands critical re-interpretation in anticipation of the future."[26] Even more significant, Okri describes his political-aesthetic impetus, like Àjẹ́ and Ifá, as predating any manner of European physical encroachment on or philosophical supposition about Africa:

> There's been too much attribution of power to the effect of colonialism on our consciousness. Too much has been given to it. We've looked too much in that direction and have forgotten about our own aesthetic frames. Even though that was there and took place and invaded the social structure, it's quite possible that it didn't invade our spiritual and aesthetic and mythic internal structure, the way in which we perceive the world. . . . There are certain areas of the African consciousness which will remain inviolate.[27]

At the conclusion of Toni Morrison's *Tar Baby,* the protagonist is described as having "forgotten her ancient properties."[28] This assessment of Jadine is also a critique of a contemporary Africana society that participates in its own subjugation by allowing its multidimensionality to be reduced by Eurocentric valuations and culturally inappropriate definitions. Okri and Morrison, all the authors discussed in this exposition, and many more weave ancient texts and tools into contemporary art to remind their audiences that in addition to terrifying spaces, there are also eternal signs and signifiers of "inviolate" and immeasurably rich "ancient properties."

Okri describes his craft as an attempt to "change the way we perceive history . . . alter the way in which we perceive what is valid and what is valuable" so that we can reach our creative, spiritual, and social apex.[29] It becomes clear to Okri's textual community, after great physical, spiritual, and social crippling, that only they can free themselves and that the tools of liberation are timeless, malleable, and Pan-African. Ayi Kwei Armah charges his audience to re-member "the way" in *Two Thousand Seasons,* and this call is taken up by Okri, who challenges us to make whole the "fragments of the Original Way":

> The Way of compassion and fire and serenity: The Way of freedom and power and imaginative life; The Way that keeps the mind open to the existences beyond our earthly sphere, that keeps the spirit pure and primed to all the rich possibilities of living, that makes of their minds gateways through which all the thought-forms of primal creation can wander and take root and flower . . . The Way that makes it possible . . . to understand the language of angels and gods, birds and trees, animals and spirits; The Way that makes them greet phenomena forever as a brother and a sister in mysterious reality; The Way that develops and keeps its secrets of transformations—hate into love, beast into man, man into illustrious ancestor, ancestor into god; The Way whose centre grows from divine love, whose roads are always open for messages from all the spheres to keep coming through. (*Songs of Enchantment,* 159–160)

The Original Way may have become fragmented, but we have the tools to reconnect and reunify those all-fortifying elements of our Divinity and Destiny. The tools are now where they have always been—waiting, sparking, and charging in our hands.

> Will the circle be unbroken
> By and by, lord,
> By and by,
>
> —African American spiritual

Coda-Continua

As a point around which many cultural realities and spiritual and historical forms and figures originate, swirl, and converge, Àjẹ́ stands at the center of the Africana worldview. Like the sixteen long livers, its binding ties are comprehensive and connect life to literature to culture to language across time and space. Even the praisenames of the Mothers enjoy cyclic reconstitution. Àgbàláàgbà Obìrin (Old and Wise One) and Ìyánlá (Great Mother) retain their force in the African American translation "Big Momma." The elision and encoding that transforms Mother Dear into the more tender and powerful "Mu Deah" is reminiscent of the transition of ìyá mi (my mother) into Ìyàmi (My Mysterious Mother). Ẹlẹ́yẹ, Owner of Birds, loses little meaning in the translation "Old Bird," a term of affection for an elder woman, especially one's mother. And compelling examples of continuity are evident in expressions, such as "Old Earth," used by members of the Nation of Gods to refer to their mothers, and the term "Earth" as a reference for young African American women.

The African American lexicon easily reaffirms the immutable yet furtive force of Ìyá Ayé and Imọlẹ̀, and ancient cosmic signs continue to signify. Itchy palms, the cycles of the moon, the untimely low of a dog or crow of a rooster, the patterns of clouds, and the screech of owls and low-winging swoops of hawks maintain their spiritual meanings in contemporary Africana communities. Africana mothers still caution their children and loved ones against behaviors that can have debilitating physical and cosmic consequences. And from Bambara country to Ngula

Bayou, Louisiana, women continue to plait/plant juju in their hair and around homes for power and protection. The vines of rootwork twist, twine, and may even be chopped down, but Àjẹ́, the original "jes grew," can't help but spontaneously generate and celestially recreate.

Constantly permeating and protecting, Àjẹ́ and its complement Ọ̀rọ̀ have always been on the scene, helping us re-member and reminding us to re-create: They were in Southampton County, Virginia, in 1831. After Nat Turner's insurrection, which resulted in the deaths of approximately fifty-five Euro-American men, women, and children, Turner and his generals were hanged and many African Americans were slaughtered. Euro-Americans made uttering the name Nat Turner a crime for which the penalty was death. The Africana community obliged and did not speak the name of the Prophet. Instead they sang praises to the vindicating Mother and her blood-libating Son:

> You might be Carroll from Carrollton
> Arrive here night afor' Lawd make creation
> But you can't keep the World from movering around
> And not turn her back from the gaining ground.[1]

Vincent Harding informs us that the last line would be repeated many times. The second, third, and fourth syllables of that line—"not turn her"—are a deftly encoded tribute to man and his divine mission, the repercussions of which, like Caucasian-American Carroll for whom Carrollton is named, although equating himself with the divine, is a stymied imposter before such a concerted, irreversible revolutionary movement. Àjẹ́, synonymous with World (Ayé), the owner of the Word (Ọ̀rọ̀), and the soul of justice (Just Us), is incapable of stasis. It is always "movering" around, hiding meaning behind seemingly innocuous words and exerting itself outright as society, soul, and art dictate, and this revolutionary movement occurs in all Africana expressive arts, especially music.

Africana artists have long been chronicling personal and social events and history along with the powers of two-headed doctors and personal use of conjure in their music. Back when rock-and-roll had a richer meaning that heralded its stimulation of the jazziest of jass, elders were lamenting the impotence of their power—"Got my mojo workin / But it just won't work on you"—and catalyzing force beyond reason:

> I got a black cat bone
> I got a mojo tooth
> I got John de Conqueroo
> I'm gonna mess with you.[2]

With spiritual-personal-aesthetic power encoded in their DNA, elders couldn't help but pass the word and the Work on to the next generations.

In the 1980s, Afrika Bambaataa and the Zulu Nation were looking for the perfect beat, and when they found it, they remixed it with a Yoruba praisechant. Oríkì Èṣù provided the ritual invocation for X Clan's songs "Tribal Jam" and "Shaft's Big Score," helping Brother J and Professor X step to and through "the crossroads, with a key!"[3] Paying respect to Òrìṣà and Àjẹ́ is not exclusive to groups with an overt Pan-African political consciousness. Hip-hop artist Mia X uses her music to remind her audience to revere what brought us here.[4] And Canibus calmly informs his audience that he practices "West Indian obeah."[5] But when Lauren Hill threatens, "I'll hex you with some witches' brew if you're do do, Hoodoo,"[6] she testifies to her own Àjẹ́ and that of the ancestors and pays homage to Master Miles Davis and one of his most sublime compilations, "Bitches' Brew," which is also a tribute to Àjẹ́. It is not unusual that rappers praise and catalyze the power of the Ancients in the contemporary era; "rap" is a Wolof word that means "soul."[7]

The word "Voodoo" also means "Soul," so it is fitting that soul singers share with us the messages of the Gods. Godfather of Soul, James Brown commanded us to expand our "soul power." D'Angelo took worship and sacrifice to womb-rocking levels with the album *Voodoo*, and he doubled-down and circled-back on his divinity with *Black Messiah*.

Erykah Badu, who emerged from Texas wearing gèlè long enough to span the Ethiopic, penned the song "Ye Yo," in which she heralds the timeless divinity within herself for her progeny and her audience:

> The sun is in the east and the moon reflects
> Like the knowledge and wisdom I manifest
> If you want to go to heaven lay up on my breast
> I'm Yeye
> Yo' Yeye[8]

The embodiment of heaven, with wisdom and knowledge—cipher—as essential and constant as the 360° rotations of the earth and moon around the sun, is Yèyé, the Good Mother who constantly blesses her progeny.

With a powerful testimony to the African spirit, Badu sparks the wisdom of rememory and takes her preappointed place within the Ẹgbẹ́ Àjẹ́. Badu joins a plethora of musical artists—such as the legendary Fela of Nigeria; African America's Robert Johnson, Chaka Khan, Parliament Funkadelic, Prince, GooDie Mob, and Billie Holiday; Senegal's Ishmael

Lo; and Nigerian hip-hopper NGO—who have moaned for and to, critiqued, and celebrated the force of Àjẹ́ in their music.

Visual artists such as James Adedayo and Bruce Onobrakpeya, Faith Ringgold, Betye Sarr, Romare Bearden, and countless Africana folk artists, carvers, and interior and exterior decorators infuse Àjẹ́ in the visual art enshrining their lives and homes.

Àjẹ́ is also a staple of the African world's most significant cinematic works. Herbert Ogunde's aptly titled classic *Aiyé* and Souleymane Cisse's *Yeelen* are powerful expositions of the profundities of spiritual force. Haile Gerima's *Sankofa* and Carlos Diegues's *Quilombo* highlight the liberational and evolutionary force of Àjẹ́ in their re-membering epics. In Charles Burnett's *To Sleep with Anger*, Oṣó takes center stage; Julie Dash's *Daughters of the Dust* depicts the unifying proclivities of Àjẹ́ in their fully paradoxical and intricate forms, and the courageous Med Hondo has re-membered the great warrior Mayya of Niger Sarraounia Aben Soro with the film *Sarraounia*.

Manifestations of Àjẹ́ in Africana literature far exceed the covers of this book. Toni Cade Bambara's *The Salt Eaters*, the valiant women of Sembene Ousmane's *God's Bits of Wood*, and Ishmael Reed's *Conjure* and his intricately woven *Mumbo Jumbo* are all overflowing with the critical and political power of Àjẹ́. Maryse Condé's *I, Tituba, Black Witch of Salem*, Njabulo S. Ndebele's "The Prophetess" and Bambara's "Maggie of the Green Bottles" also provide fertile ground for critical study of Àjẹ́. Flora Nwapa's *Efuru*, Elechi Amadi's *The Concubine*, Paule Marshall's *Praisesong for the Widow*, Akinwumi Isola's *Madam Tinubu: The Terror of Lagos*, Barbara Buford's "Miss Jessie," Jacqueline Rudet's *The Basin*, Erna Brodber's *Louisiana*, and August Wilson's *Joe Turner's Come and Gone* are all rich with the rhythms of Àjẹ́.

The poetry of such classic figures as W. E. B. Du Bois and Birago Diop; giants such as Nicholas Guillen, Nikki Giovanni, Jayne Cortez, and Ted Jones; and the resonant voices of Lorna Goodison, Olatubosun Oladapo, and Monifa Atungaye Love hum vibrations of Àjẹ́. Researchers such as Gloria Wade-Gayles with the anthology *My Soul Is a Witness*, Teresa L. Flynn Brown with *God Don't Like Ugly*, Emilie Townes with *In a Blaze of Glory*, Carlyle Fielding Stewart III with *Black Spirituality and Black Consciousness*, and Arthur Flowers with *Mojo Blues* investigate the familial, social, and artistic impacts of Àjẹ́-esque forces.

My goal was to show the timelessness of Àjẹ́ by examining mythical and historical Africana orature in classic works by such writers as Morrison, Hurston, Aidoo, and Soyinka and the art of writers who are emerging, overlooked, or considered avant-garde, such as Mary Monroe,

T. Obinkaram Echewa, and Octavia E. Butler. I used a thematic approach to emphasize the Pan-African, cross-gender, intergenerational influence of Àjẹ́, and my theoretical approach also allowed me to highlight particular themes in certain texts. However, Ọ̀rọ̀, consecration of sacred space, the relativity of negativity, neo-political Àjẹ́, and gender balance are dominant threads of continuity interwoven in all of these works, making my analysis more a quilt or tapestry than a series of segmented analyses.

These writers and their texts are talking to one another, keeping the ancient ẹsẹ and historical revisions ever relevant and easily applicable. But this is not extraordinary. It is the nature of Ọ̀rọ̀ to inspire art forms that are at once títọ́, enduring, lasting, and genuine,[9] and sísi, open to revision and reinterpretation and open to welcoming new Ọ̀rọ̀ that reconceive and complement existing art forms. Whether the arena is linguistic, political, religious, or cultural, spiritwork is inherently utilitarian: art for life's sake.

Using an infinitely rich repository of written, verbal, and visual arts, contemporary artists of the word, oils, acrylics, celluloid—any and all media—employ ancient methodology to propel us ever closer to our original state of holistic pípé, correctness and perfection, with the ultimate goal of gaining and maintaining personal, artistic, communal, and spiritual immortality, because àìkú parí ìwà—immortality completes and is the perfect manifestation of existence.[10]

* * *

The oríkì of Ìyá-Ayé, Mawu, and Nana Bùrúkù; the moans in the slave ships; the ululating field hollas; and the night-deep groans of the gut bucket reverberate from the land of Spreading Earth to campground to studio to radio. Weeping Trees, "Loving Pines," and impervious ìrókò whisper their secrets through knowing and gift-bearing limbs and ink-etched leaves. Àjẹ́ Odù's oracular utterance, with which she created all existence, rises like the impervious baobab from savannahs.

She comes equipped with her own undulating water supply and protective canopy. She is her own text; she owns her texts. And her ink is healing ink. As blood, it stains memory and mind. Chemical oil scent laced with indigo, this ink is difficult to wash from the fingertips. It tattoos the soul. It discombobulates linear time. This ink, so Black it is rainbowed, so pure it signifies despite the Ethiopic's salty waters, so rich even its clarity complicates, could only have come from Odù's infinite depths. Bound by ink-blood oaths, buried solutions, and a proclivity for evolution, Africana artists confab with the cosmic and refashion the forgotten.

Stationed at the sixteen crossroads connecting life, death, creative energies, and all times, spaces and places and dipping deep into the ink of Àjẹ́, their words dance the jubas of mothers and daughters and sons forsaken, lost, and found and offer lessons to help us re-determine our Destiny.

Not only is the circle unbroken, but it grows deeper and wider!

APPENDIX

Ìtàn-Oríkì Ìyàmi Òṣòròngà

RECITED BY OYERONKE IGBINOLA, ÌYÁLÁJÉ OF ILÉ-IFẸ̀, AWO OÒDUÀ

TRANSLATED AND TRANSCRIBED BY ADEBAYO OGUNRINU OGUNDIJO, GANIYU OYETIBO, AND TERESA N. WASHINGTON

```
        Ìyaà-mì Àbẹ̀ní
        Ẹlẹ́yinjú ẹgẹ́
        Olókìkí òru
        Ará Orífin, ará Odò Ọbà
 5      Apanì-má-hàágun
        Wọ́n n lọ sóde àti wáyé ọjọ́ àtìwọ̀ òòrùn.
        Ńbo lo kò ó?
        O kò ó lóríta mẹ́rin
        Ó kò ó lóríta mẹ́rìndínlógún.
10      Méjọ ń lọ sáyé;
        Méjọ ń lọ sọ́run.
        Kí ló kó dání?
        Ọ́ kẹ́dọ̀ gborogboro mẹ́rìndínlógún dání.
        Bí Àwọn Ìyàmi bá ń lọ sóde.
15      Wọ́n á fi apá méjéèjì
        Wọ́n á fi fò wọ́n á máa lọ
        Tí wọ́n bá darí dé
        Wọ́n á kí onílé
        Wọ́n á kí olóde
20      Wọ́n á ní ó káàbọ̀
        Gbogbo bí wọ́n ṣe ń fò, n máà ni ẹlẹyẹ ìí ṣe rí ìí o
        Gbogbo bí wọ́n ṣe máa n lọ òde
        Gẹ́gẹ́ bẹ́ẹ̀ lẹlẹyẹ ìí ṣe wà.
        Àjẹ́ funfun, n lÀjẹ́ ẹ tèmi
25      Ìyálájé ti ìlú Ifẹ̀
        . . . . . . . . . . . . . . . . . . . . . . . . . . . . . . . .
        Bí wọ́n bá ń lọ sóde
        Wọ́n á kànlèkùn nígbà mẹ́ta,
```

Wọ́n á jáde
Wọ́n á máa lo.
30 Bí wọ́n bá tún darí dé
Wọ́n á kànlèkùn nígbà mẹ́ta,
Wọ́n á ní àbọ̀
"Àbọ̀ọre. Àbọ̀ọre,
àwọn bọ̀, àwọn bọ̀
35 àwọn bọ̀ dáadáa"
Bí Àwọn Ìyàmi
Bí wọ́n bá ń jáde lọ,
Bí wọ́n bá fẹ́ẹ́ ṣiṣẹ́
Wọ́n ó sọ fónílé,
40 Wí pé àwọn ń lo.
Bí wọ́n bá tún darí dé
Wọ́n ó do páwọn bọ̀ọre
Àwọn bọ̀ọre o
Wọ́n á ní: "Ògbóni"
45 Ìdáhùn: "Ògborọ̀."
"Ipa Ògún láká ayé"
Bí aọn bá fẹ́ẹ́ kí wọn
"Ikú omi," Wọ́n á dáhùn
Ìdáhùn rẹ̀ ni: "Àrìnpa àrìnpa ọdẹ o."

50 Àwọn Ìyàmi Ẹ̀léyinjú ẹgẹ́
Olókìkí òru
Apanì-má-hàágun
Apani-má-yọdà
Atinú-jòró
55 Atinú-jòrónro Ògàlànta.
Bí wọ́n ṣe ń ní
Bẹ́ẹ̀ ni mo ṣe ń ní ìí
Kó o ṣàánú.

Àbá mọ dá fáọn Àwọn Ìyàmi,
60 Tí wón máaá rìn aago kan òru, aago kan ọ̀sán
Ìgbà tí wọn máaá rìn nìyẹn
Wọ́n sì máaá bọ̀ọre, wọ́n maa n bọ̀ọre
Wọ́n ìí foríí sọ
Wọ́n ìí fiyẹ́ẹ́ sọ.
65 Ṣùgbọ́n àwọn to ba tí jáláwọ̀ mẹ́ta?
Òru ọ̀gànjọ́ ní déédé aago mẹ́ta
N làwon Ìyá yẹn máa ń rin
Àwọn loníṣẹ́ẹbi

```
            Àwọn laláṣọ dúdú.
70          Èmi ò wàá gbà aṣọ dúdú o!
            Aṣo funfun lèmí gbà
            . . . . . . . . . . . . . . . . . . . . . . . . . . . . . . . . .
            Gégé bí wọ́n ṣe máa n lọ náà nìyìo
            Gégé bẹ́ẹ̀ ni Àwọn Ìyàmi ṣe máa ń lọ
            Bí wọ́n bá tún darí dé náà; wọ́n a sọ wí pé,
75          "Ìyáà mi òò,
            Ìyáà mi òò,
            Ìyáà mi òò."
            "A ti dé.
            A ti dé.
80          A ti dé."
            Iṣẹ́ a rángún kìí pa igún
            Iṣẹ́ tí a bá ránkọ̀ kìí pa ìkọ̀ o
            Iṣẹ́ té a bá rán wa
            Wọ́n ní kò níí bu wá ni'rú o
85          A à níí sì sọ o
            A à níí silẹ̀ tẹ̀ o
            A à níí ṣòde lọ o
            A à níí ṣòde ọ́sán lọ o
            A à níí ṣòde òru lọ o
90          A à níí ṣòde alé lọ o.
            Ìyàmi o! Ìyàmi o! Ìyàmi o!
            Hòóò, Hòóò, Hòóò."
            Bí wọ́n ṣe é dáhùn?
            Ìgbà mẹ́ta n làjé ẹ́ sọ̀rọ
95          Ìgbà mẹ́ta n loṣó ó níjọ́
            Ìgbà mẹ́ta n làwọn ọ̀n Ìyàmi dáhùn
            Wọ́n á kànlẹ̀kùn
            Wọ́n á wọlé
            Wọ́n á lónílé kúulé
100         Bí aọn bá fẹ́ẹ́ jẹfun,
            Bí aọn fẹ́ẹ́ jẹdọ̀,
            Tí aọn fẹ́ẹ́ japá,
            Tí aọn fẹ́ẹ́ jẹsẹ̀,
            Wọ́n á kànlẹ̀kùn lẹ́ẹ̀meta
105         Wọ́n á wolé tonítọ̀hún
            Wọ́n á jẹ ẹ́, Wọ́n á jẹ ẹ́
            Wọ́n á jídé
            Wọ́n á tún máa bónítọ̀lún dárò
            "Èyin Ìyàmi, ẹ má jẹ mí o! Èyin Ìyàmi, ẹ má jẹ mí o!
110         Èyin Ìyàmi ẹ má jẹ mí lápá!
```

Ẹ má jẹ mí lẹ́sẹ̀
Ẹ má jẹ mí lèfun
Ẹ má jẹ mí lẹ́dọ̀!"

     Ẹ̀yin Ìyàmi, ìbà
115 Eégún, ìbà
     Ìbà àtiwáyé ọjọ́ àtiwọ̀ oòrùn
     Àwọn Ìyàmi n ló àṣẹ ìí lé e lọ̀wọ́!
     Ẹ̀yin Ìyàmi atinú japá, Ògàlànta
     Atinú jẹ̀dọ̀
120 Atinú jòrónro,
     Ẹ̀yin lẹ ẹ́ jẹẹ̀yàn láì jẹ́ kó mọ̀
     Tẹ́ ẹ bá jẹ wọ́n tán
     Ẹ ó pẹ̀yìndà
     Ẹ ẹ́ tùn máa sọ pé kónítọ̀hún ó máa pé:
125 "Gbà mí! Gbà mí!"
     Ẹ̀yin lẹ ń ṣe é
     Ẹ̀yin lẹ́ ẹ́ gbà á lẹ̀
     Ìyàmi mo júbà o!
     Àjẹ́ má jẹ mí o!
130 Ìyàmi mo júbà o!
     Ìyàmi mo júbà o!
     Ìyàmi mo júbà o!

     Á ni: "Ògbóni! Ògborọ̀!"
     "Ògbóni! Ògborọ̀!"
135 "Ògbóni! Ògborọ̀!"
     Wọ́n lọ́ ọ kò ó
     Nbo lo kò ó o?
     Orítá mẹ́rìndínlógún ni
     Kí ló kó daní?
140 Ó kẹ́dan gbọrọgbọrọ mẹ́rìndínlógún daní
     Méjọ n lọ sáyé
     Méjọ n lọ sọ́run
     Ẹ̀yin Ìyàmi: Ìbà o

     Tá a bá fẹ́ bọwọ́ Ògbóni
145 Ọwọ́ èsì la á nà
     A nàkan síwájú
     A nàkan sádárin
     . . . .

Ìtàn Àwọn Ìyàmi nìyẹn o
Àwọn Ìyaà-mì Àbẹ̀ní
150 Ẹ̀léyinjú ẹgẹ́
Olókìkí òru
Ará Orífin, ará Odò Ọbà
Ení rán ni nṣẹ́ táà á jábọ̀ ọ́ fún
Tón tí wọ́n bá ránmọ níṣẹ́
155 Ọmọ a wáá jíṣẹ́ fún wọn o.

Ṣé ẹ ti rí bí àwọn ẹlẹyẹ yìí ṣe ń ṣe bí?
Géẹ́ bẹ́ẹ̀ ni Àwọn Ìyàmi ṣe ń jáde lọ.
Bí wọ́n bá ti ń lọ sóde
Wọ́n á fò
160 Wọ́n á júbà lọ́dọ̀ Ọlọ́run
Wọ́n á ń "Alálàfunfun, Alálàfunfun, Alálàfunfun!"
Àwọn lọ sóde rèé
Káon lọọre
Káon bọ̀ọre.

165 Nigínigín làá bójọ́,
Nigínigín làá bóṣù
Nigínigín ni wọ́n máa ń ba Àwọn Ìyámi.
Aṣojú òòrùn;
Aṣojú ọ̀sán;
170 Aṣojú alẹ́;
Nigínigín ni wọ́n máa ń ba Àwọn Ìyámi.

Àwọn Ìyàmi sọ̀kalẹ̀ nìyẹn o.

Mo pìtàn ìtàn Àwọn Ìyàmi fún o.
Kọ́ máa yéẹ́, kọ́ máa ríṣẹ
175 Korí ẹ̀ ó má gbàbọ̀dẹ̀.

GLOSSARY

Áàjálayé: The Winds of the World; a manifestation of Òrìṣà Oya
abáàra méjì: "The one with two bodies"; an oríkì of Àjẹ́
àbíkú: "born to die"; spirit children who torment mothers by entering the womb to be born and to die repeatedly
Afírìmáàkọ̀: The Greatest Strongest Elder Who if Touched Kills (the Sacrilegious One) by Magic
Afrekete: daughter and youngest child of the Loa MawuLisa and earthly parents Agbe and Naete. She is a trickster Loa and knower of secrets. Afrekete mediates between humans and the spiritual world.
Agan: force of Egúngún, overseen by Oya, that rids the earth of instability; similar to Orò
Àgbàláàgbà: wise, strong, elder; oríkì of Àjẹ́
Aido Hwedo: Rainbow Serpent of Fon Vodun who created the topography of the world with Mawu; Aido Hwedo is Damballah's counterpart
Ajalagba: Igbo term for a male with Àjẹ́ or an Oṣó
Alápò ìkà: The Owner of Wicked Bags; also an òríkì of Àjẹ́
Amusu: Igbo term for an Àjẹ́
Ani: the Igbo Earth Mother Deity, also known as Mgbara
Ala Àpẹ̀pẹ̀-Alẹ̀: one of many òríkì for and aspects of the Earth Òrìṣà
ápò ìkà: "wicked bags"; symbolizes the womb and the tomb and also medicinal-spiritual preparations
Ast: Kemetic Netcher (divinity) who is the origin of all life and perhaps Àjẹ́, also known as Isis
awo: secrets, mysteries
Àwọn Ìyá Wa: Our Mothers; a euphemism for Àjẹ́ that is literal and figurative
Àwọn Ìyàmi Òṣòròngà: the Àjẹ́ collective
Ayé: the World; a euphemism for Àjẹ́
babaláwo: father of mysteries
bokono: diviner of Fa; Fon equivalent of babaláwo
Chineke: the Igbo male supreme Deity; also called Chukwu
cigbe: the Nupe material magnifier of Ega (Àjẹ́)
Damballah: Rainbow Serpent of Fon Vodun, kin to Òṣùmàrè of Ifá; paired with Aido Hwedo
Damballah-Hwedo: the Fon Serpent Divinity amalgamated

Dan: high Serpent Loa of Fon Vodun; the elder of Damballah-Hwedo
dibia: Igbo term for diviner; equivalent of babaláwo
Dije: Ewe term for Àjẹ́
dúdú: Yoruba term for profound depth; the hue black
Ega: Nupe term for Àjẹ́
egbé: "carrier medicine"; a transportation device
Egúngún: society of the transmigrated ancestors and their worship
Èṣù Ẹlẹ́gbára: Òrìṣà of the crossroads and of human spiritual development; the Divine Linguist, Messenger, the Trickster
Ẹdan: Òrìṣà of Ògbóni Society; a progenitor of Àjẹ́
Ẹ̀fẹ̀: light-hearted yet critical songs of Gẹ̀lẹ̀dẹ́; also a son of Yemọja
ẹgbẹ́: a group, as in Ẹgbẹ́ Àjẹ́, the Àjẹ́ Collective
Ẹléyẹ: "Owner of the Bird"; Àjẹ́
ẹsẹ Ifá: divination poems of Ifá
ẹyẹ: bird (of Àjẹ́)
Ẹyẹ Òrò: the Spirit Bird of Àjẹ́
Fa: spiritual system of the Dahomey as derived from Ifá. Includes medicinal healing, ancestor reverence, and philosophy of life. As a divination system, Fa is the writing of Mawu, which contains all humans' destiny. Fa is also called Vodun and is the parent of Caribbean and American Voodoo.
funfun: the hue white
Gẹ̀lẹ̀dẹ́: the "ultimate in spectacle"; the festival of praise and placation staged by Yoruba communities to honor Àwọn Ìyá Wa; also the daughter of Yemọja
Hoodoo: African American cosmological system that includes divination, medicinal healing and protection, and power of the word
ìbà: homage
ibejì: twin Òrìṣà who represent the cycle of death and rebirth; children of Ṣàngó and Ọya
Ifá: Yoruba cosmological system and way of knowing that includes ontology, medicinal healing, divination, power of the word and metaphysics; also an Òrìṣà
ìjúbà: homage; praisesongs of invocation
Ilẹ̀ Ọgẹ́rẹ́: Slippery Earth; an oríkì of Ilẹ̀ (Earth) and Ìyàmi Òṣòròngà
ileeshin: the mystic staff of Nana Bùrúkù that is used as a protective tool
ìrókò: African teak tree; a meeting-place of Àwọn Ìyá Wa
ìtàn: oral and written literature and histories
ìtànkálẹ̀: the lands where African victims of the transatlantic enslavement were exiled; more generally, lands to which Africans migrated
ìwà: character, existence
ìwà-pẹ̀lẹ́: cool, composed character; the ideal character typical of Àwọn Ìyá Wa
ìyá: "mother" or "wife"; also a euphemism for Àwọn Ìyá Wa

Ìyá-Ayé: literally Mother of the Earth; one of many oríkì for the Earth Òrìṣà
Ìyáláwo: neologism meaning Mother of Mysteries
Ìyàmi: My Mysterious Mother
Ìyàmi Àbẹ̀ní: My Mysterious Mother, Whom We Beg to Have
Ìyàmi Òṣòròngà: the Àjẹ́ Deity
Ìyánlá: Great Mother; oríkì of Ìyàmi Òṣòròngà and Odù; Yewájọbí, Mother of all Òrìṣà and all living entities
juba: an amalgamation of praise, song, prayer, dance, planning, celebration, exultation, and pain; an African American term; origin: ìjúbà (to pay homage), Yoruba
Kemet: Ancient Egypt
Kindoki: Kongo term for Àjẹ́
Legba: youngest child of MawuLisa who knows the language of Mawu, holds her Book of Fa, and interprets Fa to humanity
Lisa: face of the sun; the Father who resides in Mawu
Loa: Fon term for Òrìṣà, Divinity, Spirit
Mani: Kongo Serpent Zambi, who are two serpents in the sky; also, a Kongo spiritual society similar to Ògbóni
Mawu: the Mother who created all life forms and wrote the Book of Fa and whose name is synonymous with Fa
MawuLisa: the combined Fon MotherFather Deity
Mayya, Mayye, Mayyu: Hausa terms for female, male, and group Àjẹ́, respectively
Nana Bùrúkù: Pan-West African Earth Mother
Ndoki: Kongo term designating a person who has/uses Kindoki (Àjẹ́)
Netcher: Kemetic term for Òrìṣà or Divinity
nganga: Kongo term for a diviner, herbal healer; a two-headed doctor
nkisi: a Kongo spiritual-material preparation that protects, heals, and avenges
Nzima Baye: Akan term for Àjẹ́ that are benevolent; also, an ethnic group
Odù: The Ìyánlá; The Àjẹ́; The Womb of Origins and Pot of Origins. Odù is also Yewájọbí, who brought all Òrìṣà into being. She is the cosmos and the creator of existence, the owner of Odù Ifá, and owner of oracular words.
Odù Ifá: divination verses of Ifá that include the ẹsẹ Ifá
Odùduwà: The child of Odù, the God who created the Earth, the Womb of Life that Creates All Existence, the progenitor of the Yoruba peoples; synonymous with Odù in some traditions
Ògbóni: ancient and still-active Yoruba political and spiritual society; also known as Imọ́lẹ̀ and Ògbóni Ibílẹ̀
Ogu: Igbo term meaning Divine Truth; also an oath
ogu: Igbo term meaning war

Ògún: Òrìṣà of Iron, technology, and creativity
orí: literally "head"; destiny
oríkì: praisename or praisesong
orin: song
ojúbọ Òrìṣà: a shrine, a sanctified place where the Òrìṣà are worshipped
Olódùmarè: Òrìṣà who maintains all life forms
olóju méjì: one with two faces; oríkì of Àjẹ́
Onílẹ̀: Òrìṣà of the Earth; material home of the ancestors; Òrìṣà of justice and divine retribution
oníṣègun: physician or healer
Òrìṣà: Select Head; Divinity
Orò: enforcement arm of Ògbóni characterized by the wailing of the bullroarers; a spiritual force of justice and retribution
Oṣó: men with a power similar to but not equal to Àjẹ́
Òṣùmàrè: Òrìṣà of the Rainbow; the Rainbow Serpent; Òrìṣà who delivers the covenant of Olódùmarè to humans
ọba: Yoruba king
Ọbà: an Òrìṣà; the first wife of Ṣàngó
Ọbàtálá: King of the White Cloth; Òrìṣà of Creation and shaper of human life forms who is paired with Odù
Ọfọ: Igbo term meaning Infinite Justice
ọfọ̀ àṣẹ: power of the word; power to pray effectively
Ọha Ndom: The Solidarity of Women
ọ̀ja: cloths with which mothers carry children on their backs
ọ̀kẹ́: the placenta
Ọlọ́mọ: Mother of Many Children; oríkì of Ìyánlá
Ọlọ́run: Owner of Heaven
Ọ̀ọ̀ni: Title for the Ruler of Ilé-Ifẹ̀ Yoruba
Ọ̀rọ̀: Word; Power of the Word; manifest in all verbal and visual art forms
Ọ̀run: The Comos; the spiritual realm
Ọ̀rúnmìlà: Òrìṣà who oversees Ifá divination, synonymous with Ifá
Ọ̀sanyìn: Òrìṣà of medicine and healing
Ọ̀sun: Òrìṣà of abundance; ancient ruler of Òṣogbo; the "leader of Àjẹ́"
Ọya: Òrìṣà of Transformation; Òrìṣà who opens the gateway to the ancestors
Petro: Vodun term signifying works of violent retribution
pupa: the hue red
Rada: Vodun term signifying benevolent works
two-headed doctor: African American term for a conjuror, medicinal healer, diviner, protector; a person with the knowledge of two heads, one material, one spiritual
Whodo(?): African American term for violent acts within the community, circa 1880; the Petro aspect of Hoodoo

Yemọja: Sacred Waters; Mother of Fishes; Mother of Many Children; "the vaginal fluid of the earth"; Òrìṣà of nurturance and healing; also Yewájọbí and the mother of many Òrìṣà; founder of the Gẹ̀lẹ̀dẹ́ festival

Yewájọbí: Oríkì of Yemọja and Odù; The Mother of Us All

Zambi: Kongo term for Spirit, Divinity

NOTES

Introduction

1. Houston A. Baker, Jr., *Workings of the Spirit* (Chicago: University of Chicago Press, 1991), 66.
2. Marjorie Pryse and Hortense Spillers, eds. *Conjuring* (Bloomington: Indiana University Press, 1985), 2.
3. Gay Wilentz, *Binding Cultures* (Bloomington: Indiana University Press, 1992), xxxiii, italics added.
4. Luisah Teish, *Jambalaya: The Natural Woman's Book of Personal Charms and Practical Rituals* (New York: Harper Collins, 1985), ix.
5. For examples of cultural difference, see Samuel G. Drake, *Annals of Witchcraft in New England, and Elsewhere in the United States; From Their First Settlement, Drawn Up from Unpublished and Other Well Authenticated Records of the Alleged Operations of Witches and Their Instigator, the Devil* (New York: B. Blom, 1967); Francesco Maria Guazzo, *Compendium Maleficarum*, ed. Montague Summers, trans. E. A. Ashwin (London: Frederick Muller, 1970); and James Randall Noblitt and Pamela Sue Perskin, *Cult and Ritual Abuse: Its History, Anthropology, and Recent Discovery in Contemporary America* (Westport, Conn.: Praeger, 1995). Wiccan informants of Frank Smyth (*Modern Witchcraft*, 1973), made it clear that Africans have no place in their system. A male Wiccan interviewed in London said, "I wouldn't admit coloured people to our meetings, simply because they have different traditions of witchcraft, and they wouldn't harmonise with us. I'm not biased of course, but that is the way it is. A foreigner could upset all our members and break the whole thing up." A female Wiccan was even more forthright: "I would never teach magic to a black or anyone else of an inferior race. They haven't the intelligence, and in the wrong hands magic can do untold harm." Quoted in J. Omosade, *Yoruba Beliefs and Sacrificial Rites* (Essex: Longman, 1979), 90.
6. Quoted in Henry L. Gates, Jr., *The Signifying Monkey* (New York: Oxford University Press, 1988), 29.
7. Quoted in Gates, *The Signifying Monkey*, 29.
8. Babatunde Lawal, *The Gèlèdé Spectacle* (Seattle: University of Washington Press, 1996), 39.

9. Queen Tiye (circa 1415–1340 b.c.e.) is an ancient Egyptian queen and the progenitor of Akhenaton and Tutankhamen. Erzulie is the Voodoo Loa of beauty and sensuality; Odù is the Great Mother of Àjẹ́. Yeye Muwo is a Yoruba Òrìṣà who is credited with creating the furrow in the backs of human beings. See Osamaro C. Ibie, *Ifism* (Lagos: Efehi, 1986), 147.

10. Wande Abimbola, *Sixteen Great Poems of Ifá* (Lagos: UNESCO, 1975), 293.

11. Awolalu, *Yoruba Beliefs and Sacrificial Rites*, 80.

12. Awo Fa'lokun Fatunmbi, *Iwà-Pẹ̀lẹ́* (Bronx, N.Y.: Original Publications, 1991), 97.

13. See Awolalu, *Yoruba Beliefs and Sacrificial Rites*, 183–192; and Simeon A. Ajayi, "The Planting of Baptist Mission Work among the Yoruba, 1850–1960: A Study in Religio-Cultural Conflict," *Ife: Annals of the Institute of Cultural Studies* 5 (1994): 49–53.

14. Fatunmbi, *Iwà-Pẹ̀lẹ́*, 97.

15. Barry Hallen and J. Olubi Sodipo, "A Comparison of the Western 'Witch' with the Yoruba 'Aje': Spiritual Powers or Personality Types?" *Ife: Annals of the Institute of Cultural Studies* 1 (1986): 3.

16. Hallen and Sodipo, "A Comparison of the Western 'Witch' with the Yoruba 'Aje,'" 4, italics added.

17. Hallen and Sodipo, "A Comparison of the Western 'Witch' with the Yoruba 'Aje,'" 5.

18. S. F. Nadel, *Nupe Religion* (London: Routledge, 1954), 170–171.

19. Nadel, Nupe Religion, 174.

20. Akin Omoyajowo, "What Is Witchcraft?" in *Traditional Religion in West Africa*, ed. E. E. Ade Adegbola (Accra: Asempa, 1983), 325.

21. Nadel, *Nupe Religion*, 176.

22. This is the case in Herbert Ogunde's film *Aiye*, in which Osetura single-handedly kills a horde of evil "African witches."

23. Hallen Barry and J. Olubi Sodipo, *Knowledge, Belief, and Witchcraft* (London: Ethnographica, Ltd., 1986; reprint, Stanford University Press, 1997), 118.

24. Diedre Badejo, *Òṣun Ṣẹ̀ẹ̀gẹ̀si* (Trenton, N.J.: Africa World Press, 1996), 27, italics in original.

1. Àjẹ́ In Yorubaland

1. G. O. Fayomi, quoted in Lawal, *Gẹ̀lẹ̀dẹ́ Spectacle*, 127–128.

2. Lawal, *Gẹ̀lẹ̀dẹ́ Spectacle*, 39.

3. Henry John Drewal and Margaret Thompson Drewal, *Gelede* (Bloomington: Indiana University Press, 1983), 7–8.

4. Badejo, *Òṣun Ṣẹ̀ẹ̀gẹ̀si*, 76.

5. Ayo Opefeyitimi, "'Women of the World' in Yoruba Culture," unpublished paper, 1993, 1.
6. Drewal and Drewal, *Gelede*, 7.
7. "Mythistories" is a compound construction of "myth" and "history." Often, when dealing with oral literature, it is difficult and unnecessary to distinguish between a historical phenomenon and an explanatory, proverbial, or fictional account. These terms are also relative, for what one ideology defines as a myth another will term history.
8. Benedict M. Ibitokun, *Dance as Ritual Drama* (Ile-Ife: Obafemi Awolowo University Press, 1993), 37.
9. The controversy surrounding the gender of Odùduwà has been discussed by a number of scholars. Space does not permit a full elaboration, but, to be brief, there are two schools of thought concerning the gender of Odùduwà. As the founder of the Yoruba nation, the Ekiti, Ado, Igbo-ora, and Ketu traditions hold that Odùduwà is a woman, while some Ife traditions maintain that Odùduwà is a man. However, as it regards spiritual traditions, most histories hold that Odùduwà is female, the creator of the earth, one and the same with Odù who is oracle, the Ìyánlá or Great Mother revered during the Gèlèdé festival, and the owner of Àjé. Lucas indirectly credits assertions that Odùduwà is a man to what I call the patriarchal shift, arguing that those assertions "are of a late origin." See also Teresa N. Washington, "Manifestations of Àjé in Africana Literature" (Ph.D. diss., Obafemi Awolowo University, Ile-Ife, 2000), chapter 1; E. Bolaji Idowu, *Olódùmarè* (1962; reprint, New York: Wazobia, 1994), 25–27; Cornelius Adepegba, "The Descent from Odùduwà," *African Historical Studies* 19, no. 1 (1986): 81; J. Olumide Lucas, *The Religion of the Yorubas* (Lagos: CMS, 1948), 93; and Lawal, *Gèlèdé Spectacle*, 24, 71, 287.
10. Samuel M. Opeola, interviews with author, Obafemi Awolowo University, 1997–1998, and Opeola, "The Ethical Influence of Yoruba Civilization," *Napatian Society* 1 (September 1993): 15.
11. Drewal and Drewal, *Gelede*, 74.
12. Drewal and Drewal, *Gelede*, 74.
13. Lawal, *Gèlèdé Spectacle*, 34.
14. Opeola, personal interviews, Obafemi Awolowo University, Nigeria, 1997; and Ibitokun, *Dance as Ritual Drama*, 36.
15. Drewal and Drewal, *Gelede*, 74.
16. Drewal and Drewal, *Gelede*, 75.
17. Many state that the word "Àjé" is never uttered at all, but this is not true. The wisdom-keepers I worked with used the word frequently, possibly due to their ownership of the force.
18. Quoted in Drewal and Drewal, *Gelede*, 7.
19. Lawal, *Gèlèdé Spectacle*, 39.

20. Modupe Oduyoye, "The Spider, the Chameleon, and the Creation of the Earth," in *Traditional Religion in West Africa*, edited by E. E. Ade Adegbola (Accra: Asempa, 1983), 383. See also Idowu, *Olódùmarè*, 25.

21. Opeola, personal interviews, Obafemi Awolowo University, Nigeria, 1997.

22. Fatunmbi, *Ìwà-Pèlé*, 38–39. The orthography is retained from the original.

23. Examples of women with Àjẹ́ who utilize Ọ̀rọ̀ can be found in Benedict M. Ibitokun's discussion of Ìyá Bọ̀kọ́lọ of Ketu in Benin Republic and Awolalu's discussion of Ekiti's Ayélála. Both women were deified for their use of divine utterance. See Ibitokun, *Dance as Ritual Drama*, 39n1; and Awolalu, *Yoruba Beliefs and Sacrificial Rites* (Essex: Longman, 1979), 41.

24. Ìtàn (history) and oríkì (praisename, praisesong) are two separate and distinct forms of orature, but they are also inseparable, for in uttering a text (ìtàn), one automatically utters praisenames (oríkì). I compound these words in an attempt to describe the holistic nature of Igbinola's utterance as a "historical praisesong." I quote from sections of the English translation of *Ìtàn-Oríkì Ìyàmi Òṣòròngà* in this text. The full text in Yoruba is included in the appendix.

25. Chief Igbinola is an Awo Oòduà (diviner in the way of Oodùa), an oníṣègùn (traditional physician), and the Ìyálájé of Ife (Ife's Mother of Prosperity).

26. Olabiyi Babalola Yai, "In Praise of Metonymy," *Research in African Literatures* 24, no. 4 (Winter 1993): 30–31.

27. Note the sixteen *ikin*, or palmnuts, the sixteen cowries used in divination, the sixteen principal olódù, the Odù Ifá composed of sixteen times sixteen (256) Odù, and the sixteen primary Òrìṣà. Sixteen is also one of the numbers associated with sacrifices to Àwọn Ìyá Wa.

28. Ibie, *Ifism*, 85–86.

29. Ayo Opefeyitimi, "Womb to Tomb: Yoruba Women Power Over Life and Death," *Ife: Annals of the Institute of Cultural Studies* 5 (1994): 63.

30. Yai, "In Praise of Metonymy," 35.

31. Ibie, *Ifism*, 49.

32. Marimba Ani, *Yurugu* (Trenton, N.J.: Africa World Press, 1984), 60.

33. Ani, *Yurugu*, 66.

34. Drewal and Drewal, *Gelede*, 22.

35. Oyeronke Igbinola, *Orin Ìyàmi Òṣòròngà;* Washington, "Manifestations of Àjẹ́ in Africana Literature," 21–29.

36. Babatunde Lawal, "New Light on Gelede," *African Arts* XI, no. 2 (1978): 66; and Lawal, *Gèlèdé Spectacle*, 66.

37. J. R. O. Ojo, "The Position of Women in Yoruba Traditional Society," *Department of History: University of Ife Seminar Papers, 1978–79* (Ile-Ife: Kosalabaro, 1980), 135.

38. Opefeyitimi, "'Women of the World' in Yoruba Culture," 17. Opefeyitimi's translation is not literal. "Eye funfun apa mi otun" should read "white bird to my right hand." "Eye funfun apa mi osi" should read "white bird to my left hand." "Eye mafunmafun" is "spotted bird." Perhaps Opefeyitimi seeks to emphasize the mystic aspects of Ẹyẹlẹ.

39. William Bascom, *Ifa Divination: Communication between Gods and Men in West Africa* (Bloomington: Indiana University Press, 1969), 469.

40. Bascom, *Ifa Divination*, 469.

41. Clement Adebooye, interviews with author, Obafemi Awolowo University, 1997.

42. Bade Ajuwon and Adebayo Faleti, interviews with author, Obafemi Awolowo University, 1998. Prior to coming to Ile-Ife, I had never encountered written or oral discussions of this color hierarchy.

43. In *Knowledge, Belief, and Witchcraft* (1986/1997), Hallen and Sodipo make this point. They assert that Lucy Mair's reliance on the term "evil" to describe "witches" is riddled with Christian eschatology and Western dichotomy. They find that "'evil' is an inappropriate concept to use as a cultural universal" (98).

44. Rowland Abiodun, "Identity and the Artistic Process in Yoruba Aesthetic Concept of Ìwà," *Journal of Cultural Inquiry* 1, no. 1 (December 1983): 15.

45. Wole Soyinka, "The African World and the Enthocultural Debate," in *African Culture: The Rhythms of Unity*, edited by Molefi Kete Asante and Kariamu Welsh Asante (Trenton, N.J.: Africa World Press, 1990), 16.

46. Rowland Abiodun, "Identity and the Artistic Process in Yoruba Aesthetic Concept of Ìwà," 13. Note that Abiodun translates pupa as "yellow" as opposed to red, possibly to give a closer approximation of certain skin tones.

47. Drewal and Drewal, *Gelede*, 71.

48. Drewal and Drewal, *Gelede*, 75, 269.

49. Pepe Carril, *Shango de Ima: A Yoruba Mystery Play*, in *Totem Voices*, edited by Paul Carter Harrison (New York: Grove, 1989), 53–54, italics added.

50. C. L. Adeoye, *Ìgbàgbọ́ àti Ẹ̀sìn Yorùbá* (Ibadan: Evans Bros., 1985), 104. Translation by Bidemi Okanlawon and Teresa N. Washington.

51. Ifayemi Eleburuibon, *The Adventures of Obatala* (Osogbo, Oyo: A. P. I., 1989), 82.

52. Abiodun, "Identity and the Artistic Process in Yoruba Aesthetic Concept of Ìwà," 15.
53. Cee-Lo, *Cee-Lo Green and His Perfect Imperfections* (New York: Arista, 2002).
54. Nikki Giovanni, "ego-tripping (there must be a reason why)," in *ego-tripping* (New York: Lawrence Hill and Co., 1973), 5.
55. Eleburuibon, *Adventures of Obatala*, 74.
56. Bascom, *Ifa Divination*, 468–489.
57. Fatunmbi, *Ìwà-Pèlé*, 184.
58. Adeoye, *Ìgbàgbó àti Èsìn Yorùbá*, 336–337.
59. Adeoye, *Ìgbàgbó àti Èsìn Yorùbá*, 336–337. Translation by Bidemi Okanlawon and Teresa N. Washington.
60. See Adeoye, *Ìgbàgbó àti Èsìn Yorùbá*, 338–339, for an allusion to the familial relationship between Àjé and Ògbóni.
61. Lawal, *The Gèlèdé Spectacle*, xviii, pl. 1.
62. Opeola, "The Ethical Influence of Yoruba Civilization," 7.
63. Kolawole Ositola, interview with author, Ibadan, Nigeria, 1999.
64. Lawal, *The Gèlèdé Spectacle*, 35.
65. Oyin Ogunba, interview with author, Obafemi Awolowo University, 1998–1999. Ogunba explains that èlèbò is the contraction of Èlè bò *oògùn*, which means "people who make sacrifices and medicine." See Awolalu, *Yoruba Beliefs and Sacrificial Rites*, 154, for a variation of this song.
66. Oyin Ogunba, interview with author.
67. Lucas, *Religion of the Yorubas*, 284.
68. Drewal and Drewal, *Gelede*, 42. Just as Àjé are misdefined as "witches," Oṣó are incorrectly called "wizards."
69. Drewal and Drewal, *Gelede*, 103.
70. Awolalu, *Yoruba Beliefs and Sacrificial Rites*, 86.
71. Drewal and Drewal, *Gelede*, 79.
72. Awolalu, *Yoruba Beliefs and Sacrificial Rites*, 85.
73. Opefeyitimi, "'Women of the World' in Yoruba Culture," 22; and Awolalu, *Yoruba Beliefs and Sacrificial Rites*, 86.
74. Ibie, *Ifism*, 159.
75. Ibie, *Ifism*, 48.
76. Adebayo Faleti, personal communication with author, Obafemi Awolowo University, August 1998.
77. Opeola, interviews with author, Obafemi Awolowo University, Nigeria, 1997.
78. Fatunmbi, *Ìwà-Pèlé*, 85.
79. Lucas, *Religion of the Yorubas*, 95.
80. Lucas, *Religion of the Yorubas*, 95. Lucas verifies that these names represent one Òrìṣà who is a woman; his findings buttress those of Oduyoye and Mason. Lawal uses "Oòduà," "Òdù," and "Odùduwà"

interchangeably while noting the connection with Ìyánlá and the controversy over gender. *Gẹ̀lẹ̀dẹ́ Spectacle*, xxii, 24. No tonal distinction between odù ("pot" or "cauldron") and Odù ("the indication of divination by the Ifá oracle") is noted in *A Dictionary of Yoruba Language* (Ibadan: Ibadan University Press, 1991), 167.

81. Ulli Beier, "Gelede Masks," *Odu* 6 (June 1958): 10–11.

82. John Mason, *Orin Òrìṣà* (Brooklyn, N.Y.: Yoruba Theological Archministry, 1992), 221. "All the Ọbàtálás" refers to the sixteen roads of the Òrìṣà.

83. Opeola, personal interviews, Obafemi Awolowo University, Nigeria, 1997. See similar statements in Drewal and Drewal, *Gelede*, 9.

84. Lucas, *Religion of the Yorubas*, 95.

85. Opeola, personal interviews, Obafemi Awolowo University, Nigeria, 1997. See similar statements in Drewal and Drewal, *Gelede*, 9.

86. *Ìgbàgbọ́ àti Ẹ̀sìn Yorùbá* describes Ìyàmi Òṣòròngà entering the earth's sphere with a group of fifteen entities and forces, including Àpẹ̀pẹ̀-Alẹ̀ (Earth personified), Ọbàtálá (The Owner of the White Cloth), and àṣẹ. Adeoye, *Ìgbàgbọ́ àti Ẹ̀sìn Yorùbá*, 32. For texts featuring Ọbàtálá and Ọ̀ṣun, see William Bascom, *Sixteen Cowries: Yoruba Divination from Africa to the New World* (Bloomington: Indiana University Press, 1980), 37; and Badejo, *Ọ̀ṣun Ṣẹ̀ẹ̀gẹ̀si*, 73–74.

87. Opeola, personal interviews, Obafemi Awolowo University, Nigeria, 1997.

88. Opeola, personal interviews; and Samuel M. Opeola, "What Is Witchcraft?" unpublished paper, Institute of Cultural Studies Seminar, Obafemi Awolowo University, 1997, 5; and Adeoye, *Ìgbàgbọ́ àti Ẹ̀sìn Yorùbá*, 203–208.

89. Ibie, *Ifism*, 47.

90. Opeola, personal interviews, Obafemi Awolowo University, Nigeria, 1997. To witness Odù containers, see Bascom, *Ifá*, pl. 21A.

91. Drewal and Drewal, *Gelede*, 9.

92. Kolawole Ositola, personal interview, Ibadan, Nigeria, 1999; and Margaret Thompson Drewal, *Yoruba Ritual* (Bloomington: Indiana University Press, 1992), 179. See also Drewal and Drewal, *Gelede*, 9; Bascom, *Sixteen Cowries*, 217–223; and Ibie, *Ifism*, 16.

93. Adeoye, *Ìgbàgbọ́ àti Ẹ̀sìn Yorùbá*, 356–357.

94. The diagram is my expansion of one drawn for me by S. M. Opeola.

95. Ibie, *Ifism*, 48.

96. Adeoye, *Ìgbàgbọ́ àti Ẹ̀sìn Yorùbá*, 356. Translation by Bidemi Okanlawon, Kasim Oladipo, and Teresa N. Washington.

97. A. P. Anyebe, *Ogboni* (Lagos: Sam Lao, 1989), 21.

98. Adeoye, *Ìgbàgbọ́ àti Ẹ̀sìn Yorùbá*, 359–360. Translation by Bidemi Okanlawon and Teresa N. Washington.

99. For the use of these praisenames for Àjẹ́, see Opefeyitimi, "Womb to Tomb," 63.

100. See Bascom, *Ifa Divination,* 229; and Opefeyitimi, "'Women of the World' in Yoruba Culture," 18.

101. Drewal and Drewal, *Gelede,* 60.

102. The supreme importance of Òṣùmàrè has Pan-African "sisters": Fon's Dan and Damballah-Hwedo, Igboland's Olisa Buluwa, and Kongo's Mani (see chapter 2 for a full discussion).

103. Solabade S. Popoola, "Your Questions Answered," *Orunmila Magazine* 6 (1993): 46. In answering a query about the difference between Olódùmarè and Ọlọ́run, Popoola states that the actual name of the Supreme Being who created the entire universe is Akamara. In *Gẹ̀lẹ̀dẹ́ Spectacle,* Lawal states, "*ayé àkámarà* refer[s] to the 'powerful mothers' as well as the evil that lurks in the physical world" (31).

104. Fatunmbi, *Ìwà-Pẹ̀lẹ́,* 84.

105. Olabiyi Babalola Yai, "Towards a New Poetics of Oral Poetry in Africa," *Ife: Annals of the Institute of Cultural Studies* 1 (1986): 49.

106. Fatunmbi, *Ìwà-Pẹ̀lẹ́,* 84.

107. Fatunmbi, *Ìwà-Pẹ̀lẹ́,* 84–85.

108. Fatunmbi, *Ìwà-Pẹ̀lẹ́,* 84–85; and Idowu, *Olódùmarè,* 34–35. Zora Neale Hurston discusses a Rainbow Python in Lake Maitland, Florida! *The Sanctified Church* (New York: Marlow & Co., 1981), 34–35. See T. N. Washington, *Manifestations of Masculine Magnificence: Divinity in Africana Life, Lyrics, and Literature* (Oya's Tornado, 2014) 61–63 for my full analysis of these divine Pan-African serpents.

109. See Lucas, *Religion of the Yorubas,* 170.

110. Bascom, *Sixteen Cowries,* 215.

111. Beier, "Gelede Masks," 10.

112. Mason, *Orin Òrìṣà,* 288.

113. Mason, *Orin Òrìṣà,* 288.

114. Fatunmbi, *Ìwà-Pẹ̀lẹ́,* 124.

115. Mason, *Orin Òrìṣà,* 288.

116. Adeoye, *Ìgbàgbọ́ àti Ẹ̀sìn Yorùbá,* 221.

117. Adeoye, *Ìgbàgbọ́ àti Ẹ̀sìn Yorùbá,* 221. Translation by Kasim Oladipo and Teresa N. Washington.

118. Raymond Prince, "The Yoruba Image of the Witch," *Journal of Mental Science* 107, no. 449 (July 1961): 796.

119. Lawal, *Gẹ̀lẹ̀dẹ́ Spectacle,* 39.

120. Lawal, "New Light on Gelede," 67. Yemọja and her daughter "Gẹ̀lẹ̀dẹ́" debunk the myth that Gẹ̀lẹ̀dẹ́ dancing is too strenuous for women: Women are the originators.

121. Mason, *Orin Òrìṣà,* 287.

122. Lawal, *Gẹ̀lẹ̀dẹ́ Spectacle,* 74.

123. Mason, *Orin Òrìṣà,* 289–290.

124. Lawal, *Gẹ̀lẹ̀dẹ́ Spectacle*, 53.
125. Lawal, *Gẹ̀lẹ̀dẹ́ Spectacle*, 50–58. Lawal discusses the important roles women hold in Gẹ̀lẹ̀dẹ́, debunking the myth that the festival is primarily a male affair.
126. Drewal and Drewal, *Gelede*, 251; Ibitokun, *Dance as Ritual Drama*, 35.
127. Mason, *Orin Òrìṣà*, 296.
128. Mason, *Orin Òrìṣà*, 294.
129. Badejo, *Ọ̀ṣun Ṣẹ̀ẹ̀gẹ̀si*, 74, italics added.
130. Mason, *Orin Òrìṣà*, 296.
131. Bascom, *Sixteen Cowries*, 419.
132. Bascom, *Sixteen Cowries*, 413.
133. Bascom, *Sixteen Cowries*, 417.
134. Bascom, *Sixteen Cowries*, 419, italics added.
135. Badejo, *Ọ̀ṣun Ṣẹ̀ẹ̀gẹ̀si*, 77. Badejo's research demonstrates that the spiritual orin refers to a historical fact. Badejo finds a queen named Ọ̀sun who ruled Òsogbo between the 1600s and 1900s and had a treaty agreement with Láróòyè and Òlútímíhin.
136. Mason, *Orin Òrìṣà*, 294.
137. Bascom, *Sixteen Cowries*, 407, 417.
138. Badejo, *Ọ̀ṣun Ṣẹ̀ẹ̀gẹ̀si*, 25.
139. Akinwumi Isola, "Ọya: Inspiration and Empowerment," Cultural Studies Seminar, Obafemi Awolowo University, March 1998, and unpublished paper, 3.
140. Fatunmbi, *Ìwà-Pẹ̀lẹ́*, 39.
141. Bascom, *Ifá Divination*, 479.
142. Mason, *Orin Òrìṣà*, 292; see also Bascom, *Sixteen Cowries*, 231.
143. Bascom, *Sixteen Cowries*, 231.
144. Drewal and Drewal, *Gelede*, 251.
145. Fatunmbi, *Ìwà-Pẹ̀lẹ́*, 39.
146. S. O. Babayemi, *Egungun among the Oyo Yoruba* (Ibadan: Board Publications, 1980), 4.
147. Babayemi, *Egungun among the Oyo Yoruba*, 7.
148. Mason, *Orin Òrìṣà*, 293.
149. Babayemi, *Egungun among the Oyo Yoruba*, 10.
150. Babayemi, *Egungun among the Oyo Yoruba*, 10.
151. Cheikh Anta Diop, *The Cultural Unity of Black Africa* (1959; reprint, Chicago: Third World Press, 1963), 120, italics added.
152. 'Biodun Adediran, "Women, Rituals and Politics in Pre-Colonial Yorubaland," unpublished paper 1992, 10–11.
153. Funso Afolayan, "Women, Politics and Society in Pre-Colonial Igbomina," unpublished paper, 1992, 98.
154. Ekpo Eyo, "Recent Excavations at Ife and Owo and Their Implications for Ife, Owo and Benin Studies" (Ph.D. diss., University of

Ibadan, 1974); Adediran, "Women, Rituals and Politics in Pre-Colonial Yorubaland," 4; and interview with author, Obafemi Awolowo University, 1998.
155. R. A. Olaniyan and I. A. Akinjogbin, "Sources of the History of Ife," in *The Cradle of a Race: Ife,* edited by I. A. Akinjogbin (Lagos: Sunray, 1992), 41–42.
156. Adediran, "Women, Rituals and Politics in Pre-Colonial Yorubaland," 3.
157. See Washington, "Manifestations of Àjẹ́ in Africana Literature," 98–119.
158. Nina Mba, *Nigerian Women Mobilised* (Berkeley: University of California Press, 1982), 10.
159. Mba, *Nigerian Women Mobilised,* 10.
160. Mba, *Nigerian Women Mobilised,* 11.
161. Mba, *Nigerian Women Mobilised,* 9, italics added.
162. Mba, *Nigerian Women Mobilised,* 143.
163. Mba, *Nigerian Women Mobilised,* 146.
164. Bascom, *Sixteen Cowries,* 263–265 and 673–679.
165. Mba, *Nigerian Women Mobilised,* 150.
166. Mba, *Nigerian Women Mobilised,* 153.

2. Àjẹ́ across the Continent and an the Ìtànkálẹ̀

1. Adeoye, *Ìgbàgbọ́ àti Ẹ̀sìn Yorùbá,* 340.
2. Emefie Ikenga Metuh, *God and Man in African Religion* (London: Geoffrey Chapman, 1981), 100.
3. Nadel, *Nupe Religion,* 170. Lawal found that barren women carry a buffalo horn smeared with camwood to promote fertility. The buffalo and its horns are symbols of Ọya; it is logical that women would beseech the mother of nine children for children. See B. Lawal, *The Gẹ̀lẹ̀dẹ́ Spectacle,* 50n20.
4. I do not argue that the Yoruba are the sole originators, as these systems are clearly Pan-African. However, the Ewe peoples, largely of Togo, Benin, and Ghana, and the Ga peoples of Ghana state that their place of origin is Ife. G. K. Nukunya, "Traditional Cultures and Modern International Boundaries: A Study of the Ewe and Their Eastern Neighbours," in *African Unity: Cultural Foundations,* edited by Zaccheus Sunday Ali (Lagos: Centre for Black and African Arts and Civilization, 1988), 68; and field research in Legon, Ghana, by author, 1995. In compiling lists of Odùduwà's progeny, notable inclusions were Oninana, "who founded his kingdom in what is known as Gold Coast [Ghana] today," and Obarada, "who was driven to found latterly the Kingdom of Dahomey." I. A. Akinjogbin, "Dispersal from Ife," in *The*

Cradle of a Race: Ife: From the Beginning to 1980, edited by I. A. Akinjogbin (Lagos: Sunray, 1992), 250–251.

5. Gabriel Bannerman-Richter, *The Practice of Witchcraft in Ghana* (Elk Grove: Gabari, 1982), 22.

6. Simon Bockie, *Death and the Invisible Powers* (Bloomington: Indiana University Press, 1993), 43.

7. Bockie, *Death and the Invisible Powers*, 43–67.

8. Bockie, *Death and the Invisible Powers*, 56.

9. Bockie, *Death and the Invisible Powers*, 45.

10. Bockie, *Death and the Invisible Powers*, 65.

11. Abubacar Mamane, interview with author, Obafemi Awolowo University, Ile-Ife, 1999.

12. Mary E. Modupe Kolawole, *Womanism and African Consciousness* (Trenton, N.J.: African World Press, 1997), 46.

13. Kolawole, Womanism and African Consciousness, 45–48.

14. In *Religion of the Yorubas,* J. Olumide Lucas undertakes a detailed comparative analysis of Kemet and Yorubaland.

15. Barbara J. Walker, *The Woman's Encyclopedia of Myths and Secrets* (San Francisco: Harper San Francisco, 1983), 453.

16. Walker, *Woman's Encyclopedia of Myths and Secrets*, 453.

17. Walker, *Woman's Encyclopedia of Myths and Secrets*, 454.

18. Diop, *Cultural Unity of Black Africa*, 59–60.

19. According to Sir Gaston Maspero, "The Egyptians made their first appearance on the stage of history about 8,000 to 10,000 B.C.E." Quoted in Anthony Browder, *Nile Valley Contributions to Civilization* (Washington, D.C.: Institute of Karmic Guidance, 1992). Browder finds that "oral records indicate that a considerable amount of activity was taking place as early as 20,000 B.C.E." (62).

20. Walker, *Woman's Encyclopedia of Myths and Secrets*, 455.

21. Opeola, "What Is Witchcraft?" 5.

22. Browder, *Nile Valley Contributions to Civilization*, 82.

23. Browder, *Nile Valley Contributions to Civilization*, 82.

24. Dele Layiwola, "Womanism in Nigerian Folklore and Drama," *African Arts* XI, no. 1 (1987): 29.

25. Browder, *Nile Valley Contributions to Civilization*, 91.

26. Browder, *Nile Valley Contributions to Civilization,* 91. Heru, son of Ast and Ausar, is symbolized by the falcon. Falcons and serpents often adorn the traditional headgear of the Kemetic rulers. The significance of the ibis and *benu* birds of Kemet, indicative of transcendence and regeneration, are also relevant to this discussion. A remarkably exquisite profile of Khafre, the architect of Her-em-aket (erroneously called the Sphinx by Europeans), is rendered with a falcon cresting his headdress (222).

27. Diop, *Cultural Unity of Black Africa*, 76.

28. Peter Sarpong, *Ghana in Retrospect* (Accra: Ghana Publications, 1974), 18.
29. T. N. O. Quarcoopome, *West African Traditional Religion* (Ibadan: African Universities Press, 1987), 53.
30. J. P. Clark-Bekederemo, *The Ozidi Saga* (Washington, D.C.: Howard University Press, 1991), 83.
31. Teish, *Jambalaya*, 54.
32. Lawal, *Gèlèdé Spectacle*, 11.
33. B. B. O. Emeh, *The Treasures of Nnobi* (Enugu, Nigeria: Ochumba Press, n.d. [1986]), 38.
34. Mason, *Orin Òrìṣà*, 260.
35. Mason, *Orin Òrìṣà*, 262.
36. Mason, *Orin Òrìṣà*, 276–277.
37. Mason, *Orin Òrìṣà*, 262.
38. Mason, *Orin Òrìṣà*, 281.
39. See Metuh, *God and Man in African Religion*, 26.
40. Adeoye, *Ìgbàgbọ́ àti Ẹ̀sìn Yorùbá*, 325–326. Translation by Bidemi Okanlawon and Teresa N. Washington.
41. Mason, *Orin Òrìṣà*, 227.
42. Mason, *Orin Òrìṣà*, 227.
43. Adeoye, *Ìgbàgbọ́ àti Ẹ̀sìn Yorùbá*, 326.
44. Adeoye, *Ìgbàgbọ́ àti Ẹ̀sìn Yorùbá*, 327.
45. Robert Farris Thompson, *Flash of the Spirit* (New York: Vintage, 1983), 71.
46. Mason, *Orin Òrìṣà*, 260.
47. Melville J. Herskovits, *Dahomey: An Ancient West African Kingdom*, vol. 2 (Evanston: Northwestern University Press, 1967), 125.
48. Herskovits, *Dahomey: An Ancient West African Kingdom*, 101.
49. Lucas, *Religion of the Yorubas*, 95.
50. Jan Knappert, *Myths and Legends of the Congo* (Ibadan: Heinemann, 1971), 182.
51. Knappert, *Myths and Legends of the Congo*, 182.
52. Melville J. Herskovits and Frances S. Herskovits, *Dahomean Narrative: A Cross Cultural Analysis* (Evanston: Northwestern University Press, 1958), 135.
53. Teish, *Jambalaya*, 54.
54. Metuh's definitions allude to interesting links between Yoruba's Nana Bùrúkù and the Fon Deity MawuLisa. He translates Olisa as "container of the universe," and Buluwa as "one who permeated the world." Thus, Olisa N'buluwa is "he who is spread out everywhere and carrying the world." The Fon word "Olisa" is strikingly similar in composition and definition to the Yoruba "Òrìṣà"; likewise, the Fon "Buluwa" could be a linguistic sibling of the Yoruba "Bùrúkù." *God and Man in African Religion*, 26.

55. Herskovits, *Dahomey: An Ancient West African Kingdom*, 203.
56. Herskovits, *Dahomey: An Ancient West African Kingdom*, 176.
57. Herskovits, *Dahomey: An Ancient West African Kingdom*, 155.
58. Herskovits, *Dahomey: An Ancient West African Kingdom*, 170.
59. Christian R. Gaba, *Scriptures of an African People* (New York: Nok, 1973), 79.
60. Thompson, *Flash of the Spirit*, 109; and Metuh, *God and Man in African Religion*, 10, respectively.
61. Clarence Major, *From Juba to Jive* (New York: Penguin, 1994), 313.
62. Gaba, *Scriptures of an African People*, 58–59.
63. Gaba, *Scriptures of an African People*, 61.
64. Gaba, *Scriptures of an African People*, 128.
65. Clark-Bekederemo, *Ozidi Saga*, 26, 73, 318.
66. Thompson, *Flash of the Spirit*, 74.
67. Clark-Bekederemo, *Ozidi Saga*, 97.
68. Clark-Bekederemo, *Ozidi Saga*, liv.
69. Egbe Ifie, *A Cultural Background to the Plays of J. P. Clark-Bekederemo* (Ibadan: Time End Press, 1994), 90.
70. Ifie, *A Cultural Background to the Plays of J. P. Clark-Bekederemo*, 73.
71. Ifie, *A Cultural Background to the Plays of J. P. Clark-Bekederemo*, 91.
72. Ifie, *A Cultural Background to the Plays of J. P. Clark-Bekederemo*, 91.
73. Ogunsola John, "The Role of the Towns in the Creation and Development of Yoruba Oral Literature," in *Yoruba Oral Tradition*, edited by Wande Abimbola (Ibadan: Ibadan University Press, 1975), 340.
74. See William Harrison Pipes, "Old Time Religion: Benches Can't Say Amen," in *Black Families*, 3rd ed., edited by Harriet Pipes McAdoo (Thousand Oaks, Calif.: Sage, 1997), 43.
75. Igue, "Role of the Towns in the Creation and Development of Yoruba Oral Literature," 340.
76. Sandra L. Richards, "Cultural Tourism to Slave Sites," *Black Theater Network News* 9 (Winter/Spring 1999): 14.
77. Thompson, *Flash of the Spirit*, 73–74; Clark-Bekederemo, *Ozidi Saga*, 26; and author's field research with The Old Lady, Kissehman, Ghana, 1995.
78. Colin A. Palmer, *Slaves of the White God* (Cambridge: Harvard University Press, 1976), 152–153.
79. Palmer, *Slaves of the White God*, 161.
80. Palmer, *Slaves of the White God*, 161.
81. Palmer, *Slaves of the White God*, 162.

82. For an African American example, see "Praying for Rain," in Zora Neale Hurston, *Mules and Men* (New York: Harper Perennial, 1935), 88.
83. See Browder, *Nile Valley Contributions to Civilization*, 97 (especially the quote from Joceyln Rhys's *Shaken Creeds*) and 109.
84. George Eaton Simpson, "The Belief System of Haitian Vodun," in *People and Culture of the Caribbean*, edited by Michael A. Horowitz (Garden City: Natural History Press 1971), 493.
85. Simpson, "Belief System of Haitian Vodun," 493.
86. David Barry Gaspar, *Bondmen & Rebels* (Baltimore: Johns Hopkins University Press, 1985), 244–245.
87. Simpson, "Belief System of Haitian Vodun," 493.
88. Simpson, "Belief System of Haitian Vodun," 493–494.
89. Karla Gottlieb, *The Mother of Us All* (Trenton, N.J.: Africa World Press, 1997), 24.
90. Gottlieb, *Mother of Us All,* 49; for examples of pot-boiling Àjẹ́ in African America, see Georgia Writers' Project, *Drums and Shadows* (Athens: University of Georgia Press, 1940), 28, 121, 176.
91. Gottlieb, *Mother of Us All,* 68. In her poem "Nanny," Lorna Goodison describes Nanny being trained in Africa and sent to Jamaica to free the Africans; *Daughters of Africa*, edited by M. Busby (New York: Ballantine, 1992), 723–724.
92. George P. Rawick, *From Sundown to Sunup: The Making of the Black Community* (Westport: Greenwood Press, 1972), 33.
93. Teresa N. Washington, "Readily Apparent: Rarely Understood: Africanisms in the Rural South," *A Pilgrimage of Color: 2001 National Conference: Culture Monograph Series* (Houston: NAAS, NAHLS/ NANAS/ IAAS, 2000), 285–323.
94. Melvin Dixon, "Singing Swords: The Literacy Legacy of Slavery," in *The Slave's Narrative,* edited by Charles T. Davis and Henry Louis Gates, Jr. (New York: Oxford University Press, 1985), 302, italics added.
95. Soyinka, "The African World and the Enthocultural Debate," 18.
96. George P. Rawick, ed., *Virginia Narratives*, in Vol. 16 of *The American Slave: Kansas, Kentucky, Maryland, Ohio, Virginia and Tennessee Narratives* (Westport: Greenwood Press, 1972), 12, italics added.
97. Rawick, *From Sundown to Sunup*, 39–40.
98. Rawick, *From Sundown to Sunup*, 42.
99. Rawick, *From Sundown to Sunup*, 43.
100. Quoted in Lawrence W. Levine, *Black Culture and Black Consciousness* (New York: Oxford University Press, 1977), 34.
101. Levine, *Black Culture and Black Consciousness*, 45–46, 34, respectively.

102. George P. Rawick, ed., *The Unwritten History of Slavery*, Vol. 18 of *The American Slave* (Westport: Greenwood Press, 1972), 138, 134, also see 118.

103. Rawick, ed., *Unwritten History of Slavery*, 105.

104. A sugar tit is a rag dipped in sweetened water. While writing this passage, I developed a poignant understanding of why my elders, many of whom have become ancestors, so craved "sugar water," which they would ask me to prepare for them when I was a child. See Zora Neale Hurston, *Their Eyes Were Watching God* (New York: Harper Perennial, 1937), 27.

105. Mason, *Orin Òrìṣà*, 266–267.

106. Angela Davis, "Reflections on the Black Woman's Role in the Community of Slaves," in *Words of Fire*, edited by Beverly Guy-Sheftall (New York: The New Press, 1995), 209.

107. Davis, "Reflections on the Black Woman's Role," 209.

108. Levine, *Black Culture and Black Consciousness*, 78.

109. Bockie, *Death and the Invisible Powers*, 84–85. Also see John S. Mbiti, *African Religions and Philosophy*, 2nd ed. (London: Heinemann, 1989), 41.

110. George P. Rawick, ed., *Georgia Narratives*, Vol. 13 of *The American Slave* (Westport: Greenwood Press, 1972), Part 4, 261.

111. George P. Rawick, ed., Kentucky Narratives, in Vol. 16 of *The American Slave: Kansas, Kentucky, Maryland, Ohio, Virginia and Tennessee Narratives* (Westport: Greenwood Press, 1972), 59.

112. Rawick, ed., *Georgia Narratives*, Part 3, 345.

113. Note the linguistic variations on the same root word for West African spiritual systems: Ifá, Afa, Fa (Yoruba, Ewe, and Fon spiritual systems, respectively); and Vodun, Voodoo, Hoodoo (Fon, Haitian, and African American spiritual systems, respectively). Gaba states that the Anlo adopted their system of divination, Afa, from Yoruba Ifá; *Scriptures of an African People*, 125.

114. Bockie, *Death and the Invisible Powers*, 66–67, italics added.

115. Quoted in Levine, 58. This quote is from DuBois's classic, *The Souls of Black Folk*.

116. Rawick, ed., *Georgia Narratives*, Part 4, 295–296.

117. Rawick, ed., *Georgia Narratives*, Part 2, 130, and Part 4, 298–299.

118. Rawick, ed., *Unwritten History of Slavery*, 51.

119. Rawick, ed., *Unwritten History of Slavery*, 81, 84; and Rawick, ed., *Kentucky Narratives*, 62.

120. Levine, *Black Culture and Black Consciousness*, 71. BaKongo spiritual works often involve the movement of the sun. See Esteban Montejo, *The Autobiography of a Runaway Slave*, edited by Miguel Barnet (London: The Bodley Head, 1968), 34; and Thompson, *Flash of the Spirit*, 108–113.

121. Levine, *Black Culture and Black Consciousness*, 71. Reciprocal retribution, where the person administering a beating falls victim to adverse physical damage, is also found in Hausaland. Abdul-Rasheed Abdu, conversation with author, Obafemi Awolowo University, Ile-Ife, 1998.
122. Hurston, *Mules and Men*, 234–236.
123. Levine, *Black Culture and Black* Consciousness, 75.
124. Levine, Black Culture and Black Consciousness, 75.
125. Rawick, ed., *Kentucky Narratives*, 121–122.
126. The Yoruba trickster is the turtle Ijapa. Harold Courlander's *A Treasury of African Folktales* gives examples of Ijapa tales on pages 221–230. The lizard's tales are interspersed throughout African oral literature.
127. Quoted in Thompson, *Flash of the Spirit*, 117.
128. Bockie, *Death and the Invisible Powers*, 67–71.
129. Quoted in Hallen and Sodipo, *Knowledge, Belief, and Witchcraft*, 108.
130. Ibitokun, *Dance as Ritual Drama*, 8.
131. John A. Umeh, *After God Is Dibia*, Vol. 1 (London: Karnak House, 1997), 42–43.
132. Levine, Black *Culture and Black Consciousness*, 87, italics added.
133. Georgia Writers' Project, *Drums and Shadows*, 151, 169, respectively. In Haile Gerima's film *Sankofa*, Mona/Shola and Nunu journey through time and space with the assistance of a buzzard. Julius Lester's "People Who Could Fly" is an oral testimony turned folktale in which humans transform into buzzards; Lester, *Black Folktales* (New York: Grove, 1969), 147–152. In the twentieth century, Mrs. E. L. Smith described how a "hoodoo woman" from Aberdeen, Mississippi, prepared medicine to rid her aunt of conjure. In the course of the healing, the woman spun rapidly around on her heel until she transformed into a large turkey; Richard M. Dorson, *American Negro Folktales* (Greenwich, Conn.: Fawcett, 1956), 189.
134. Montejo, *Autobiography of a Runaway Slave*, 43–44.
135. Montejo, *Autobiography of a Runaway Slave*, 131, italics added.
136. Georgia Writers' Project, *Drums and Shadows*, 154.
137. Georgia Writers' Project, *Drums and Shadows*, 145. For a fictionalized tribute to Ryna, Theresa, Rosa, and other Ancestors, see Toni Morrison's *Song of Solomon* (New York: Plume, 1977).
138. Dorson, *American Negro Folktales*, 279.
139. See Toni Cade Bambara, "Broken Field Running," in *The Sea Birds Are Still Alive* (New York: Vintage, 1977), 43–70; Bambara, *The Salt Eaters* (New York: Random House, 1980); Earl Lovelace, *Salt* (New York: Persea, 1996); Ishmael Reed, *Flight to Canada* (New York: Simon

& Schuster, 1976); and Toni Morrison, *Song of Solomon* (New York: Plume, 1977).

55. Among the Igbo, disembodied spirits are called *ndi mmuo*. According to Metuh, "The spirits of evil men, and all who have not reached *Ani Mmuo* [the Spirit Land], roam around restlessly in ... an intermediate state between the spirit-land and the visible world of men." *God and Man in African Religion*, 55. See Hurston, *Mules and Men*, 273, for a similar African American belief.

141. Rawick, ed., *Georgia Narratives*, Part 4, 351.

142. Although often discussed in absolute terms, the role of salt in flight and spiritual ritual is complex, riddled with cultural specificity and biochemical fact. See Monica Schuler, *Alas, Alas Kongo* (Baltimore: Johns Hopkins University Press, 1980), 89–96; and Bambara, "Broken Field Running," 43–70.

143. Levine, *Black Culture and Black Consciousness*, 74. See Bannerman-Richter, *Practice of Witchcraft in Ghana*, 29.

144. Rawick, ed., *Georgia Narratives*, Part 4, 266.

145. Rawick, ed., *Kentucky Narratives*, 67.

146. While such gifts and abilities as invisibility, shape-shifting, and astral flight are often discussed interchangeably, each is distinct, and not every empowered person can do every powerful thing. For example, it is not necessarily the case that all Àjẹ́, who move about astrally, can fly physically. Just as kánàkò, egbé, and ọfẹ̀ are different terms for different abilities, so too do African American spiritual mobility devices and powers vary. Compare the testimonies in Georgia Writers' Project, *Drums and Shadows*, 7, 24, 31, 79, 80.

147. Jean McMahon Humez, ed., *Gifts of Power* (Amherst: University of Massachusetts Press, 1981), 77, 97, 107–108, 220.

148. Humez, ed., *Gifts of Power*, 95.

149. Humez, ed., *Gifts of Power*, 95.

150. Humez, ed., *Gifts of Power*, 222.

151. Humez, ed., *Gifts of Power*, 153–154. Humez doubts (and undermines) the veracity of Jackson's words because the Shakers also believed in a mother deity as an aspect of god. However, the Shakers have no monopoly on the Great Mother! Jackson describes an Ìyánlá as a woman she must emulate and follow early on in her memoirs (93, 133). Jackson's spiritual guide, described as having long black hair, may well have become physically embodied in Jackson's African American companion, Rebecca Perot (225). She also describes an astral visit from her grandmother and an unknown woman, and both women bless her with astral-material gifts (119). Jackson's spiritual instruction comes from a number of gendered and ungendered spiritual sources. But her visions, astral mobility, and spiritual ability clearly align her with Àjẹ́. It is important to note that Jackson's African consciousness is the very

reason she leaves the Shakers, at one point, to minister to her enslaved people and build a sanctuary for them. It is telling that Jackson's society forced her to veil her gifts under Methodist or Shaker affiliations although she clearly fit neither and was physically and spiritually threatened by these sects of Christianity.

152. Ibitokun, *Dance as Ritual Drama*, 39n12, italics added.
153. Hurston, *Mules and Men*, 185.
154. Levine, *Black Culture and Black Consciousness*, 87; Harold Courlander, *A Treasury of Afro-American Folklore* (New York: Marlow, 1996), 286.
155. Rawick, ed., *Georgia Narratives*, Part 2, 158.
156. Vircy Dickey, interview with author, Mississippi, 1995.
157. Hurston, *Mules and Men*, 197–198.
158. Hurston, *Mules and Men*, 195; italics added.
159. Mbiti, *African Religions and Philosophy*, 74.
160. See Teresa N. Washington, "Afraifalang: A Literary Gẹ̀lẹ̀dẹ́" (master's thesis, University of Mississippi, 1996), 58–61.
161. Hurston, *Mules and Men*, 184.
162. Opeola, "What Is Witchcraft?" 2–3. See also Lawal, "New Light on Gelede," 6.
163. Hurston, *Mules and Men*, 31–34.
164. Hurston, *Mules and Men*, 31.
165. Hurston, *Mules and Men*, 32.
166. Hurston, *Mules and Men*, 33.
167. Bascom, *Ifa Divination*, 557.
168. Hurston, *Mules and Men*, 165.
169. Hurston, *Mules and Men*, 168.
170. Rawick, ed., *Georgia Narratives*, Part 4, 262.
171. Hurston's *Every Tongue Got to Confess* attributes an oral text very similar to "Why Women Always Take Advantage of Men" to Old Man Drummond. As communal art is uttered to be shared, not owned, it could be the case that Mosely shared her own version, which was recorded by Hurston and included in *Mules and Men*, or it could be the case that Hurston revised the orature and attributed it to Moseley to call attention to gender relationships in Eatonville. *Every Tongue Got to Confess*, edited by Carla Kaplan (New York: Harper Collins, 2001), 7–8.
172. Zora Hurston, *Dust Tracks on a Road* (New York: Harper Perennial, 1942), 138.
173. Hurston, *Mules and Men*, 175.
174. Hurston, *Mules and Men*, 179.
175. The Odù Ifá has texts of talking skulls, explications of how the snake got its rattles, how the crocodile got its protective teeth and hide, and the wiles of the rabbit which are almost identical to African American orature.

176. Hurston, *Mules and Men*, 127, 148, 175.
177. Hurston, *Mules and Men*, 154.
178. Hurston, *Mules and Men*, 192.
179. Hurston, *Mules and Men*, 199, 201.
180. Hurston, *Mules and Men*, 239.
181. Baker, *Workings of the Spirit*, 92.
182. Zora Hurston, *Tell My Horse* (New York: Harper Perennial, 1938), 114.
183. Baker, *Workings of the Spirit*, 72.
184. Carole Boyce Davies, *Black Women, Writing, and Identity* (New York: Routledge, 1994), 17.
185. Toni Morrison, *Beloved* (New York: Plume, 1987), 199.
186. Thomas LeClair, "The Language Must Not Sweat: A Conversation with Toni Morrison," in *Toni Morrison*, edited by Henry Louis Gates, Jr., and K. A. Appiah (New York: Amistad, 1993), 371, italics added. Also see Bessie W. Jones and Audrey Vinson, "An Interview with Toni Morrison," *Conversations with Toni Morrison*, edited by Danille Taylor-Guthrie (Jackson: University Press of Mississippi, 1994), 173. Here Morrison discusses how her own ancestry, as sung by her "mothers and aunts," is interwoven into *Song of Solomon*.
187. Christina Davis, "An Interview with Toni Morrison," in *Conversations with Toni Morrison*, edited by Danille Taylor-Guthrie (Jackson: University Press of Mississippi, 1994), 225, italics added.
188. Anne Koenen, "The One Out of Sequence," in *Conversations with Toni Morrison*, edited by Danille Taylor-Guthrie (Jackson: University Press of Mississippi, 1994), 79, 80.
189. Koenen, "The One Out of Sequence," 81.
190. Quoted in Adeola James, ed., *In Their Own Voices* (London: Heinemann, 1990), 146.
191. James, ed., *In Their Own Voices*, 146, italics added.
192. Igbinola chanted the *Ìtàn-Oríkì Ìyàmi Òṣòròngà* with a white pigeon in her hand. At the conclusion of her recitation, Ìyàmi Òṣòròngà spiritually entered the pigeon. See Washington, "Manifestations of Àjẹ́ in Africana Literature," chapter 1.
193. James, ed., *In Their Own Voices*, 146, italics added.
194. James, ed., *In Their Own Voices*, 152.
195. Gloria Naylor, "A Conversation: Gloria Naylor and Toni Morrison," in *Conversations with Toni Morrison*, edited by Danille Taylor-Guthrie (Jackson: University Press of Mississippi, 1994), 214.
196. Nellie McKay, "An Interview with Toni Morrison," in *Conversations with Toni Morrison*, edited by Danille Taylor-Guthrie (Jackson: University Press of Mississippi, 1994), 153–154.

197. Alice Walker, "Saving the Life That Is Your Own," in *In Search of Our Mothers' Gardens* (New York: Harcourt Brace Jovanovich, 1983), 11.

198. Alice Walker, "The Revenge of Hannah Kemhuff," in *In Love and Trouble* (New York: Harvest, 1973), 69.

199. Rowland Abiodun, "Verbal and Visual Metaphors: Mythical Allusions in Yoruba Ritualistic Art of *Orí*," *Word and Image Journal of Verbal-Visual Inquiry* 3, no. 3 (1987): 255.

200. Lawal, "New Light," 136.

201. Yai, "Towards A New Poetics of Oral Poetry in Africa," 48.

202. A. I. Asiwaju, "Èfè Poetry as a Source for Western Yoruba History," in *Yoruba Oral Tradition,* edited by Wande Abimbola (Ibadan: Ibadan University Press, 1975), 210.

203. Asiwaju, "Èfè Poetry as a Source for Western Yoruba History," 211.

204. Asiwaju, "Èfè Poetry as a Source for Western Yoruba History," 203.

205. Asiwaju, "Èfè Poetry as a Source for Western Yoruba History," 203.

206. Alice Walker, *The Color Purple* (New York: Pocket Books, 1982), 213, italics added.

207. Walker, *The Color Purple,* 213.

208. Walker, *The Color Purple,* 214.

209. Teresa N. Washington, *The Architects of Existence: Àjẹ́ in Yoruba Cosmology, Ontology, and Orature* (Oya's Tornado, 2014), 159–160.

210. Flora Nwapa, *Efuru* (London: Heinemann, 1966), 275.

211. See Gates, *The Signifying Monkey,* 78.

212. Hallen and Sodipo, *Knowledge, Belief, and Witchcraft,* 68, italics added.

213. Quoted in Jane Wilkinson, ed., *Talking with African Writers* (London: Heinemann 1992), 88. 2004.

214. Hallen and Sodipo, *Knowledge, Belief, and Witchcraft,* 68.

3. Word Becoming Flesh and Text

1. Chukwuemeka Godfri Avajah, e-mail communication with author, July 2004.

2. Emeh, *Treasures of Nnobi,* 78.

3. F. A. Arinze, *Sacrifice in Ibo Religion* (Ibadan: Ibadan University Press, 1970), 65.

4. Arinze, *Sacrifice in Ibo Religion,* 65.

5. Gloria Naylor, *Mama Day* (New York: Vintage, 1988), 3, italics added. All subsequent references are to this edition and will be given parenthetically in the text.

6. For a few examples, see Susan Meisenhelder, "'The Whole Picture' in Gloria Naylor's *Mama Day*," *African American Review* 27, no. 3 (1993): 405–419; Lindsey Tucker, "Recovering the Conjure Woman: Texts and Contexts in Gloria Naylor's *Mama Day*," *African American Review* 28, no. 2 (1994): 173–187; David Cowart, "Matriarchal Mythopoesis: Naylor's Mama Day," *Philological Quarterly* 77, no. 4 (Fall 1998): 439–459; Gary Storhoff, "'The Only Voice Is Your Own': Gloria Naylor 's Revision of *The Tempest*," *African American Review* 29, no. 1 (Spring 1995): 35–45; Kathleen M. Puhr, "Healers in Gloria Naylor's Fiction," *Twentieth Century Literature* 40, no. 4 (Winter 1994): 518–527.

7. Tucker, "Recovering the Conjure Woman," 174.
8. Cowart, "Matriarchal Mythopoesis," 449; see also 445, 447, 450.
9. Meisenhelder, "'The Whole Picture' in Gloria Naylor's *Mama Day*," 412.
10. Fatunmbi, *Ìwà-pèlé*, 36.
11. See Cowart, "Matriarchal Mythopoesis," 444.
12. Knappert, *Myths and Legends of the Congo*, 185.
13. Cowart mentions Nana Bùrúkù as a progenitor but is unable to convincingly relate her force to Sapphira's; "Matriarchal Mythopoesis," 451–455.
14. Paula G. Eckerd, "The Prismatic Past in 'Oral History' and *Mama Day*," *Multi-Ethnic Literature of the United States* 20, no. 3 (Fall 1995): 130.
15. Drewal and Drewal, *Gelede*, 22, 24, 29, 43, 90.
16. Tucker, "Recovering the Conjure Woman," 17–18.
17. It appears that Naylor is extending an intertextual nod to Toni Morrison's novel *Sula* (1973) which focuses on the Peace women, Eva, Hannah, and Sula, who, with different but interconnected aspects of Àjé and actualizations of "peace," offer critiques of Western Sapphire, witch, and Jezebel stereotypes.
18. Chinua Achebe, *Things Fall Apart* (London: Heinemann, 1958), 54. Puhr mentions Achebe's work but is unable to make a convincing connection between the events in *Things Fall Apart* and *Mama Day;* "Healers in Gloria Naylor's Fiction," 523.
19. Fatunmbi, *Iwà-Pèlé*, 38.
20. Bella Brodzki, "History, Cultural Memory, and the Tasks of Translation in T. Obinkaram Echewa's *I Saw the Sky Catch Fire*," *Publications of the Modern Language Association* 114, no. 2 (1999): 210.

21. T. Obinkaram Echewa, *I Saw the Sky Catch Fire* (New York: Dutton, 1992), 7. All subsequent references are to this edition and will be given parenthetically in the text.
22. Zora Hurston, *Tell My Horse* (New York: Harper Perennial, 1938), 114.
23. Emeh, *Treasures of Nnobi*, 1.
24. Emeh, *Treasures of Nnobi*, 1.
25. Emeh, *Treasures of Nnobi*, 1.
26. Metuh, *God and Man in African Religion*, 100.
27. Metuh, *God and Man in African Religion*, 100.
28. Metuh, *God and Man in African Religion*, 67.
29. Metuh, *God and Man in African Religion*, 66.
30. Metuh, *God and Man in African Religion*, 67.
31. Metuh, *God and Man in African Religion*, 38.
32. Mba, *Nigerian Women Mobilised*, 69–70.
33. Mba, *Nigerian Women Mobilised*, 72.
34. Women's battles against colonialism also occurred in the late 1920s, the early 1930s, the 1950s, and the 1980s. And in the spring of 2003, 600 women from the Nigerian Delta, which abuts Igboland, took over Chevron-Texaco's Escravos terminal, trapping 700 employees for a week. The women made numerous social and environmental demands, including correction of river erosion, clean water, electricity, and schools and health clinics. Chevron agreed to the terms. "Shell, Chevron, and Elf all Quit Nigerian Delta," *SRi Media: Corporate Governance News*, March 24, 2003. Available online: http://www.srimedia.com/artman/publish/article466.shtml (accessed March 15, 2004).
35. Zaynab Alkali, *The Stillborn* (Essex: Longman, 1988), 53.
36. Bascom, *Sixteen Cowries*, 423.
37. Prince, "Yoruba Image of the Witch," 799.
38. Akinwumi Isola, *Madam Tinubu: The Terror of Lagos* (Ibadan: Heinemann, 1998), 105.
39. "Nigerian Women Take Over More Oil Facilities," *USA Today.com*, July 17, 2002. Available online: http://www.usatoday.com/news/world/2002/07/17/ nigerian-women.htm (accessed March 15, 2004).
40. Lawal, *Gèlèdé Spectacle*, 33, 241, 246.
41. Old heads and wisdom teeth will recognize the pun on "pot liquor," the juice that remains, rich and seasoned, after the collard greens have been eaten and can be a social drink.
42. Prince, "Yoruba Image of the Witch," 799.
43. Mba, *Nigerian Women Mobilised*, 77.
44. Mba, *Nigerian Women Mobilised*, 77.
45. B. Hallen and O. Sodipo address the same issues from a male standpoint in *Knowledge, Belief, and Witchcraft*, 9.

46. Brodzki, "History, Cultural Memory, and the Tasks of Translation," 217.
47. Anthonia Kalu, telephone conversation with author, July 2004.
48. Hallen and Sodipo, *Knowledge, Belief, and Witchcraft*, 68. My italics.
49. John A. Umeh, *After God Is Dibia*, Vol. 1, 42–43.

4. Initiations into the Self, The Conjured Space of Creation and Prophetic Utterance

1. Ayi Kwei Armah, *Two Thousand Seasons* (Ibadan: Heinemann, 1973), 16. Armah's *Osiris Rising* (Popenguine: Per Ankh, 1995) also elaborates on the curse and its modern manifestations.
2. Armah, *Two Thousand Seasons*, 17.
3. Armah, *Two Thousand Seasons*, 13–14.
4. "Tàn" as a root word of "itànkálẹ̀," and "itàn" is a powerful word with profound and exact meaning for Africans displaced in the West. "Tàn" means to lure, to deceive, to decoy; to spread and to scatter. But it also means light, lamp, and to shine.
5. Ama Ata Aidoo, *Anowa* (Essex: Longman, 1965), 68. All subsequent references are to this edition and will be given parenthetically in the text.
6. Ntozake Shange, *Sassafrass, Cypress & Indigo* (New York: St. Martin's Press, 1982), 3. All subsequent references are to this edition and will be given parenthetically in the text.
7. For example, "she so Black, she blue."
8. Bascom, *Sixteen Cowries*, 479–481.
9. Teish, *Jambalaya*, 13.
10. Armah, *Two Thousand Seasons*, 61.
11. Thompson, *Flash of the Spirit*, 44.
12. Adebayo Faleti, conversation with author, Obafemi Awolowo University, Ile-Ife, Nigeria, October 1998.
13. Thompson, *Flash of the Spirit*, 44; and Palmer, Slaves of the White God, 164.
14. In *The Autobiography of a Runaway Slave*, Esteban Montejo offers a rich explication of how minkisi can be fashioned in a pot (130).
15. Thompson, *Flash of the Spirit*, 117, italics added. Also see *Flash of the Spirit*, 117–131, for doll depictions of nkisi.
16. Teish, *Jambalaya*, 191–195. Teish's work complements Shange's novel perfectly in many ways.
17. Quoted in Gail Hanlon, "Homegrown Juju Dolls," in *My Soul Is a Witness*, edited by Gloria Wade-Gayles (Boston: Beacon, 1995), 287.
18. Thompson, *Flash of the Spirit*, 125.

19. Arlene Elder, "*Sassafrass, Cypress & Indigo:* Ntozake Shange's Neo-Slave/ Blues Narrative," *African American Review* 26, no. 1 (Spring 1992): 100.
20. Levine, *Black Culture and Black Consciousness*, 7.
21. Levine, *Black Culture and Black Consciousness*, 209.
22. Eleburuibon, *Adventures of Obatala*, 81–82.
23. Zora Neale Hurston, *Jonah's Gourd Vine* (New York: Harper Perennial, 1934), 29.
24. Thompson, *Flash of the Spirit*, 42–43.
25. Quoted in Alan P. Merriam, "African Music," in *"Les Bambara," Continuity and Change in African Cultures*, edited by William Bascom and Melville Herskovits (Chicago: University of Chicago Press, 1959), 49–86. Translation by Ibrahim Seck.
26. Armah, *Two Thousand Seasons*, 73.
27. Quoted in James, ed., *In Their Own Voices*, 21.
28. Ama Ata Aidoo, *Dilemma of a Ghost* (Essex: Longman, 1965), 19.
29. Aidoo, *Dilemma of a Ghost*, 17.
30. Hurston, *Their Eyes Were Watching God*, 15.
31. Hurston, *Dust Tracks on a Road*, 83.
32. Also see Gay Wilentz's discussion of the revolutionary nature of Aidoo's craft in *Binding Cultures*, 41.
33. Rebecca Carroll, "Back At You," *Mojo Wire* (1995). Available online: http://www.motherjones.com/arts/qa/1995/01/carroll.html (accessed August 14, 2000).
34. Yanque Orandoh Bigboi, conversation with author, Obafemi Awolowo University, Ile-Ife, 1998; Joseph Holloway and Winifred K. Vass, *The African Heritage of American English* (Bloomington: Indiana University Press, 1993), 141.
35. Carroll, "Back At You."

5. Un/Complementary Complements

1. Lawal, *Gẹ̀lẹ̀dẹ́ Spectacle*, 288.
2. Chinua Achebe, "Work and Play in Tutuola's *The Palm-Wine Drinkard*," in Achebe, *Hopes and Impediments* (New York: Double Day, 1988), 105.
3. Achebe, "Work and Play in Tutuola's *The Palm-Wine Drinkard*," 109–112.
4. Amos Tutuola, *The Palm-Wine Drinkard* (Boston: Faber and Faber, 1952), 39–40. All subsequent references are to this edition and will be given parenthetically in the text.
5. In *Zora Neale Hurston: A Literary Biography*, Hemenway notes in her 1931 *Journal of American Folklore* article, "Hoodoo in America,"

that the gentleman identified as Luke Turner in *Mules and Men* (1935) was called Samuel Thompson. Hemenway, *Zora Neale Hurston: A Literary Biography* (Urbana: University of Illinois Press, 1977), 120.
   6. Hurston, *Dust Tracks on a Road*, 139–149.
   7. Hurston, *Mules and Men*, 200.
   8. Adeoye, *Ìgbàgbọ́ àti Ẹ̀sìn Yorùbá*, 304. Translation by Abdul-Rasheed Abudu and Teresa N. Washington.
   9. See Bascom, *Ifa Divination*, 229; Adeboye Babalola, "The Delights of Ìjálá," in *Yoruba Oral Tradition*, edited by Wande Abimbola (Ibadan: Ibadan University Press, 1975), 639.
   10. Adeoye, *Ìgbàgbọ́ àti Ẹ̀sìn Yorùbá*, 304.
   11. 11. Adeoye, *Ìgbàgbọ́ àti Ẹ̀sìn Yorùbá*, 307.
   12. Rachel Stein, "Remembering the Sacred Tree: Black Women, Nature and Voodoo in Zora Neale Hurston's *Tell My Horse* and *Their Eyes Were Watching God,*" *Women's Studies* 25 (1996): 471–472.
   13. Zora Neale Hurston, *Their Eyes Were Watching God* (New York: Harper Perennial, 1937), 12. All subsequent references are to this edition and will be given parenthetically in the text.
   14. Gates, *The Signifying Monkey*, 205.
   15. Ogunba, "The Performance of Yorùbá Oral Poetry," 865.
   16. Tejumola Olaniyan, "God's Weeping Eyes: Hurston and the Anti-Patriarchal Form," *Obsidian II* 5, no. 2 (Summer 1990): 36.
   17. See Susan Willis, "Wandering: Hurston's Search for Self and Method," in *Zora Neale Hurston: Critical Perspectives*, eds. Henry L. Gates, Jr., and K. A. Appiah (New York: Amistad, 1993), 125.
   18. Claire Crabtree, "The Confluence of Folklore, Feminism and Black Self-Determination in Zora Neale Hurston's *Their Eyes Were Watching God,*" *Southern Literary Journal* 17, no. 2 (Spring 1985): 60.
   19. Mary Helen Washington, "Foreword," in Hurston, *Their Eyes Were Watching God* (New York: Harper Perennial, 1937), xiv.
   20. Drewal and Drewal, *Gelede*, 74.
   21. Hear Fela Anikulapo Kuti, *Beasts of No Nation*, 1989; reissued FAK/ MCA Records, Santa Monica, 2001.
   22. Hemenway, *Zora* Neale Hurston: A Literary Biography, 247.
   23. Teish, *Jambalaya*, 120.
   24. Mason, *Orin Òrìṣà*, 314.
   25. Metuh, *God and Man in African Religion*, 101.
   26. Zora Hurston, *Jonah's Gourd Vine* (New York: Harper Perennial, 1934), 167.
   27. Hurston, *Jonah's Gourd Vine*, 169.
   28. Certain social realities compound the significance of Janie's "silence": *Their Eyes Were Watching God* occurs during the multidecade era, including the Red Summer of 1919, during which America's national pastime was lynching innocent African men and women. Some

European Americans might well have interpreted the act of one African in America killing another as a form of social "assistance." At any rate, the lack of value placed on Africana lives in this era is mentioned in both *Mules and Men* (60) and *Their Eyes Were Watching God* (179–180).

29. Adeoye, *Ìgbàgbọ́ àti Ẹ̀sìn Yorùbá*, 304.
30. Drewal and Drewal, *Gẹlẹdẹ*, 79.
31. Crabtree, "The Confluence of Folklore, Feminism and Black Self-Determination," 57.
32. Adebayo Faleti, interview with author, Obafemi Awolowo University, Ile-Ife, Nigeria, October 1998. Faleti, a highly regarded scholar of Gẹ̀lẹ̀dẹ́, stated that the close and, at times, conflicting relationship between Àjẹ́ and the Deity Ọ̀sanyìn is due to the fact that while Ọ̀sanyìn is the master herbalist, with all knowledge of leaves, Àjẹ́, as the owners of the earth and all that comes from the earth, are superior to Ọ̀sanyìn. Àjẹ́ can render an herbal preparation useless if an herbalist prepares leaves without their permission; by contrast, their blessing imparts effectiveness.
33. Randall Keenan, "An Interview with Octavia E. Butler," *Callaloo* 14, no. 2 (Spring 1991): 499.
34. Hanlon, "Homegrown Juju Dolls," 287.
35. Octavia Butler, *Wild Seed* (New York: Popular Library, 1980), 19–20. All subsequent references are to this edition and will be given parenthetically in the text.
36. Wole Soyinka, *Madmen and Specialists, Six Plays* (Ibadan: Spectrum Books, 1988), 252. All subsequent references are to this edition and will be given parenthetically in the text.
37. Mason, *Orin Òrìṣà*, 296.
38. Mason, *Orin Òrìṣà*, 221.
39. Fatunmbi, *Ìwà-pẹ̀lẹ́*, 64.
40. Jeyifous Biodun and Wole Soyinka, "Wole Soyinka, A Transition Interview," *Transition* 42 (1973): 62, italics in original.
41. T. S. Eliot, "Gerontion," in Eliot, *Complete Poems and Plays: 1909–1950* (New York: Harcourt Brace Jovanovich, 1952), 22.
42. Fela Anikulapo Kuti, *Teacher Don't Teach Me Nonsense*, 1986; reissued FAK/ MCA Records, Santa Monica, 2001.
43. Sandra Y. Govan, "Connections, Links, and Extended Networks: Patterns in Octavia Butler's Science Fiction," *Black American Literature Forum* 18, no. 2 (Summer 1984): 87n19. Although Butler's comments are made in reference to *Kindred* (1979), they shed light on the rather glossed depictions of slavery in *Wild Seed*.
44. Govan, "Connections, Links, and Extended Networks," 84.
45. Pre–*Wild Seed* Patternist novels include *Patternmaster* (1976) and *Mind of My Mind* (1977).
46. Keenan, "An Interview with Octavia E. Butler," 500, italics added.

47. T. Obinkaram Echewa, *I Saw the Sky Catch Fire* (New York: Dutton, 1992), 14. Also recall the "truth" Dr. Holly educated Hurston about during her trip to Haiti; *Tell My Horse* (New York: Harper Perennial, 1938), 114.
48. Armah, *Two Thousand Seasons*, 9.
49. Frances Harding, "Soyinka and Power: Language and Imagery in Madmen and Specialists," *African Literatures and Cultures* 4, no. 1 (1991): 96.
50. Ruth Salvaggio, "Octavia Butler and the Black Science-Fiction Heroine," *Black American Literature Forum* 18, no. 2 (Summer 1984): 81.

6. The Relativity of Negativity

1. Jean Pliya, "The Watch-Night," in *Jazz and Palm Wine,* edited by Willfried F. Feuser (Essex: Longman, 1981), 83. All subsequent references are to this edition and will be given parenthetically in the text.
2. See James H. Neal, *Ju-Ju in My Life* (London: George G. Harrap, 1966), for the testimony of a European who thought he was immune to spirit-work.
3. Eric J. Sundquist's offer a wonderful analysis of Hurston's use of Pan-African orature in "'The Drum With the Man Skin': *Jonah's Gourd Vine,*" in *Zora Neale Hurston,* edited by Henry L. Gates, Jr., and K. A. Appiah (New York: Amistad, 1993), 39–66.
4. Zora Neale Hurston, *Jonah's Gourd Vine* (Philadelphia: J. B. Lippincott, 1934), 145–146. All subsequent references are to this edition and will be given parenthetically in the text.
5. Herskovits and Herskovits, *Dahomean Narrative,* 135.
6. Hurston, *Mules and Men,* 184.
7. For more on the use of water in traditional African spiritual systems, see Hurston *Mules and Men,* 200. See also Pipes, "Old Time Religion: Benches Can't Say Amen," 43.
8. Olaudah Equiano, *The Interesting Narrative of the Life of Olaudah Equiano, or Gustavas Vassa, the African, in The Classic Slave Narratives,* edited by Henry Louis Gates, Jr. (New York: Mentor, 1987), 22.
9. Camera Laye, *The Dark Child: The Autobiography of an African Boy,* trans. James Kirup and Ernest Jones (New York: Hill and Wang, 1954), 22–26.
10. Hurston, *Mules and Men,* 154–155 and 194–202.
11. Hurston, *Dust Tracks on a Road,* 41.

12. Toni Cade Bambara, "Blues Ain't No Mocking Bird," in *Gorilla My Love* (New York: Vintage, 1992), 133–134; Tina McElroy Ansa, *Baby of the Family* (New York: Harcourt Brace, 1989), 243, 249.

13. For contemporary examples, listen to GooDie Mob's, "Soul Food," on *Soul Food*, LaFace Records, Atlanta, 1995; and Wu-Tang Clan's "Wu-Gambinos" on *Wu-Chronicles*, Priority Records, New York, 1999.

14. These customs are well known. See Hurston, *Mules and Men*, 229.

15. Naylor makes many subtle intertextual nods to Toni Morrison and Zora Hurston in her works. It could also be the case that Naylor's Ruby is an intertextual nod to Mary Monroe's Mama Ruby of *The Upper Room*. See the analysis of Mama Ruby in chapter 8.

16. Gloria Naylor, *Mama Day* (New York: Vintage, 1988), 69. All subsequent references are to this edition and will be given parenthetically in the text.

17. Meisenhelder, "'The Whole Picture' in Gloria Naylor's *Mama Day*," 416.

18. Rawick, ed., *Georgia Narratives*, Part 4, 279.

19. See also Susan Meisenhelder, "False Gods and Black Goddesses in Naylor's *Mama Day* and Hurston's *Their Eyes Were Watching God*," *Callaloo* 23, no. 4 (2000): 1445.

20. Teish, *Jambalaya*, 120.

21. Quoted in Georgia Writer's Project, *Drums and Shadows*, 246n68c.

22. Palmer, *Slaves of the White God*, 161.

23. Rawick, *Georgia Narratives*, Part 4, 271. See Emmaline Heard's discussion on page 259.

24. Bockie, *Death and the Invisible Powers*, 47.

25. Bockie, *Death and the Invisible Powers*, 46–47.

26. The WPA testimonies are replete with examples. See Rawick, ed., *Kansas, Kentucky, Maryland, Ohio, Virginia and Tennessee Narratives*, vol. 16.

7. The Womb of Life is a Wicked Bag

1. Lawal, *Gẹ̀lẹ̀dẹ́ Spectacle*, 34.

2. Amos Tutuola, *My Life in the Bush of Ghosts* (1954; reprint, New York: Grove, 1994), 114–118.

3. Audre Lorde, *Zami* (Freedom, N.Y.: Crossing Press, 1982), 7. All subsequent references are to this edition and will be given parenthetically in the text.

4. Quoted in Wilentz, *Binding Cultures*, 85.

5. Hurston, *Their Eyes Were Watching God*, 85.

6. Zami is a refreshing liberation from "lesbian," which, like "feminism" and "witchcraft," is a specific term created by and/or for members of a specific racial group. Lorde is referring to woman-to-woman sensual love and a love of nonsensual respect and equality. She is also referring to a community of women who subscribe to these values. For a powerful example of the holistic woman-love of Zami, see the bathing and climax of Avatara in Paule Marshall's *Praisesong for the Widow* (New York: Plume, 1983), 219–224.

7. See Karla Provost, "Becoming Afrekete: The Trickster in the Work of Audre Lorde," *Multi-Ethnic Literature of the United States* 20, no. 4 (Winter 1995): 45–59.

8. Jamaica Kincaid, "My Mother," in Kincaid, *At the Bottom of the River* (New York: Adventura, 1983), 53. All subsequent references are to this edition and will be given parenthetically in the text.

9. Fatunmbi, *Ìwà-Pèlé*, 84–85.

10. Knappert, *Myths and Legends of the Congo*, 49–50.

11. Toni Morrison, *Beloved* (New York: Plume, 1987), 23. All subsequent references are to this edition and will be given parenthetically in the text.

12. Joan H. Grant-Boyd, personal communication, Black Expressive Cultural Studies Conference, University of Maryland Eastern Shore, Princess Anne, Maryland, 2000; and Catherine Yronwode, "Bluestone and Blueing," *Lucky Mojo.* Available online: http://www.luckymojo.com/ bluestone.html (accessed January 3, 2003).

13. Ousseynou B. Traore, "Figuring Beloved/*Beloved*: Re/membering the Body African and Yoruba Mythography," unpublished paper, Black Expressive Cultural Studies Association Conference, University of Maryland Eastern Shore, Princess Anne, Maryland, 2000.

14. Gaba, *Scriptures of an African People*, 79.

15. Toni Morrison, *Paradise* (New York: Plume, 1997), 272–273; and Morrison, *Sula* (New York: Alfred A. Knopf, 1973), 89.

16. Toni Morrison, *Jazz* (New York: Alfred A. Knopf, 1992), 176. Morrison has discussed *Beloved; Jazz;* and *Paradise* as being a quasi-trilogy in which Beloved is re-embodied in each text. See Martha J. Cutter, "The Story Must Go On and On: The Fantastic, Narration, and Intertextuality in Toni Morrison's *Beloved* and *Jazz*," *African American Review* 34, no. 1 (2000): 61–75.

17. Morrison, *Sula*, 46–47.

18. Morrison, *Sula*, 75–76.

19. Quoted in Angela Y. Davis, *Women, Race & Class* (New York: Vintage, 1983), 21. See Morrison's elaboration on the importance of the history of Garner and other sacrificed/sacrificing figures in her work in Gloria, "A Conversation: Gloria Naylor and Toni Morrison," 206–208.

20. Rawick, ed., Unwritten History of Slavery, 283–284.

21. Rawick, ed., *Unwritten History of Slavery*, 284, italics added.

22. For one woman to "naked" (strip) another in a battle is a common fighting tactic that I have witnessed several times in West Africa. The goal of "nakeding" is public humiliation. See Alkali, *The Stillborn*, 84–85. However, as is depicted in the film *Sankofa* (when Nunu performs a caesarian section on Kunta and when Mona/Shola returns to the Castle at Elmina), African women also encircle and hide a sister's nakedness during birth or at a time of crisis. It is said that while you may see a mentally debilitated man go about naked in Africa, you will never see a naked woman because other women will clothe her. Nne-nne makes this point in Echewa, *I Saw the Sky Catch Fire*, 45.

23. Rawick, ed., *Unwritten History of Slavery*, 287.

24. Rawick, ed., *Unwritten History of Slavery*, 288.

25. Rawick, ed., *Unwritten History of Slavery*, 289.

26. Elsie B. Washington, "Talk with Toni Morrison," in *Conversations with Toni Morrison*, ed. Danille Taylor-Guthrie (Jackson: University Press of Mississippi, 1994), 235.

27. Achebe, *Things Fall Apart*, 55. See also Ben Okri, *The Famished Road* (New York: Anchor, 1991), 4.

28. Marsha Darling, "In the Realm of Responsibility: A Conversation with Toni Morrison," in *Conversations with Toni Morrison*, edited by Danille Taylor Guthrie (Jackson: University Press of Mississippi, 1994), 247.

29. Rawick, ed., *Kansas Narratives*, in Vol. 16 of *The American Slave: Kansas, Kentucky, Maryland, Ohio, Virginia and Tennessee Narratives* (Westport: Greenwood Press, 1972), 91–92; and Rawick, ed., *Georgia Narratives*, Part 1, 338.

30. Mason, Orin Òrìṣà, 308.

31. In her review of J. Brooks Bouson's *Quiet As It's Kept: Shame Trauma, and Race in the Novels of Toni Morrison*," Martha Cutter stated, "my students report that Morrison's novels unsettle and perhaps even traumatize them as readers." *African American Review* 35, no. 4 (Winter 2001): 671–672.

32. Naylor, "A Conversation: Gloria Naylor and Toni Morrison," 208.

33. Lawal, *Gẹ̀lẹ̀dẹ́ Spectacle*, 261; and Metuh, *God and Man in African Religion*, 69–70, respectively.

34. Darling, "In the Realm of Responsibility," 248.

35. Excuse me while I riff with the elders of Toni Cade Bambara's "Broken Field Running."

36. See Maggie Sale, "Call and Response as Critical Method: African American Oral Traditions and Beloved," *African American Review* 26, no. 1 (1992): 42, and William R. Handley, "The House a Ghost Built," *Contemporary Literature* 36, no. 4 (Winter 1995): 691. Handley

discusses Morrison's "incantory powers [to] summon not only ghosts but also readers."

37. Abiodun, "Verbal and Visual Metaphors: Mythical Allusions in Yoruba Ritualistic Art of *Orí*," 252.

38. Abiodun, "Verbal and Visual Metaphors: Mythical Allusions in Yoruba Ritualistic Art of *Orí*," 253–255.

8. Twinning across the Ocean

1. Parliament, "Chocolate City," on *Chocolate City*, Polygram Records, New York, 1975.

2. Mary Monroe, *The Upper Room* (New York: St. Martin's Press, 1985), 285. All subsequent references are to this edition and will be given parenthetically in the text. For an African literary version of marked birth, see Alkali, *The Stillborn*, 6–7.

3. Beier, "Gelede Masks," 10–11.

4. Beier, "Gelede Masks," 10–11.

5. Actor Rudy Ray Moore has made quite a name for himself as screen star "Dolomite," an update of the ever-signifying, virile, butt-kicking "Devil's only son-in-law."

6. Ralph Ellison, *Invisible Man* (New York: Vintage, 1952), 173.

7. Toni Morrison, *Sula* (New York: Quality Paper Back Book Club, 1973), 116.

8. Herskovits and Herskovits, *Dahomean Narrative*, 124, 126.

9. Ifie, *A Cultural Background to the Plays of J. P. Clark-Bekederemo*, 91.

10. Anyebe, *Ogboni*, 55. Orò is a secret Yoruba organization dedicated to cleansing society.

11. Hurston, *Mules and Men*, 60. This same type of anti-law is evident when Ruby is acquitted of the murder of her husband but is sentenced for leaving the Euro-American children she was babysitting unattended.

12. Hurston, *Mules and Men*, 179.

13. Clark-Bekederemo, *The Ozidi Saga*, 26.

14. Ben Okri, *The Famished Road* (New York: Doubleday, 1991), 36–37. All subsequent references are to this edition and will be given parenthetically in the text.

15. A Nigerian expression and action. See chapter 7, note 22.

16. Lawal, *Gẹ̀lẹ̀dẹ́ Spectacle*, 42. See also John C. Hawley, "Ben Okri's Spirit Child: *Abiku* Migration and Postmodernity," *Research in African Literatures* 26, no. 1 (Spring 1995): 30–39.

17. Echewa, *I Saw the Sky Catch Fire*, 179–180, italics added.

18. Mattie A. Harris, conversation with author, Rienzi, Miss., 2004.

19. Holloway and Vass, *The African Heritage of American English*, 98.
20. In 1998, Okri published *Infinite Riches* (London: Phoenix), which continues the saga of Dad, Mum, Koto, and Azaro.
21. Bockie, *Death and the Invisible Powers*, 64–66.
22. Ben Okri, *Songs of Enchantment* (New York: Nan A. Talese, 1993), 91. All subsequent references are to this edition and will be given parenthetically in the text.
23. Morrison, *Beloved*, 31.
24. Fela Ransome-Kuti & The Africa 70, "Unknown Soldier," on *Greatest Hits*, Leader Records, Lagos, 1997.
25. Quoted in Wilkinson, ed., *Talking with African Writers*, 85.
26. Olatubosun Ogunsanwo, "Intertextuality and Post-Colonial Literature in Ben Okri's *The Famished Road*," *Research in African Literatures* 26, no. 1 (Spring 1995): 45.
27. Quoted in Wilkinson, ed., *Talking with African Writers*, 86.
28. Toni Morrison, *Tar Baby* (New York: A. A. Knopf, 1981), 305.
29. Quoted in Wilkinson, ed., *Talking with African Writers*, 87.

Coda-Continua

1. Vincent Harding, *The Other American Revolution* (Atlanta: Center for Afro-American Studies, 1980), 36.
2. Quoted in Thompson, *Flash of the Spirit*, 131.
3. X Clan, *To The East Blackwards*, Island Records, New York, 1990.
4. Charlie R. Braxton, "Mia X: All Tru Woman," *XXL* 1, no. 1 (1997): 98.
5. Canibus, "Patriots," on *Can-I-Bus*, Universal, New York, 1998.
6. Fugees, "Ready or Not," on *The Score*, Sony, New York, 1996.
7. Ibrahim Seck, conversation with author, Oxford, Mississippi, 1995.
8. Erykah Badu, "Ye Yo," on *Live*, Universal, New York, 1997.
9. Abiodun, "Identity and the Artistic Process in Yòrúba Aesthetic Concept of Ìwà," 26.
10. Abiodun, "Identity and the Artistic Process in Yòrúba Aesthetic Concept of Ìwà," 23, 14.

WORKS CITED AND SELECTED BIBLIOGRAPHY

Abimbola, 'Wande. *Ifá: An Exposition of Ifá Literary Corpus.* Ibadan: Oxford University Press, 1967.
-----. *Ifa Divination Poetry.* New York: Nok, 1977.
-----. *Sixteen Great Poems of Ifa.* Lagos: UNESCO, 1975.
-----. *Yoruba Oral Tradition.* Ibadan: Ibadan University Press, 1975.
Abiodun, Rowland. "Identity and the Artistic Process in Yoruba Aesthetic Concept of *Ìwà*." *Journal of Cultural Inquiry* 1, no. 1 (December 1983): 13–30.
"Verbal and Visual Metaphors: Mythical Allusions in Yoruba Ritualistic Art of *Orí*." *Ife: Annals of the Institute of Cultural Studies* (1985): 8–38.
Achebe, Chinua. *Hopes and Impediments.* New York: Anchor Books, 1988. Adediran, A. Abiodun, and S. O. Arifalo. "The Religious Festivals of Ife." In *The Cradle of a Race: Ife—From the Beginning to 1980,* edited by I. A. Akinjogbin, 305–317. Lagos: Sunray, 1992.
Adediran, 'Biodun. "A Descriptive Analysis of Ife Palace Organisation." *The African Historian* VIII (1976): 3–30.
-----. "The Early Beginnings of Ife State." In *The Cradle of a Race: Ife—From the Beginning to 1980,* edited by I. A. Akinjogbin, 77–95. Lagos: Sunray, 1992.
-----. "Women, Rituals and Politics in Pre-Colonial Yorubaland." Unpublished paper, Women in African and the African Diaspora Seminar. 1992.
Adeeko, Adeleke. "The Language of Head-Calling: A Review Essay on Yoruba Metalanguage: Ede Iperi Yoruba." *Research in African Literatures* 24 (Winter 1993): 198–201.
Adegbola, E. E. Ade, ed. *Traditional Religion in West Africa.* Accra: Asempa, 1983.
Adeoye, C. L. *Ìgbàgbọ́ àti Ẹ̀sìn Yorùbá.* Ibadan: Evans Bros., 1985.
Adepegba, Cornelius. "The Descent from Odùduwà: Claims of Superiority among Some Yoruba Traditional Rulers and the Arts of Ancient Ife." *African Historical Studies* 19, no. 1 (1986): 77–92.

Adisa, Opal Palmer. *Bake-Face and Other Guava Stories.* Berkeley: Kelsey St. Press, 1986.
-----. *It Begins with Tears.* Portsmouth: Heinemann, 1997.
Afolayan, Funso. "Women, Politics and Society in Pre-Colonial Igbomina." Unpublished paper, 1992.
Aidoo, Ama Ata. *The Dilemma of a Ghost* and *Anowa.* Essex: Longman, 1985.
-----. *No Sweetness Here and Other Stories.* New York: Feminist Press, 1970.
Ajayi, Simeon A. "The Planting of Baptist Mission Work among the Yoruba, 1850–1960: A Study in Religio-Cultural Conflict." *Ife: Annals of the Institute of Cultural Studies* 5 (1994): 45–56.
Akinjogbin, I. A., ed. *The Cradle of a Race: Ife: From the Beginning to 1980.* Lagos: Sunray, 1992.
Ali, Zaccheus Sunday, Anthony Ijaola Asiwaju, and Benjamin Olatunji Oloruntimehin, eds. *African Unity: The Cultural Foundations.* Lagos: Centre for Black and African Arts and Civilization, 1988.
Alkali, Zaynab. *The Stillborn.* Essex: Longman, 1988.
Amuta, Chidi Nnanna. *The Theory of African Literature: Implications for Practical Criticism.* London: Zed, 1989.
Angelou, Maya. *I Know Why the Caged Bird Sings.* New York: Bantam, 1969.
Ani, Marimba. *Yurugu: An African-Centered Critique of European Cultural Thought and Behavior.* Trenton: Africa World Press, 1994.
Anyebe, A. P. *Ogboni: The Birth and Growth of the Reformed Ogboni Society.* Lagos: Sam Lao, 1989.
Arinze, Francis. *Sacrifice in Ibo Religion.* Ibadan: Ibadan University Press, 1970. Armah, Ayi Kwei. *The Beautyful Ones Are Not Yet Born.* Oxford: Heinemann, 1968.
-----. *The Healers.* Oxford: Heinemann, 1978.
-----. *Osiris Rising.* Popenguine: Per Ankh, 1995.
-----. *Two Thousand Seasons.* Oxford: Heinemann, 1973.
Asante, Molefi K. *Afrocentricity.* Trenton: Africa World Press, 1988.
Asante, Molefi K., and Kariamu Welsh Asante. *African Culture: The Rhythms of Unity.* Trenton: Africa World Press, 1990.
Asiwaju, A. I. "Èfè Poetry as a Source for Western Yoruba History." In *Yoruba Oral Tradition,* edited by Wande Abimbola, 199–266. Ibadan: Ibadan University Press, 1975.
Awolalu, J. Omosade. *Yoruba Beliefs and Sacrificial Rites.* Essex: Longman, 1979. Babalola, Adeboye. "The Delights of Ìjálá." In *Yoruba Oral Tradition,* edited by Wande Abimbola, 631–676. Ibadan: Ibadan University Press, 1975.

Babayemi, S. O. *Egúngún among the Oyo Yoruba.* Ibadan: Board Publications, 1980.

Badejo, Diedre. *Òṣun Ṣèègèsi: The Elegant Deity of Wealth, Power and Femininity.* Trenton: Africa World Press, 1996.

Baker, Houston A. "Workings of the Spirit: Conjure and the Space of Black Women's Creativity." In *Zora Neale Hurston: Critical Perspectives Past and Present,* edited by Henry Louis Gates, Jr., and K. A. Appiah, 280–308. New York: Amistad, 1993.

-----. *Workings of the Spirit: The Poetics of Afro-American Women's Writing.* Chicago: University of Chicago Press, 1991.

Bambara, Toni Cade. "Broken Field Running." In *The Sea Birds Are Still Alive,* 43–70. New York: Vintage, 1977.

-----. "Maggie and the Green Bottles." In *Gorilla My Love,* 149–160. New York: Vintage, 1972.

-----. *The Salt Eaters.* New York: Random House, 1980.

Bannerman-Richter, Gabriel. *The Practice of Witchcraft in Ghana.* Elk Grove, Calif.: Gabari, 1982.

Bascom, William. *Ifa Divination: Communication between Gods and Men in West Africa.* Bloomington: Indiana University Press, 1969.

-----. *Sixteen Cowries: Yoruba Divination from Africa to the New World.* Bloomington: Indiana University Press, 1980.

Beier, Ulli, ed. *Black Orpheus.* Ikeja: Longman, 1964.

-----. "Gelede Masks." *Odu* 6 (June 1958): 4–23.

-----. *Yoruba Poetry: An Anthology of Traditional Poems.* Cambridge: Cambridge University Press, 1970.

Bhely-Quenum, Olympe. "A Child in the Bush of Ghosts." In *African Rhapsody,* edited by Nadezda Obradovic, 58–72. Trans. Willifried F. Feuser. New York: Anchor, 1994.

Bockie, Simon. *Death and the Invisible Powers: The World of Kongo Belief.* Bloomington: Indiana University Press, 1993.

Boudreau, Kristin. "Pain and the Unmaking of Self in Toni Morrison's *Beloved.*" *Contemporary Literature* 36, no. 3 (Fall 1995): 447–465.

Brodzki, Bella. "History, Cultural Memory, and the Tasks of Translation in T. Obinkaram Echewa's *I Saw the Sky Catch Fire.*" Publications of the Modern Language Association 114, no. 2 (March 1999): 207–220.

Browder, Anthony T. *Nile Valley Contributions to Civilization.* Washington, D.C.: Institute of Karmic Guidance, 1992.

Busia, Abena, P. A. "Parasites and Prophets: The Use of Women in Ayi Kwei Armah's Novels." In *Ngambika: Studies of Women in African Literature,* edited by Carole Boyce Davies and Anne Adams Graves, 89–113. Trenton: Africa World Press, 1986.

Butler, Octavia E. *Wild Seed.* New York: Popular Library, 1980.

Campbell, Mavis C. *The Maroons of Jamaica, 1655-1796: A History of Resistance, Collaboration and Betrayal.* Trenton: Africa World Press, 1990.
Carew, Jan. *Fulcrums of Change: Origins of Racism in the Americas and Other Essays.* Trenton: Africa World Press, 1988.
Carril, Pepe. *Shango de Ima: A Yoruba Mystery Play—Totem Voices,* edited by Paul Carter Harrison. New York: Grove, 1989.
Chesnutt, Charles W. *The Conjure Woman.* 1899. Reprint, Ridgewood: Gregg Press, 1968.
Chinweizu, Onwuchekwa Jemie, and Ihechukwu Madubuike. *Toward the Decolonization of African Literature.* Enugu: Fourth Dimension, 1980.
Ciuba, Gary. "The Worm against the Word: The Hermeneutical Challenge in Hurston's *Jonah's Gourd Vine.*" *African American Review* 36, no. 1 (Spring 2000): 119–133.
Clark-Bekederemo, John P. *The Ozidi Saga.* Washington, D.C.: Howard University Press, 1991.
Clarke, John Henrik, and Yosef ben-Jochannan. *New Dimensions in African History.* Trenton: Africa World Press, 1991.
Cliff, Michelle. *No Telephone to Heaven.* New York: Plume, 1987.
Coker, Syl Cheney. *The Last Harmattan of Alusine Dunbar.* Ibadan: Heinemann, 1990.
Cook, Mercer, and Stephen E. Henderson. *The Militant Black Writer in Africa and the United States.* Madison: University of Wisconsin Press, 1969.
Courlander, Harold A., ed. *A Treasury of African Folklore.* New York: Marlowe and Company, 1996.
-----. *A Treasury of Afro-American Folklore.* New York: Crown Publishers, 1976.
Cowart, David. "Matriarchal Mythopoesis: Naylor's *Mama Day.*" *Philological Quarterly* 77, no. 4 (Fall 1998): 439–459.
Crabtree, Claire. "The Confluence of Folklore, Feminism and Black Self Determination in Zora Neale Hurston's *Their Eyes Were Watching God.*" *Southern Literary Journal* 17, no. 2 (Spring 1985): 55–66.
Cutter, Martha J. "The Story Must Go On and On: The Fantastic, Narration, and Intertextuality in Toni Morrison's *Beloved* and *Jazz.*" *African American Review* 34, no. 1 (Spring 2000): 61–75.
Darling, Marsha. "In the Realm of Responsibility: A Conversation with Toni Morrison." In *Conversations with Toni Morrison,* edited by Danille Taylor-Guthrie, 246–254. Jackson: University Press of Mississippi, 1994.
Davies, Carole Boyce. *Black Women, Writing, and Identity.* New York: Routledge, 1994.

-----. "Introduction: Feminist Consciousness and African Literary Criticism." In *Ngambika: Studies of Women in African Literature*, edited by Carole Boyce Davies and Anne Adams Graves, 1–23. Trenton: Africa World Press, 1986.

-----. "Maidens, Mistresses and Matrons: Feminine Images in Selected Soyinka Works." In *Ngambika: Studies of Women in African Literature*, edited by Carole Boyce Davies and Anne Adams Graves, 75–88. Trenton: Africa World Press, 1986.

Davies, Carole Boyce, and Anne Adams Graves. *Ngambika: Studies of Women in African Literature*. Trenton: Africa World Press, 1986.

Davis, Angela Y. *Women, Race & Class*. New York: Vintage, 1983.

Dictionary of the Yoruba Language. Ibadan: University of Ibadan Press, 1991.

Diop, Cheikh Anta. *The Cultural Unity of Black Africa*. 1959. Reprint, Chicago: Third World Press, 1963.

Dixon, Melvin. "Singing Swords: The Literacy Legacy of Slavery." In *The Slave's Narrative*, edited by Charles T. Davis and Henry Louis Gates, Jr., 298–317. New York: Oxford University Press, 1985.

Drewal, Henry John, and Margaret Thompson Drewal. *Gẹlẹdẹ: Art and Female Power among the Yoruba*. Bloomington: Indiana University Press, 1983.

Drewal, Margaret Thompson. *Yoruba Ritual: Play, Performers, Agency*. Bloomington: Indiana University Press, 1992.

Dundes, Alan, ed. *Mother Wit from the Laughing Barrel*. Englewood Cliffs, N.J.: Prentice Hall, 1973.

Echewa, T. Obinkaram. *I Saw the Sky Catch Fire*. New York: Dutton, 1992.

Egejuru, Phanuel Akubweza. *Towards African Literary Independence: A Dialogue with Contemporary African Writers*. Westport: Greenwood Press, 1980.

Elder, Arlene. "*Sassafrass, Cypress & Indigo:* Ntozake Shange's Neo-Slave/ Blues Narrative." *African American Review* 26, no. 1 (Spring 1992): 99–107.

Eleburuibon, Ifayemi. *The Adventures of Obatala: Ifa and Santeria God of Creativity*. Oyo: A. P. I., 1989.

Ellison, Ralph. *Invisible Man*. New York: Vintage, 1952.

Emeh, B. B. O. *Treasures of Nnobi*. Enugu, Nigeria: Ochumba Press, n.d. [1986]. Emovon, Aminu. "Ominigbon Divination." *Nigeria Magazine* 151 (1984): 1–9. Epega, Afolabi A., and Philip John Neimark. *The Sacred Ifa Oracle*. New York: Harper, 1995.

Equiano, Olaudah. *The Interesting Narrative of the Life of Olaudah Equiano, or Gustavas Vassa, the African* In *The Classic Slave*

Narratives. Edited by Henry Louis Gates, Jr. New York: Mentor, 1987.
Evans, Mari, ed. *Black Women Writers (1950–1980): A Critical Evaluation.* Garden City, N.Y.: Anchor Books, 1984.
Fatunmbi, Awo Fá'lokun. *Iwà-pèlé: Ifá Quest: The Search for the Source of Santería and Lucumí.* Bronx, N.Y.: Original Publications, 1991.
Fernandez, James W. *Bwiti: An Ethnography of the Religious Imagination in Africa.* Princeton: Princeton University Press, 1982.
Fortes, Meyer. "Ancestor Worship." In *African Systems of Thought,* edited by Meyer Fortes and Germain Diterlen, 16–20. New York: Oxford University Press, 1965.
Fox, Robert Elliot. "Blacking the Zero: Toward a Semiotics of Neo-Hoodoo." *Black American Literature Forum* 18, no. 3 (Autumn 1984): 95–99.
Gaba, Christian R. *Scriptures of an African People: Ritual Utterances of the Anlo.* New York: Nok, 1973.
Gaspar, David Barry. *Bondmen & Rebels: A Study of Master-Slave Relations in Antigua.* Baltimore: Johns Hopkins University Press, 1985.
Gates, Henry Louis, Jr. *The Signifying Monkey: A Theory of African American Literary Criticism.* New York: Oxford University Press, 1988.
Gates, Henry Louis, Jr., and K. A. Appiah, eds. *Toni Morrison: Critical Perspectives Past and Present.* New York: Amistad, 1993.
Gayle, Addison. *The Black Aesthetic.* New York: Anchor Books, 1971.
Georgia Writers' Project. *Drums and Shadows: Survival Studies among the Georgia Coastal Negroes.* Athens: University of Georgia Press, 1940.
Giovanni, Nikki. *ego-tripping.* New York: Lawrence Hill and Co., 1973.
Gonzalez-Whippler, Migene. *Santeria: The Religion.* St. Paul: Llewellyn Publications, 1989.
Gottlieb, Karla. *The Mother of Us All: A History of Queen Nanny, Leader of the Windward Jamaican Maroons.* Trenton: Africa World Press, 1997.
Govan, Sandra Y. "Connections, Links, and Extended Networks: Patterns in Octavia Butler's Science Fiction." *Black American Literature Forum* 18, no. 2 (Summer 1984): 82–87.
Gover, Robert. "An Interview with Ishmael Reed." *Black American Literature Forum* 12, no. 1 (Spring 1978): 12–19.
Greer, T. J. *One People: The Ancient Glory of the African Race.* Chicago: Karnak, 1984.
Griaule, Marcel, and Germaine Dieterlen. *The Pale Fox.* 1965. Reprint, Chino Valley: Continuum, 1986.

Hallen, Barry, and J. Olubi Sodipo. "A Comparison of the Western 'Witch' with the Yoruba Àjẹ́: Spiritual Powers or Personality Types?" *Ife: Annals of the Institute of Cultural Studies* 1 (1986): 1–7.

Knowledge, Belief, and Witchcraft: Analytic Experiments in African Philosophy. London: Ethnographica, Ltd., 1986; reprint, Stanford: Stanford University Press, 1997.

Handley, William R. "The House a Ghost Built: *Nommo*, Allegory, and the Ethics of Reading Toni Morrison's *Beloved.*" *Contemporary Literature* 36, no. 4 (Winter 1995): 677–701.

Harding, Frances. "Soyinka and Power: Language and Imagery in *Madmen and Specialists.*" *African Literatures and Cultures* 4, no. 1 (1991): 87–98.

Harding, Vincent. *The Other American Revolution.* Atlanta: Center for Afro-American Studies, 1980.

Harrison, Paul Carter. *Kuntu Drama.* New York: Grove, 1974.

Hawley, John C. "Ben Okri's Spirit Child: *Abiku* Migration and Postmodernity." *Research in African Literatures* 26, no. 1 (Spring 1995): 31–39.

Hemenway, Robert. *Zora Neale Hurston: A Literary Biography.* Urbana: University of Illinois Press, 1977.

Herskovits, Melville J. *Dahomey: An Ancient West African Kingdom.* Vol. 2. New York: J. J. Augustin, 1938.

-----. *The Myth of the Negro Past.* 1941. Reprint, New York: Harper and Row Publishers, 1970.

Herskovits, Melville J., and Frances S. Herskovits. *Dahomean Narrative: A Cross-Cultural Analysis.* Evanston: Northwestern University Press, 1958.

Hill-Lubin, Mildred. "The Grandmother in African and African-American Literature." In *Ngambika: Studies of Women in African Literature,* edited by Carole Boyce Davies and Anne Adams Graves, 257–270. Trenton: Africa World Press, 1986.

Holloway, Joseph, ed. *Africanisms in American Culture.* Bloomington: Indiana University Press, 1990.

Holloway, Joseph E., and Winifred K. Vass. *The African Heritage of American English.* Bloomington: Indiana University Press, 1993.

Honwona, Luis Bernardo. "Papa, Snake and I." In *African Rhapsody,* edited by Nadezda Obradovic, 19–34. Trans. Dorothy Guedes. New York: Anchor, 1994.

hooks, bell. *Ain't I a Woman: Black Women and Feminism.* Boston: South End Press, 1981.

Horowitz, Michael A., ed. *People and Culture of the Caribbean: An Anthropological Reader.* Garden City: Natural History Press, 1971.

Hudson-Weems, Clenora. *Africana Womanism: Reclaiming Ourselves*. 3rd rev. ed. Troy: Bedford, 1995.
Hurston, Zora Neale. *Dust Tracks on a Road*. New York: Harper Perennial, 1942.
-----. *Jonah's Gourd Vine*. Philadelphia: J. B. Lippincott, 1934.
-----. *Mules and Men*. New York: Harper Perennial, 1935.
-----. *The Sanctified Church*. New York: Marlowe & Co., 1981.
-----. *Tell My Horse*. New York: Harper Perennial, 1938.
-----. *Their Eyes Were Watching God*. New York: Harper Perennial, 1937.
Ibie, Cromwell Osamaro. *Ifiim: The Complete Work of Orunmila*. Lagos: Efehi, 1986.
Ibitokun, Benedict M. *Dance as Ritual Drama and Entertainment in the Gelede of the Ketu-Yoruba Subgroup in West Africa*. Ile Ife: Obafemi Awolowo University Press, 1993.
Idowu, Bolaji E. *Olódùmarè: God in Yoruba Belief*. 1962. Reprint, New York: Wazobia, 1994.
Ifie, Egbe. *A Cultural Background to the Plays of J. P. Clark-Bekederemo*. Ibadan: Time End, 1994.
Igue, Ogunsola John. "The Role of the Towns in the Creation and Development of Yoruba Oral Literature." In *Yoruba Oral Tradition*, edited by Wande Abimbola, 331–355. Ibadan: Ibadan University Press, 1975.
Irele, Abiola. *The African Experience in Literature and Ideology*. Bloomington: Indiana University Press, 1990.
Isola, Akinwumi. *Madam Tinubu: The Terror of Lagos*. Ibadan: Heinemann, 1998.
"Oya: Inspiration and Empowerment." Unpublished paper, 1998.
Iwara, Alexander U. "Unity and Diversity in West African Folktales." In *African Unity: The Cultural Foundations*, edited by Zaccheus Sunday Ali, Anthony Ijaola Asiwaju, and Benjamin Olatunji Oloruntimehin, 101–109. Lagos: Centre for Black and African Arts and Civilization, 1988.
Jackson, Bruce. *"Get Your Ass in the Water and Swim Like Me."* Cambridge: Harvard University Press, 1974.
Jackson, Rebecca. *Gifts of Power: The Writings of Rebecca Jackson, Black Visionary, Shaker Eldress*. Amherst: University of Massachusetts Press, 1981.
Jahn, Janheinz. *Muntu: The New African Culture*. New York: Grove, 1961. James, Adeola. In *Their Own Voices: African Women Writers Talk*. London: James Currey, 1990.
Jeyifous, Biodun, and Wole Soyinka. "Wole Soyinka, A Transition Interview." *Transition* 42 (1973): 62–64.

Joyce, Joyce-Ann. *Warriors, Conjurers and Priests*. Chicago: Third World Press, 1993.
Jules-Rosette, Benetta. "Women in Indigenous African Cults and Churches." In *The Black Woman Cross-Culturally*, edited by Filomina Chima Steady, 185–207. Cambridge: Schenkman, 1981.
Kennan, Randall. "An Interview with Octavia E. Butler." *Callaloo* 14, no. 2 (Spring 1991): 495–504.
Kincaid, Jamaica. "My Mother." In *At the Bottom of the River*. New York: Adventura, 1983.
Knappert, Jan. *Myths and Legends of the Congo*. Ibadan: Heinemann, 1971. Kolawole, Mary E. Modupe. *Womanism and African Consciousness*. Trenton: Africa World Press, 1996.
Lawal, Babatunde. *The Gèlèdé Spectacle: Art Gender and Social Harmony in an African Culture*. Seattle: University of Washington Press, 1996.
"New Light on Gelede." *African Arts* XI, no. 2 (1978): 65–70, 94. Layiwola, Dele. "Womanism in Nigerian Folklore and Drama." *African Notes* XI, no. 1 (1987): 26–33.
LeClair, Thomas. "The Language Must Not Sweat: A Conversation with Toni Morrison." In *Toni Morrison: Critical Perspectives Past and Present*, edited by Henry Louis Gates, Jr., and K. A. Appiah, 269–377. New York: Amistad, 1993.
Lester, Julius. *Black Folktales*. New York: Grove Weidenfeld, 1969.
Levine, Lawrence W. *Black Culture and Black Consciousness*. New York: Oxford University Press, 1977.
Lindroth, James. "Images of Subversion: Ishmael Reed and the Hoodoo Trickster." *African American Review* 30, no. 2 (Summer 1996): 185–196.
Lorde, Audre. *Zami: A New Spelling of My Name*. Freedom: Crossing Press, 1982.
Lucas, Olumide J. *The Religion of the Yorubas*. Lagos: Christian Missionary Society, 1948.
Magubane, Bernard M. *The Ties That Bind: African-American Consciousness of Africa*. Trenton: Africa World Press, 1987.
Major, Clarence, ed. *From Juba to Jive: A Dictionary of African American Slang*. New York: Penguin, 1994.
Makinde, Akin Moses. *African Philosophy, Culture and Traditional Medicine*. Athens: Ohio University Center for International Studies, 1988.
Marshall, Paule. *Praisesong for the Widow*. New York: Plume, 1983.

Marwick, M. G. "Witchcraft and Sorcery." In *African Systems of Thought*, edited by Meyer Fortes and Germain Diterlen, 21–27. New York: Oxford University Press, 1965.

Mason, John. *Orin Òrìṣà: Songs for Selected Heads*. Brooklyn: Yoruba Theological Archministry, 1992.

Mba, Nina. *Nigerian Women Mobilised*. Berkeley: University of California Press, 1982.

Mbiti, John S. *African Religions and Philosophy*. 2nd ed. London: Heinemann, 1969.

Meisenhelder, Susan. "False Gods and Black Goddesses in Naylor's *Mama Day* and Hurston's *Their Eyes Were Watching God*." *Callaloo* 23, no. 4 (2000): 1440–1463.

-----. "'The Whole Picture' in Gloria Naylor's *Mama Day*." *African American Review* 27, no. 3 (Fall 1993): 405–419.

Merriam, Alan P. "African Music." In "*Les Bambara*." *Continuity and Change in African Cultures*, edited by William Bascom and Melville Herskovits, 49–86. Chicago: University of Chicago Press, 1959.

Metraux, Alfred. *Voodoo in Haiti*. 1959. Reprint, New York: Schocken, 1972.

Metuh, Emefie Ikenga. *God and Man in African Religion: A Case Study of the Igbo of Nigeria*. London: G. Chapman, 1981. Mokoso, Ndeley. "God of Meme." In *African Rhapsody*, edited by Nadezda Obradovic, 278–288. New York: Anchor, 1994.

Monroe, Mary. *The Upper Room*. New York: St. Martin's Press, 1985.

Montejo, Esteban. *Autobiography of a Runaway Slave*. Edited by Miguel Barnet. Translated by Jocasta Innes. London: The Bodley Head, 1968.

Morrison, Toni. *Beloved*. New York: Plume, 1987.

-----. *Jazz*. New York: Alfred A. Knopf, 1992.

-----. *Paradise*. New York: Plume, 1997.

-----. *Song of Solomon, Tar Baby* and *Sula*. New York: Quality Paperback Book Club, 1987.

"The Mother Tongue." *U.S. News & World Report*, November 5, 1990, 60–70.

Nadel, S. F. *Nupe Religion: Traditional Beliefs and the Influence of Islam in West African Chiefdom*. London: Routledge, 1954.

Naylor, Gloria. *Mama Day*. New York: Vintage, 1988.

Ndebele, Njabulo. "The Prophetess." In *African Rhapsody*, edited by Nadezda Obradovic, 35–46. New York: Anchor, 1994.

Neal, James H. *Ju-Ju in My Life*. London: George G. Harrap, 1966.

Nnameka, Obioma, ed. *Sisterhood, Feminism and Power in Africa*. Trenton: Africa World Press, 1997.

Nunley, John W. *Moving with the Face of the Devil*. Chicago: University of Illinois Press, 1987.

Nwapa, Flora. *Efuru.* London: Heinemann, 1966.
Obayemi, Ade. "The Phenomenon of Oduduwa in Ife History." In *The Cradle of a Race: Ife: From the Beginning to 1980,* edited by I. A. Akinjogbin, 62–76. Lagos: Sunray, 1992.
Obradovic, Nadezda, ed. *African Rhapsody.* New York: Anchor, 1994.
Oduyoye, Modupe. "The Spider, the Chameleon and the Creation of the Earth." In *Traditional Religion in West Africa,* edited by E. E. Ade Adegbola, 374–388. Accra: Asempa, 1983.
Ogunba, Oyin. "The Performance of Yorùbá Oral Poetry." In *Yoruba Oral Tradition,* edited by Wande Abimbola, 807–876. Ibadan: Ibadan University Press, 1975.
Ogunsanwo, Olatubosun. "Intertextuality and Post-Colonial Literature in Ben Okri's *The Famished Road.*" *Research in African Literatures* 26, no. 1 (Spring 1995): 41–52.
Ojo, J. R. O. "A Cross-Cultural Study of Some African Masquerades." In *African Unity: The Cultural Foundations,* edited by Zaccheus Sunday Ali, Anthony Ijaola Asiwaju, and Benjamin Olatunji Oloruntimehin, 119–123. Lagos: Centre for Black and African Arts and Civilization, 1988.
"The Position of Women in Yoruba Traditional Society." In *Department of History: University of Ifè Seminar Papers, 1978–79,* 132–157. Ile-Ife: Kosalabaro, 1980.
Okonjo, Kamene. "Women's Political Participation in Nigeria." In *The Black Woman Cross-Culturally,* edited by Filomina Chima Steady, 79–106. Cambridge: Schenkman, 1981.
Okpewho, Isidore. African Oral Literature: Backgrounds, Character and Continuity. Bloomington: Indiana University Press, 1992.
"The Ozidi Saga: A Critical Introduction." In *The Ozidi Saga,* edited by J. P. Clark-Bekederemo, vii–lvii. Washington, D.C.: Howard University Press, 1991.
Okri, Ben. *The Famished Road.* New York: Doubleday, 1991.
———. *Songs of Enchantment.* New York: Nan A. Talese, 1993.
Olajubu, Oludare. "Composition and Performance Techniques of Iwì Egúngún." In *Yoruba Oral Tradition,* edited by Wande Abimbola, 877–933. Ibadan: Ibadan University Press, 1975.
Olaniyan, R. A., and I. A. Akinjogbin. "Sources of the History of Ife." In *The Cradle of a Race: Ifè—From the Beginning to 1980,* edited by I. A. Akinjogbin, 39–50. Lagos: Sunray, 1992.
Olaniyan, Tejumola. "God's Weeping Eyes: Hurston and the Anti-Patriarchal Form." *Obsidian II* 5, no. 2 (Summer 1990): 30–45.
Olayemi, Val. "The Supernatural in the Yoruba Folktale." In *Yoruba Oral Tradition,* edited by Wande Abimbola, 958–971. Ile-Ife: Department of African Languages and Literature, 1975.

Olomola, Isola. "Ife Before Oduduwa." In *The Cradle of a Race: Ife: From the Beginning to 1980*, edited by I. A. Akinjogbin, 51–61. Lagos: Sunray, 1992.
Omole, Bamitale Idowu. "Oyo Palace: An Historical Analysis of its Organisation." *The African Historian* III (1976): 31–55.
Omoyajowo, Akin. "What Is Witchcraft?" In *Traditional Religion in West Africa*, edited by E. E. Ade Adegbola, 317–336. Accra: Asempa, 1983.
Opefeyitimi, Ayo. "Womb to Tomb: Yoruba Women Power Over Life and Death." *Ife: Annals of the Institute of Cultural Studies* 5 (1994): 57–67.
-----. "'Women of the World' in Yoruba Culture." Unpublished paper, 1993.
Opeola, Samuel M. "The Ethical Influence of Yoruba Civilization," *Napatian Society: A Society in Search of Ancient African Knowledge* 1 (September 1993): 5–13.
"What Is Witchcraft?" Unpublished paper, Institute of Cultural Studies Seminar, Obafemi Awolowo University, 1997.
Oyesakin, Adefioye. "The Image of Women in Ifa Literary Corpus." *Nigeria Magazine* 141 (1982): 16–23.
Palmer, Colin A. *Slaves of the White God: Blacks in Mexico, 1570–1650.* Cambridge: Harvard University Press, 1976.
Parrinder, Geoffrey. *Witchcraft: European and African*. London: Faber, 1963.
Pennington, Dorothy L. "Time in African Culture." In *African Culture: The Rhythms of Unity*, edited by Molefi K. Asante and Kariamu Welsh Asante, 123–139. Trenton: Africa World Press, 1990.
Picton, Sue. "The Visual Arts of Nigeria." In *Nigerian History and Culture*, edited by Richard Olaniyan, 235–238. Ibadan: Longman, 1985.
Pliya, Jean. "The Watch-Night." In *Jazz and Palmwine*, edited by Willfried F. Feuser, 85–102. London: Longman, 1981.
Popoola, Solabade S. "Your Questions Answered." *Orunmila Magazine* 6 (1993): 46.
Priebe, Richard K. *Myth, Realism and the West African Writer*. Trenton: Africa World Press, 1988.
Prince, Raymond. "The Yoruba Image of the Witch." *Journal of Mental Science* 107, no. 449 (July 1961): 795–805.
Provost, Karla. "Becoming Afrekete: The Trickster in the Work of Audre Lorde." *MELUS* 20, no. 4 (Winter 1995): 45–59.
Pryse, Marjorie, and Hortense J. Spillers, eds. *Conjuring: Black Women, Fiction and Literary Tradition*. Bloomington: Indiana University Press, 1985.

Rawick, George P., ed. *From Sundown to Sunup: The Making of the Black Community*. Vol. 1 of *The American Slave: A Composite Autobiography*. Westport: Greenwood Press, 1972.

-----. *Georgia Narratives*. Vol. 13 of *The American Slave*. Westport: Greenwood Press, 1972.

-----. *God Struck Me Dead*. Vol. 19 of *The American Slave: A Composite Autobiography*. Westport: Greenwood Press, 1972.

-----. *Kansas Narratives*. In Vol. 16 of *The American Slave: Kansas, Kentucky, Maryland, Ohio, Virginia and Tennessee Narratives*. Westport: Greenwood Press, 1972.

-----. *Kentucky Narratives*. In Vol. 16 of *The American Slave: Kansas, Kentucky, Maryland, Ohio, Virginia and Tennessee Narratives*. Westport: Greenwood Press, 1972.

-----. *The Unwritten History of Slavery*. Vol. 18 of *The American Slave: A Composite Autobiography*. Westport: Greenwood Press, 1972.

-----. *Virginia Narratives*. In Vol. 16 of *The American Slave: Kansas, Kentucky, Maryland, Ohio, Virginia and Tennessee Narratives*. Westport: Greenwood Press, 1972.

Reed, Ishmael. *Conjure: Selected Poems, 1963–1970*. Amherst: University of Massachusetts Press, 1972.

-----. *Mumbo Jumbo*. New York: Atheneum, 1972.

Richards, Dona. "The Implications of African American Spirituality." In *African Culture: The Rhythms of Unity*, edited by Molefi K. Asante and Kariamu Welsh Asante, 207–231. Trenton: Africa World Press, 1990.

Richards, Sandra. "Under the Trickster's Sign: Toward a Reading of Ntozake Shange and Femi Osofisan." In *Critical Theory and Performance*, edited by Janell G. Reinelt and Joseph R. Roach, 65–78. Ann Arbor: University of Michigan Press, 1990.

Sale, Maggie. "Call and Response as Critical Method: African-American Oral Traditions and *Beloved*." *African American Review* 26, no. 1 (Spring 1992): 41–50.

Salvaggio, Ruth. "Octavia Butler and the Science-Fiction Heroine." *Black American Literature Forum* 18, no. 2 (Summer 1984): 78–81.

Schuler, Monica. *Alas, Alas Kongo: A Social History of Indentured African Immigration into Jamaica 1841–1865*. Baltimore: Johns Hopkins University Press, 1980.

Sekora, John, and Darwin T. Turner, eds. *The Art of Slave Narrative: Original Essays in Criticism and Theory*. Macomb: Western Illinois University Press, 1982.

Sertima, Ivan Van. *They Came Before Columbus: The African Presence in Ancient America*. New York: Random House, 1976.

Shange, Ntozake. *for colored girls who have considered suicide when the rainbow was enuf.* In *Totem Voices*, edited by Paul Carter Harrison, 225–274. New York: Grove, 1989.
-----. *nappy edges.* New York: St. Martin's Press, 1978.
-----. *Sassafrass, Cypress & Indigo.* New York: St. Martin's Press, 1982.
-----. *three pieces: spell #7, a photograph: lovers in motion, boogie woogie landscapes.* New York: St. Martin's Press, 1981.
Soyinka, Wole. "The African World and the Ethnocultural Debate." In *African Culture: The Rhythms of Unity,* edited by Molefi K. Asante and Kariamu Welsh Asante, 13–38. Trenton: Africa World Press, 1990.
-----. *Madmen and Specialists. Six Plays.* Ibadan: Spectrum, 1988.
-----. *Myths, Literature and the African World.* Cambridge: Cambridge University Press, 1976.
Spencer, Jon Michael. *Rhythms of Black Folk: Race, Religion, and Pan-Africanism.* Trenton: Africa World Press, 1995.
Steady, Filomina Chima, ed. *The Black Woman Cross-Culturally.* Cambridge: Schenkman, 1981.
Stein, Rachel. "Remembering the Sacred Tree: Black Women, Nature and Voodoo in Zora Neale Hurston's *Tell My Horse* and *Their Eyes Were Watching God.*" *Women's Studies* 25, no. 5 (1996): 465–482.
Steiner, Roland. "Braziel Robinson: Possessed of Two Spirits." In *Mother Wit from the Laughing Barrel,* edited by Alan Dundes, 377–379. 1973. Reprint, Jackson: University of Mississippi Press, 1990.
Sudarkasa, Niara. "The 'Status of Women' in Indigenous African Societies." In *Women in Africa and the African Diaspora,* edited by Rosalyn Terborg-Penn, Sharon Harley, and Andrea Benton Rushing, 25–41. Washington, D.C.: Howard University Press, 1987.
The Strength of Our Mothers: African and African American Families—Essays and Speeches. Trenton: Africa World Press, 1997.
Sundquist, Eric J. "'The Drum with the Man Skin': *Jonah's Gourd Vine.*" In *Zora Neale Hurston: Critical Perspectives Past and Present,* edited by Henry Louis Gates, Jr., and K. A. Appiah, 39–66. New York: Amistad, 1993.
Taiwo, Oladele. *An Introduction to West African Literature.* London: Nelson, 1967. Tate, Claudia, ed. *Black Women Writers at Work.* New York: Continuum, 1983. Taylor-Guthrie, Danille, ed. *Conversations with Toni Morrison.* Jackson: University Press of Mississippi, 1994.
Teish, Luisah. *Jambalaya: The Natural Woman's Book of Personal Charms and Practical Rituals.* New York: Harper Collins, 1985.

Terborg-Penn, Rosalyn, Sharon Harley, and Andrea Benton Rushing, eds. *Women in Africa and the African Diaspora.* Washington, D.C.: Howard University Press, 1987.

Thomas, H. Nigel. *From Folklore to Fiction: A Study of Folk Heroes and Rituals in the Black American Novel.* Westport: Greenwood Press, 1988.

Thompson, Robert Farris. *Dancing between Two Worlds: Kongo-Angola Culture and the Americas.* New York: Caribbean Cultural Center, 1991.

-----. *Flash of the Spirit: African & Afro-American Art and Philosophy.* New York: Vintage, 1983.

Tucker, Lindsey. "Recovering the Conjure Woman: Texts and Contexts in Gloria Naylor's *Mama Day.*" *African American Review* 28, no. 2 (1994): 17–18.

Turner, Victor. "Ritual and Symbolism." In *African Systems of Thought,* edited by Meyer Fortes and Germain Diterlen, 9–15. New York: Oxford University Press, 1965.

Tutuola, Amos. *The Palm-Wine Drinkard and My Life in the Bush of Ghosts.* New York: Grove, 1994.

Twinning, Mary A., and Keith E. Baird, eds. *Sea Island Roots: African Presence in the Carolinas and Georgia.* Trenton: Africa World Press, 1992.

Verger, Pierre F. *Ewe: The Use of Plants in Yoruba Society.* Sao Paulo: Odebrecht, 1995.

Wade-Gayles, Gloria, ed. *My Soul Is a Witness: African-American Women's Spirituality.* Boston: Beacon, 1995.

No Crystal Stair: Visions of Race and Sex in Black Women's Fiction. New York: Pilgrim, 1984.

Walker, Alice. *The Color Purple.* New York: Harcourt, 1982.

-----. *In Love and in Trouble: Stories of Black Women.* New York: Harvest, 1967.

-----. *In Search of Our Mother's Gardens.* New York: Harcourt Brace Jovanovitch, 1983.

Walker, Barbara J. *The Woman's Encyclopedia of Myths and Secrets.* San Francisco: Harper San Francisco, 1983.

Wall, Cheryl A. "Zora Neale Hurston: Changing Her Own Words." In *Critical Perspectives on Zora Neale Hurston,* edited by Henry Louis Gates, Jr., and K. A. Appiah, 76–97. New York: Amistad, 1993.

Washington, Joseph R., Jr. *Black Sects and Cults.* Garden City: Doubleday, 1972.

Washington, Teresa N. "Afraifalang: A Literary Gèlèdé." Master's thesis, University of Mississippi, 1996.

-----. *The Architects of Existence: Àjẹ́ in Yoruba Cosmology, Ontology, and Orature.* Qya's Tornado, 2014.
-----. "Manifestations of Àjẹ́ in Africana Literature." Ph.D. diss., Obafemi Awolowo University, Ile-Ife, 2000.
-----. *Manifestations of Masculine Magnificence: Divinity in Africana Life, Lyrics, and Literature.* Qya's Tornado, 2014.
-----."Readily Apparent, Rarely Understood: Africanisms in the Rural South." In *A Pilgrimage of Color 2001 National Conference Monograph Series,* 285–323. Houston: National Association of African American Studies.
Wilentz, Gay. *Binding Cultures: Black Women Writers in African and the Diaspora.* Bloomington: Indiana University Press, 1992.
Wilkinson, Jane, ed. *Talking with African Writers: Interviews with African Poets, Playwrights and Novelists.* London: James Currey, 1990.
Willis, Susan. "Wandering: Hurston's Search for Self and Method." In *Zora Neale Hurston: Critical Perspectives Past and Present,* edited by Henry Louis Gates, Jr., and K. A. Appiah, 110–129. New York: Amistad, 1993.
Wilson, August. *They Tell Me Joe Turner's Come and Gone.* In *Three Plays,* 196–289. New York: Plume, 1988.
Yai, Olabiyi Babalola. "In Praise of Metonymy: The Concepts of 'Tradition' and 'Creativity' in the Transmission of Yoruba Artistry over Time and Space." *Research in African Literatures* 24, no. 4 (Winter 1993): 29–37.
"Towards A New Poetic of Oral Poetry in Africa." *Ife: Annals of the Institute of Cultural Studies* 1 (1986): 40–55.
Youngblood, Shay. "Shakin the Mess Outta Misery." In *Colored Contradictions: An Anthology of Contemporary African American Plays,* edited by Harry J. Elam, Jr., and Robert Alexander, 4–45. New York: Penguin Books, 1996.
Zamir, Shamoon. "An Interview with Ishmael Reed." *Callaloo* 17, no. 4 (Autumn 1994): 1131–1157.

INTERVIEWS AND COMMUNICATIONS

Adebooye, Clement. Interviews with author. Obafemi Awolowo University, 1997.
Adedayo, James Isola. Interview with author. Obafemi Awolowo University, 1997.
Adediran, 'Biodun. Personal communications. Obafemi Awolowo University, 1998.
Ajuwon, Bade. Interviews with author. Obafemi Awolowo University, 1998.

Akingbade, John, and Charles Oladapo. Interview with author. Obafemi Awolowo University, 1998.
Dickey, Vircy. Conversation with author. Mississippi, 1994.
Faleti, Adebayo. Conversations and interview with author. Obafemi Awolowo University, 1998.
Harris, Lenell. Conversation with author. Mississippi, 1995.
Harris, Mattie A. Conversation with author. Mississippi, 2004.
Ibitokun, Benedict M. Conversations and interviews with author. Obafemi Awolowo University, 1997.
Igbinola, Oyeronke. Conversations with author. Ile-Ife, Nigeria, 1997–1998.
Makinde, Moses Akin. Conversations with author. Obafemi Awolowo University, 1998.
Mamane, Aboubacar. Conversations with author. Obafemi Awolowo University, 1999.
Ogunba, Oyin. Conversations and interviews with author. Obafemi Awolowo University, 1998.
Ogundijo, Bayo. Conversations with author. Obafemi Awolowo University, 1998.
Opeola, Samuel Modupe. Interviews with author. Obafemi Awolowo University, 1997–1998.
Ositola, "Abdifa" Kolawole. Interview with author. Ibadan, Nigeria, 1999.
Patterson, Betty Jo. Conversations with author. Mississippi, 1995.
Seck, Ibrahim. Conversations with author. Mississippi, 1995.
Shange, Ntozake. Conversations with author. University of Maryland Eastern Shore, 2000.
Washington, Cornelius, Jr. Conversations with author. Missouri, 1993.
Yanque, Orandoh Bigboi. Conversations with author. Obafemi Awolowo University, 1998.

INDEX

Áàjálayé, 50, 75, 91, 118, 180, 210, 283
aásàn, 17, 177
abáàra méjì, 16, 35, 283
àbíkú, 46, 186, 243, 265, 283, 258
Abimbola, Wande, 5
Abiodun, Rowland, 28, 106, 235, 242
Achebe, Chinua, 123, 166, 178, 235
Adeoye, C. L., 27, 168
Afa (Ewe), 80, 90
Afa (Igbo), 80, 93, 113, 114
Afaro, 69, 251
Afírìmáàkọ̀, 62, 115, 211, 283
Afrekete, 66, 72, 222, 244, 248, 253, 283
African Cult, 75–80
After 7, 109
After God Is Dibia (Umeh), 86
Àgbàláàgbà (or Àgbàláàgbà Obìrin), 13, 16, 56, 150, 151, 273. *See also* Àjẹ́
Aido Hwedo, 65–66, 202, 225
Aidoo, Ama Ata, 9, 142, 144, 155–156, 159, 240; analysis of *Anowa*, 141–164
Ajalagba, 56, 127, 128, 131, 133, 181, 186, 283
Àjẹ́, 4, 6, 9, 10, 171, 172, 175, 179, 181,183, 184, 188–189, 190, 276–277; African powers similar to, 57–69; and Àràká 168; attributes of, 13–36;

color and color symbolism of, 25–27, 198–216; compared to witchcraft, 7–8; defined, 13–16, 17; Deities of, 36–51; Ẹgbẹ́ Àjẹ́, 34, 148, 168–169, 184; flight (astral and physical), 86–90; and historical Yoruba women, 51–55; and Hoodoo and Whodo(?) 82–85; justice, political power and, 29–35; manifestations in African America, 75–100; manifestations in the Caribbean and Latin America, 70–75; and the mother-daughter relationship, 217–245; and neo-political power, 245–272; origin and origin texts of, 18–19, 94; Ọ̀rọ̀ (Power of the Word), 16–17, 90–92, 106, 141–142, 177–179, 274; relationship with Oṣó,31–34, 138–197; and Zora Neale Hurston, 97–101. *See also* Àgbàláàgbà; Amusu; Àwọn Ìyá Wa; Ayé; Dije; Ẹléyẹ; and Odù
Ajuwon, Bade, 25
Ajuziogu (*I Saw the Sky Catch Fire*), 114, 125–139
Akan, 57, 61, 74, 80, 142, 205
Akinshegun, Riua, 150, 185
Alkali, Zaynab, 132, 143, 309nn2, 22

Amusu, 56, 127, 128, 131, 133, 185, 283
An' Dangie Dewoe (*Jonah's Gourd Vine*), 204, 205, 206, 215
Ani (or Ala), 22, 61, 125, 127
Ani, Marimba, 22
Anikulapo-Kuti, Fela, 53, 193, 268, 275
Anlo, 67, 118, 137, 228
Anowa (Aidoo), 9, 141–164
Anowa (also Anoa), 141–144, 154–159, 163, 166, 174–175, 176
Ansa, Tina McElroy, 203
Anyanwu (*Wild Seed*), 185–186, 187–188, 189, 195, 220
Àràká, 168–170, 173, 181
Armah, Ayi Kwei, 141, 147, 196, 271
Asase Yaa, 61, 156, 164
àṣẹ, 14, 21, 47, 60, 149, 228, 261
Asiwaju, A. I., 101 Ast, 58–61, 78, 289n23
Aunt Gussi ("The Watch-Night"), 198–199
Ausar, 59, 61, 295n26
Awolalu, J. Omosade, 5, 33, 289n23
Àwọn Ìyá Wa, 13, 14, 22, 24, 27, 33, 34, 35, 38, 39, 43, 61, 71, 107, 115, 148, 217, 242, 252, 266, 283. *See also* Àjẹ́
AWU (Abeokuta Women's Union), 53 Ayé, 13, 39, 43, 107, 283. *See also* Àjẹ́
Ayele ("The Watch-Night"), 9, 199, 200–201, 206–207, 215
Azaro (*The Famished Road* and *Songs of Enchantmen*t), 257–262, 267, 270

Ba, 60, 270

babaláwo, 6, 7, 80, 100, 200, 283
Babayemi, S. O., 50
Baby of the Family (Ansa), 203
Baby Suggs, holy, 227–229, 237, 245
Badejo, Diedre, 8, 293n135
Badu, Erykah, 275
Baker, Houston, 1, 98, 99, 101
BaKongo, 57, 67, 74, 84, 85, 87, 88, 117
Bambara, Toni Cade, 1, 203, 276, 299n139
Bascom, William, 24, 26
Bascombe Wade (*Mama Day*), 119, 121, 122, 124, 211, 214, 215
Beloved (Morrison), 9, 102, 218, 219, 226, 227, 230, 233, 238, 239
Beloved (*Beloved*), 232, 233, 235–236, 237, 239, 240, 241, 242, 243, 244
Big Sweet (*Mules and Men*), 97–99, 214
Binding Cultures (Wilentz), 2
Bockie, Simon, 57–58, 81, 215, 264
Boukman, 74, 78
Bradley, Margaret, 79
Braxton, Charlie R., 4
Brodzki, Bella, 125, 135
Brother J, 242, 275
Brown, Kitty, 99–100
Butler, Octavia E., 9, 165, 184, 186, 194, 196, 197, 278; analysis of *Wild Seed*, 184–197

Carril, Pepe, 27
Chi, 86, 239
Chineke, 129, 283. *See also* Chukwu
Christian, Barbara, 2

Chukwu, 127–128. *See also* Chineke
Cocoa (*Mama Day*), 114, 123–124, 140, 209, 212, 213, 214
The Color Purple (Walker), 107–108
Cowart, David, 116
Crabtree, Claire, 178, 183

Damballah-Hwedo, 66, 84, 202, 203, 206, 211, 212, 213, 214, 224, 232, 244, 283
Dan (Vodun Deity), 66, 212, 283
Davies, Carole Boyce, 101
Davis, Angela Y., 79
de Isla, Leonor, 71–74, 92, 213, 250
Death and the Invisible Powers (Bockie), 215
Denver (*Beloved*), 227, 229, 232, 233, 236, 237, 238
Devil (also Lucifer, Ole Scratch), 72, 95–96, 242, 247, 248, 250
dibia, 86, 113, 114, 235, 283
Dije, 57, 65–66, 67, 283
Dilemma of a Ghost (Aidoo), 156, 158
Diop, Cheikh Anta, 58, 165
Dixon, Melvin, 76
Doro (*Wild Seed*), 186–187, 188, 189, 193–196
Dr. Bero (*Madmen and Specialists*), 185, 189–191
Dr. Buzzard (*Mama Day*), 207, 208, 209, 211–212
Dr. Holly (*Tell My Horse*), 100
Drewal, Henry, 13, 15
Drewal, Margaret, 13, 15
DuBois, W. E. B., 81, 276
Dust Tracks on a Road (Hurston), 167
Echewa, T. Obinkaram, 9, 113, 114, 125, 276; analysis of *I Saw the Sky Catch Fire*, 113–114, 125–139

Efunsetan, Aniwura, 52, 53, 58, 245
Efuru (Nwapa), 108, 143
Egreja da Santa Efigênia, 71, 77
Egúngún, 43, 47, 50, 52, 60, 265, 284
18 & 23 (*Mama Day*), 114–124, 213, 214
ekili, 86, 118
Elder, Arlene, 151
Elders of the Night, 15, 25
Eleburuibon, Yemi, 28
Eliot, T. S., 193
Elizabeth Ashby-Jones (*I Saw the Sky Catch Fire*), 135–137, 139
Ellison, Ralph, 247
Emeh, B. B. O., 127, 128
Equiano, Olaudah, 203
Ewe, 57, 71, 80
Ẹdan, 30–31, 35, 40, 56, 60, 265, 283
ẹsẹ Ifá, 19, 25, 48, 93, 284
Ẹléyẹ, 22–23, 46, 206, 273, 284. *See also* Àjẹ́; Ẹyẹ Òrò
Èṣù Ẹlẹ́gbára (also Legba), 4, 27, 66, 72, 73, 95, 97, 227, 247, 248, 253, 265, 284
Ẹyẹ Àjẹ́, 23, 24, 25. *See also* Ẹléyẹ
Ẹyẹ Òrò, 22, 23, 27–28, 61, 149, 229, 232, 233, 239, 261. *See also* Ẹléyẹ

Fa, 66, 93, 122, 221, 284
Faleti, Adebayo, 25, 306n32
The Famished Road (Okri), 9, 245, 256–272
Farrow, Stephen, 213

Fatunmbi, Awo F., 17, 36, 42, 117, 124, 192, 232
Flash of the Spirit (Thompson), 71
flight (astral and human), 1–2, 86–88, 261, 298n133, 299n139
Fon, 80, 84

Gaba, Christian, 66–68
Garner, Margaret, 230, 233, 237
Gates, Henry Louis, Jr., 4, 93, 95, 176
Gbàgbọ́, 109–111, 214
Gẹ̀lẹ̀dẹ́, 16, 22, 32, 43, 45–46, 71, 106, 107, 150, 184, 186, 224, 229, 251, 265, 268, 270, 284
The Gẹ̀lẹ̀dẹ́ Spectacle (Lawal), 165, 291n80 George Andrews (*Mama Day*), 114, 116, 124, 140, 209, 211, 212–213
Gifts of Power (Jackson), 89
Giovanni, Nikki, 28, 234, 276
God and Man in African Religion (Metuh), 127
goofer dust (also goober dust), 261
Govan, Sandra, 194
Grandmother (Anlo Deity), 67–68, 118, 137
Grant, Rosa, 87–88
Green, Cee-Lo, 28

Haiti, 74, 80
Hall, Shad, 86
Hallen, Barry, 6, 7, 8, 109
"harmonious dualism" (Diop), 51, 58, 165
Harris, Donnie, 90
Hattie (*Jonah's Gourd Vine*), 9, 204, 205–206, 208

Holy Office of Inquisition, 72–73
Hoodoo, 5, 80–85, 93, 147, 205, 215, 284
"Hoo-dooism," 82–85
hooks, bell, 2
Hudson-Weems, Clenora, 2
Hull, Gloria T., 2
Hurston, Zora Neale, 4, 9, 82, 92, 93–101, 105, 109, 126, 152, 159, 165, 167, 168, 180, 182, 198, 201, 215, 253, 297n104; analysis of *Jonah's Gourd Vine*, 201–206, 215; analysis of *Mules and Men*, 93–100; analysis of *Their Eyes Were Watching God*, 167–183; Morrison on, 104; and Ọya, 167–168

I Saw the Sky Catch Fire (Echewa), 9, 113–114, 125–139, 196, 259
Ibie, Osamaro, 20, 22
Ibitokun, Benedict M., 90, 289n23
Idemilli, 61, 128
Ifá, 6, 13, 29, 44, 47, 72, 76, 80, 93, 94, 113, 114, 122, 149, 271, 284
Ifism: The Complete Works of Orunmila (Ibie), 22
Ìgbàgbọ́ àti Ẹ̀sìn Yorùbá (Adeoye), 168, 291n86
Igbinola, Oyeronke, 11, 18, 20, 21, 23, 71, 104, 235, 279, 289nn24, 25
Igbo, 56, 61, 63, 65, 66, 74, 80, 104, 113, 125–138, 181, 235
Igue, Ogunsola, 70
Ijọ, 61, 68, 93
ìjúbà, 73, 94, 95, 284
ileeshin, 64

Ìmọlẹ̀, 14, 35, 40, 273. *See also* Ìyá-Ayé
Indigo (*Sassafrass, Cypress, & Indigo*), 9, 143, 145–146, 148–154, 160–164
Invisible Man (Ellison), 247
Isaki, Nsemi, 85, 149
Isola, Akinwumi, 134, 276
Ìtànkálẹ̀, 48
Ìtàn-Oríkì Ìyàmi Òṣòròngà (Igbinola), 18, 19, 20, 21, 25, 29, 33–34, 93, 100, 165, 289n24
Ìwà, 26–29, 116, 284
ìwà-pẹ̀lẹ́, 15
Ìwà-Pẹ̀lẹ́: Ifá Quest (Fatunmbi), 17
Ìyá Bọ̀kọ́lọ, 9i, 267, 289n23
Ìyá-Ayé (or Àpẹ̀pẹ̀-Àlẹ̀), 30, 33, 35, 39–42, 60, 61, 67, 225, 232, 277, 284. *See also* Ìmọlẹ̀
Ìyàmi Àbẹ̀ní, 23, 30, 41, 284
Ìyàmi Òṣòròngà, 4, 18, 19, 20, 22, 26, 29, 59, 60, 68, 91, 93, 104, 119, 120, 224, 225, 232, 235, 239, 257, 269. *See also* Àjẹ́; Àwọn Ìyá Wa; Odù
Ìyánlá, 26, 118, 149, 248, 259–261, 273

Jackson, Rebecca, 89–90, 101, 245, 299n151
Jamaica, 74
Jambalaya (Teish), 3, 150
James, Adeola, 103
Janie (*Their Eyes Were Watching God*), 108, 165, 170–183, 210, 217, 223
Jazz (Morrison), 229
Jeyifous, Biodun, 193

Jody (or Joe) Starks (*Their Eyes Were Watching God*), 108, 173–178, 205
John Pearson (*Jonah's Gourd Vine*), 182, 201–206
John-Paul (*Mama Day*), 122, 211, 214
Johnson, Robert, 5
Jonah's Gourd Vine (Hurston), 9, 152, 181,198, 201–206, 211, 215
juba, 74, 94, 226, 227, 228, 284

Ka, 60
Kalu, Anthonia, 137–138
Keenan, Randall, 185, 194
Kemet, 58, 60, 61, 284
Kincaid, Jamaica, 9, 218, 219, 222, 223, 232, 239; analysis of "My Mother," 222–226
Kindoki, 57–58, 215, 284
Kofi Ako, 154–156, 158–159, 160, 163, 166, 167, 174–175
Kolawole, Mary E. M., 2

Lawal, Babatunde, 30, 165, 239, 291n80
Laye, Camera, 203
Lee, Barbara, 245
Leonard, George, 80
Leveau, Marie, 91–92, 99, 105, 106, 168, 203, 267
Lorde, Audre, 9, 236; analysis of *Zami*, 218–222
Lucas, J. Olumide, 37, 291n80
Lucy (*Jonah's Gourd Vine*), 202–206, 210, 215

Maat, 60, 61
Madame Koto (*The Famished Road* and *Songs of Enchantment*), 9, 245, 246, 257–268, 269, 270

Madame Tinubu, 52, 58, 245
Madmen and Specialists (Soyinka), 165, 184–197, 269
Mama Day (*Mama Day*), 9, 115, 123–124, 207–209, 211, 212–213, 214, 215, 245
Mama Day (Naylor), 9, 113–124, 136, 139–140, 198, 206–216, 270
Mama Dyumbo, 67, 118, 214
Mama Ruby (*The Upper Room*), 9, 245– 256, 262, 263, 269, 270
Mami Wota, 66, 72
Mani, 65, 84, 284
Mason, John, 37, 63, 189
Maureen (*The Upper Room*), 251, 253, 255–256, 260, 261
MawuLisa (also Mawu), 64–66, 67, 122, 222, 247, 248, 277, 284–285
Mba, Nina, 53, 129, 131
Mbiti, John, 92, 94
McCullough, Priscilla, 87
Meisenhelder, Susan, 116, 210
Metuh, Emefie Ikenga, 127, 239
minkisi, 84–85
Monroe, Mary, 9, 245, 249, 269, 307n15; analysis of *The Upper Room,* 245– 257, 267, 269
Montejo, Esteban, 87
Morrison, Toni, 1, 9, 102–105, 111, 121, 217, 219, 226, 234, 235, 247, 271, 299nn138, 139, 302n17; on artistic creation and critique, 102; analysis of *Beloved,* 226–244; on Hurston, 104
Moseley, Mathilda, 94, 300n170
Mules and Men (Hurston), 83, 92–100, 106, 114, 167, 254

My Life in the Bush of Ghosts (Tutuola), 217 "My Mother" (Kincaid), 218, 222–226

Nadel, Siegfried F., 7
Nana Burúkú, 59, 62, 63–65, 66, 91, 119, 265, 277
Nanny (*Their Eyes*), 157, 171–172, 180, 183, 217, 221
Naylor, Gloria, 9, 113, 114, 139, 198, 206, 215, 307n15; analysis of *Mama Day,* 113–124, 139, 207–216
Ndoki, 57–58, 224, 285
Neo-Hoodoo, 1, 11
nganga, 81, 285
ngoni (harp), 153–154, 160
Nigerian Women Mobilised (Mba), 129
nkisi (plural: minkisi), 84–85, 149, 285
Nne-nne (*Fire*), 114, 125–139
Nupe, 7
nwaobiala, 129, 133
Nwapa, Flora, 108, 143

Odù (also Odùduwà, Oòduà), 14, 16, 17, 18, 19, 23, 25, 26–28, 29, 36–39, 40, 41, 42, 43, 44, 51, 54, 58, 59, 60, 64, 72, 75, 77, 90, 102, 108, 111, 113, 117, 119, 139, 141, 189, 205, 221, 225, 232, 243, 244, 267, 277, 287n9, 291n80
Odù Ifá, 13, 38, 113–114, 115, 119, 122, 124, 213, 214
Oduyoye, Modupe, 16, 89
ogbanje, 124, 186, 235
Ògbóni (also Ògbóni Ibílẹ̀, Imọlẹ̀, Òṣugbó), 30–31, 33, 40, 41, 52

Ogu (Divine Truth, Moral Authority), 113–114, 125, 128, 285
ogu (war), 114, 125, 130, 131, 133, 134, 138, 285
Ògún, 38, 44, 47, 48–49, 64, 74, 97, 168–169, 173, 230, 285
Ogunba, Oyin, 32, 177–178
Ogundipe, Ayodele, 27, 114
Ogunsanwo, Olatubosun, 270
ogwu, 138–139
Ojo, J. R. O., 23
Okri, Ben, 9, 109, 245, 268, 270; analysis of *The Famished Road* and *Songs of Enchantment*, 256–272
Olaniyan, Tejumola, 178
The Old Man (*Madmen and Specialists*), 188–193
Olódùmarè, 28, 37, 42–43, 94, 95, 117, 176, 232
Olúkòsì Èpé, 169, 170, 178, 182
Omoyajowo, Akin, 7 124 (*Beloved*), 227, 234, 235, 236, 242, 243
oníṣègun, 6, 7, 80, 166, 261, 285
Opefeyitimi, Ayo, 13, 23–24, 26
Opeola, Samuel M., 15, 31, 36, 37
Orífín, 19, 57, 121
Orò (society of judicial enforcement), 52, 54, 285
Oṣó, 31–33, 34, 56, 57, 80, 95, 127, 189, 191, 228, 254, 285; neo-Oṣó, 188, 190, 192, 194, 196; relationship with Àjé, 31–34. See also Ajalagba
Òṣùmàrè, 42–43, 65, 84, 93, 221, 224, 232, 243, 266, 286
Othella (*The Upper Room*), 244, 250, 251, 267
The Ozidi Saga, 68–69, 71

Ọbà, 19, 62–63, 101
Ọbalúaiyé, 38, 47, 64
Ọbàtálá, 26–29, 36–37, 38, 61, 64, 117, 119, 139, 153, 189, 236
Ọfọ (Infinite Justice), 113–114, 136, 139, 285
ọfọ àṣẹ (the power to pray effectively), 17, 47, 285
Ọha Ndom, 114, 125, 130, 136, 137, 138, 285
Ọlọ́run, 20, 21, 37, 47, 285
Ọrẹamẹ (*The Ozidi Saga*), 68–69, 254
Òrò (Power of the Word), 14, 17, 38, 47, 54, 59, 61, 90, 92, 105, 106, 107, 108, 110, 120, 141, 157, 159, 176, 177, 178, 221, 234, 242, 261, 262, 265, 285; Pan-African examples, 90–92
Òrò Èfè, 106–107, 128, 132, 268
Òrúnmìlà, 24, 25, 29, 38, 39, 44, 118
Òsanyìn, 44, 60, 64, 146, 149–151, 153, 189, 285, 306n32
Òṣun, 44–45, 46–48, 53, 63, 78, 97–98, 176, 246, 269, 286
Ọya, 47, 48–51, 57, 59, 62, 75, 84, 89, 91, 97–98, 108, 118, 139, 167, 177, 180, 196, 207, 210, 211, 229, 269, 286; as Àràká, 168–170, 173, 181; Hurston's connection with, 167–168

The Palm-Wine Drinkard (Tutuola), 143, 165–167, 178
Paques, Viviana, 153
Parable of the Sower (Butler), 143 *Parable of the Talents* (Butler), 143, 196 *Paradise* (Morrison), 102, 229
Parrinder, Geoffrey, 7

Paul D (*Beloved*), 235, 236, 238, 240
Pleasant, Mary Ellen, 245
Pliya, Jean, 9, 198, 215; analysis of "The Watch-Night," 196–201
Prince, Raymond, 45, 133
Pryse, Marjorie, 1

Quarterman, Wallace, 86
Queen Makeda of Sheba, 90
Queen Nanny, 74
Queen Omu (Sofola), 103–104, 128

Ransome-Kuti, Olufunmilayo, 52, 53–54, 58, 245, 263, 268–269
Rawick, George P., 75
Reed, Ishmael, 1, 11, 158–159, 299n139
Rei, Chico, 71
"The Revenge of Hannah Kemhuff" (Walker), 105–107
Richards, Sandra, 71
Ruby (*Mama Day*), 9, 207–209, 211, 215, 210

Salvaggio, Ruth, 197
Şàngó, 44–45, 48–49, 62, 118, 168, 173, 246
Sapphira Wade (*Mama Day*), 115–123, 139, 210, 213, 245, 252, 267
Sarpong, Peter, 61
Sarraounia Aben Soro, 58, 276
Sassafrass, Cypress & Indigo (Shange), 9, 141–164
Scriptures of an African People: Ritual Utterances of the Anlo (Gaba), 66–68
Sethe (*Beloved*), 226, 227, 229–230, 233, 234, 235, 237, 238–244, 254, 260

Shange, Ntozake, 9, 108, 143; analysis of *Sassafrass, Cypress & Indigo,* 141–164
Shango de Ima (Carril), 27, 47, 139
Si Bero (*Madmen and Specialists*), 184–185, 189, 190
The Signifying Monkey (Gates), 4, 95, 176
Sixo (*Beloved*), 231
Smith, Barbara, 2
Sodipo, Olubi J., 6, 7, 8, 109
Sofola, Zulu, 103–104
Song of Solomon (Morrison), 1, 102, 299n138
Songs of Enchantment (Okri), 9, 245, 265–268
Soyinka, Wole, 9, 26, 165, 184, 191, 193; analysis of *Madmen and Specialists*, 184–197
Spillers, Hortense, 1
Stein, Rachel, 170
The Stillborn (Alkali), 132, 143, 309nn2,22
Strickland, Ellis, 97
Styles, Amanda, 80
Suggs, James D., 87
Sula (Morrison), 217, 229, 247

Tamara (Ijọ Deity), 61, 69, 93
Tar Baby (Morrison), 271
Tate, Claudia, 2
Tea Cake (*Their Eyes Were Watching God*), 178–183, 205
Teish, Luisah, 3, 147, 150, 211
Their Eyes Were Watching God (Hurston), 108, 157, 167–183, 210, 214, 217, 221, 297n104
Things Fall Apart (Achebe), 123–124, 235
Thompson, Robert F., 71
Treasures of Nnobi (Emeh), 127

Truth, Sojourner, 79
Tubman, Harriet, 79, 245
Tucker, Lindsey, 116, 122, 123
Turner, Luke, 92, 99, 167–168
Turner, Nat, 1, 78, 274
Tutuola, Amos, 9, 143, 165–166, 178, 217; analysis of *The Palm-Wine Drinkard,* 165–167
Two Thousand Seasons (Armah), 141–142, 144, 147, 155, 196, 271
two-headed doctor, 80, 81, 102

Ugbala (*I Saw the Sky Catch Fire*), 131, 134–137
Umeh, John A., 56, 138
The Unwritten History of Slavery (Rawick), 231
The Upper Room (Monroe), 9, 245–257, 267, 269

Vodun, 76, 80, 95
Voodoo, 80, 147, 180

Walker, Alice, 2, 292; *The Color Purple,* 107–108; "The Revenge of Hannah Kemhuff," 105–107
Wallace, Michelle, 108
Washington, Elsie B., 234
Washington, Mary Helen, 2, 170
"The Watch-Night" (Pliya), 9, 198–201, 211
Whodo(?), 85, 106, 204–205, 207, 208, 209, 210, 211, 212, 213, 215, 286
Wicca, 3, 287n3
Wild Seed (Butler), 165, 184–197, 220
Wilentz, Gay, 112–113
witch, 3, 5, 287n3; concept of the African, 6–8

witchcraft, 3, 5, 287n3; construct of African, 6–8
Wolof, 74
Word, Sophia, 88

Yai, Olabiyi Babalola, 18, 20, 42, 56
Yemọja, 43–46, 47, 66, 72, 77, 118, 146, 164, 225, 236, 246, 286
Yéwà, 62, 101, 115, 166
Yewájọbí, 5, 13, 16, 44, 58, 71, 93, 109, 118, 119, 122
Yoruba, 4, 8, 9, 14, 25, 29, 51, 61, 80, 84, 86, 87, 109, 113, 224, 233
Yurugu (Ani), 22

Zambi, 118, 286
Zami: A New Spelling of My Name (Lorde), 9, 218–222, 226, 240
Zannu ("The Watch-Night"), 199–201, 209, 215

Teresa N. Washington, Ph.D. is the author of *The Architects of Existence: Àjẹ́ in Yoruba Cosmology, Ontology, and Orature*; *Manifestations of Masculine Magnificence: Divinity in Africana Life, Lyrics, and Literature*; and *Our Mothers, Our Powers, Our Texts: Manifestations of Àjẹ́ in Africana Literature*. Dr. Washington's analyses are published as chapters in *Harold Bloom's Modern Critical Interpretations: Toni Morrison's <u>Beloved</u>: New Edition*; *Yemọja: Gender, Sexuality, and Creativity in the Latina/o and Afro-Atlantic Diasporas*; *Èṣù: Yoruba God, Power, and the Imaginative Frontiers*; and *Step into a World: A Global Anthology of the New Black Literature*. Her articles have been published in many noted journals, including the *African American Review*, the *Journal of American Folklore*, *FEMSPEC*, and the *Journal of Pan African Studies*.

MORE "BOOKS TO BLOW YOUR MIND" FROM QYA'S TORNADO!

Ah Jubah! A PleaPrayerPromise (a novel)
Asiri Odu, Author
ISBN: 9780991073047 (pbk), also available on Kindle and Google Books

Six Pan-African collectives organize to unite warring gangs, exterminate "good old boys," turn tables—and barrels—on trigger-happy cops, and heal victims of genital excision, rape, and sodomy. Want a blueprint for complete elevation and liberation? Check out the novel *Ah Jubah!* It's a revolution in ink.

The African World in Dialogue: An Appeal to Action!
Teresa N. Washington, editor
ISBN: 9780991073078 (Cloth); 9780991073061 (pbk); 9780991073085 (ebook)

In this contemporary anthology, elders, warriors, scholars, artists, and activists address some of the most significant political, cultural, and social issues facing the African world. What is more, they offer viable solutions to facilitate progress, evolution, and elevation.

The Architects of Existence: Àjẹ́ in Yoruba Cosmology, Ontology, and Orature
Teresa N. Washington, Author
ISBN: 9780991073016 (pbk); 9780991073030 (cloth); also available at Google Books

The Architects of Existence is the companion to Teresa N. Washington's *Our Mothers, Our Powers, Our Texts: Manifestations of Àjẹ́ in Africana Literature*, and it is the only book-length exposition of the power of Àjẹ́ and the African Gods and Divine Mothers who own and control this power in Yoruba cosmology and ontology.

Manifestations of Masculine Magnificence: Divinity in Africana Life, Lyrics, and Literature
Teresa N. Washington, Author
ISBN: 9780991073009 (pbk); 9780991073023 (cloth); also available at Google Books

Teresa N. Washington uses a compelling historical and spiritual foundation as a lens by which to analyze the proliferation of humanodivinity in contemporary Africana life, in some of the deepest lyrics ever spit, and in some of the richest literature ever written.

Our Mothers, Our Powers, Our Texts: Manifestations of Àjẹ́ in Africana Literature
By Teresa N. Washington, Author
ISBN: 9780991073054 pbk also available at Google Books

Using orature and historical documents, this book explores Àjẹ́'s forces and figures throughout the African continuum. From this rich foundation, Teresa N. Washington analyzes the impact and influence of Àjẹ́ in the contemporary literature of Africana writers. Oya's Tornado is proud to publish the revised and expanded edition of Washington's groundbreaking study!

www.ingramcontent.com/pod-product-compliance
Lightning Source LLC
Chambersburg PA
CBHW021115300426
44113CB00006B/165